Central Banking, Asset Prices, and Financial Fragility

The current literature on central banking contains two distinct branches. On one side, research focuses on the impact of monetary policy on economic growth, unemployment, and output-price inflation, while ignoring financial aspects. On the other side, some scholars leave aside macroeconomics in order to study the narrow, but crucial, subjects of financial behaviors, and financial supervision and regulation. This book aims at merging both approaches by using macroeconomic analysis to show that financial considerations should be the main preoccupation of central banks. Éric Tymoigne shows how different views regarding the conception of asset pricing lead to different positions regarding the appropriate role of a central bank in the economy. In addition, Hyman P. Minsky's framework of analysis is used extensively and is combined with other elements of the Post-Keynesian framework to study the role of a central bank.

Tymoigne argues that central banks should be included in a broad policy strategy that aims at achieving stable full employment. Their sole goal should be to promote financial stability, which is the best way they can contribute to price stability and full employment. Central banks should stop moving their policy rate frequently and widely because that creates inflation, speculation, and economic instability. Instead, Tymoigne considers a pro-active financial policy that does not allow financial innovations to enter the economy until they are certified to be safe and that focuses on analyzing systemic risk. He argues that central banks should be a guide and a reformer that allow a smooth financing and funding of asset positions, while making sure that financial fragility does not increase drastically over a period of expansion.

This book will be of interest to students and researchers engaged with central banking, macroeconomics, asset pricing, and monetary economics.

Éric Tymoigne is Assistant Professor of Economics at California State University Fresno.

Routledge international studies in money and banking

Central Banking, Asset Prices, and Financial Fragility

Éric Tymoigne

Routledge
Taylor & Francis Group

LONDON AND NEW YORK

First published 2009
by Routledge
2 Park Square, Milton Park, Abingdon, Oxon, OX14 4RN

Simultaneously published in the USA and Canada
by Routledge
270 Madison Avenue, New York, NY 10016

*Routledge is an imprint of the Taylor & Francis Group,
an informa business*

© 2009 Éric Tymoigne

Typeset in Times New Roman by Keyword Group Ltd
Printed and bound in Great Britain by TJI Digital Padstow, Cornwall

British Library Cataloguing in Publication Data
A catalogue record for this book is available from the British Library

Library of Congress Cataloging-in-Publication Data
Tymoigne, Éric, 1976-
Central banking, asset prices and financial fragility / Éric Tymoigne.
    p. cm.
  Includes bibliographical references and index.
  1. Banks and banking, Central. 2. Capital assets pricing model.
  3. Monetary policy. I. Title.

HG1811.T96 2008
332.1'1–dc22   2008025843

ISBN10: 0-415-77399-7 (hbk)
ISBN10: 0-203-88517-1 (ebk)

ISBN13: 978-0-415-77399-7 (hbk)
ISBN13: 978-0-203-88517-8 (ebk)

To my Parents

Contents

Illustrations

Figures

Tables

Acknowledgments

This book grew out of my dissertation and I wish to thank the members of my Committee for their guidance. Among them, Professor L. Randall Wray and Professor Jan A. Kregel deserve additional acknowledgments for their patience and constant availability during the entire Ph.D. program at the University of Missouri-Kansas City (UMKC). I have benefited greatly from their knowledge of economics.

This project gained from the discussions and interactions with many people. At UMKC, I benefited from discussions about Post-Keynesian economics and economic systems with Professor Frederic S. Lee and Professor John F. Henry. Additional discussions with Professor James I. Sturgeon, Professor Mathew Forstater, and Professor Stephanie A. Kelton were very helpful. Outside UMKC, Edwin le Héron and Marc Lavoie deserve a special mention; they encouraged me to go to UMKC, and we had several interesting discussions that were always profitable. I have benefited also from discussions with Basil Moore, Alain Parguez, Warren Mosler, Paul Davidson, Mario Seccareccia, Louis-Philippe Rochon, Sasan Fayazmanesh, Bernard Vallageas, Giuseppe Fontana, Thomas Palley, Michael Radzicki, Linwood Tauheed, Robert Parenteau, John Smithin, and Scott Fullwiler.

The project was made possible by the financial assistance of several institutions. I would like to thank the Center for Full Employment and Price Stability (CFEPS), the Department of Economics of UMKC and of California State University Fresno (CSUF), the Interdisciplinary Doctoral Student Council of UMKC, the Dean of the College of Arts and Sciences of UMKC and CSUF, and the School of Graduate Studies of UMKC for their financial support.

Finally, I would like to thank my wife, Yan Liang, for her support and encouragements over the years and for carefully reading the final draft of the book.

1 Introduction

For most contemporary economists, the main goal of a central bank is to achieve price stability, that is, low and stable inflation. Financial management, regulation, and supervision are additional concerns that represent the prophetical element or "extension" of a central bank (Greenspan 1996). This position is rooted in a presupposition that goes back to the quantity theory of money, i.e. inflation has monetary origins and the central bank is the institution that controls the money supply. In the past, this view has been shared with more or less conviction by economists, but with the emergence of the New Neoclassical Synthesis, output-price stability has become the overriding goal of a central bank, which is supposed to promote robust economic growth and financial stability.

The position taken in this book is the opposite. Financial matters should be the primary preoccupation of a central bank, and other public institutions should deal with inflation. Central banks have been created to take care of financial matters, not price stabilization or the fine-tuning of economic activity, and it is only recently that their role has changed dramatically (Goodhart 1988). The problem becomes determining how a central bank can improve its current framework to deal with financial concerns. Indeed, one may wonder if the current supervisory and regulatory policies, together with the lender of last resort, are enough, and if focusing on financial matters substantially changes the way central banking should be practiced.

To provide an answer to these questions, this book uses a macroeconomic framework that emphasizes financial aspects. Most of the literature on central banking written by macroeconomists focuses on the impact of monetary policy on the production side of the economy (economic growth, unemployment, output-price inflation), while totally ignoring the financial implications. On the other side, some economists leave aside macroeconomic implications in order to concentrate on the narrow, but crucial, subjects of financial behaviors, and financial supervision and regulation. This book aims at bridging the gap by using macroeconomic arguments to show that financial considerations should be at the center of the preoccupation of central banks. By focusing on the financial side of the economy, this book shows that the current manipulation of interest rates in order to fine-tune the economy is inappropriate because its effects are weak and uncertain, and they may generate financial instability and speculation. Central banks would be much more effective in their management of the economic system if they concentrated their efforts on direct management of the financial positions and financial practices.

The book argues in favor of the creation of a highly developed proactive financial policy that takes into account both the actual and expectational sides of the financial frame. A Financial Oversight and Resolution Commission (FORC) should be created to monitor constantly developments in the financial sector, in the same way the FOMC monitors economic activity today. This Commission would approve financial innovations before they are used, and would foster research toward financial systems and instruments that promote financial stability and social welfare. The Commission would also aim at constantly improving its supervisory and regulatory framework by concentrating its research toward a better understanding of the aggregate, sectoral, and individual sensitivity of balance-sheet positions, cash-flow positions, and position-making sources, to changes in variables such as asset prices, income, and expectations. The goal would be to develop a cash-flow-oriented approach to systemic risk and to monitor financial innovations. The current focus on capital requirement is not enough, not only because the level of capital equity may have non-linear impacts on risk aversion, but also because capital requirements may reinforce financial instability. In addition, capital equity is not the appropriate variable to check financial fragility because equity is a residual variable, and a growing equity may not reflect economic success and a higher capacity to meet contractual and compulsory payments. Only present and future cash flows provide a good picture of the financial fragility of an economic unit.

CAMELS supervision (supervision of Capital adequacy, Asset quality, Management, Earnings, Liquidity, and Sensitivity to market risk) is a good supervisory tool, but it should be developed much further, should be generalized to all financial institutions without exceptions, and should include all off-balance sheet items. In addition, by staying at the level of individual banks, and by applying a reactive financial policy that waits until catastrophes unfold to decide what to do about financial innovations (which are validated *ex post* because of the fear of weakening further the economy), central banks impair the efficacy of their lender of last resort interventions and supervisory activities. Indeed, the profit motive that drives economic units, combined with the social rationality that they use to justify their decisions, leads private agents to believe that the lender of last resort will guarantee a privatization of economic gains and a socialization of economic losses. This behavior endangers the long-term financial stability of the economic system and the capacity of the central bank to maintain short-term and long-term financial stability.

Institutions similar to the FORC already exist in other parts of the economic system. For example, the Food and Drug Administration approves new drugs and the National Highway Traffic Safety Administration defines and monitors safety standards for vehicles while promoting further safety improvements. Those institutions exist because of the potential health hazard of medical treatments and of driving motored vehicles. Financial activities may also have substantial adverse impacts on the well-being of the population, and so financial innovations should be tested extensively in a controlled setting before they are used in daily transactions.

Another conclusion of the book is that constant interest-rate manipulations are not an appropriate policy, whatever the rule followed. The central bank has a role of contrarian, which was well illustrated by the two colorful expressions of William McChesney Martin that the role of the Federal Reserve is "to take away the punch bowl just when the party gets going" or "to lean against the wind." However, the main way this should be done is not by fine-tuning the economy with interest rates, a rather ineffective tool because of its passivity, cumulative effects, and *ex post* response to problems, but by intervening dynamically in the credit and placement policies, as well as refinancing practices, of financial institutions.

The book contains five core chapters. Chapter 2 reviews the literature in the New Consensus and Post-Keynesian schools regarding the role of asset prices and financial fragility for central banking. Because the frame of thought used by each school is central to understanding their respective views, the chapter spends some time presenting some of the characteristics of each view. The New Neoclassical Synthesis relies extensively on the work of Fisher and Wicksell and assumes that the framework of a barter economy patched with money provides a good understanding of a capitalist economy. In this type of framework, money is neutral, at least in the long run, and market imperfections are essential to explain government intervention and the importance of financial aspects. The Post-Keynesian framework relies on the work of Keynes, Sraffa, Kalecki, Marx, and others, and argues that a capitalist economy is a monetary production economy. In the latter, people care about nominal values, money is never neutral, and financial instability is intrinsic. Contrary to the New Consensus, the importance of money and financial institutions is integrated from the very beginning because monetary accumulation, not physical accumulation, drives economic decisions. Since the bubble of the 1990s, there has been an increasing debate in the New Consensus about the role of financial matters in the decisions of a central bank. This debate has been intense and has concerned several subjects, from the relation between financial stability and price stability to the importance of asset prices for monetary-policy decisions and central banking. The debate among Post-Keynesians has been much less intense because there is a broad consensus about the importance of financial matters for central banking. Discussions of the relationship between financial stability, price stability, and full employment have been settled. The debate focuses more on the appropriate goal and interest-rate rule for a central bank. Overall, the chapter concludes that financial matters are an important element that central banks should consider in their daily preoccupations. More precisely, central banks should pay much more attention to the financial imbalances that accumulate in the economic system. The role of a central bank is not to determine if assets are well priced, nor to figure out how to use them to improve inflation targeting, but to understand the implications of changes in asset prices on financial positions.

Chapter 3 narrows the discussion by reviewing three views regarding asset pricing and their implications for central banking. Indeed, views about the way assets are priced have a strong impact on the position taken regarding the role of central banks in the economy. The rational approach assumes that there is an a priori fundamental value toward which the market price converges. The convergence process is more or less fast, depending on the efficiency of financial markets and the rationality of individuals. Speculation is possible, but can persist only as a correcting force that accelerates the convergence process. In this approach, bubbles and crashes are mainly the result of informational problems. In terms of central banking, the essential conclusion of the rational approach is that central banks are not qualified to enter directly in the pricing mechanisms of assets. However, central banks should promote fundamental pricing by contributing to the formation of equity analysts, accountants, and other agents necessary to price assets properly. The irrational approach aims at showing that, contrary to the claim of the rational approach, disruptive speculation may prevail and be permanent in financial markets. This approach focuses on both microeconomic factors (behavioral finance) and macroeconomic factors that promote "irrational exuberance," and shows that bubbles are not necessarily the result of informational problems. Behavioral "biases" or "anomalies," relative to the *homo-economicus* standard, can be explained by psychological, institutional, and social factors. In this context, a self-justification process may exist in which it is the fundamental value that converges toward the market price. The role of the central bank is to help educate people in order to eliminate behavioral anomalies, to help create institutions that promote fundamentalist behaviors, and, when appropriate, to use either moral suasion or margin requirements to constrain the growth of asset prices. The convention approach states that rationality is not hedonistic but social, which implies that most behaviors in financial markets are assumed to be reasonable, given the existing institutional and socio-economic setup. Liquid financial markets, by their nature, promote speculation, and so, contrary to the irrational approach, speculative behaviors are not seen as anomalies and providing all the information necessary will not eliminate speculation. In this context, asset prices are subject to a self-justification process like in the irrational approach but, contrary to the latter, this self-justification process is not necessarily doomed. The structure of the economy may change and may provide solid foundations to the prevailing convention. In the end, what matters is not how well priced assets are, but the sensitivity of balance-sheet positions, cash-flow positions, and position-making activities to changes in asset prices. The central bank should focus its attention on the financial implications of a change in asset-price configurations, and not on the asset-price level *per se*. Thus, preoccupations about the correctness of the level of asset prices are irrelevant and can be dangerous. Even if there is no bubble, checking asset prices is still central to the formulation of a good financial policy.

Chapter 4 explains why interest-rate-based policies are not a good practice in central banking; this is especially the case for rules that aim at targeting a real interest rate. It is argued that the best monetary policy a central bank can have is to set permanently at zero the overnight nominal policy rate on central bank advances. By using theoretical and empirical arguments, the first part of the chapter provides a critique of the notion of real interest rate. It is claimed that the notion of real interest rate is flawed and that Fisher's theory of interest rates cannot provide a good justification for interest-rate policies. Financial market participants may care about purchasing power considerations but, contrary to Fisher, the latter are included in portfolio strategies that include preoccupations regarding liquidity and solvency. In addition, many empirical studies have shown that interest rates have failed consistently to adjust for expected inflation until the mid-1950s in the United States. It is argued that the reason interest rates have responded more strongly (but not fully) to inflation after 1953 is because the Federal Reserve, not financial market participants, has become more Fisherian. The second part of the chapter focuses on interest-rate rules that aim at managing nominal interest rates. It is claimed that the liquidity preference theory has to be understood in the broader context of financial market configurations, and that under specific configurations interest-rate policy creates more volatility than stability. All this provides a foundation to critique the alternative interest-rate rules provided by some Post-Keynesians. Indeed, some of them are for an active interest-rate policy, even though for different goals than the New Consensus. The chapter concludes by providing some arguments for the idea that economic stability is promoted by setting forever at zero the central bank rate on overnight advances. Constantly moving interest rates may promote output-price instability, financial speculation, and lower economic growth.

Chapter 5 studies in detail Minsky's Financial Instability Hypothesis and uses System Dynamics within a stock-flow-consistent framework to model some insights of the Minskian analysis. It is shown that the dynamics of the analysis are complex, and that the instability of capitalist economies does not rest on arguments based on irrationality, the loanable funds theory, asymmetric information, or fallacies of composition. There are psychological, social, economic, institutional, and policy reasons that promote instability. The chapter goes on to argue that the best way to model the Minskian framework is to use models that emphasize the preeminence of nominal cash-flow considerations and in which shifting parameters and the model structure, not *ad hoc* non-linear equations, explain the dynamics of the system. The chapter also provides suggestions for empirically testing the Minskian framework. Overall, this is an important chapter because it lays out a framework that is very helpful to drawing some implications for central banking. Central banks should develop regulatory and supervisory tools that emphasize cash-flow aspects rather than capital requirements. Capital-equity requirement may help constrain the growth of credit by setting minimum standards in terms of collaterals. However, the concept of capital equity has important limitations in terms of preventing risky behaviors, of promoting financial stability in periods of instability, and in understanding how financially sound a financial institution is. Present cash flows and cash balance (liquidity) and future cash flows (solvency) should be the focus of attention of a central bank. Unfortunately, today, there is no macroeconomic accounting framework that focuses exclusively on cash-flow relationships. It is suggested that the stock-flow-consistent framework might be a fruitful tool to develop, in order to help central banks to manage systemic risk and to understand macroeconomic cash-flow implications. However, a large amount of research needs to be devoted to those very important problems in terms of both data availability and conceptual framework. The central bank should also manage financial innovations and should direct financial market participants toward non-speculative financing practices.

Chapter 6 uses the insights obtained in previous chapters to study how the members of the FOMC took into account financial matters in their decision-making process, and how the economic model that they have used to analyze the economy has been challenged. The analysis relies extensively on the FOMC transcripts available at the website of the Federal Reserve System. In the first section of the chapter, it is argued that financial matters have usually been a secondary consideration when setting interest rates. The emphasis is first and foremost on inflation, and most FOMC members do not have a frame of thought that incorporates financial considerations well. The latter are only emphasized in time of financial instability rather than over the whole business cycle. Consequently, FOMC members have been reactive rather than proactive in their management of financial problems. The second section studies how successful FOMC members have been in their analysis of the economic system. It is shown that most of the beliefs of FOMC members have been challenged, from the capacity of the central bank to control the money supply, the determinants of interest rates, the monetary origins of inflation, to the capacity of the central bank to manage inflation. Overall, it is shown that the Post-Keynesian framework would have provided some valuable insights to FOMC members. It is also shown that political considerations are an important determinant in the decisions of the FOMC members. For example, the shift to Monetarism was not based exclusively, or even mainly, on economic arguments. Several, if not a majority of, FOMC members were skeptical about Monetarism and knew that it was impractical in terms of policy. In addition, the Federal Reserve has been reluctant to implement strongly its regulatory framework because of political pressures to leave alone major financial institutions and financial market participants. All this provides some support for a central banking framework that emphasizes financial stability and leaves the management of inflation, economic growth, and income distribution to other government institutions.

2 Central banking, asset prices, and financial fragility

Today, a majority of economists and most central bankers assume that the main goal of a central bank should be to promote price stability, i.e. a stable and low rate of inflation. This goal is considered as the only reasonable objective that can be attributed to a central bank, all other objectives "having failed." Recently, however, an intense debate has taken place among economists about the role that should be given to asset prices and other financial considerations in central bank operations. Most economists have concluded that financial matters have no role in usual policy-making unless they help to improve inflation targeting. However, not all economists agree and some of them would like central banks to put more focus on the management of financial imbalances.

This chapter reviews the literature concerning the role of asset prices and financial fragility within central bank operations by studying the views of the New Consensus (also called New Neoclassical Synthesis) and the Post-Keynesian schools of thought. Other approaches may have dealt with this subject but will not be presented here. It is shown that all authors recognize that financial aspects are important. However, they have different ways of dealing with them and including them into their analysis. Some authors think that price stability will guarantee financial stability and others want a more direct consideration of financial factors in the daily activities of central banks. To get a good grasp of the position of each school, this chapter also presents the main hypotheses that sustain their analysis. It is argued that the Post-Keynesian framework provides a better starting point to understand the inner working of capitalist economies.

Asset prices, financial fragility, and central banking in the new consensus

What is the New Consensus?

The New Consensus finds its roots in Monetarism and in the debate that occurred during the 1970s and 1980s between New Classical, New Keynesian, and Real Business Cycle theorists. The period of stagflation of the mid-1970s led to a rejection of the Neoclassical Synthesis that favored counter-cyclical policies in order to promote high stable economic growth. Several authors provided an explanation of the stagflation period. Friedman (1968) put forward a fooling-and-lag argument, while Weintraub (1978), Lerner (1961, 1979), and Davidson (1978) showed that stagflation could be explained by using Keynes's framework; however, because the rejection of the Neoclassical Synthesis led to a rejection of Keynes's ideas altogether, Friedman's explanation was considered to be the only valid one. The triumph of Monetarist ideas in academia manifested itself at the policy level by the modification of the strategy of central bankers all over the world, the most preeminent changes being at the Federal Reserve in 1979 and at the Bank of England in the early 1980s.

Several authors have surveyed this period and the failure of monetary-aggregate targeting (Greider 1987; Mayer 2001; Crow 2002). Central bankers were never able to target any monetary aggregates and the high variability of short-term interest rates helped to precipitate one of the worst recessions since 1946 in the US. By 1982, Volcker had given up any monetary-aggregate targeting, and the disarray was summarized well by Richard Pratt at the Federal Home Land Bank: "I don't know what money is today [...]. And I don't think anybody at the Fed does, either" (Mayer 1984: 21).

The failure of Monetarist ideas, however, has not led to a total rejection of Monetarism. The idea that "inflation is always and everywhere a monetary phenomenon" (Friedman 1987 (1989): 32) has always been a very appealing argument for central bankers, economists, and the general public. It has provided central bankers a way to legitimize their role in the prevention of inflation. Therefore, given the failure to target inflation by targeting monetary aggregates, central bankers decided that they should directly target inflation by preemptively raising or lowering interest rates. The New Consensus states that monetary policy should be preoccupied with inflation only, and Goodhart summarizes well the current state of affairs:

> In contrast to the previous two decades, there is presently, at the outset of the 1990s, a considerable degree of consensus about the appropriate objectives and functions for a central bank in the conduct of macro monetary policy. [...] The core of the monetarist position remains untouched, or has even strengthened. There has been no serious challenge to the claim that the medium- and long-term Phillips curve is vertical, and hence that monetary policy should focus, primarily, if not solely, on controlling the level of some intermediate nominal variable, so as to anchor the rate of inflation at zero, or some very small positive number. [...] Thus the current consensus is that the central bank should use its (short-run) control over money market interest rates to achieve price stability.
>
> (Goodhart 1992 (1995): 216–217)

The central bank should maintain its inflation target by being "prepared to vary nominal interest rates sharply, both up and down, over the cycle" (Goodhart 1992 (1995): 234). In the following sections, a more detailed justification of this position is provided.

The underlying theoretical framework of the new consensus

The benchmarks are the Real Business Cycle (RBC) and New Classical (NEC) models because, by assuming pure and perfect competition, they give "the efficient response of the economy to [a] shock" (Gilchrist and Leahy 2002: 87), and so do not necessitate any government intervention. However, in the real world, "the existence of credit-market frictions, that is, problems of information incentives, and enforcement in credit relationships" as well as "the existence of nominal rigidities [give] the central bank [...] some control over the short-term real interest rate" (Bernanke and Gertler 1999: 23–24). Then, "the goal of policy should be to mimic [the RBC/NEC models] response as closely as possible" (Gilchrist and Leahy 2002: 87). To understand why, it is necessary to look more closely at the underlying hypotheses of this New Consensus, which can be classified into two categories: long-run neutrality of money and short-term non-neutrality of money.

The long-run neutrality of money manifests itself through two old theoretical elements: the natural rate of interest and the quantity theory of money. The notions of "natural" growth and unemployment rates are also important but will not be presented. They assume that a free market economy leads, in the long run, to a specific state determined by the structure of the economy. This state is an a priori norm toward which the economic system converges, with or without any help from economic policies, and beyond which all intervention only generates inflation or other disturbances. Supply and demand forces are independent of each other.

If money is neutral in the long run, this is not the case in the short run; otherwise there would be no role for an active monetary policy in the New Consensus. To explain this short-term non-neutrality, New Consensus economists assume the existence of "frictions" in goods market, the labor market, and the credit market that take the form of price rigidities and asymmetries of information.[1] In addition, the non-transparency of information is essential to explain financial crises (Bernanke 1983; Bernanke and Gertler 1989, 1995; Mishkin 1991, 1997). Indeed, in a world of efficient financial markets, there would be neither crashes nor bubbles and so it is necessary to assume that agents do not have all the information necessary to make good judgments. The role of the government is to correct the effects of those frictions in order to put back the economy on its natural path. Policy intervention, thus, may be good as long as the government does not try to push the economy above its natural path, which it may have a tendency to do for electoral reasons, or other reasons related to politicians' self-interests (Friedman 1968; Kydland and Prescott 1977; Barro and Gordon 1983). Therefore, having policy institutions that are isolated from political influence is important, which is why the independence of central bank should be promoted.

NATURAL RATE OF INTEREST AND NEUTRALITY OF MONEY

By encapsulating the work of Wicksell and other Neoclassical authors, Fisher (1907, 1930) developed a theory of interest rates that provides a foundation for the idea that money is neutral. To do so, he distinguished the real interest rate (r) and the nominal interest rate (i), and provided an explanation for both. These explanations are very important for the New Consensus and so it is necessary to present them in detail. First, the determination of real rates is explained, followed by the explanation of nominal rates.

The theory starts with the microeconomic decisions of individuals who want "to increase or decrease the flow of their income at different periods of time, and it is through their efforts to do so, by bargaining with each other, that the rate of interest is itself determined" (Fisher 1907: 256). The aim of individuals is to smooth their consumption pattern according to their time preference by arbitraging between their present and future incomes through lending and borrowing operations. These operations are done "under the guise of money" (Fisher 1907: 122), but money is just a veil that helps to transfer across time "enjoyable income." Monetary income is not what matters for individuals, they only care about physical income, i.e. "nourishment, clothing, shelter, amusements, the gratification of vanity, and other miscellaneous items" (Fisher 1907: 91). Enjoyable income is approximated by real income, i.e. price-adjusted monetary income. In terms of interest rates, all this means is that what really matters for individuals is "the rate of interest [...] described as the percentage premium on present goods over future goods of the same kind" (Fisher 1930: 36) determined by "the supply and demand of present and future [enjoyable] income" (Fisher 1907: 131).

Each economic activity provides a specific yield in terms of output. In the "first approximation,"[2] this yield is fixed and known with certainty because it depends on the technique of production. By planting 100 bushels of wheat today, a producer knows that he will obtain 110 bushels in the future, and the real rate on wheat is 10%. Thus, if someone lends wheat, one expects to receive at least a 10% return, and inversely, if someone borrows wheat, one will be willing to pay no more than 10% in the wheat market. In this context, given their time preference, individuals have to decide what asset(s) to buy (where to lend) or to sell (where to borrow) in order to get the highest yield in terms of output, or to pay the lowest cost in terms of output. The higher the preference for the present of individuals, i.e. their impatience, the higher the yield required by lenders, and the higher rate borrowers are ready to pay.

At the aggregate level, assuming that a representative rate exists because of perfect competition (Roberston 1940: 84; Fisher 1907: 328) and that there is only one "commodity" (aggregate real income), there is a unique, required real rate that makes the marginal individual indifferent between borrowing and lending aggregate income. This required rate is equivalent to Wicksell's natural rate of interest. It is the one that equalized the marginal productivity of capital and the time preference of individuals. The easier it is for existing production capacities to satisfy the preference for the present of individuals, the lower the required real interest rate will be. The required real rate will be more stable when a large choice of physical yields is available and when social factors, among which the time preference is the most important, are stable over time (Fisher 1907: 328–330). The stability usually holds except during periods of "fashion" (Fisher 1907: 333). Thus, the level and change in the real interest rate are explained, in first approximation, by several factors, two of which being "(1) The extent of the effective range of choice of different incomes which are open to each individual; (2) the dependence of 'time preference' upon prospective income" (Fisher 1907: 328).

Following this explanation of real rates, Fisher turns to nominal interest rates. Indeed, to be able to compare the rate on different activities, individuals need to define a common denominator, which can be any asset. Once a standard has been chosen, changes in the standard will affect all standard rates; therefore, individuals have to consider this effect in the arbitrage process. Say, following Fisher, that individuals have a choice between two assets, gold and wheat, and that gold is a monetary asset. Table 2.1 shows the real rates on gold and wheat.

Individuals can choose between lending (borrowing) B bushels of wheat today and getting from the crop (having to pay) $B(1+r_w)$ bushels of wheat in the future, or lending (borrowing) D dollars at r_g and getting (paying) $D(1+r_g)$ dollars in the future. Individuals will be indifferent if

$$B(1+r_w) \text{ bushels} \Leftrightarrow D(1+r_g) \text{ dollars.}$$

However, the comparison cannot be done in this way because the denomination is not the same. In the real world, all rates are money rates and so it is necessary to calculate the money rate (or, in this case, the gold rate) on wheat. To do so, arbitragers must take into account the change in the price of a bushel of wheat (p_w) in terms of dollars during the carrying (or production) period, so that purchasing power is not altered. Say that p_w changes by π_w, in order to obtain B bushels of wheat in the future, arbitragers will have to pay $D(1+\pi_w)$ dollars, which means that D dollars will buy $B/(1+\pi_w)$ bushels of wheat. Therefore, if individuals lend (borrow) D dollars today, they know that getting (paying) $D(1+r_g)$ will allow them to buy (to deliver) $B(1+r_g)/(1+\pi_w)$ bushels of wheat in the future. If the latter amount is superior (inferior) to $B(1+r_w)$ bushels, individuals buy/lend (sell/borrow) gold. Thus, individuals are indifferent when they will obtain/pay the same amount of goods by lending/borrowing in gold or wheat:

$$B(1+r_w) = B(1+r_g)/(1+\pi_w).$$

That is

$$(1+r_w)(1+\pi_w) = (1+r_g).$$

By developing, we have

$$r_w + \pi_w + r_w \cdot \pi_w = r_g.$$

Table 2.1 Real rates on wheat and on gold

Assets	Today	Future	Real rates
Gold (dollars)	D	$D(1+r_g)$	r_g
Wheat (bushels)	B	$B(1+r_w)$	r_w

The gold rate on wheat is $i_w \equiv r_w + \pi_w + r_w \cdot \pi_w$ and, when no arbitrage is profitable, it is equal to the gold rate on gold ($i_g \equiv r_g$). However, today, π_w is unknown and so individuals can only base their decisions on expectations about the change in the wheat price. Thus, the actual condition of indifference is not the previous one but

$$r_w + E(\pi_w) + r_w \cdot E(\pi_w) = r_g.$$

These expectations are used to rationalize transactions in spot and forward markets. Indeed, if at time 0, $i_{w0} > i_{g0}$, it is profitable for individuals to borrow gold to buy wheat spot,[3] and to sell wheat forward. At the settlement date, individuals sell wheat for gold, obtaining a rate of return i_{w0}, and reimburse their gold loan (contracted at i_{g0}). This arbitrage process leads to an increase (decrease) in the spot price (S) of wheat (gold), and a decrease (increase) in the forward price (F) of wheat (gold) so that $E(\pi_w) = \left(\frac{F_w/F_g - S_w/S_g}{S_w/S_g}\right)$ decreases, and so i_w decreases, until $i_w = i_g$. If r_w and $E(\pi_w)$ are small, $r_w \cdot E(\pi_w)$ is negligible and the condition of indifference can be written as $i_g = r_w + E(\pi_w)$.

Assuming the condition of arbitrage between two assets also holds at the aggregate level,[4] the arbitrage can be reduced to a choice between aggregate real income and money. The arbitrage equalizes the (expected) real rate $r \equiv i - E(\pi)$ on real income to the required real rate r^* on real income:

$$i = r^* + E(\pi) \Leftrightarrow r^* = i - E(\pi).$$

In addition, at the aggregate level, the adjustment does not go via $E(\pi)$, but via i. r^* is still given by technology and impatience, and inflation expectations are derived from the quantity identity. This provides an explanation of what drives the nominal rates of interest; they are "connected with [expected] changes in the standard of value" while the real rates are "connected with the other and deeper economic causes" that were presented above (Fisher 1907: 327). A high nominal rate of interest on money results from high expectations of inflation or high required real return on aggregate real income.

This conclusion is exceedingly important for the New Consensus. It shows that the central bank should manage inflation because "the really important disturbance is this discrepancy between real interest rate and money rate" (Fisher 1932: 38–39). Indeed, if price instability prevails, two things happen. First, the actual purchasing power gain/cost of income arbitrages, $i - \pi$, is different from the real rate, which leads to a Wicksellian positive feedback loop unless i adjusts by a large enough amount. Indeed, if, for example, $\pi_t > E_{t-1}(\pi_t)$ so that $i_t - \pi_t < r_{t-1} = r^*_{t-1}$, then, borrowers (investors) are encouraged and lenders (savers) are discouraged, which generates more inflation, unless i rises fast enough to offset any incentive to borrow. In the real world (third approximation), this requires the intervention of a central bank because, as shown in chapter 4, expected inflation and actual inflation are not well integrated in the decision process of private agents. Second, in case of price instability, $E(\pi)$ will be unstable and so r will vary a lot relative to r^*. This will lead borrowers and lenders to limit their arbitrages, and so will generate a suboptimal level of income and economic growth, because of the lack of visibility of the future.

A central bank, thus, should guide inflation expectations so that price stability prevails and errors of expectation are limited. If necessary, it should intervene to adjust i so that disequilibrium between investment and saving do not persist. By providing a stable r and $i - \pi$ relative to r^*, the central bank will stabilize the confidence of borrowers and lenders and so economic activity.[5] While implementing this policy, the central bank should not hesitate to be very aggressive:

> The human race should forget its primitive notions about interest. One of the greatest of all economic reforms would be, on the one hand, to get rid of the popular prejudice against raising, promptly and drastically, rates of interest when conditions justify; and, on the other hand, to get rid of the inertia which keeps rates high when conditions call for reduction.
>
> (Fisher 1932: 127)

The central bank should use a wide variety of clues to assess price stability. And, even if there are no clues, it should not hesitate to implement preemptive actions if it has any doubts that price stability is threatened:

> The point is to quell the inflation as soon as the price level is even slightly affected by it. Even in cases (like 1923–1929) in which the commodity price level fails to register the inflation, there is still the stock market as an indicator; and even if inflation altogether escapes observation or is neglected, then to prevent the sequel, deflation will become all the more important.
>
> (Fisher 1932: 121)

If the central bank fails to do that, its interest-rate policy will become ineffective (Fisher 1932: 130) and, eventually, price instability will generate financial instability.

THE MODIFIED QUANTITY THEORY OF MONEY

In this framework of analysis, money is neutral in the long run, in the sense that it does not have long-term impacts on production. Putting the quantity identity in terms of growth rates and making some assumptions, we have:

$$m + v \equiv \pi + g_Q \Rightarrow \pi = m - g_{Qn} + \bar{v},$$

with v constant, because of habits of payments (Friedman 1987), and $g_Q = g_{Qn}$ the natural rate of growth of the economy. If monetary authorities increase the money supply more rapidly than the natural growth of output, prices will increase by a proportional amount. This theory complements the Fisherian approach by showing that the central bank can control inflation by controlling m; therefore, it is well suited to deal with the management of real interest rates.

There is, however, a twist to the New Consensus approach because now m is endogenous and so the previous equation should be rewritten:

$$m = \pi + g_{Qn} - \bar{v}.$$

This endogeneity is supposed, not because of the nature of money, which is assumed to be a pure asset (a commodity) best represented by precious metals, but because of the procedure used by central banks to manage the economy, i.e. central banks always have had an interest-setting procedure.[6]

The quantity equation, however, still has its use as a medium-/long-term guide for monetary policy. Meyer (2001) shows how the central bank should determine a reference value for m (m^*) that is consistent with its inflation target π^T, the prevailing g_{Qn}, and the existing trend of velocity:

$$m^* = \pi^T + g_{Qn} - \bar{v}.$$

If $m > m^*$, inflation will be above target. This provides a medium-term view for central bankers:

> The purpose of the reference value, in my view, is not to read short-run deviations from it as signals of the need for adjustments in policy. The short-term variability in velocity makes the extraction of such a signal too difficult. Instead, the purpose of the reference value is to provide a check that might help avoid significant and persistent errors that undermine the Fed's medium-term inflation objective.
>
> (Meyer 2001: 11)

Thus, if in the short run the causality $m \rightarrow \pi$ disappears, in the medium/long run it is still present.

THE SHORT-RUN NON-NEUTRALITY OF MONEY AND NOMINAL RIGIDITIES

Three equations represent the reduced form of a dynamic general equilibrium model of real business cycle, like the one presented by Bernanke *et al.* (1999). These equations are the core of the New Consensus (Clarida *et al.* 1999; Meyer 2001; Walsh 2002):

$$x_t = \gamma_1 x_{t-1} + \gamma_2 E_t(x_{t+1}) - \gamma_3(i_t - E_t(\pi_{t+1})) + u_t,$$

$$\pi_t = \gamma_4 x_t + \gamma_5 \pi_{t-1} + \gamma_6 E_t(\pi_{t+1}) + z_t,$$

$$i_t = r^* + E_t(\pi_{t+1}) + \gamma_7 x_{t-1} + \gamma_8(\pi_{t-1} - \pi^T),$$

where $x_t \equiv (g_{Qt} - g_{Qn})/g_{Qn}$ is the percentage point difference between actual and natural output growth rates, $\gamma_5 + \gamma_6 = 1$ (current inflation is a weighted average of past and future inflation), and u_t and z_t are stochastic variables that represent shocks on demand and supply. The use of lagged variables illustrates the effect of policy lags and price rigidities (Friedman 1968; Gordon 1990). The first equation is an IS curve that represents the demand side of the model, which is a function of the previous output gap, the expected output gap, and the expected real rate of interest. The second equation represents the supply side of the model. It is the New Phillips curve, which is a positive relationship between output gap and inflation that includes expected inflation and price stickiness. The last equation is an interest-rate rule. "The" interest rate (the central bank sets the short-term rate and "all other interest rates and asset prices are linked, directly or indirectly, to the policy rate through stable and predictable arbitrage relationships" (Meyer 2001: 5)), is a function of the expected nominal rate on non-monetary assets corrected for past output gap and the difference between past inflation and targeted inflation.

The underlying dynamics of the model are simple (Walsh 2002). They rest on the same principle as the one set by Friedman (1968), except that here the central bank manages interest rates, expectations are rational, and some imperfections are added in terms of nominal rigidities. At equilibrium, the economy grows at its potential rate, expectations of inflation are realized, and inflation is on target: $x_t = 0, E_t(\pi_{t+1}) = \pi_t = \pi_{t-1} = \pi^T$. Say that the economy is at equilibrium and that the central bank decides to decrease its inflation target. In this case, $E_t(\pi_{t+1}) = \pi_t = \pi_{t-1} > \pi^T$ and so the central bank increases its interest rate. This raises the real interest rate $i_t - E_t(\pi_{t+1})$, which discourages investment and consumption and so puts the economy below its potential growth rate, $x_t < 0$. With the economy growing below potential, inflation declines progressively and so the inflation gap is reduced ($\Delta(\pi_{t-1} - \pi^T) < 0$). This leads to a progressive decline in expectations of inflation ($\Delta E_t(\pi_{t+1}) < 0$), which shifts the New Phillips curve downward. Given the tendencies of output and inflation, the central bank lowers its nominal interest rate in order to stimulate economic activity and to help to close the output gap. Note that when it changes its interest rate, the central bank should be "aggressive." Indeed, absolute changes in nominal interest rates must be superior to absolute changes in expected inflation; otherwise, $i_t - E_t(\pi_{t+1})$ goes up when expectation of inflation goes down, which discourages further economic activity (Clarida *et al.* 1999: 1663; Walsh 2002: 344).[7] The process of adjustment to a new inflation target continues until a new long-term equilibrium is reached.[8] The more flexible prices are the less real impact monetary policy has, and if prices can adjust immediately, no real effects are recorded because real interest rates are unchanged.

As an aside, one may note that all this illustrates well that the New Neoclassical Synthesis is much more Fisherian than Wicksellian in its nature. Indeed, even though it draws on the concept of natural rate of interest, "Wicksell viewed inflation as being a disequilibrium phenomenon [whereas] inflation in the New-Keynesian model is an equilibrium phenomenon" (Weber *et al.* 2008: 54).

Forward transactions that allow the implementation of optimal forward-looking decisions over a set of complete markets are involved.

One assumption of the New Consensus is that financial markets are efficient: "the primary role of the capital market is allocation of ownership of the economy's capital stock. [It is] [...] a market in which prices provide accurate signals for resource allocation" (Fama 1970: 383). In this context, "prior to the introduction of informational asymmetries, the framework resembles a simple real business cycle model; financial structure is irrelevant" (Gertler 1988: 581) and "banks and other financial institutions are simply veils over real economic behavior" (Gertler 1988: 575). Therefore, in the New Consensus, the use of asymmetries of information is essential to explain how money, or more broadly the financial structure, can have an influence on the economy. Mishkin (1991, 1997) provides a comprehensive statement of this position.

The economy always records "shocks" in terms of higher interest rates, declines in balance-sheet quality, stock market declines, or higher uncertainty. Mishkin does not provide an explanation of how those shocks emerge but focuses on their consequences through the impact of information asymmetries. For example, an increase in perceived risk surrounding the quality of the borrowers leads lenders to increase the real interest rate they charge on their loans. However, higher interest rates reduce the proportion of good borrowers because risky borrowers, who potentially get a higher return and so care less about the cost of borrowing, will not be discouraged as much as good borrowers. To avoid this adverse selection, lenders can either ration credit, which is bad for economic activity, or demand collateral: "With collateral, therefore, the fact that there is asymmetric information between the borrower and lender is no longer as important a factor in the market" (Mishkin 1991: 72). However, once loans have been granted, all borrowers may have an incentive to cheat either by not implementing exactly the project funded or by becoming careless. This also gives the incentive to lenders to limit their supply of loans so that "lending and investment will be at suboptimal levels" (Mishkin 1991: 73). One way to diminish moral hazard is to supervise the balance sheet of borrowers by making sure that their net wealth is high enough. Indeed, borrowers with little net wealth have nothing to lose and so they will take greater risks.

According to Mishkin, the preceding implies three ways through which shocks on the economy can be amplified and generate debt-deflation tendencies in an efficient market economy. First, shocks in the financial markets increase real interest rates, which increase the adverse selection problem, leading to an increase in credit rationing. Second, financial market crashes decrease the value of financial assets used as collateral, which increases the risk of adverse selection and moral hazard. Finally, unanticipated deflation increases the real value of debts and the resulting decline in real net worth increases moral hazard. All this leads to credit rationing, and the credit squeeze decreases investment and economic activity, which has potential feedback effects on the financial structure through the emergence of bank runs, and ultimately, debt-deflation processes (Bernanke 1983; Mishkin 1991, 1997; Kiyotaki and Moore 1997).

Suarez and Sussman (1997, 1999, 2007) have completed this imperfection view of financial crisis by focusing on the reversion mechanisms rather than the propagation mechanisms. They show how the moral hazard leads to an endogenous business cycle. As the boom proceeds, agents become more indebted and the loss of equity decreases the incentive of borrowers to run their business conscientiously, which increases the probability of default.

Conclusion: The role of monetary policy in the New Consensus

Both the long-term neutrality of money and the existence of market imperfections are essential for the New Consensus. They provide a justification for the role given to central banks in the management of inflation. Because real rates of return are assumed to be what matter for entrepreneurs and financial market participants, inflation should be the central preoccupation of the government. Because excessive monetary creation is the main source of inflation, monetary authorities have to be given the objective to control inflation by managing the money supply directly (money-supply targeting) or indirectly (interest-rate targeting).

In terms of monetary policy, this leads to a framework called "Inflation Targeting," which is characterized by "the announcement of official target ranges for the inflation rate at one or more horizons, and by explicit acknowledgement that low and stable inflation is the overriding goal of monetary policy" (Bernanke and Mishkin 1997: 97). Practically, this means that Inflation Targeting is a framework of decisions for central bankers. Discretion is still possible to accommodate for output stabilization, financial stability, and exchange rate problems, but it is a "constrained discretion" (Bernanke and Mishkin 1997: 104). Indeed, any discretionary decision must be justified by "its impact on conditional forecast of target variables," otherwise judgment should not influence the rule (Disyatat 2005: 11). This can be implemented, for example, by allowing short-term inflation to be off target, or by having a wider range for the inflation target. Another way to accommodate for short-term problems is by having a definition of inflation that excludes supply shocks, volatile prices, and other distorting elements (Bernanke and Mishkin 1997: 99, 101).

In the end, the New Consensus reaches conclusion very similar to Fisher. The aim of the central bank is to target inflation by managing expectations of inflation in order to stabilize real interest rates. A central bank should change its short-term interest rates each time its long-term expectations of inflation change, even if today there is no sign of inflation at all:

> Monetary authorities need to be brave in the face of uncertainty, and be prepared to vary interest rates earlier and more violently than their natural caution would normally entertain.
>
> (Goodhart 1992 (1995): 227)

By changing its short-term rate, the central bank will affect directly the other short-term rates, and indirectly (via expectations of future monetary policy) long-term rates, allowing i to compensate for changes in $E(\pi)$. Laubach and Williams (2003) have shown that r^* fluctuated widely in the US over the past 40 years.[9] In this case, an even greater variability of i, is needed in order to avoid a too accommodative or too restrictive policy (Meyer 2004: 182).

Inflation targeting, asset prices, and financial fragility

Now that the theoretical framework of the New Consensus, as well as its monetary policy recommendations have been presented, it is possible to review the literature about the role of financial considerations in the decision process of central bankers. This literature can be divided into three parts. The first part studies the relationship between price stability and financial stability. The second part questions if it is necessary to include asset prices in monetary policy decisions. The third part of the literature goes beyond inflation targeting and studies the appropriate use of asset prices by the central bank in order to promote financial stability.

Price stability and financial stability

There are two positions in the New Consensus regarding the relation between price stability and financial stability. The first one argues that price stability guarantees financial stability and so a central bank should not be preoccupied with financial stability and asset prices in its daily operations. Only when a financial crisis occurs, which is very rare, should a central bank intervene by acting as a lender of last resort. The second position argues that price stability can trigger financial instability; therefore, financial considerations have an active role to play in monetary policy decisions.

PRICE STABILITY GENERATES FINANCIAL STABILITY

Schwartz (1988, 1998) has been the main advocate of this position. Relying on an earlier work with Friedman (Friedman and Schwartz 1963), she argues that inflation is the major threat to financial stability. More precisely, she argues that high unexpected changes in prices generate financial instability:

> The reason that price instability confounds financial stability is related to the way financial institutions conduct credit analysis. [...] The lender bases both the estimate of a would-be borrower's balance sheet ratios and the valuation of collateral on his presumption of the continuation for the life of the loan of the current price level or inflation rate. Unexpected changes in the price level or inflation rate can invalidate the assumptions on which the loan was based. [...] The original price level and inflation rate assumptions are no longer valid. The change in monetary policy makes rate of return calculations on the yield of

projects, based on the initial price assumptions of both lenders and borrowers, unrealizable. Borrowers lose the sums they have invested. Lenders have to contend with loses on loans.

(Schwarz 1998: 38–39)

Schwartz states that both lenders and borrowers live in the same state of uncertainty when they evaluate a project and so "asymmetric information is not the problem confronting lenders and borrowers" (Schwarz 1998: 39). The problem is that monetary authorities vainly try to stimulate the economy above its natural path, which generates inflation. By generating persistent high inflation, the central bank encourages optimistic expectations of nominal income by lenders and borrowers. Thus, the economy becomes more sensitive to changes in prices, and, in periods of high inflation, even disinflation can be harmful by decreasing the speed of nominal income gains relative to the interest rate. This is true for both entrepreneurs and bankers whose "perceptions of credit and interest rate risk both on the upswings and the downswings of price movements" are distorted by price instability (Schwartz 1988: 41).

Therefore, by promoting price stability, the central bank "will do more for financial stability than reforming deposit insurance or reregulating" (Schwartz 1988: 55). The price stability policy should be implemented at a low level of inflation, because "the variability of changes in relative prices seems to rise as the overall rate of inflation rises" (Schwartz 1998: 34). By doing this, central banks will reduce the variability of the nominal rate of interest and make it easier for banks to access creditworthiness, which promote economic growth and financial stability.

Bordo *et al.* (2002) and Bordo and Wheelock (1998) have tested the "Schwartz Hypothesis" that (expected) price stability promotes financial stability. They found a positive correlation between price instability and financial instability (taken in the narrow sense of bank panics (Schwartz (1988)) and go on to argue that

This circumstantial evidence is largely consistent with the Schwartz Hypothesis. At a minimum, the historical association of severe financial instability with fluctuations in the price level would seem to support the arguments of those who favor a price stability mandate for monetary policy.

(Bordo and Wheelock 1998: 42)

Bernanke and Gertler share this view and state that "central banks should view price stability and financial stability as highly complementary and mutually consistent objectives, to be pursued within a unified policy framework" called Inflation Targeting (Bernanke and Gertler 1999: 18).

PRICE STABILITY MAY TRIGGER FINANCIAL INSTABILITY

While adhering to the Inflation Targeting framework, some authors have critiqued the preceding view. They argue that the relationship between price stability and financial stability is not as simple. McGee (2000) and Bean (2003) show that output-price stability and solid growth may lead to the development of bullish expectations in financial markets, which, by generating optimistic views about the future and by increasing the value of collateral, may trigger a credit boom that reinforces the bullish financial market.

Borio and Lowe (2002, 2003) give four reasons why financial stability may not result from price stability. First, a successful monetary policy can improve the optimism of economic agents by improving the possibility of long-term planning. This optimism will be transferred to asset prices, particularly real estate, which will affect credit markets. The boom in the credit market, by generating looser creditworthiness criteria, may trigger financial instability in the future when borrowers cannot meet their income expectations. Second, a positive supply-side shock by, for example, increasing productivity may increase profitability and optimism about the future. Then "the combination of rising asset prices, strong economic growth and low inflation can lead to overly optimistic expectations of the future, [...] [and can generate] increases in asset and credit markets significantly beyond those justified by the original improvement in productivity" (Borio and Lowe 2002: 21). Third, and this is quite problematic in the inflation-targeting framework, a highly credible monetary policy may anchor inflation expectations so well that wages and prices on long-term contracts may not respond as fast to demand pressures. Finally, related to the previous ideas, output-inflation expectations may manifest themselves first in asset markets rather than goods markets. Thus, a central bank that focuses on goods markets may find little reasons to tighten its policy while financial imbalances are growing. Kaufman (1998) also notes that low output-price inflation leads to low interest rates target by central banks following a "strict inflation targeting" regime (Borio *et al.* 2003: 41). The resulting cheap cost of external funds can contribute to "the acceleration in stock prices as well as accelerating a budding rise in real estate prices" (Kaufman 1998: 34).

Finally, Borio and Lowe (2002) note that unexpected output-price instability may generate financial instability only if financial imbalances are strong. Indeed, the stronger the imbalances, the higher are the dependency of borrowers and lenders on the realization of a certain price level. Mishkin (1997: 92) concludes that price stability and financial stability are mutually reinforcing goals and so both should be pursued independently by central bankers.

Should monetary policy take into account asset prices?

The first debate about the role of asset prices for monetary policy concerns the importance of asset prices for smoothing inflation and output growth. The overall conclusion of this debate is summarized by Smets (1997) and Disyatat (2005): If asset-price misalignments (bubbles) can be identified and if they provide relevant information about future inflation and future growth, it may be useful to include them in the reaction function to "achieve the optimal price level" and growth rate.

The Bank of International Settlements (1997) concluded that asset prices are good indicators of future inflation and output growth. However, for the BIS, asset prices should not be included in the reaction function but should be used as additional indicators for policy formulation. This may be seen as a middle position in the current state of the debate. Some authors argue for an inclusion of asset prices in the reaction function, others are for a "benign neglect."

INCLUSION OF ASSET PRICES IN THE REACTION FUNCTION OF THE CENTRAL BANK

The first side of the debate argues that inflation targeting would be improved by including asset prices in the reaction function of central banks. This is so because asset-price misalignments, even if they are hard to measure, are measurable by central banks, and because asset prices are reliable indicators of future inflation. The inclusion of asset prices can be done through a broader measure of inflation, or through a direct inclusion in the reaction function.

Alchian and Klein (1973) argued early that asset prices are relevant to improve the measure of expected output-price inflation. Schinasi (1994), Goodhart (1992, 1993, 1999, 2001), Goodhart and Hofmann (2000, 2001), the International Monetary Fund (2000), and Christoffersen and Schinasi (2003) argue that there is a positive correlation between asset prices and CPI, and that the former, especially housing prices, help to predict inflation. Thus, by including asset prices in a broader measure of inflation, the central bank can improve its inflation targeting and potential-output targeting because it will react faster to emerging problems. This policy suggests that variations of interest rates would be wider than current monetary policy, and so it would be necessary to protect the banking system (Goodhart 1993).

This position implies that it would be redundant to include asset prices directly in the reaction function because they would be already included in the inflation measure. However, another group of economists (Smets 1997; Cecchetti *et al.* 2000; Cecchetti 2003; Cecchetti *et al.* 2003) wants to go further. They argue that asset prices have their own place in the reaction function. They agree with the preceding authors that asset prices help to predict inflation (Bryan *et al.* 2001), but they argue that inflation targeting is improved by reacting directly to asset-price misalignments. They recognize that the calculation of misalignments is difficult, but they consider that they are not harder to calculate than, for example, potential output. In this context, the central bank should react to all asset prices if they are misaligned (Cecchetti *et al.* 2000: 59). This does not mean that the central bank should target asset prices or should try to burst asset bubbles; it only means that the central bank should automatically move its interest rates to respond to asset-price misalignments, with the objective to improve inflation targeting and nothing else. By doing so, the central bank will reduce the variability of inflation and output (Cecchetti *et al.* 2000: 35).

Filardo (2001, 2004), Dupor (2002, 2005), Roubini (2006), and Berger *et al.* (2007) have complemented this view by showing that, once the weight put on asset prices is derived from an optimization strategy, and not randomly like in Bernanke and Gertler (1999, 2001) or Cecchetti *et al.* (2000), the loss is always minimized by reacting to asset-price misalignments. Contrary to Cecchetti (2003), they show that this holds true even if the central bank cannot distinguish between fundamental and non-fundamental components of a bubble, and if asset prices are volatile. In those cases, the weight will be lower but, usually, it will not be zero.

Contrary to Goodhart, these authors do not argue that the Fed should rapidly move its interest rates: "A crucial element of our proposal is that interest rates would move gradually in response to deviations of asset prices from perceived fundamentals" (Cecchetti *et al.* 2000: 53). Filardo (2001), however, notes that a central bank that cares about interest-rate smoothing may not include asset-price inflation in the reaction function. This is especially the case because there is more to monetary policy than inflation and output variability. Indeed, financial fragility is an important factor to take into account that is not included in previous models.

BENIGN NEGLECT TOWARD ASSET PRICES

The other side of the debate views the inclusion of asset prices as counterproductive or unnecessary. This is the conventional view in the New Consensus. The authors holding this position agree that asset prices should be included if they had the potential to improve inflation forecasting and output-growth forecasting, but they find that either asset prices do not help to improve inflation forecasting, or the inclusion of asset prices is not beneficial (the loss is not lower) if appropriate weights are put on inflation and output in the reaction function.

Borio *et al.* (1994), Shiratsuka (1999), Stock and Watson (2003), and Filardo (2000) conclude that aggregate asset-prices indexes, or individual asset prices, are not reliable leading indicators for inflation or output growth. The authors usually can find a predictive power but "the strength and regularity of the relationship, however, are open to question" (Borio *et al.* 1994: 66):

> Some asset prices have substantial and statistically significant marginal predictive content for output growth at some times in some countries. Whether this predictive content can be exploited reliably is less clear [...]. Finding an indicator that predicts well in one period is no guarantee that it will predict well in later periods.
>
> (Stock and Watson 2003: 789)

One explanation provided by those studies is that the predictive capacity of asset prices depends on the institutional context (Spaventa 1998; Stock and Watson 2003), and on the nature of asset-price growth. For example, if one asset is highly represented in the portfolios of households, it has more chance to generate a wealth effect, and growth of asset prices due to productivity growth will not trigger inflation. Thus, the main conclusion of these studies is that "hard and fast rules are clearly inappropriate; considerable judgment is called for" (Borio *et al.* 1994: 66).

At the theoretical level, Goodfriend (1998a, 2001, 2003) argues that equity prices are a misleading indicator for inflation forecasting; a role already fulfilled by the spot-rate yield curve (Goodfriend 1998b). More generally, a preemptive monetary policy is, for him, usually in conflict with taking into account asset prices. This is so because in order to prevent inflation, a central bank may have to increase its interest rate, even if asset prices are decreasing and there are no signs of inflation. Another point of Goodfriend's argument (Goodfriend 2001) is that the capacity of the central bank to affect long-term rates rests on a relative inertia of its policy. However, as shown above, the proponents of an inclusion of asset prices concluded that wider fluctuations in short-term rates would be necessary.

Putting aside cases of financial crisis, Bernanke and Gertler (1999, 2001), Artus (2000), Bullard and Schaling (2002), and Fuhrer and Moore (1992) argue that the improvement of inflation targeting is insignificant, nil, or even negative by adding asset prices into the reaction function of the central bank. Gilchrist and Leahy (2002) summarize the position by arguing that asset prices should not be included in an inflation index or be used to forecast inflation, and by showing that strong inflation targeting by the central bank leads to an efficient response to a shock. However, Artus (2003) has amended his view by arguing that if the central bank wants to stabilize output prices, it should react to asset prices. Only if the central bank tries to stabilize output after a demand shock should it not react to asset prices.

Bernanke and Gertler (1999, 2001) argue that a flexible inflation targeting that is aggressive enough provides both price stability and financial stability. This is so because this policy focuses strongly on the stabilization of aggregate demand; therefore, it already includes the possibility of a wealth effect. In addition, the absence of disinflation or deflation promotes financial stability as Schwarz argues, and lower inflation decreases interest rates and asset-price volatility and so limits adverse balance-sheet effects. Finally, the awareness of economic agents that the central bank will react to asset prices if they affect output-price inflation limits the possibility of overreactions and bubbles. This result is similar to Furher and Moore (1992), who show that the higher the weight on asset prices, the lower the control of inflation. Bernanke and Gertler claim that Cecchetti *et al.* found their results because they made special assumptions. They assumed that the central bank could know if stock markets are driven by fundamentals, and they assumed that the central bank knows when the bubble will burst.

Asset prices and financial stability: Beyond inflation targeting

While the previous debate examines the role of asset prices within the framework of inflation targeting, the following two debates focus purely on financial aspects. The positions taken in those debates affect the position taken in the previous debates. The first debate wonders if central banks should try to prick bubbles and under what conditions they could do so. The second debate argues that it is not asset-price bubbles that really matter but the fragility of the financial system. Some authors are for a proactive reaction to financial matters, while others argue in favor of a reactive approach by the central bank.

BUBBLES AND CENTRAL BANKING

Bubbles can be very harmful for the economy when they burst because they generate a shift in expectations and a decline in the value of collateral, which may lead to a credit crunch and a recession. This concern led Kent and Lowe (1997) to wonder if it may be preferable to burst bubbles early. A central bank can increase its interest rate in order to increase the chance of collapse of a bubble. This may lead to a small contraction or stagnation, but "it reduces the probability of the much larger medium-term swings in output and inflation that would eventuate if the bubble was allowed to continue unchecked" (Kent and Lowe 1997: 19). Cecchetti *et al.* (2000) agree with this position, and, as shown earlier, argue that the central bank can get information about asset-price misalignments. Finally, Gruen *et al.* (2003) and Bordo and Jeanne (2002) show that the bursting of the bubble is desirable under some circumstances but not others. They argue in favor of an intervention by central banks when

> The asset-price bubble is small enough, [...] [that is to say, if] the probability that the bubble will burst of its own accord over the next year is assessed to be small; the bubble's probability of bursting is quite interest sensitive; efficiency losses associated with the bubble rise strongly with the bubble's size; or, the bubble's demise is expected to occur gradually over an extended period, rather than in a sudden burst.
>
> (Gruen *et al.* 2003: 275–276)

This implies that the central bank can measure quickly misalignments and can assess the impact of the burst on the economy. If the bubble is strong and rational, meaning that the expectations of future growth are well anchored so that many decisions are based on them, large variations in interest rates will be necessary to burst the bubble and this is not recommended. Indeed, large variations in interest rates are harmful for economic activity, especially when financial imbalances are high. Roubini, however, argues that recent experiences in Australia, New Zealand, and the United Kingdom show that small increases in interest rates can be sufficient to stop a bubble smoothly. This is all the more the case that bubbles and financial imbalances are not necessarily related. Higher interest rates should be coupled with dispassionate speeches about the state of the economy, something the Fed, especially Greenspan, failed to do during the 1990s (Roubini 2006; Meyer 2004).

The majority of the authors in the New Consensus (including central bankers) do not agree with the preceding position. The main argument put forward is that financial markets are efficient and so it is very daring for a central bank to claim that it knows better than the market. It is impossible for a central bank to know when there is a bubble before the market does and, if the market knows that there is a bubble, it will correct the misalignment automatically (Mishkin 1988;

Goodfriend 1998a, 2001; Issing 1998; Cogley 1999). Bernanke (2002) and the European Central Bank (2005) argue that "safe popping" is not feasible by using interest rates because large variations in interest rates are always needed. In addition, Posen (2006) argues that there is considerable evidence that bubbles do not have monetary origins.

Borio and Lowe (2002, 2003) and Ferguson (2005) argue that bubbles are too difficult to measure, and involve political interests because of their impact on the wealth of economic agents. The latter put strong pressures on central bankers not to try to burst bubbles (Mishkin 1988; Borio *et al.* 2003; Meyer 2004: 143–144). Finally, Posen (2006), Mishkin and White (2003a, 2003b), Detken and Smets (2004), and Trichet (2005) argue that bubbles are not in themselves harmful for the economy. They argue that not all market crashes have been followed by economic instability and that the heart of the problem lies more in the fragility of financial positions.

FINANCIAL FRAGILITY AND ASSET PRICES

The final discussion in the New Consensus concerns the relation between financial fragility and asset prices. As shown at the end of the preceding discussion, the sensitivity of the economy to asset prices is an important matter. Borio and Lowe (2002, 2003), Mussa (2003), and Filardo (2004) argue that the level of asset prices does not matter or is an inappropriate target. "Financial imbalances" are what matters and are measured independently of the measurement of a bubble. According to those authors, these imbalances can be checked by looking at the growth of credit, the growth of investment, and the rapid growth of asset prices. To these different measures, it is possible to attribute thresholds, based on historical values, that will define if there is an unsustainable boom in the economy. The role of a central bank should be to respond to both inflation forecasting and financial imbalances:

> Under such a regime the central bank might opt for higher interest rates than are justified simply on the basis of the short-term inflation outlook if there are clear signs of financial imbalances, such as if credit growth is rapid and asset prices are rising quickly.
>
> (Borio and Lowe 2003: 261)

This inclusion of financial imbalances into the reaction function may lead central banks to leave aside short-term inflation considerations. The "new-environment view" of the New Consensus (Borio *et al.* 2003) argues that short-term conflict between the goal of price stability and of financial stability may be resolved by focusing on the greater good of long-term price stability (Brousseau and Detken 2001). All this could be complemented by a macro-oriented prudential regulation (Borio and Lowe 2002; Borio *et al.* 2003).

Bordo and Jeanne (2002), Filardo (2001), the European Central bank (2005: 54), Bean (2003), Disyatat (2005), and Bell and Quiggin (2006) concur that financial imbalances are important for the daily policy of a central bank, but they also note that the macroeconomic model underlying inflation targeting lacks important elements to deal with financial issues:

> If there is scope for proactive monetary policy, it is highly contingent on a number of factors for which output, inflation and the current level of asset prices do not provide appropriate summary statistics. It depends on the risks in the balance sheets of private agents assessed by reference to the risks in asset markets. The balance of these risks cannot be summarized in two or three macroeconomic variables.
>
> (Bordo and Jeanne 2002: 144)

Disyatat also notes that simply lengthening the horizon of output-price expectations will not help to solve potential conflict between goals: "financial imbalances [...] must [...] be introduced into the forecasting model" (Disyatat 2005: 24). In the end, the central bank may have to deviate from the Taylor-rule framework and use judgments; flexible inflation targeting should be implemented to account for financial imbalances (Bean 2003).

Most authors agree with the idea that financial fragility matters (Mishkin and White 2003a, 2003b; Bernanke and Gertler 1990; Gertler 1998; Illing 2001; Schwartz 2003; Ferguson 2005; Posen 2006; Detken and Smets 2004); however, they may not agree with the implications that Borio and Lowe draw from their results. Indeed, again some of them argue that central banks are not able to measure those financial imbalances quickly and accurately. A better solution would be to let financial imbalances grow and burst, and to concentrate efforts on the protection of the private sector. Ultimately, it is more a question of financial regulation and supervision than a question of monetary policy. In addition, the central bank, by acting as lender of last resort, promotes orderly declines in asset prices.

Asset prices, financial fragility, and central banking: A Post-Keynesian view

The Post-Keynesian school of thought starts with a completely different theoretical framework, leading to the conclusion that the main goal of a central bank is not the management of output-price inflation. Beyond that, what the goal of a central bank should be and what interest-rate rule should be followed is subject to great debates that will be reviewed briefly in this chapter and will be presented more extensively in chapter 4. In terms of the role that should be given to financial matters in the decisions of central bankers, the debate is settled. Post-Keynesians have integrated financial aspects in their macroeconomic analysis far before any other school of thought, and there is a broad agreement about what the central bank should do. Some authors, however, would put much more emphasis on financial factors and argue that financial stability should be the main goal of a central bank. Again, in order to get a better understanding of the position held by the Post-Keynesian school, its basic theoretical framework is presented.

What is the Post-Keynesian school of thought?

King (2002) and Lee (2000, 2002) have studied the origins of the Post-Keynesian school of thought. The Post-Keynesian approach of economics may be considered to start with Keynes's *General Theory* and following articles, even though some authors would start earlier with Sraffa's and Kahn's contributions in the 1920s. This approach combines some elements of Marx, Kalecki, Keynes, Schumpeter, and Sraffa and departs completely from the Pigouvian and Fisherian views of the economic system. As Kregel (1994) recognizes, a complete application of Post-Keynesian ideas would require a profound change of mentality at the national and at the international level, in order to promote institutional changes that favor full employment. The basic hypotheses of the Post-Keynesian framework can be summarized by one concept: monetary production economy. In this type of economy, money is never neutral, inflation does not have necessarily monetary origins, liquidity and solvency concerns are primordial, and aggregate supply and aggregate demand are interdependent forces.

The non-neutrality of money

The fact that money is not neutral manifests itself through different theoretical elements: the financial power of money, the intrinsic endogeneity of money, the distinction between financing and funding (or initial finance and final finance), the monetary theory of interest rates, and the rejection of the existence of a natural path for the economic system. This last point will not be developed below, the main idea being that there is no predetermined state that the economy will reach for sure. The structure of the economy is endogenous to current economic decisions (Kregel 1976, 1986b), which makes NAIRU and potential output weak theoretical and policy concepts (Sawyer 1985b, 1999; Anthony 1986; Setterfield *et al.* 1992; Issac 1993; Lavoie 2004; Palacio-Vera 2005; Fontana and Palacio-Vera 2007; Gnos and Rochon 2007). Stated alternatively, supply and demand are not independent, which is best expressed by the concept of effective demand: expected aggregate demand determines current aggregate supply.

FINANCIAL POWER VERSUS PURCHASING POWER OF MONEY

The central importance of the purchasing power of money for most economists has been restated by Hahn:

> Let us begin with an axiom that I think most economists would accept, and that I have already used in the previous lecture: the objectives of agents that determine their actions and plans do not depend on any nominal magnitudes. Agents care only about 'real' things, such as goods [...] leisure and effort. We know this as the axiom of the absence of money illusion, which it seems impossible to abandon in any sensible analysis.
>
> (Hahn 1982: 34)

For example, entrepreneurs are interested in the additional amount of output they will get from acquiring an investment good (the marginal productivity of capital), not in the amount of money the sale of output will provide. In the "'peasant' barter economy" of the New Consensus, money is a veil, which implies that the realization of surplus value is unimportant and is guaranteed by the prevalence of Say's Law (Kenway 1980; Henry 2003).

In the Post-Keynesian framework money matters, and as Minsky puts it, "Money isn't everything, it is the only thing" (Minsky 1990a: 369). This is so because, as Marx noted, the capitalist economy is a monetary production economy – the economic process starts with money in expectation of ending with more money:

> The firm is dealing throughout in terms of sums of money. It has no object in the world except to end up with more money than it started with. That is the essential characteristic of an entrepreneur economy.
>
> (Keynes 1933b (1979): 89)

Thus, when entrepreneurs produce and invest, they are not interested in producing more goods and services for their personal consumption or to exchange them for other goods; they want to obtain more money. As Mr. Nardelli, Chief Executive of Chrysler LLC stated, for private companies "cash is king" (Nardelli in Valcourt 2007).

Contrary to a real-exchange economy, in a monetary/entrepreneur economy, "money plays a part of its own and affects motives and decisions" (Keynes 1933a (1973): 408). Pecuniary emulations and invidious comparisons are at the center of economic dynamics (Veblen 1899, 1904), and the primary goal of businesses is "vendibility," not productivity (Veblen 1901):[10]

> The classical theory supposes that [...] only an expectation of more *product* [...] will induce [an entrepreneur] to offer more employment. But in an entrepreneur economy this is a wrong analysis of the nature of business calculation. An entrepreneur is interested, not in the amount of product, but in the amount of *money* which will fall to his share. He will increase his output if by so doing he expects to increase his money profit, even though this profit represents a smaller quantity of product than before. [...] Thus the classical theory fails us at both ends, so to speak, if we try to apply it to an entrepreneur economy. For it is not true that the entrepreneur's demand for labour depends on the share of the product which will fall to the entrepreneur; and it is not true that the supply of labor depends on the share of the product which will fall to labour.
>
> (Keynes 1933c (1979): 82–83)

Thus, in a monetary economy, the purchasing power of money is a secondary property; what really matters for individuals is the "financial power" of money. Economic units are happier if their buying power increases; but, rather than focusing on this narrow problem, economic agents pay a lot more attention to risks of insolvency and liquidity:

> The borrower is only interested in the prospect of an excess of his money receipts over his money outgoings. [...] In short, it is not the prospect of rising prices as such which stimulates employment, but the prospect of an increased margin between sales proceeds and variable costs.
>
> (Keynes 1933c (1979): 84–85)

> Liquidity is a fundamental recurring problem whenever people organize most of their income receipt and payment activities on a forward money contractual basis. For real world enterprises and households, the balancing of their checkbook inflows against outflows to maintain liquidity is the most serious economic problem they face everyday of their lives.
>
> (Davidson 2002: 78)

Financial power considerations outweigh, and are inclusive of, purchasing power considerations.

Economists may be interested only in changes in real variables, because they reflect an increase in standard of living and welfare. However, the economic units primarily responsible for raising standards of living, entrepreneurs, are not interested directly in improving welfare. They are interested in making money and results are judged in relation to that end. Thus, given the nature of capitalist economies, "real" considerations cannot be understood without first studying monetary relations, because the latter determines the former. Real consequences are the end results of a decision-making process entirely based on monetary terms for the sake of monetary terms. The role of real variables should be left for historical comparison, not for what drives current economic activity (Keynes 1933b (1973): 408–411; Keynes 1936a: 40). Monetary illusion is a different matter; it deals with the incapacity of economic agents to determine if the purchasing power of their monetary hoards has increased or not. It does not deal with what is most important for economic agents in their daily life.

This idea will be developed further in the book and will be illustrated several times; but, in order to be more concrete, the following example is provided. Say that workers earn a wage $W = \$5$, and that they have to pay a cash commitment of $CC = \$2$ each month to service their debts, and assume that the general price level is $P = \$1$. The real wage earned by workers is $W/P = 5$ and the net wage of workers is $W - CC = \$3$. Say now that workers get a raise that doubles their wage so that $W = \$10$, and that the general price level is also doubled $P = \$2$. The real wage is unchanged and New Neoclassical economists, following Ricardo,[11] Fisher, and Hahn, would say that workers are not better off. Post-Keynesians on the other side would say that the situation of workers has considerably improved. Indeed, the financial power of money, the capacity of workers to meet their debt commitments (the liquidity of their position), is much improved, $W - CC = \$8$. This improvement in financial power increases their financial wealth (assuming that their real consumption level is unchanged)[12] and gives them easier access to bank loans and financial independence. As Keynes says, the recommendations of Classical economists ignore this:

> Nor are they based on indirect effects due to a lower wages-bill in terms of money having certain reactions on the banking system and the state of credit.
>
> (Keynes 1936a: 11)

Actually, the improvement in the financial position is not necessary to conclude that workers are better off. Say that CC is also doubled so that CC/P and W/P are unchanged, still, providing that consumption level is at a comfortable level (and so could be adjusted downward without much consequences), the situation of workers has improved financially because their financial position is more liquid, and so bankers will consider them as safer because they have a bigger monetary buffer ($W - CC = \$6$).

Finally, the real burden of debts (CC/P) is not a relevant concept for borrowers because price changes may leave their financial burden unchanged. What matters is the nominal value of income inflows compared to the nominal value of debt services; therefore, as long as inflows or debt services are not affected (or are only partly affected) by inflation, the notion of "real" (defined in the Neoclassical senses) loses its importance. For workers, only changes in nominal wage income will affect the burden of debt, CC/W is what matters. For firms also, higher prices do not reflect automatically a better capacity of meeting debt payments because prices are only one component of cash inflows. The following quote is a good illustration of the professional mental deformation that comes with "the economist who automatically thinks in terms of real" (Gale 1982: 154) when trying to analyze a monetary economy.

> Inflation causes a reduction in the real value of the manufacturer's indebtedness and this increase in net wealth ought, in some sense, to have counted as income [...] had there been some way to realize this income [...]
>
> (Gale 1982: 157)

An increase in real net wealth does not represent in any sense a direct improvement of the financial situation of firms, and bankers will be indifferent to change in real net worth *per se*. Similarly, real net wealth may decline but as long as nominal net worth goes up, everything is fine from the point of view of entrepreneurs and bankers.

In the end, output prices are only a partial element of cash inflows and outflows, or not a component at all. In a monetary economy, real improvements are, at best, notional gains that are irrelevant for capitalist economic operations. Real financial improvements are only relevant in a perfectly competitive barter economy, where there are complete markets that allow immediate accounting of real gains/losses (Gale 1982: 157). This framework of analysis is inappropriate for the study of capitalist economies.

THE ENDOGENEITY OF MONEY AND RESERVES

In the New Consensus, the supply of money and reserves are made endogenous to conform to the reality of central bankers' practices. The Post-Keynesian school of thought has argued for a long time that money is endogenous, that is to say, its creation results from a flow-demand for money, i.e. a willingness to get advances from banks (Keynes 1936a;[13] Kaldor 1982; Davidson 1978; Minsky 1975a; Moore 1988; Graziani 1990, 2003a; Wray 1990; Lavoie 1984, 1992; Rochon 1999). Bankers cannot create money if nobody asks for bank advances. The endogeneity of money results from the nature of monetary instruments. All monetary instruments, public or private, are always asset/debt relationships; there are never, and never have been, pure assets (Tymoigne 2007b).[14]

Given the liquidity and profitability considerations of banks (Dow 1996; Wray 1990; Minsky 1975a; Le Héron 1986), the supply of bank money is completely driven by the demand for advances from creditworthy borrowers (even though, as shown in chapter 5, recent developments in financial markets have changed this; individuals' creditworthiness is no longer an essential requirement to obtain loans). To start an economic activity, individuals usually need to borrow money. The granting of a loan (assets side of banks) leads to the creation of money (liabilities side of banks). At the end of the economic process, loans are reimbursed and money is destroyed, the payments of interest to banks destroying an additional amount of bank money. Thus, the creation and the destruction of money are intrinsic counterparts to the inner working of capitalist economic systems. In this process, banks are not understood as intermediaries that indirectly channel saving toward investment by granting loans. Banks do not need any prior depositors ("savers") to create additional demand deposits for borrowers ("investors"). They provide a demand deposit to borrowers first by recording *ex nihilo* an amount on a book, and then fund their positions by borrowing or by selling assets in order to get the reserves they need. Leaving aside cost considerations, this could be logically all done, and ultimately must be all done, by going to the central bank, i.e. without the help of hoarders of central bank money. Indeed, the central bank is the entity that creates reserves.[15]

The central consequence of what precedes is that "money is never neutral" (Minsky 1993b: 78; Davidson 2002: 78) because it is necessary both at the beginning and at the end of the economic process. In both cases, the absence of money has detrimental effects. As Gale states "Neutrality is [...] restricted to the realm of 'helicopter economics'" (Gale 1982: 15).

In terms of monetary policy and of the analysis of the financial system, the consequences of money endogeneity have led to a long debate between the Structuralist Post-Keynesians (Dow 2006) and the Horizontalist/Accommodationist Post-Keynesians (Lavoie 2006). A concise summary is provided by Wray (2007a). For our concerns, the central consequence of the endogeneity of money is that central banks of sovereign countries (in monetary terms) do not, and cannot, control the reserves they supply (Minsky 1967a: 268; Kaldor 1982; Moore 1988; Wray 1990; Lavoie 1992, 2006). Ultimately, the central bank must be the supplier of reserves. This is so either to prevent financial crises, or to maintain the parity between bank money and central bank money in the clearing process, or, more simply, to maintain its targeted rate on non-borrowed reserves (Wray 2003b, 2004a). All a central bank can do is to set the rate of interest at which it supplies reserves, and to supply and to withdraw reserves on demand so as to maintain its interest-rate target. Stated alternatively, the daily amount of reserves added or withdrawn by central bankers is not driven by their will, it is a defensive operation not a proactive targeting of reserves.

Finally, the amount of reserves to supply, or to withdraw, is independent of the interest rate targeted. Thus, a low interest-rate target does not mean that the central bank is "pumping lots of money" in the economy. Indeed, not only are reserve supply and money supply not automatically related, but also the maintenance of a targeted interest rate of 9% may require as much, or more, net supply of reserves as a 2% target; it all depends on the needs of private financial institutions. The central bank "only" controls the nominal cost of central bank money ("reserves").

FINANCING (INITIAL FINANCE) AND FUNDING (FINAL FINANCE)

The distinction between financing and funding is essential in the Post-Keynesian analysis (Davidson 1986b) and goes back to Keynes's essays written after the *General Theory* (Keynes 1937a, 1937c, 1937d, 1938c, 1939); Keynes's 1939 article is maybe the clearest of all those articles. Making this difference improves the understanding of the aggregate income creation process by showing logically that (current) saving cannot finance (current) investment (Tymoigne 2003; Keynes 1938a, 1938b); investment must come first, saving can only be used to fund investment.

The first stage of the economic process is the production phase whose counterpart is the creation of monetary income. For this phase to start, labor time and raw materials must be purchased and this purchase must be financed (Parguez 1984; Lavoie 1992; Graziani 1990, 2003a). This initial financing cannot rest on *ex ante* saving (i.e. desired saving), like in the loanable funds theory, because individuals can desire to save as much as they want until "they are blue in the face" (Keynes 1937d (1973): 222), and this wishful thinking will never provide an actual source of funds. The initial financing cannot depend on current saving either. Indeed, current saving depends on the income of the same period and saving cannot occur before income exists, and so it cannot be a source of funds for the creation of current income. The only sources of funds are accumulated past savings and *ex nihilo* monetary creation:

> Dishoarding and credit expansion provides not an *alternative* to increased saving, but a necessary preparation for it. It is the parent, not the twin, of increased saving.
>
> (Keynes 1939 (1973): 281)

In fact, logically, only monetary creation is a source of financing for the creation of income. Indeed, past savings were generated by past incomes, which were financed partly by further past savings. This circularity about the origins of past savings can only be broken by recognizing that ultimately only the (*ex nihilo*) granting of monetary advances is an initial financing source.[16] This takes care of the first stage of economic activity and the financing of output production.

The second stage of the economic process concerns the acquisition of the output produced. Once income has been created, it is spent on the acquisition of goods, which generates an aggregate level of profit for firms. In the simplest model, the income that is not spent is recorded by the saving of households and the net profit of firms. The former can be captured, in part or totally, by firms via the issuance of securities. In the end, aggregate expenditures contribute as much as aggregate saving to the funding of aggregate investment by generating a profit for firms:

> The Committee have overlooked the fact that *spending* releases funds just as much as saving does, [...].
>
> (Keynes 1939 (1973): 282)

Actually, spending is the best way to release funds for the funding of production because it limits the need to resort to borrowing operations. As shown later, Kalecki's equation of profit clearly explains why.

The funding process also includes refinancing activities, that is, the rollover (i.e. the renewal of the same loans), renegotiation (change in the terms of debt contracts), or consolidation (borrowing to reimburse several debts) of existing financial contracts. At the macroeconomic level, the need to refinance emerges, in the simplest models, from the desire of households to keep part of their saving in monetary form (Davidson 1978; Lavoie 1987, 1992; Parguez 1984). At the microeconomic level, all economic units that have a maturity of their assets that is longer than the maturity of their debts need to refinance their asset positions at one point.

A MONETARY THEORY OF INTEREST RATES

With Fisher and Wicksell, the theory of the rate of interest rests on impatience and the state of machinery. Post-Keynesians reject this theory because it assumes a long-run neutrality of money. There is no a priori natural rate of interest; interest rate is a monetary phenomenon (Veblen 1909; Rogers 1989; Seccareccia 1998; Smithin 2003; Fontana 2006). As Kregel puts it, money is "a 'real' factor, and the rate of interest is a 'monetary' factor" (Kregel 1988a: 236). The preceding section explained why money is a "real" factor. This non-neutrality of money can also be expressed through the theory of the rate of interest developed by Keynes.

Keynes proposed a monetary theory of the total monetary rate of return of all assets based on the marginal "efficiency" or "productivity"[17] of those assets. The context is the same as Fisher's, in the sense that individuals have to decide in which assets they want to take a position; but the reasoning is reversed (see Appendix 1).

Each asset has its own rate of return measured in terms of itself. However, returns can only be compared if they are measured in a similar standard. The standardized total rate of return is

$$R_j = q_j + r_j - c_j + l_j + a_j.$$

Assuming that a monetary standard is chosen, the marginal efficiency of asset j depends on the expected monetary yield generated by the income obtained from operations or contracts (q), on the risk premium (r) needed "to cover the unknown possibilities of the actual yield differing from the expected yield" (Keynes 1936a: 68),[18] on the expected monetary carrying cost (c) of an asset due to maintenance and insurance, on the implicit monetary yield (l) attributed to the perceived liquidity of an asset, and by the expected rate of change (a) in the price of asset j. The liquidity premium should be differentiated from the risk premium and "it is evident [...] [that] we must allow for both" (Keynes 1936a: 240) because

> I am rather inclined to associate risk premium with probability strictly speaking, and liquidity premium with what in my *Treatise on Probability* I called "weight." An essential distinction is that a risk premium is expected to be rewarded on the average by an increased return at the end of the period. A liquidity premium, on the other hand, is not even expected to be so rewarded.
>
> (Keynes 1938d (1979): 293–294)

Thus, contrary to l, r is an explicit yield on assets, i.e. its owner will be rewarded in money terms.

Marginal efficiencies are not the equivalent of the marginal productivities of the Classicals. Indeed, the capacity of some assets to generate physical output is not of direct importance for their valuation. The money rates are usually positive because assets are scarce and their detention is purposeful, i.e. they help to stay liquid and solvent. Thus, if "capital becomes less scarce, the excess yield will diminish, without its having become less productive – at least in the physical sense" (Keynes 1936a: 213). As Veblen notes, in a monetary economy, the "vendibility" of the output generated by an asset or of the asset itself, not its productivity, is what matters to value an asset.

Differences in total money rates of return result in portfolio arbitrages until all the money rates "of comparable term and risk" (Keynes 1936a: 68) are equal so that economic agents are indifferent between holding any asset. The arbitrage process depends on the state of expectations and the liquidity preference of individuals, which affect the money rates via their effects on the forward and spot prices of assets. To see more clearly why, it is first necessary to remember that the money rates are "a sum of money contracted for forward delivery, [...] over what we may call the 'spot' or cash price of the sum thus contracted for forward delivery" (Keynes 1936a: 222):[19]

$$R_j \equiv (F_j - S_j)/S_j.$$

Say that there are two assets. Asset 1 is a risky capital asset that is expected to generate monetary profits from the sale of its output ($q_1 > 0$). Asset 2 is a riskless demand deposit at a bank that does not pay any interest ($q_2 = 0$) and that is highly liquid ($l_2 > 0$). Assuming to simplify that risk is given, we have

$$R_1 = q_1 + \bar{r}_1 - c_1,$$

$$R_2 = l_2.$$

And at equilibrium $R_1 = R_2 + \bar{r}_1$, that is, $q_1 - c_1 = l_2$. Note that R_2 is an implicit rate because l is not remunerated but represents the minimum required rate on illiquid assets before risk adjustment. Thus, $\Delta R_2 > 0$ means that the minimum required rate on asset 1 increases.

If the state of expectations rises (the prospect of monetary profits improves or confidence in expectations rises), liquidity preference decreases, and so the value attached to ls declines, whereas that of qs increases. The first effect of this improvement in expectations is to change the forward prices ($\Delta F_1 > 0, \Delta F_2 < 0$), which leads to $q_1 - c_1 > l_2$ and so $R_1 > R_2 + \bar{r}_1$. Then, assets that have a total return that depends mainly on their liquidity premium are sold, which decreases their spot price ($\Delta S_2 < 0$) so that $\Delta R_2 > 0$. On the contrary, the return on asset 1 decreases as arbitragers bid up its spot prices ($\Delta S_1 > 0$). In addition, the more intensive use (longer use) or extensive use (investment) of asset 1 generates an increase in output 1. As the market for output 1 gets saturated, q_1 goes down and so F_1 goes down too.[20] Thus, movements in the spot price and forward price of asset 1 work together to decrease the total return R_1. Under perfect competition, the arbitrage stops when the risk-adjusted money rates are equalized across assets.

During this arbitrage process, the marginal efficiency of money leads the arbitrage decisions because of the special properties of money that make the interest rate on money sluggish relative to the quantity of money (Keynes 1936a: 222ff.).[21] For Keynes, this last point is the essential difference from the Neoclassical interest theory:

> Put shortly, the orthodox theory maintains that the forces which determine the common value of the marginal efficiency of various assets are independent of money, which has, so to speak, no autonomous influence, and that prices move until the marginal efficiency of money, i.e. the rate of interest, falls into line with the common value of the marginal efficiency of other assets as determined by other forces. My theory, on the other hand, maintains that this is a special case and that over a wide range of possible cases almost the opposite is true, namely, that the marginal efficiency of money is determined by forces partly appropriate to itself, and that prices move until the marginal efficiency of other assets fall into line with the rate of interest.
>
> (Keynes 1937b (1973): 103)

In essence, therefore, both the "complex of rates of interest on loans of various maturities and risks" (Keynes 1936a: 28) and the marginal efficiencies of non-monetary assets are explained via the use of a monetary theory. Indeed, monetary conditions affect the determination of those marginal efficiencies in several ways: through the expectations of monetary incomes and capital gains, through the state of liquidity preference of economic agents, and through the amount of liquid assets available to match the liquidity preference of individuals. The more optimistic the state of expectations, the lower the state of liquidity preference, and the lower the marginal efficiencies of liquid assets compared to illiquid assets. Thus, rates of return change for other reasons than changes in productivity or thrift, and the impacts of the latter go through their effects on monetary variables: "Productivity and thrift exist, but in a capitalist economy their impact is always filtered by uncertainty" (Minsky 1972b: 114).

Non-monetary theory of output prices

In the New Consensus, the results of the quantity theory of money hold in the long run. However, this explanation of the general price level has been critiqued by Keynes and his followers (Keynes 1930, 1936a; Kahn 1956a, 1956b, 1959; Lerner 1961, 1979; Davidson 1985; Weintraub 1969, 1978; Kregel 1975; Minsky 1986a; Le Héron 1991; Lavoie 1996a). Indeed, it assumes that full employment is reached so that output is given (or grows at its given natural rate), and that the demand for money is stable.[22] Post-Keynesians reject these hypotheses; therefore, another macroeconomic explanation of prices has to be provided. The latter can be illustrated by starting with national accounting identities. Indeed, the income approach to the GDP identity tells us (ignoring discrepancies between national income and gross domestic product) that

$$PQ \equiv W + \Pi \equiv W + Z + \Pi_{nD} + T_\Pi \Rightarrow P \equiv w/\mathrm{AP}_L + Z/Q + \Pi_{nD}/Q + T_\Pi/Q,$$

with, Π gross profit of firms, Π_{nD} the disposable net profit of firms (i.e. profit after accounting for corporate income tax, distribution, and subsidies), their "retained earnings," W employees' compensations, Z the gross non-wage incomes paid by firms (dividends, interests, rental income), and T_Π corporate income tax. Knowing that d is a linear operator and extracting the growth rate $g_X = dX/X$, we have

$$\pi \equiv g_{w/\mathrm{AP}_L} \times s_w + g_{Z/Q} \times s_Z + g_{\Pi_{nD}/Q} \times s_{\Pi_{nD}} + g_{T_\Pi/Q} \times s_{T_\Pi}.$$

where $s_w, s_Z, s_{\Pi nD}$, and s_{T_Π} are, respectively, the national income shares of wages, other incomes, retained earnings, and corporate income tax. We can go a little further by decomposing the rate of growth of each ratio into the growth rate of each of its components:[23]

$$\pi \equiv \frac{g_w - g_{\mathrm{AP}_L}}{1 + g_{\mathrm{AP}_L}} \times s_W + \frac{g_Z - g_Q}{1 + g_Q} \times s_Z + \frac{g_{\Pi_{nD}} - g_Q}{1 + g_Q} \times s_{\Pi_{nD}} + \frac{g_{T_\Pi} - g_Q}{1 + g_Q} \times s_{T_\Pi}.$$

For small values of g_Q and g_{AP_L}, we have

$$\pi \approx (g_w - g_{AP_L})s_w + (g_z - g_Q)s_z + (g_{\Pi_{nD}} - g_Q)s_{\Pi_{nD}} + (g_{T_\Pi} - g_Q)s_{T_\Pi}.$$

The previous equations do not provide an explanation of inflation, they are just identities. An explanation requires making some assumptions about the behavior of the variables involved in the identity so that some causalities are drawn. The assumptions are that g_w results from a bargaining process between employees and firms (e.g. conflict-claims models of inflation (e.g. Lavoie 1992: 391 ff.; Rowthorn 1977)). g_z results from, among others, monetary policy and the state of liquidity preference. g_{AP_L} is determined by the constraints existing on the process of production. The exact way g_{AP_L} changes depends on the institutional framework of an economy. In general, in a period of labor-time scarcity, g_{AP_L} goes up and, during an economic slowdown, g_{AP_L} goes down before people are laid off. The strength of this relationship depends on how expensive and time consuming it is to hire and to lay off individuals. For example, in an economy in which employment is based on a long-term relationship between employers and employees, labor productivity acts as a buffer between desired production and employment. On the contrary, in an economy with flexible employment contracts, until the economy is close to full employment, labor productivity is less variable and employment does the adjustment. The point is that g_{AP_L} is not constant because full employment is rarely reached. g_Q is determined by expectations of monetary profits (i.e. effective demand) (Keynes 1936a). As shown below, $g_{\Pi_{nD}}$ is determined by the Kalecki equation of monetary profit.[24] Finally, the growth of taxes depends on the tax rates and economic activity. For the sake of the argument, one can assume that national income shares are constant, even though they can also be explained by using a monetary theory of distribution.[25]

All this shows that an explanation of inflation or deflation is not necessarily based on money, and as shown below, even if money is a cause of inflation, it is due to different mechanisms than what the New Consensus puts forward. Conflicts over income distribution, innovations in the processes of production (better organization, better formation of workers, invention of new machines, etc.), and the state of the economy are important elements to explain continuous and general price movements. Prices can go up and down as $g_{\Pi_{nD}}$, g_w, g_z, and g_{T_Π} go up and down, but their effects will be mitigated by changes in productivity growth and output growth. Only when the last two are fixed or sluggish relative to the former four can inflation permanently take place, and this is, as Keynes called it, a state of true inflation. One economic condition during which this can occur is full employment, but this is not the only one. Prices may go up because of, for example, uncontrolled wage-price spiral induced by high expectation of inflation, competition between unions for relative wage improvements, competition between employers for a scarce labor force (Kahn 1959), or a rise in costs not controlled by residents. Rising interest rates, by affecting g_z, can also promote inflation given everything else.

The previous explanation of inflation does not discard the possibility of a monetary source of inflation, but it requires that several conditions be met. First, if funds are injected via portfolio transactions, output-price inflation may occur only if desired stocks of money are fulfilled, if receivers of money decide to spend their excess funds on existing goods and services rather than financial assets, and if the economy is in a sluggish state. Second, if funds are injected in the private domestic sector via income transactions like government spending or exports, inflation will occur only if the economy is slow to respond (so that Π_n/Q increases). More formally, national accounting identities tell us that

$$W + Z + \Pi_{nD} + T_\Pi \equiv C + I + G + X - J,$$

with C the consumption level, I the level of investment, G the level of government spending, X exports, and J imports. Accounting for net tax payments induced by taxes and transfer payments in all sectors, one gets

$$W_D + Z_D + \Pi_{nD} \equiv C + I + DEF + NX,$$

with the subscript D indicating disposable income (i.e. after tax and transfer payments), DEF the government budget deficit (including transfer payments), and NX net exports. Subtracting $W_D + Z_D$ from each side and defining C_Π as the consumption out of disposable net profit one has

$$\Pi_{nD} = C_\Pi - S_H + I + DEF + NX,$$

with $S_H(= S_W + S_Z)$ the saving level of wage earners and rentiers. The identity has been transformed into an equality by the behavioral and causal mechanisms that are assumed to exist in the economy. As Kalecki (1971a: 78–79) argues, Π_{nD} is not under the control of firms, whereas variables on the right side (expenditures) depends on discretionary choices.[26] Thus

$$g_{\Pi_{nD}} = (g_{C_\Pi} s_{C_\Pi} - g_{SH} s_{SH} + g_I s_I + g_g s_g - g_T s_T + g_X s_X - g_J s_J)/s_{\Pi_{nD}},$$

where s_i is the share of variable i in national income (or GDP), which are assumed to be constant. In the end, one gets an explanation of aggregate output price that is far more general and consistent than the New Consensus, and that can explain both forward-price (i.e. income or "cost-push") and spot-price (or "demand-pull") inflation. Below full employment, the main problem is cost-push inflation due to, for example, rising interest rates, rapid growth in compensations of workers, and higher tax rates on profit.

In terms of policy (Kaldor 1950; Kahn 1959; Weintraub 1979; Davidson 2006; Palma 1994; Wray 2001), the previous theory means that inflation is managed best by buffer-stock policies and fiscal policy (to prevent spot-price inflation), and income policies (to prevent income inflation), or a combination of both such as an employer of last resort program (Minsky 1986a; Wray 1998b). Monetary policy does not have much direct impact on inflation and actually can contribute to inflation through the cost and demand impacts of rising interest rates, the latter impact coming from the increase in consumption by interest-income earners (Lavoie 1995, 1996a; Tauheed and Wray 2006; Kelton and Wray 2006).

Liquidity and uncertain: Financial markets and debt deflation

In the New Consensus, asymmetries of information are essential to explain the periods of speculation and financial crisis that would not occur otherwise because the financial market participants would arbitrage immediately any possibilities of speculation. In the Post-Keynesian framework, asymmetries are not essential.[27] Like Monetarists, Post-Keynesians assume that lenders and borrowers live in the same state of uncertainty (Schwartz 1998: 38; Kregel 1992a: 87; Minsky 1975a, 1986a; Wolfson 1996: 450ff.). However, the agreement stops here because Monetarists believe in the efficiency of financial markets, and see the origins of financial crises in the incompetence of a central bank that refuses to act as a lender of last resort, or that "creates too much money" (Friedman and Schwartz 1963).

In the Post-Keynesian analysis, the origins of financial crises have to be found in the inner working of the capitalist system. In chapter 5, the timing and origins of a financial crisis will be explained, and here it is enough to state that the financial weakening of the economy is a normal result of prolonged periods of stable economic expansion. As the economy grows, the financial positions of economic agents have a tendency to become more fragile. Here again, the liquidity of financial positions (financial power) is crucial because it determines the impact of financial crises on the production side of the economy. Forced sales induced by the need to liquidate illiquid positions may trigger output-price deflation. The latter may reinforce the depressive effects of asset-price deflation by diminishing cash inflows from normal operations.

Conclusion: Monetary policy in the Post-Keynesian framework

The preceding should lead the reader to conclude that, according to Post-Keynesian economists, the role of a central bank is not to manage output-price stability:

> Both full employment *and* relatively stable prices are the responsibility of fiscal policy.
>
> (Wray 1995: 209)

> Monetary [policy] [...] should not be concerned with price level problems *per se*.
>
> (Davidson 1968c (1991): 106)

> It would, I submit, be a great mistake for the Committee to accept the view that it is the proper function of monetary policy, together with budgetary policy and the like, to secure a tolerable behavior of prices.
>
> (Kahn 1959 (1972): 140)

A central bank has only a very indirect impact on inflation because it cannot control the supply of means of payments, and, more importantly, because inflation usually does not have monetary origins. In addition, the impact of a central bank on aggregate profit is also indirect because it goes through investment and other interest-sensitive expenditures, in which the most important determining variable is not the long-term rate (Keynes 1936a: 145; Fazzari *et al*. 1988; Fazzari 1993; Glyn 1997). Most of the time, large variations of interest rates are necessary to influence the production side of the economy, and these may have the opposite effect of the one desired, i.e. rather than smoothing economic activity, strong disruptive financial effects may be generated. In addition, raising interest rates to limit investment will not have a large impact if the rise in long-term rates is expected to be temporary relative to the length of investment projects (Kaldor 1958 (1964): 131–137). Finally, raising interest rates may promote inflation, by pushing up costs and by providing interest-income earners with more money to spend. Overall, therefore, "the official rate of interest should be treated as an 'anchor' rather than a 'battle-ax'" (De-Juan 2007: 664) and other tools, which more directly influence the production and financial sides of the economy, should be used to complement the fixed nominal-interest-rate policy of a central bank.

In this context, the main role of a central bank is on the financial side of the economic system, not the production side. The main influence of a central bank is on the price of existing financial assets and on the liquidity of financial positions. A central bank can complement the full-employment policy and income policy of the federal government by promoting financial stability in several ways (Keynes 1936a; Minsky 1975a, 1986a; Kregel 1984, 1992a; Wray 1990, 1992d, 1995, 1996a, 1996b, 1996c, 1997a, 1998a, 1998b, 2003b).

First, a central bank should be ready to intervene as a lender of last resort any time it is necessary. One way to do this is by buying or discounting eligible papers at a low rate of interest:

> It was not simply the conversion of the bills into money that provided the possibility of liquidation, but the conversion at particular prices relative to other assets. [...] The Bank of England thus provided liquidity not so much by purchasing or rediscounting these bills, but by doing so at their prior prices and at market interest rates.
>
> (Kregel 1984: 224–225)

Second, a central bank should promote a stable yield curve (Keynes 1936a: 202; Kregel 2003), which helps to preserve the liquidity of financial positions (Hannsgen 2005). Third, nominal interest rates should be pushed as low as necessary in order to promote full employment (Davidson 1968c, 2006; Minsky 1986a; Kregel 1984, 1992a), which is achieved most effectively by a zero percent interest rate on overnight central bank advances (Wray 2004c, 2007b; Mosler and Forstater 2004). At full employment, higher central bank rates might be a last resort choice if inflationary pressures persist, but, given the relative ineffectiveness of this type of policy and its uncertain effects on inflation (even more so at full employment), one could argue that it is better left untouched. Fourth, selective credit controls (Kaldor 1982; Wray 1991a; Rousseas 1994; Lavoie 1996a) and supervision that are applied to the whole financial system should be developed in order to promote both aggregate and micro financial stability (Wray 1995; Minsky 1975b; Shull 1993; Guttentag and Herring 1988; Palley 2000, 2004). Fifth, a central bank should help in the provision of financial services to the least developed sectors of the economy (Wray 2003b).

Like in the New Consensus, there are debates inside the Post-Keynesian school. Some authors want a more active interest-rate policy in order to manage economic growth and income distribution. Starting with distribution matters, some Post-Keynesian authors like Smithin, Lavoie, and Seccareccia are for an involvement of the central bank in the setting of real rates to limit the unequal distribution of income between lenders and borrowers. Other Post-Keynesian economists like Dalziel, Sawyer, Arestis, Fontana, and Palacio-Vera welcome interest-rate manipulations to manage output growth. These views will be presented more fully in chapter 4. For reasons developed previously and in the following chapters, one may be skeptical about these views. The position taken in this book is that the role of a central bank is to promote financial stability while targeting nominal overnight interest rates at a permanent zero level. The effectiveness of a central bank regarding anything else is limited and uncertain, especially compared to other tools.

Asset prices, financial fragility, and central banking

Now that the framework of the Post-Keynesian analysis has been presented, it is possible to study the role of financial matters in the making of central bank policies. Two topics can be found in the Post-Keynesian literature. One is the relationship between full employment, price stability, and financial fragility, and the other is a role of the central bank in the valuation process of asset prices. Views of Post-Keynesians on these topics are quite similar and seem to have been settled quickly, which explains the limited amount of literature on the subject.

Financial fragility, full employment, and price stability

Post-Keynesians argue that financial stability, price stability, and full employment are highly complementary goals. By promoting a stable financial structure, a central bank will promote price stability and will help the private sector to get closer to full employment. By guaranteeing full employment and price stability, a stable financial structure will be promoted, at least to a point. As Minsky remarked, there are no definitive solutions to the management of a capitalist system because periods of stability lead to instability.

FULL EMPLOYMENT AND FINANCIAL FRAGILITY

Following Keynes's statement that *laissez-faire* capitalism is flawed because it fails to provide full employment and generates unequal and arbitrary distribution of resources, the goal of the government should be to tackle those problems. To do so, the government should be systematically, permanently, and actively involved in the affairs of the economic system. It should do so by applying neither fascism nor socialism, but by following a "third course" that involves removing "certain substantial spheres of activity from the hands of private enterprise" (Robinson 1943 (1966): 86).

The government should socialize investment by fixing the reward received by entrepreneurs, and by allocating resources toward the most socially needed investment projects, without necessarily leading their construction nor removing ownership from the private sector (Keynes 1936a: 378ff.):

> It is not quite correct that I attach primary importance to the rate of interest [...]
> I should regard state intervention to encourage investment as probably a more important factor than low rates of interest taken in isolation.
>
> (Keynes 1943 (1980): 350)

The goal is to remove the scarcity of capital equipment so that the marginal efficiency of capital, "apart from any allowance for risk and the like" tends toward zero (Keynes 1936a: 221). That is, "the return from [capital equipment] would have to cover little more than their exhaustion by wastage and obsolescence together with some margin to cover risk and the exercise of skill and judgment" (Keynes 1936a: 375) so that $q - c \approx 0$.

This investment policy should be complemented by a low and stable (nominal) interest-rate policy that only rewards the skills and judgment of lenders, that decreases uncertainty about future rates and so lowers the risk premium and liquidity premium, and that helps to reduce transaction costs between borrowers and lenders (Keynes 1936a: 208, 309). Pure interest rates should be nil, which means that the central bank rate should be zero (Keynes 1936a: 208, 221; Wray 2007b). Treasury bond rates equally should be set low by the Treasury because of the absence of default risk and the low liquidity risk.

In addition, policies that promote higher propensity to consume by reducing income inequalities should be implemented. Finally, the government should guarantee full employment by putting in place a government employment program that provides a buffer for individuals who cannot find a job in the private sector (Minsky 1986a; Wray 1998a).

For most Post-Keynesians, this central management of some aspects of economic life is a necessary condition "to avoid the destruction of existing [capitalist] economic forms in their entirety, and [to guarantee] the successful functioning of individual initiative" (Keynes 1936a: 380). This will allow full employment to prevail while containing inflationary pressures and helping to distribute output fairly. All this, of course, has nothing to do with the typical fine-tuning of the textbook Keynesian analysis or the "Keynesian" period of the 1950s–1960s. Counter-cyclical policies are ineffective and impractical to deal with full-employment problems (Robinson 1945; Wray 1994; Kregel 1994; Minsky 1975a).

By guaranteeing stable full employment, the government will promote financial stability because full employment stabilizes the liquidity preference of individuals by decreasing economic uncertainty:

> If the level of government investment is sufficiently high and sufficiently stable to provide full employment, liquidity will be automatically provided to the system via stable incomes and stable sales receipts which assure that debts can be liquidated through the sale of assets. [...] The best way to reduce liquidity demands is by assuring that they are provided by the steady full employment cash flows of firms and incomes of households.
>
> (Kregel 1984: 230–231)

Indeed, a steady inflow of cash makes it easier for the private sector to plan ahead to fulfill its debt obligations and limits its needs to go into debt (Minsky 1962, 1986a).

However, full employment does not guarantee financial stability because, if the private sector becomes too confident, its liquidity preference can decrease dangerously, and this may lead to financial fragility. The latter still can have a strong impact on the economic system even if full employment is guaranteed by the government. Indeed, during the expansion, financial fragility may generate inflationary pressures, and, during the contraction, it may lead to bankruptcies and other adverse financial consequences as some people are laid off from private jobs that pay more, and may provide raises at a faster and more frequent pace than the employment programs set by the government. A full-employment policy, therefore, should be complemented by a financial policy. It is here that a central bank can make its best contribution. Without a stable financial structure, the private sector of a market economy cannot expect to get close to, or to sustain, full employment (Minsky 1975a, 1978).

FINANCIAL FRAGILITY AND PRICE STABILITY

Minsky (1975a: 163) noted that a fragile financial structure is characterized by financial positions built upon expectations of high output- and asset-price growth in the hope of a bonanza. This may promote output-price instability under specific conditions. First, during an expansion, high output-price expectations may be self-fulfilling. This is all the more the case that firms have some market power and that they are pressured to meet some cash commitments. Second, following a crisis, financial fragility may generate a debt-deflation process if it is allowed to go on by the government. Third, if the government intervenes, or is expected to intervene, to limit financial instability during a downturn, this may promote inflation under some specific conditions presented earlier.

Thus, financial policies and anti-inflation policies are complementary. In addition, because financial stability and full employment are compatible, full employment and price stability are also compatible if the right economic set up is put in place:

> A full-employment economy, where full employment is guaranteed by government employment programs for both youth and adults, in the context of competitive markets and stable money wages, is a possible offset to the inflationary pressures which follow from the way threats of a deep depression are offset.
>
> (Minsky 1983a: 276)

The employment program of the government plays the same role as an income policy (by anchoring wages on the government program wage) while at the same time generating full employment (by guaranteeing access to a job) and helping to promote financial stability (by guaranteeing a certain level of monetary income). Applying this type of program will create a horizontal Phillips curve, i.e. as the economy approaches full employment, wage growth would be contained.

Finally, price stability may also promote financial strength by making it easier for the private sector to realize its expectations. As the Schwartz Hypothesis notes, price stability is good for financial stability. However, contrary to this hypothesis, Post-Keynesians share the idea that the causality runs both ways. In addition, even though agents can realize their inflation expectations, it does not guarantee that their financial position is strong. As shown in chapter 5, their expectations may include refinancing needs and their financial position may depend heavily on the continuation of the inflationary process. Therefore, price stability is, in itself, a poor guide to judge the extent of financial fragility, and a strong focus by a central bank on inflation, or one or two other variables like credit growth, will not help to promote financial stability (Palley 2006; Bell and Quiggin 2006). A comprehensive and systematic understanding of financial interrelations is needed, which starts by using a theoretical framework that recognizes that monetary and financial relations are an integral part of the economic system, not patches that can be added at convenience to the "real economy." Focusing research on finding correlations to manage financial stability (as the New Consensus tends to do), rather than on developing causal explanations, will lead to unpleasant surprises similar to the Monetarist experience. It is well known that correlations tend to break down at the least expected and least convenient times and as financial innovations enter the economic system (Sahel and Vesala 2001; Goodhart 1989: 377).

The role of a central bank is, thus, to participate in a policy that promotes stable full employment, which is done by promoting financial stability and so financial strength:

> The maintenance of a robust financial structure is a precondition for effective anti-inflation and full employment policies without a need to hazard deep depressions.
>
> (Minsky 1978 (1985): 27)

By promoting financial stability, reliance on the expected growth of output price will be limited, the use of lender of last resort will be contained, and the private sector will be able to reach a state close to full employment. In terms of asset prices, this has several implications for a central bank.

Asset prices, financial fragility, and central banking

The first implication is that a central bank should promote interest-rate stability in both short-term and long-term maturities. Variations in interest rates, even relatively small, can have large disruptive effects (Kaldor 1982; Keynes 1936a: 202) because it raises uncertainty about future interest rates, which is not desirable for both liquidity and solvency reasons. Concerning liquidity matters, an economy in which the financing process depends on short-term external funds, and in which the two sides of balance sheets have different maturity terms, is sensitive to changes in interest rates. In terms of insolvency, too high variations in the long-term rates will affect the value of assets and liabilities (Hannsgen 2005).

The stability of short-term interest rates is easy to obtain because a central bank controls the discount rate and can closely target the federal funds rate. This is the case whether the financial system is an asset-based or an overdraft system (Lavoie 2005), whether or not banks are required to hold reserves, and whether or not most economic transactions use central bank money (Fullwiler 2006). The central bank is the monopoly supplier of reserves and so is price setter in the reserve market no matter what. Bank loan rates are related to the previous rates through a cost function (Kaldor 1982; Moore 1988). Long-term rates could be directly targeted by central banks, but the latter usually prefer to let financial market participants do the job and to influence them indirectly by credible policies, i.e. policies of stable short-term rates (Keynes 1936a: 202ff.; Bibow 2006; Siscú 2001; De-Juan 2007). In this case, the expectations of financial market participants concerning future short-term rates (Keynes 1936a; Kaldor 1982; Moore 1988) and future long-term rates (Keynes 1936a; Robinson 1951; Kahn 1954) are central for the determination of the long-term rates of interest.

The second implication is that, during a period of asset-price inflation in financial markets, the capacity of a central bank to influence the economy via interest rates is low and ineffective (Toporowski 1999, 2000, 2002). Indeed, like in a period of high expected output-price inflation or strong economic activity, high variations in interest rates are necessary to compensate for high marginal efficiencies of financial assets. This policy may stop speculation but will come at a high cost in terms of economic activity. These conclusions are similar to some of the authors in New Consensus. The bubble must be interest-rate sensitive and recent (so that financial positions do not depend too much on it) to justify a popping by a central bank.

Concerning the targeting of asset prices, Post-Keynesians are against it. This is so either because it is not possible to define an equilibrium, or fundamental, value (Davidson 2002: 193), or because the central bank already provides a cushion by acting as a lender of last resort (Minsky 1986a). The main role of a central bank is to guide financial market participants by providing an anchor for the valuation of asset prices, and by guiding borrowers toward the most reliable source of refinancing (Minsky 1986a; Kregel 1992a). First, a central bank can provide an anchor in the valuation of asset prices by an extended use of the Discount Window:

> Minsky's support of discount policy is an attempt to introduce monetary policy at the beginning, rather than at the end, of the process which determines capital asset prices, i.e., at the moment when banks and firms evaluate the future profitability of investment in drawing up lending agreements. [...] If the Fed were to return to creating reserves by discounting against banks' commercial lending, it would be 'cofinancing business' and be 'participating in and encouraging hedge financing.' [...] Indeed, such a policy would find the Central Bank situating itself at the interface between firms' anticipations of future profits and banks' anticipations of ability to pay interest; the point at which the price of capital assets is determined. [...] It is clear that [...] [an] increased use of discount policy would involve making a wider range of assets eligible for discount. Indeed, Minsky suggests that asset eligibility be part of policy discretion.
>
> (Kregel 1992a: 88, 100–101)

By providing an anchor via the discount rate, a central bank can guide the expectations of the private sector and so their liquidity preference (Kregel 1984: 231). Second, by having the discretion to select and to change the securities acceptable at the Discount Window, a central bank can influence the methods of (re)financing of the private sector.

Conclusion

The different conclusions concerning the appropriate role for a central bank come from the use of a different framework of analysis. Even though the New Consensus may use money in its analysis, it does not imply that it studies a monetary economy, because ultimately, money is not essential to economic decisions. Post-Keynesians start with a monetary economy, not a barter economy patched with money.

Both New Consensus and Post-Keynesian economists agree that asset prices and financial fragility are important elements to include in the decision-making process of central banks, even though they differ in terms of degree and method. For the former, financial fragility is an additional preoccupation that a central bank should tackle. In terms of asset prices, this implies that their relevance depends on the capacity of a central bank to provide to financial market participants additional information in the pricing process, and on the reliability of asset prices as predictors of future inflation and output. For Post-Keynesians, inflation should not be the main concern of a central bank. What the goal of a central bank should be is subject to debate, but some Post-Keynesian authors argue that financial fragility is the main problem that a central bank has to confront. By promoting financial strength, a central bank will promote financial stability and so will help to maintain a stable and healthy (i.e. non-inflationary) state of full employment. Asset prices matter in terms of their effects on financial fragility. What a central bank needs to study is not how well asset prices are priced, but the impact of their variability on the financial positions of economic agents.

If one follows the Post-Keynesian approach and the authors of the New Consensus that focus on financial imbalances, the central problem that needs to be explored is, therefore, the relationship between asset prices, financial fragility, and central bank policy. For example, the lender of last resort policy is usually critiqued because it may promote moral hazard and inflation. The floor put on asset prices may promote instability by increasing the confidence of the private sector and decreasing its liquidity preference. This may lead to a higher leveraging of economic decisions and so may increase the financial fragility of the economy. Thus, a too aggressive (i.e. too high) floor on asset prices is bad for financial stability, price stability, and private-sector-led full employment. The problem becomes to know if it is possible to improve the lender of last resort policy, and one may wonder how a central bank could improve its management of financial fragility. The rest of the book is devoted to providing the beginning of an answer to those questions. An enormous amount of research should be devoted to the study of these difficult but highly important questions.

3 Asset-price theories and central banking

The way economists conceive the price mechanism of assets has a definite influence on the way they position themselves in the previous debates, and on their view regarding the role of a central bank. To clearly see why, and to get additional insight about the role of asset prices for central banking, the present chapter narrows the discussion to the theories of asset prices that underlie two previous competing views, and shows the consequences of each theory in terms of central bank policy. It is argued that it is possible to classify all the immense[1] literature regarding asset pricing into three categories: the rational approach, the irrational approach, and the convention approach. The chapter shows that the irrational and convention approaches share some commonalities, and are, at least in part, an extension of Keynes's liquidity preference theory. Each section starts with a presentation of the basic concepts and hypotheses of each approach.

The rational approach to asset prices

Hypotheses

This approach is the most common in economic analysis.[2] Three hypotheses are essential. First, the rational approach supposes that economic agents are rational in the sense that they only act based on public or private information available without looking at what others do. This implies that individuals hedonistically maximize their utility by taking only into account the price signals given to them by the market. This allows them to get a portfolio with the optimal risk-return combination, given risk preference (Tobin 1958). The ultimate aim for each agent is to smooth his consumption pattern over time, as shown in chapter 2.

The second core hypothesis is the existence of an a priori "fundamental value" for each asset. This fundamental value is the sum of the discounted expected real incomes y obtained from an asset plus the estimated resale real market value P_A of the asset. If the discount rate is constant over time, the present value V of any asset at any time t is defined by

$$V_t \equiv \sum_{s=1}^{T} \frac{E_t(y_s)}{(1+r)^s} + \frac{E_t(P_{AT})}{(1+r)^T},$$

with r the risk-free real interest rate plus a risk premium, and $E_t(P_{AT})$ the expected market value of the asset at time T. The authors of the rational approach call the present value, which is a definition, the fundamental value because it is supposed to be an anchor for portfolio decisions.

Third, following Fama (1965, 1970), the rational approach assumes that capital markets are efficient. This claim emerged as a direct reaction to the chartist approach that assumes that it is possible to extract information about future asset-price movements from past data. The efficient market theory claims that asset prices follow a random walk, because they integrate immediately all the information arriving randomly in the market.

Asset-price valuation

Before purchasing any asset, a rational individual is supposed to ask himself if it is worth buying the asset. This is done by comparing the current market value P_A (the cost of the asset) to the fundamental value V (the benefit from holding the asset), both being expressed in real terms. If $P_A > V$, the marginal net benefit from buying an asset is negative and so there is no point in buying, and if an individual already bought the asset he is better off selling it, because the current amount of goods and services obtained from the sale of the asset is superior to the present value of the future amounts of goods and services obtained from its ownership. This puts a downward pressure on P_A. On the contrary, if $P_A < V$, there is an incentive for individuals to buy (or to buy more of) the asset concerned, which puts an upward pressure on P_A. In the end, thus, the quantity to buy is determined when $P_A = V$. Because individuals are supposed to be rational and to react immediately to price signals, this equality holds all the time:

$$P_{At} = \sum_{s=1}^{T} \frac{E_t(y_s)}{(1+r)^s} + \frac{E_t(P_{At})}{(1+r)^T}.$$

If one supposes that there is an "infinite planning horizon," that is to say, if individuals live indefinitely and if there is a complete set of future markets for all future periods (Shell and Stiglitz 1967), then one can apply the transversality condition:

$$\lim_{T \to \infty} \frac{E_t(P_{AT})}{(1+r)^T} = 0.$$

which is true $\forall r > 0$, given $E_t(P_{At})$. Therefore

$$P_{At} = \sum_{s=1}^{\infty} \frac{E_t(y_s)}{(1+r)^s}.$$

This can be called the "intrinsic" fundamental value.

The consequence of all this is that, if capital markets are efficient, if agents are rational, and if planning can be done over an infinite period of time, the emergence of bubbles is either impossible or, if markets are less than strongly efficient, cannot persist because market participants would bring the market price back to its fundamental value:

> We saw earlier that the independence of successive price changes is consistent with an "efficient" market, that is, a market where prices at every point in time represent best estimates of intrinsic values. This implies in turn that, when an intrinsic value changes, the actual price will adjust "instantaneously" where instantaneously means, among other things, that the actual price will initially overshoot the new intrinsic value as often at it will undershoot it.
>
> (Fama 1965: 94)

However, these conditions are not the ones that exist in the economy, where individuals are mortal and there are "futures markets for only a few commodities, and those that do exist, extend only for a few periods in the future" (Shell and Stiglitz 1967: 604–605). In this case, it is only if rational agents have perfect foresights, or adjust their expectations instantaneously that the market price will converge to its intrinsic value. Finally, if individuals do not have perfect foresight or do not adjust their expectations instantaneously, then bubbles cannot emerge only if financial markets are "nonexistent or imperfect" so that the possibility to make capital gains is very low or nil (Shell and Stiglitz 1967: 608). If capital markets on which second-hand assets are traded are liquid and if uncertainty prevails, then a bubble can occur:

$$B_t = P_{At} - \sum_{s=1}^{\infty} \frac{E_t(y_s)}{(1+i)^s}.$$

The problem becomes to know if this bubble can persist over time, or if there are forces that will constrain the persistence, or even the emergence, of the bubble.

Speculation is stabilizing

Speculation can be defined in different ways (Chick 1992), but the definition proposed by Kaldor (1939) is used in what follows. Authors of the rational approach agree that there are individuals who are preoccupied only by changes in P_A, i.e. who do not really plan to keep assets in their portfolio to gain real incomes from their ownership or their use. However, authors of the rational approach argue that this is not a problem for two reasons. First, following a logic that goes back at least to Marshall's "well-informed dealer," they claim that speculation will tend to correct asset-price misalignments (Kregel 1992b; Raines and Leathers 2000). And second, Friedman and others claim that, even if "destabilizing," "exaggerated," or "harmful" speculation is possible, it will vanish because it is unprofitable:

> I am very dubious that in fact speculation in foreign exchange would be destabilizing. [...] People who argue that speculation is generally destabilizing seldom realize that this is largely equivalent to saying that speculators lose money, since speculation can be destabilizing in general only if speculators on the average sell when the currency is low in price and buy when it is high.
>
> (Friedman 1953: 175)

Thus, speculation is a force that will correct, not promote, price misalignments induced by the previous "imperfections." Indeed, well-informed speculators are supposed to be rational agents that act upon the information available to calculate the intrinsic value of an asset. If $P_A > V$, speculators expect that the price will go back to its fundamental value; therefore, they anticipate capital losses by selling the assets for which this is the case. This decreases the market price and brings it back to its intrinsic fundamental value. Inversely, when $P_A < V$, speculators anticipate capital gains by buying the assets concerned, which increases P_A and brings it back to V. Thus, well-informed speculators complement rational individuals seeking to keep assets in their portfolio, which helps to speed up the adjustment process in imperfect markets.[3]

Rational bubble

Because of the contrast with economic reality, which recorded several periods of destabilizing speculations in a wide variety of markets (Kindleberger 1996), many authors have critiqued the position that speculation is stabilizing and that destabilizing speculation is unprofitable. However, these critiques have not been considered satisfying because they are based on the assumption of market imperfections or irrational expectations (Hart and Kreps 1986). A true rejection of Friedman's argument is supposed to show that rational agents under perfect competition can generate a bubble.

This was done first by Blanchart (1979) and Blanchart and Watson (1982), who explained how a bubble could grow in the context of an efficient financial market with rational agents, perfect foresight, and infinite life. They concluded that usually financial markets are not a good estimator of the intrinsic value because multiple equilibrium prices exist, and for only one of those is the market price equal to the fundamental intrinsic value. Therefore, individual rationality does not lead to market rationality. However, these two authors cannot explain why a bubble appears and why it bursts. They have to suppose that the bubble already exists at issuance. Moreover, as Tirole (1982) shows, if agents do not have "myopic" rational expectations but have a fully dynamic rational behavior over an infinite period, then nobody can profit from differences of information because markets are efficient and so a bubble can never occur. This leads Tirole to conclude that

> More research should be devoted to the explanation of actual price bubbles by non-rational behavior as well as to the study of the manipulability and controllability of speculative markets.
>
> (Tirole 1982: 1180)

This is why other authors (e.g. Avery and Zemsky 1998; Banerjee 1992; Bikhchandani *et al.* 1992; Welch 1992) have tried to make rational bubbles endogenous by relaxing to a certain degree the hypothesis of rationality.

Agents continue to maximize their expected utility but through Bayesian probabilities. This implies that financial actors take into account the behaviors of preceding agents to make their choices. Behaviors are supposed to reflect perfectly the information that individuals have about an asset. A herd behavior can occur when there is an "information cascade," that is to say, when individuals are led to ignore their own information in front of the unanimous decisions of previous agents. In this context, authors find several interesting results. First, herd behaviors can be rational and can help to correct price misalignments. Indeed, if the herd behaviors are based on following well-informed individuals, they can contribute to bring back the market price to its fundamental value (Avery and Zemsky 1998; Banerjee 1992). Second, the more complex the information, the higher the probability of the emergence of a bubble is (Avery and Zemsky 1998). Finally, Bikhchandani *et al.* (1992) show that the higher the number of market participants, the higher the probability of harmful herd behaviors, because the information upon which the herd is based has a higher probability not to reflect the a priori fundamental intrinsic value. This leads Banerjee (1992) to argue that the destruction of information can actually be beneficial by decreasing the probability of an information cascade. In the same line, Bikhchandani *et al.* (1992) claim that the intervention of a public authority during an information cascade (but not before because this could generate one) can be beneficial. In the end, the emergence of a rational bubble is explained by the fact that there are information problems that are not due to inefficient capital markets but due to "rational herding" (Avery and Zemsky 1998: 737). With this theory, it is possible to explain the 1987 crash by the incapacity of the clearing system to integrate all the stop-loss orders programmed into the computers that managed portfolios (Greenwald and Stein 1991). Another important conclusion of these developments is that the chartist approach becomes rational because of the multiple risks financial actors have to tackle (Avery and Zemsky 1998: 740). Traders should be aware of what happened in the past. Finally, this endogenization of the rational bubble gives importance to the role of experts and gurus who can try to manipulate the crowd in their favor.

Critique

The emergence of a bubble in a rational framework is impossible if agents are rational, have perfect foresight, and live indefinitely, and if there is a set of complete markets for all periods and contingencies in the future. To prove the existence of a bubble in the rational/efficiency framework, some hypotheses have to be relaxed about the rationality of agents (Bayesian probabilities rather than Benthamian probabilities), about the capacity of agents to see into the future, about the institutional framework in which agents act, and about the accuracy of information. Thus, the idea that a bubble cannot occur rests on special assumptions about individuals and the institutional framework. As long as individuals live a finite period and long enough, rational speculation can occur (Tirole 1985; Leach 1991).

The main merit of this approach is to show that whatever the market (efficient or not), a bubble can appear because of informational problems (asymmetry, herding) that lead market makers and other financial actors to act rationally in a wrong way. Thus, individuals acting in the financial markets are not responsible for the bubble; it is the quality of the information provided to them that is the real cause of the problem. This imperfection of information is a reality, for example, as Peter Fisher (who managed the System Open Market Account) admitted: "Every time somebody publishes a period-end balance sheet, required by the SEC, it's a lie" (Quoted in Mayer (2001: 308)). Large banks keep four sets of books: "one for the internal management information system, which hopes to keep the bosses informed of what's happening; one for the regulators; one for the Internal Revenue Service; and one for the stockholders" (Mayer 2001: 308).

However, this approach has several weaknesses. First, it leaves aside "non-rational" behaviors that can become dominant in the market. Second, the herd theory supposes that individuals act one by one in an exogenously predefined order. This approach does not take into account the social interaction that exists in the market: everybody looks at everybody at the same time (Keynes 1936a; Glickman 1994; Shiller 1995; Wärneryd 2001: 202). Third, this explanation supposes that it is possible to discover the information possessed by an individual from his behavior. However, Shiller (2000) shows that sometimes individuals do not remember why they acted in a certain way when someone asks them. In addition, during collective actions, what is important is the interpretation of information, not the information itself (Livet and Thevenot 1994; Glickman 1994). Finally, this approach states that, eventually, a "true" value always imposes itself. As shown later, this idea ignores one important characteristic of financial markets – the self-justification process. In this case, it is the fundamental value that moves toward the market price.

Implications in terms of central banking

Because individuals are rational and capital markets are efficient, the current price is usually equal to the fundamental value. Price misalignments are possible but are rare events that do not last and that are not caused by market participants but by the bad quality of the information. In this context, a central bank has no role to play unless it possesses information that is relevant to correct price misalignments. However, for the authors of this approach, this is doubtful because central banks are usually viewed as incompetent to determine the fundamental value:

> Central bankers have no particular expertise in valuing future corporation earnings, that is, in pricing equities, which is a full-time job carried on by armies of stock analysts and investors. On this basis, central bankers should feel no obligations to make public their personal views on equity prices.
>
> (Goodfriend 1998a: 18)

The best a central bank can do is to promote fundamental analyses by taking "an active role in investing in the development of the base of professionals – actuaries, financial analysts, appraisers, and insolvency experts – to perform these sophisticated functions" (Hunter *et al.* 2003: xxiii). It is also important for a central bank to promote market efficiency and deregulation so that market forces can improve the allocation of resources.

The irrational approach to asset prices

Following the conclusion reached by Tirole that economists should concentrate their efforts on the non-rational explanations of bubbles, and because "observations of reality, in particular single observations at single points in time, have cast much doubt on the assumptions that people behave rationally, even in the restricted sense 'as if'" (Wärneryd 2001: 119), the irrational approach has been developed. As shown below, this approach has obtained very interesting results even though there is still a close tie to the rational approach.

Hypotheses

In this approach, authors argue that individuals are usually rational but they can become irrational for a while because of psychological factors, human nature, or by pure accident:

> Deviations from economic rationality are often ascribed to limited cognitive capacity, [...] but are also often blamed on feelings, emotions, and deep-seated driving forces over which the individual has little control.
>
> (Wärneryd 2001: 96)

Therefore, the authors go further in the re-examination of the rational hypotheses by considering that, sometimes, there are some "anomalies" in behaviors. An irrational individual is one that does not make a decision (buys, sells, or stays neutral) on the basis of fundamentals but on the basis of "noises," which is why they are also called "noise traders," contrary to the "informed" traders (speculators or not). The concept of noise, borrowed from physics, was first introduced by Black (1986) to explain the erratic movements in financial asset prices. Thus, noise traders "trade for other reasons than maximizing expected [real] return for a given level of risk" (Black 1986: 530, n. 2), or, as De Long *et al.* put it:

> Noise traders falsely believe that they have special information about the future price of the risky asset. They may get their pseudosignals from technical analysts, stockbrokers, or economic consultants and irrationally believe that these signals carry information.
>
> (De Long *et al.* 1990: 706)

Even though noise traders create volatility, the authors of the irrational approach argue that they are essential for the existence of liquid markets because without them there would be no, or limited trading, because all informed traders know the predefined fundamental value.

Regarding the efficiency of financial markets, authors like Shiller (1981) or De Bondt and Thaler (1985) doubt that it applies all the time because of excessive volatility, and Black concurs that in the "long run prices are efficient but short run prices need not to be" (Black 1986: 532, n. 4). This overreaction of market prices to changes in fundamentals is considered an anomaly that can be explained by the "biases" of individual behaviors.

Asset-price valuation

It is possible to make a distinction between the microeconomic approach of irrationality, called behavioral finance, and the macroeconomic approach, which extends the explanation of irrationality by including other factors than purely individualistic ones. Several surveys on the microeconomic literature are available (De Bondt and Thaler 1995; Shiller 1999; Wärneryd 2001), and Shiller (2000) provides a comprehensive macroeconomic explanation and review of irrationality.

The microeconomic explanation of irrationality

The microeconomic approach of irrationality emerged in the 1990s to counter Friedman's statement that traders who do not act rationally are eliminated from the market. The main explanation rests on overconfidence and other psychological and human characteristics that lead some financial actors to choose probability distributions that are not identical to that of the fundamental value (higher expected value and lower variance). From an overlapping model with rational traders and noise traders, De Long *et al.* (1990, 1991) show that noise traders can survive and can become more and more numerous over time. This is due to a double mechanism of invasion and imitation. First, rational traders must take into account the risk generated by noise trading; this leads them to imitate the behaviors of noise traders. Second, if noise traders perform better than rational traders, more and more young traders will behave like noise traders.

However, these authors do not explain why some traders are irrational in the first place. To do so, economists have used some results obtained in psychology, anthropology, and sociology (Shiller 1999). For example, Daniel *et al.* (1998) show that psychological factors are important to explain overconfidence. Indeed, traders often have a biased vision of the results related to their past decisions, that is to say, they have a tendency to attribute good results to their competence rather than chance, whereas errors are analyzed as noises. Thus, the more experienced a trader is, the more overconfident he will be. Gervais and Olean (2001) show that novices are not immune from this tendency. Indeed, they do not know how to interpret the results of their past decisions, and tend to attribute good results to their own competence rather than chance. However, as they become more experienced, they learn that they can be wrong and so become more rational. Overall, anomalies like excess optimism, excessive confidence, excessive rationalization, or excessive agreement among analysts (De Bondt 2003), can be explained in several ways, two main explanations being heuristics and bounded rationality (Wärneryd 2001).

The first explanation of irrationality is that individuals tend to use mental frames and heuristics to interpret information. Tversky and Kahneman have been two important psychologists in this area (Kahneman and Tversky 1973; Tversky and Kahneman 1974, 1983; Harvey 1998). The heuristics that they analyzed are representative heuristics, conservatism principle, availability, adjustment, and anchoring. The first two heuristics mean that, in order to make a decision, individuals use "good stories" or "good hypotheses" and once this judgment is made, they are reluctant to change it. Thus, individuals are used to using a predefined mental model to judge a situation and to act in consequence. For example, they are prompt to judge other individuals (type of work, clever or not, etc.) based on their appearance. On financial markets, individuals use the chartist method, assimilating preceding situations with current situations, and claim to recognize the same trends at different periods of time. The third heuristic, availability, means that, in order to judge the probability of an event, individuals look for past similar occurrences of this event. However, individuals have a tendency to discount highly past information: "One particular kind of overconfidence that appears to be common is a tendency to believe that history is irrelevant, not a guide to the future [...]" (Shiller 1999: 1325). The fourth heuristic implies that to judge a situation with which they are not familiar, individuals first rely on an approximately similar situation that they know well and make an adjustment relative to it. Finally, anchoring means that in order to make decisions, individuals usually use easy points of reference. Shiller (2000) shows that financial actors use anchors to make decisions. There are quantitative anchors like a psychological price level or the past trend of prices. There are also moral anchors provided to financial actors to help them in their arbitrages. Moral anchors are based on explanations/rationalizations that aim at boosting confidence about, for example, the liquidity of assets in portfolios. All these heuristics have led to the development of the prospect theory[4] by Kahneman and Tversky (1979, 1992), which has been embraced by economists because it can be applied to the utility maximization framework and can explain some of the puzzles that standard expected utility theory cannot.

A second explanation of noise trading is that individuals have limited cognitive capacities. This leads them to try to satisfy their utility rather than maximize it (Simon 1955). With the bounded-rationality approach, the importance of the interpretation and of the processing of information is put forward. However, as the cognitive capacities of individuals increase (because of computers for example), the capacity of individuals to analyze a large quantity of information also increases and so their behaviors come closer to rationality. The prospect theory also reaches the same result; if experience can be repeated, behaviors tend to conform to the expected utility theory (Wärneryd 2001: 109).

The macroeconomic approach to irrationality

The macroeconomic approach to irrationality is mainly represented by Galbraith (1961, 1993), Kindleberger (1996), and Shiller (2000). Galbraith extended Keynes's analysis by studying periods of massive speculation. This led him to analyze the relationship between men and money. Rich persons are assumed to be cleverer rather than luckier, individuals are fundamentally greedy and want to earn a maximum amount of money with a minimum amount of effort. He also included in his analysis the importance of financial innovations that let individuals believe that it is safe to enter financial markets and to manage portfolios with very high leverages. The institutional and cultural factors are, thus, very important in the promotion or the limitation of speculation.

Kindleberger provides an extensive analysis of the history of financial crises to show that, contrary to the Monetarist view, too much money in the economy is not a sufficient condition for speculation. He also shows that there is an endogenous weakening of the economy and that "manias" (i.e. the irrationality of financial market participants (Kindleberger 1996: 13)) may result in crashes.

Shiller, by regrouping many past psychological and sociological studies, gives importance to regret (those who have not yet placed their money see some individuals making massive gains, and so try to enter quickly into the market), to rumors, and to the way information is dispersed (progressive deformation of the original information). He shows the importance of representativeness (decisions based on rough assimilations) and of the conservatism principle in the valuation of financial assets. These two elements are sufficient to influence the sentiments of traders concerning the future changes in market prices (Barberis *et al.* 1998).

Shiller and Galbraith also point out the importance of mass media and financial analysts in the spreading of overconfidence. Media help to homogenize and to spread a positive or negative sentiment in the market and, in a period of boom, newspapers try to rationalize a posteriori market prices to put traders' minds at rest, in spite of the rapid changes in the financial asset prices that do not seem to reflect fundamentals. There is a self-justification process during the boom. A market price may be judged irrational relative to the long-term expectations of incomes, but it can be justified by other explanations, or indicators, that make the "old" explanations "irrelevant." For example, during the speculative boom of the 1920s, Galbraith states that new fundamentals were created:

> The mass escape into make-believe, so much a part of the true speculative orgy, started in earnest. It was still necessary to reassure those who required some tie, however tenuous, to reality. And, [...] the process of reassurance – of inventing the industrial equivalents of the Florida climate – eventually achieved the status of a profession.
>
> (Galbraith 1961: 16–17)

This new explanation of asset-price levels is necessary to reassure the individuals already in the market and push them to buy more, and to attract new individuals, so that the speculative process can continue. The main pattern that is found in each bubble is that a "new-era" explanation emerges "as reporters scramble to justify stock market price moves" (Shiller 2000: 99). In the 1920s, the new era concerned electronics and motor vehicles; in the 1960s, it was mass production; in the 1980s–1990s, it was the information industry and biotechnologies; and each time the new era promises a higher productivity trend and more profitability. Thus, it is V that moves toward P_A, with V using more optimistic expectations of the same fundamentals, or different kinds of fundamentals than the "old era."

Figure 3.1 synthesizes Shiller's explanation of the emergence of irrational exuberance in the stock market. He puts forward not only psychological factors but also cultural and structural factors. At the macroeconomic level, individual behaviors are sustained, promoted, or repressed by cultural and structural factors, and the latter two can have positive feedback effects that contribute to irrational exuberance.

Critique

One can see that in this approach speculation is not necessarily stabilizing, and that the process of correction of misalignments can be the reverse of the rational approach, with V adjusting to P_A. This approach also puts forward the importance of the interpretation of information by individuals. This interpretation is socially determined and homogenized via mass media and financial analysts. All this is in common with the convention approach that will be presented below. However, this approach (except for Galbraith and Kindleberger) still supposes that, intrinsically, agents are rational in an orthodox way. Non-*homoeconomicus* behaviors are "irrational," "anomalies," "cognitive bias." Thus, if one could teach people to behave properly in the market, by using options to hedge their positions and by looking only at the relevant information and not at what other market participants do, it would be possible to eliminate "irrational exuberance."

However, this proposition puts aside the self-justification process. A market price may be judged irrational relative to a given set of long-term expectations of

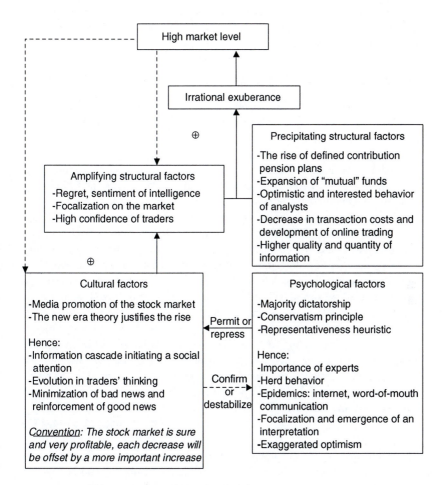

Figure 3.1 Shiller's explanation of irrational exuberance.

profits, but it can be justified by other explanations or indicators. In addition, the idea that more information leads to more rationality is not valid, only confidence is boosted:

> The relationship between availability of information and confidence is surprising. Intuitively, it is assumed that more information leads to better decisions and more confidence in judgments and decisions. Only the second part is confirmed by research. More information inspires more confidence, but the quality of decisions tends to increase only up to a point and then deteriorate[s].
>
> (Wärneryd 2001: 168)

This goes against the bounded-rationality approach and the prospect theory that still supposes that, ultimately, if information were perfect and immediately available and interpretable, individual rationality would prevail.

Implications in terms of central banking

Contrary to the Monetarist view, the authors of the irrational approach, especially the authors concerned with macroeconomics, claim that the main source of speculation is not monetary:

> The long accepted explanation that credit was easy and so people were impelled to borrow money to buy common stocks on margin is obviously nonsense. On numerous occasions before and since credit has been easy, and there has been no speculation whatever. Furthermore, much of the 1928 and 1929 speculation occurred on money borrowed at interest rates which for years before, and in any period since, would have been considered exceptionally astringent. [...] Far more important than rate of interest and the supply of credit is the mood. Speculation on a large scale requires a pervasive sense of confidence and optimism and conviction that ordinary people were meant to be rich. People must also have faith in the good intentions and even in the benevolence of others, for it is by the agency of others that they will get rich. [...] Such a feeling of trust is essential for a boom. When people are cautious, questioning, misanthropic, suspicious, or mean, they are immune to speculative enthusiasm. Speculation, accordingly, is most likely to break out after a substantial period of prosperity, rather than in the early phases of recovery from a depression.
>
> (Galbraith 1961: 174–175)

Thus, raising interest rates is not a good policy because it is ineffective given the confidence of individuals and the return they can obtain, and because it can be harmful for the economy (Shiller 2000: 223; Galbraith 1961: 34–37). Chapter 2 shows that most economists share this view. Galbraith proposes instead to use margin requirements and strong and repeated moral suasion by public figures (President, Secretary of the Treasury, central bankers) in order to stop the speculative process (Galbraith 1961: 31, 37). However, he recognizes that the latter may be too effective at stopping a bubble, and in addition, it may have adverse consequences for the person who denounces forcefully speculation:

> Of all the weapons in the Federal Reserve arsenal, words were the most unpredictable in their consequences. Their effect might be sudden and terrible. Moreover, these consequences could be attributed with the greatest of precision to the person or persons who uttered the words. Retribution would follow.
>
> (Galbraith 1961: 38)

Kindleberger shares Galbraith's opinion that margin requirements should be used more often and extended in order to manage speculative propensities (Kindleberger 1996, 1997). However, he does not share Galbraith's position about moral suasion that he considers "futile" (Kindleberger 1996: 86). This is so because warnings about speculation need to be issued at the right time and need to be convincing. In addition, strong moral suasion may be too effective and may precipitate a crisis rather than provide a smooth management of the economy (Kindleberger 1996: 83–86). Shiller shares the same view:

> The trouble with such exercises of moral authority is that, although views that the market is either very overpriced or very underpriced may become commonplace among the experts, they are never universally held. The leaders who make such statements find themselves doing so based on personal opinion: an intuitive judgment about the state of market fundamentals and psychology, a judgment that is so hard to prove that they probably feel that it takes an act of courage to make such a statement in the first place. There probably is a role for such actions by opinion leaders, but it is only a minor one. If they are genuinely disinterested in their pronouncements and are perceived as true moral leaders, their pronouncements may have a small stabilizing effect on the market.
>
> (Shiller 2000: 225)

Another device rejected by both Shiller (2000: 225ff.) and Kindleberger (1996: 132–133) is the discouragement of trade (taxes on transactions) or, during a financial crisis, the interruption of trading (use of "circuit breakers" by closing the market in the hope that spirits will calm down). Both argue that these tools are not very effective, they just postpone the drop in prices. In the end, therefore, Kindleberger is led to recommend the use of the lender of last resort during a period of financial crisis, and to use more intensively margin requirement ratios to prevent manias (Kindleberger 1997). However, he recognizes that the latter works only when "the virus [...] is speculation with borrowed funds" (Kindleberger 1996: 201). When this is not the case, like the speculative era of the 1990s (Toporowski 2000), changing margin requirement ratios will not be effective (Kindleberger 1997). Shiller, following Brennan (1998), argues that new institutions internal to financial markets should be created in order to "encourage public attention to long-run fundamentals and deflect attention away from short-run speculation" (Shiller 2000: 229). For example, one may put in place futures markets for dividends that explicitly materialize the expectations of dividends of financial market participants so they can be compared to past data.

The convention approach to asset prices

The macroeconomic irrational approach already takes into account the role of conventions but still considers that the rational approach is a good approximation of reality, irrationality being an anomaly. Galbraith and Kindleberger, however, do not suppose this and clearly assume that irrationality, or mania, is socially constructed. It is not an anomaly. The convention approach goes one step further and assumes that most behaviors in the financial markets are rational, but rationality is social not hedonistic. Irrationality is only the last stage of a speculative process or a financial distress, when herd behaviors occur. This convention approach is shared by Post-Keynesians and other heterodox economists like the French Conventions school, and it leads to completely different recommendations in terms of central bank policy.

Hypotheses

In this approach, the role of uncertainty, the importance of the institutional context, the importance of liquidity, and the irrelevance of the notion of an a priori fundamental value are put forward. At the basis of the convention approach is the recognition that the economic system is uncertain. Uncertainty is different from risk (Knight 1921; Keynes 1921) or ambiguity (Ellsberg 1961). A situation is risky when it is possible to determine all the contingencies and their probability of occurrence. Under risk, "the relation between given states of nature is known precisely, and although the random variation in the state of nature which 'obtains' may be considerable, its stochastic properties are often known confidently and in detail" (Ellsberg 1961: 666). This applies to closed and controlled situations like games, and some particular economic situations that involve routines, like insurance or the daily production process (Keynes 1936a: 24, 46ff.; Lavoie 1985).

A situation is ambiguous when there is an ambiguity of information, "a quality depending on the amount, type, reliability and 'unanimity' of information, and giving rise to one's degree of 'confidence' in an estimate of relative likelihoods" (Ellsberg 1961: 657). This is an intermediate situation between Ignorance *à la* Shackle and Risk *à la* Savage. Stated alternatively, ambiguity is defined as *unknown* risk (contrary to "known 'risk'" (Ellsberg 1961: 649, n. 5)). Finally, uncertainty, as defined by Knight, Keynes, and Schakle, means *unknowable* risk. Under uncertainty, "the probability relation itself is unknown, or more importantly, is numerically indeterminate in the literal sense that there is no basis upon which it could be determined" (Lawson 1985: 915). Even if one can come up with a probability assessment, under uncertainty a probability of one does not imply certainty.

Convention and rationality

Some institutions exist to deal with uncertainty and to manage complexity. Conventions are one kind of institution: "conventional decision making creates a significant degree of continuity, order and conditional stability [...] in spite of the potential for chaos and perpetual instability seemingly inherent in the assumption of true uncertainty" (Crotty 1992 (1993): 65). These institutions are the product of social interactions. Thus, contrary to the preceding approaches, which analyze financial markets through the use of representative hedonistic agents or sequential analysis, the convention approach fully takes into account the fact that humans are social animals. The rationality of economic agents in an uncertain world is different from the rationality defined in the previous sections. Preferences are endogenous, they are changed and shaped by social interactions, and decisions and opinions are confronted and compared to the social consensus to judge their normality and good sense. This position has been held for a long time in other disciplines like psychology or sociology (Wärneryd 2001: 80), and Veblen (1898) was among the first to critique the utilitarian approach on such a point:

> Most social influences and interactions are by definition incompatible with economic rationality [...]. Social influence may mean to follow a market leader, to react simultaneously with other investors on identical information, or simply imitate behavior, spurred directly by one's own observations or indirectly by mass media reports on what significant other people are doing. [...] Social influence is not only the strongest when the individual feels uncertain and finds no direct applicable earlier experience of her/his own, but such situations may lead to an active search for some kind of *social support* and confirmation.
>
> (Wärneryd 2001: 202–203)

Thus, in an uncertain world, in which the future is unknown and cannot be known, it is rational for individuals to look at what others do, and so a social behavior is rational (Glickman 1994; Orléan 1999; Keynes 1936a). In this case, the behaviors observed by Kahneman, Tversky and others, even under very simple and familiar situations for which probability calculus could be used easily, are more prone to appear.

Coupled with the dynamic competitive institutional set up of capitalist economies, uncertainty implies that its actors must turn their attention toward the future, and that they are subject to the "unseen pressure of society" to estimate monetarily an "unseen future" (Commons 1934 (1959): 440). This implies that the market valuation of securities depends on confidence, speculation, manipulations, propaganda, the state of the banking system, and sentiments (Commons 1934 (1961): 455, 602). In this context, speculative behaviors are a rational response to the set up of financial markets, they are not an aberration (Orléan 1999: 50). As Keynes says:

> This behavior is not the outcome of a wrong-headed propensity. It is the inevitable result of a market organized along the lines described. [...] [T]he professional investor is forced to concern himself with the anticipation of impending changes, in the news or in the atmosphere, of the kind by which experience shows that the mass psychology of the market is most influenced. This is the inevitable result of investment markets organized with a view of so-called "liquidity."
>
> (Keynes 1936a: 155)

This individual social rationality does not necessarily result in collective rationality because of the liquidity paradox, i.e. as a whole, financial markets are illiquid even though they are liquid for each individual. Thus, the fact that, for the convention approach, it is rational to look at what other individuals do does not result from a lack of information. In addition to uncertainty, this behavior results from the existence of institutional factors that promote this kind of behavior, like the promotion of liquid markets or a reward mechanism based on relative performances (Palley 1995; Trichet 2003; Kyle and Wang 1997; Orléan 1999).

A convention can be defined by three characteristics: (1) Some norms of behavior that determine the normality of a situation and give anchors to implement decisions; (2) A particular vision of the future that justifies the norms chosen; and (3) A level of confidence in the expectations provided by the convention. A convention gives confidence to individuals to implement their decisions in a situation of uncertainty because it gives them an interpretation of the current situation, it defines the appropriate ("rational" or "reasonable") mode of behavior to adopt, and it provides an objective that reduces the darkness of the future (a projection of the future that society would like to create). This social evaluation rests on rationality based on three elements (Keynes 1937b (1973): 114): (1) The present situation is a good indicator of the future state of the economy, and old past experiences are put aside or judged less important; (2) The current opinion reflected in asset prices is a correct estimation of the expectations of future profits, and there is an self-justification process; and (3) To make a decision, individuals check the opinion of the other agents, and adjust their judgement relative to what the majority thinks. There is a self-referential rationality that generates a convention that stabilizes the opinion of the financial community (Orléan 1999). This is the famous beauty contest of Keynes.

This, however, does not imply that individuals are always rational in the sense just defined. There is a place for irrationality in the convention analysis because the latter makes a distinction between mimetic behavior and herding. The former results from an interactive process in which everybody looks at everybody else, knowing that everybody else does the same thing. The point is to anticipate (not to follow) the move of the average opinion (not of everybody else) that is created through an imitative process (Keynes 1936a; Dupuy 1989; Orléan 1999). On the contrary, herding (the sequential analysis developed in the rational approach) is a behavior that consists in following the beliefs of the preceding persons without any consideration for the environment. Mimetism is rational at the individual level, contrary to herding (Orléan 1999: 83). Stated alternatively, people have self-referential, or social, rationality, and this is perfectly normal in an uncertain environment where there is no obvious point of reference from which one can make a decision. Herding is an exceptional case and the ultimate point of a crash (bubble) process where everybody tries to sell (to buy) whatever information they have. In a herding process, no point of reference (no convention) exists or can exist; it is just pure panic (mania), and the market price goes down (up) steeply and fast. These cases are rare. A stable financial market implies that market participants have a mimetic behavior that generates an average opinion (Orléan 1999; Glickman 1994; Keynes 1936a: 156; Dupuy 1989). Finally, conventions do not wash out individual initiatives, they "*guide* rather than *completely determine* behaviour" (Setterfield 2004b: 211).

Liquidity concerns, behaviors, and asset-price valuation

As shown in chapter 2, in a monetary economy, economic agents are concerned primarily with liquidity and solvency of their financial positions. This can be used to analyze behaviors in financial markets. Following Robinson (1951) and Kahn (1954), one can distinguish two types of economic agent; both are concerned about the financial power of their positions but in different ways. On one side, there are income-risk sensitive individuals who buy assets to earn an income (interest, dividend, rent). These "gentlemen" tend to hold securities in their portfolios for a long time because "the fear of income loss more than offsets a mild change of capital loss" (Kahn 1954 (1972): 83). On the other side, there are capital-risk sensitive persons who buy financial assets to trade them and make capital gains; they are afraid of increases in interest rates[5] and of missing an opportunity for capital gains. This is the typical behavior of "fund managers."

The higher the liquidity of an asset, the more individuals have a fund-manager behavior on the market for that asset (Keynes 1936a: 149–151). However, even "gentlemen" who buy assets for long-term purposes care about the resale value of assets because their solvency and creditworthiness depend on it. Liquidity also gives incentives to gentlemen to care about asset prices because, in case of emergency or when some large financial commitments become due, their liquidity may be at risk if asset prices drop too much.

Fundamentals and convention

All this has practical consequences for the valuation of asset prices because uncertainty, competition for monetary accumulation, and convention bring forward the role of liquidity preference. Indeed, the preceding implies that it is necessary to propose another theory of asset-price valuation in which P_A never has to be equal to, nor tend toward, V:

> Unlike economists, financial analysts do not appear to be making the key normative assumption that the Fundamentals *do* and *should* drive prices.
>
> (Harvey 2001: 5)

The rational and irrational approaches pay so much attention to the fundamental value because of their assumption about the nature of arbitrages by individuals. Individuals want to smooth enjoyable income over time. But, once the primacy of liquidity over purchasing power is recognized, the concept of intrinsic fundamental value loses its importance, and expectations of future prices and the timing of their occurrence become more important to determine asset prices. This does not deny that individuals own assets to try to smooth consumption, but especially for liquid assets, this consideration has little influence on daily prices and expectations of future prices are central.

The convention approach to asset prices even goes further and states that V in itself does not exist a priori. Indeed, the preceding approaches assume that "[f]uture real returns of the underlying real assets are the inevitable outcomes predetermined by today's fundamentals and unalterable by human activity" (Davidson 2002: 183, 1998). However, in a uncertain world, economic reality is changed and created by the decisions taken by economic actors, "*crucial decisions* by humans (under uncertainty) alter the fundamental real forces of the economic system as decision makers create (and therefore affect) the future" (Davidson 2002: 64). Or, as Bernstein notes, "The very idea of 'undervaluation' or 'overvaluation' implies some identifiable norm to which value will revert. [...] The lesson of history is that norms are never normal forever" (Bernstein 1993 (1993): 76). There is no a priori future that the economy will follow with certainty.[6] However, because individuals who trade in the capital markets need to be reassured, some sort of "fundamentalist" arguments have to be provided to justify the current price level. Another type of individual that needs a fundamental-value calculation, but does not base all his decision on it, is the entrepreneur who invests in capital assets for the long term (Davidson 1978: 278, 262; Keynes 1936a). The convention offers this fundamental analysis by providing a vision of the future, but these expectations do not need to reflect any past economic trends. The convention may provide *ad hoc* justifications, hypotheses, and methods of evaluation to create a foundation for the current market level:

> The fundamentals are a social construct. They evolve through the interaction of convention, information-gathering, market activity, investor psychology, and economic events.
>
> (Goldstein 1995: 723)

Therefore, the self-justification process shows that economic myopia is a social construction and not an irrational phenomenon (Orléan 1999: 155), because it is not in the interests of financial actors to look at anomalies, and because the current mode of interpretation leads to unconscious ignorance of bad information, or to a minimization of its importance, or even to turn it into good news:

> Above all, it is evident that the capacity of the financial community for ignoring evidence of accumulating trouble, even of wishing devoutly that it might go unmentioned, is as great as ever.
>
> (Galbraith 1961: xxi)

Thus, the present value has nothing fundamental; it is just the way to calculate the fair value of an asset. Market prices may be determined independently of V, and V may have to catch up to provide a fundamentalist justification to P_A. One then may define a normal price P_{An} that represents the consensus, i.e. the average opinion, in the market about what the price level should be on average. The normal price is not determined by market forces but by the mimetic process described above.

The role of financial markets: Efficiency versus liquidity

The convention approach does not assume that financial markets are efficient in the sense of the rational approach (Wray 1995; Glickman 1994, 2000; Pressman 1996; Davidson 2002). The role of financial markets is not primarily to allocate resources:

> For the most part financial market activity is speculative and independent of both real investment activity and the rate at which new securities are being floated since the latter is very small relative to the total number of transactions and the outstanding stock of existing securities. The lower the transaction cost of organized security market activity, the more the focus of market participants will be on the capital gains or losses due to expected changes in the very near future of spot market prices of financial assets.
>
> (Davidson 2002: 107–108)

The role of financial markets is to make illiquid capital goods liquid for individuals (Keynes 1936a: 150ff.; Davidson 2002: 187). This may promote investment by giving an incentive to economic agents with idle money to buy the liquid financial claims issued to fund investment spending. However, the main result of creating an organized market, in which claims upon the property of underlying capital assets can be exchanged quickly at low cost, is to promote concerns about short-term expectations of prices. In addition, the liquidity of financial markets is imperfect because it exists only if they are not one-sided. There is no such thing as liquid financial markets at the market level (Keynes 1936a: 153) and "the existence of a *variety* of opinion about what is uncertain" (Keynes 1936a: 172) is essential to preserve the liquidity of financial markets.

Adding this to the preceding, all this implies that the market price of financial assets does not reflect technology and tastes, and that observed excess volatility in financial markets does not necessitate the loose concept of "noise." The volatility of the capital markets increases with their liquidity and is the normal result of the latter because of the variety of opinions necessary to ensure liquidity: "Price volatility is therefore an integral part of the story and requires no *deus ex machina* to account for it" (Glickman 1994: 348). This relation between liquidity and volatility was observed by Fields in 1933. He studies the US stock market from 1872 to 1927 and splits the period into three parts: 1872–1896, which he called the "formative [period] in American Stock Exchange history" (Fields 1933: 359); 1897–1914, which "marks the beginning of the first major combination movement in American industry" (Fields 1933: 360); and 1914–1927, when "short selling first assumed major proportions" (Fields 1933: 360). He shows that each period witnessed an increase in the volatility of stock prices (Fields 1933: 365) and is the highest for the last period "when all the facilities of the highly organized New York Stock Exchange were open to traders" (Fields 1933: 366).

Asset-price valuation

In the convention view, the explanation of the asset-price level and movements is based on the liquidity preference theory of asset prices. This theory, created by Keynes (1936a), has been developed by Townshend (1937), Boulding (1944, 1950, 1966), Robinson (1951), Kahn (1954), Davidson (1968a, 1968b, 1978, 1988b, 2002), Minsky (1975a), Kregel (1988a, 1992a, 1998a), and Wray (1991b, 1992b, 1992c). All these authors show that the liquidity preference theory developed by Keynes is not a simple theory of money demand *à la* Hicks but a theory of asset prices.

This theory makes a difference between the price of new issues and the price of old issues, especially when assets have a well-organized secondary market:

> The stock of financial assets is very large compared to the flow of new assets entering the market. This was recognized by Keynes, who argued that [...] the prices of new issues of both long-term and short-term debt are influenced by the prices of existing debt. This means that the price of new credit instruments must continually compete with the prices of existing assets. To some extent, competition is imperfect because secondary markets do not exist for many types of loans, and because banks (and other financial institutions) are prohibited from entering many financial markets. Thus, market segmentation can maintain price differentials, although deregulation and innovation are rapidly breaking down such barriers. In any case, prices of existing assets will influence (and place ceilings and floors on) interest rates on new financial assets. However, even if new flows are relatively small, they can play a large role in affecting the prices of existing assets by affecting expectations and by the leadership role played by the central bank and by large ("money center") banks. That is, those who operate in secondary markets will pay close attention to wholesale and retail rates announced by the central bank and commercial banks. They will also try to guess the prices that will be announced in the future.
>
> (Wray 1992c: 1164)

If Wray concentrates the argument on financial assets, this is also true for the price of capital assets, and the comparison between the flow price of capital assets (i.e. the price of new capital assets, or price of investment goods) and the stock price of capital assets (or price of old capital assets) has an impact on investment (Keynes 1936a; Minsky 1975a). Post-Keynesians have provided an explanation of both the flow-equilibrium price and the stock-equilibrium price of assets.

The price and level of transactions in the secondary market

Because the flow of new assets created is very small relative to the size of the existing stock of assets, the price that results from the equilibrium between the stock of existing assets and the demand for them dominates. The stock-equilibrium price is an anchor toward which the flow-equilibrium price will tend (even though expectations regarding the latter influence the former). To understand how the volume of transactions and prices are determined in the market, one needs to distinguish between price-determining factors and quantity-determining factors (Boulding 1944).

PRICE-DETERMINING FACTORS

The position of each individual is defined by the type of assets in portfolio. As shown in chapter 2, each asset has special characteristics in terms of expected earnings, risk, liquidity, carrying cost, and capital gains. The more optimistic and confident agents are, the more they will accept to hold assets with low liquidity premium, and risky and uncertain earnings. However, because the future is uncertain and individuals care about the liquidity of their financial position, they will tend to keep liquid assets in their portfolio, even if a probabilistic assessment gives them a probability of success of one on risky assets. Therefore, each individual j has a desired proportion of asset i and money that he wants to keep in portfolio:

$$\alpha_{ij} \equiv \frac{(P_{Ai}A_{ij})_d}{W_j} \quad \alpha_{Mj} \equiv \frac{M_{jd}}{W_j} \quad \text{with} \quad W_j \equiv M_j + \sum_{k=1}^{K} P_{Ak}A_{kj},$$

with W_j the nominal wealth owned by an individual j and $(P_{Ai}A_{ij})$ the nominal amount of asset i desired by individual j and

$$\sum_{k=1}^{K} \alpha_{kj} + \alpha_{Mj} = 1 \quad \forall j.$$

If an individual has more (less) of one type of asset than desired, he will be willing to sell (buy) an amount at the prevailing market price P_{Ai} so that his money stock will increase (decrease). D_{ij} is the excess demand of an asset i by an individual j. If $D_{ij} > 0$ an individual is a net buyer of asset i. If his money stock was also in disequilibrium in an opposite way (so that no more transaction occurs), the wealth of an individual is redistributed as follows:

$$W_j = \left(M_j - P_{Ai}D_{ij}\right) + \left(\sum_{k=1}^{K} P_{Ak}A_{kj} + P_{Ai}D_{ij}\right).$$

More generally, after all transactions are done, each individual has the nominal stock of assets and money that he desires:

$$\alpha_{ij} = \frac{P_{Ai}A_{ij} + P_{Ai}D_{ij}}{W_j} \quad \alpha_{Mj} = \frac{M_j - \sum_{k=1}^{K} P_{Ak}D_{kj}}{W_j}.$$

Given the quantity of assets (including money), α_{ij}, and α_{Mj}, the null price is obtained by first determining the excess demand function. By substituting W in α_{Mj} and rearranging, we obtain the excess demand for an individual j:

$$\frac{\alpha_{Mj}}{\alpha_{ij}} = \frac{M_j - \sum_{k=1}^{K} P_{Ak}D_{kj}}{P_{Ai}A_{ij} + P_{Ai}D_{ij}} \Rightarrow D_{ij} = \frac{\alpha_{ij}(M_j - \tilde{S}_j)}{(\alpha_{ij} + \alpha_{Mj})P_{Ai}} - \frac{\alpha_{Mj}}{\alpha_{ij} + \alpha_{Mj}}A_{ij} \quad \forall i, \forall j,$$

with $\tilde{S}_j \equiv \sum_{k=1, k \neq i}^{K} P_{Ak}D_{kj}$ the sum of all trades made by an individual j excluding his trades on asset i. The null price for an individual j is the price at which he has no incentive to trade asset i: $D_{ij} = 0$. Thus, the null price for the individual j is

$$P_{Aij}^0 = \frac{\alpha_{ij}}{\alpha_{Mj}} \cdot \frac{\left(M_j - \tilde{S}_j\right)}{A_{ij}} \quad \forall i, \forall j.$$

The null price of individual j depends on the quantity of asset i, the quantity of money held by individual j, the preference of individual j in terms of assets, as well as on the volume of other transactions he made. The higher the liquidity preference of an individual, the higher α_{Mj}, and so the lower the individual null price on the asset i is. One can also see that there is an interdependence between markets because the individual null price of any assets depends on the price at which other assets are traded by individual j.

The problem becomes to aggregate this in order to find the equilibrium price of the market for asset i. In practice there are many obstacles to aggregation; however, if the excess demand functions are supposed to be linear, it is possible to show that the market price is a weighted average of the null prices of all individuals with the slopes of the individual excess demand curves as a weight (Boulding 1944: 57, n. 3). At the market equilibrium for asset i, the market price P_{Ai} is such that:

$$D_i\left(P_{Ai}^*\right) = \sum_{j=1}^{J} D_{ij}\left(P_{Ai}^*\right) = 0 \quad \forall i.$$

Therefore, by developing and simplifying, the equilibrium price of the market is

$$P_{Ai}^* = \frac{\sum_{j=1}^{J} \alpha_{ij}\left(M_j - \tilde{S}_j\right)}{\sum_{j=1}^{J} \alpha_{Mj}A_{ij}} \quad \forall i.$$

To simplify this function, one may either assume that individuals have all the same portfolio preferences, a very strong assumption,[7] or may calculate the desired aggregate average ratio $\bar{\alpha}_M$ and $\bar{\alpha}_i$. In the latter case, Boulding (1944: 59, n. 1) shows that, when there are only two assets, these ratios are a complex weighted average that depends not only on α_{ij}s and α_{Mj}s but also on A_{ij}s and M_js. As shown in Appendix 2, this weighted average is even more complex when there are K assets because it also depends on $\tilde{S}_j$. This again shows that there is an interdependence between markets. Once the market-preference ratios have been determined, one has

$$P^*_{Ai} = \frac{\bar{\alpha}_i M - \bar{\alpha}_i \sum_{j=1}^J \tilde{S}_j}{\bar{\alpha}_M \sum_{j=1}^J A_{ij}} \quad \forall i.$$

We know that each trade implies a buyer and a seller; therefore, $\sum_{j=1}^J \tilde{S}_j = 0$. In the end, the equilibrium market price of an asset i is given by:

$$P^*_{Ai} = \frac{\bar{\alpha}_i}{\bar{\alpha}_M} \cdot \frac{M}{A_i} \quad \forall i.$$

The equilibrium price of any asset i, at the market level, depends on the average liquidity preference of market participants, the stock of money in the economy, and the quantity of asset i. The volume of trade in other assets is still present indirectly through the average preference ratios. The higher the uncertainty about the future, the higher the average liquidity preference of individuals, the faster α_i will drop, and the lower the equilibrium price of asset i will be. As noted earlier, a diversity of opinions about the future path of the asset price is essential for price stability. If everybody is pessimistic then $\bar{\alpha}_M \to \infty$ and so $P^*_{Ai} \to 0$, and inversely if everybody is optimistic. The price-determining factors will be analyzed further below.

THE QUANTITY-DETERMINING FACTORS

Prices and volumes of transactions are not directly related because prices can change without any transactions occurring:

> Thus, in the simplest case, where everyone is similar and similarly placed, a change in circumstances or expectations will not be capable of causing any displacement of money whatever – it will simply change the rate of interest in whatever degree is necessary to offset the desire of each individual, felt at the previous rate, to change his holding of cash in response to the new circumstances or expectations; and, since everyone will change his ideas as to the rate which would induce him to alter his holdings of cash in the same degree, no transactions will result.
>
> (Keynes 1936a: 198)

Thus, there is no stable relationship between price and quantity exchanged; both have to be explained separately.[8] It has been shown that the appropriate price for an individual is given by his null price. The level of transactions in the market for an asset i depends on the divergence of null prices. Individuals with a null price below the market price have an incentive to sell, whereas individuals with a null price above the market price have an incentive to buy. The higher the divergence of opinion, the higher the volume of trade is. Boulding (1944: 60) shows that "a rise in liquidity preference, or a fall in the total quantity of money held in the market will have a general tendency to increase the volume of transactions."

GENERALIZATION OF THE MODEL OF ASSET-PRICE DETERMINATION

Knowing how the equilibrium stock price of each asset is determined, one can explain how the latter change by explaining how $\bar{\alpha}_M$, $\bar{\alpha}_i$, M, and A_i grow:

$$\pi_{A_i}^* = g_{\bar{\alpha}_i} - g_{\bar{\alpha}_M} + m - g_{A_i}.$$

Boulding (1944, 1950, 1966) already provides some explanations, but the model has been extended by Wray (1992b), who provides a model that generalizes Boulding's by endogenizing all the variables, and by making the distinction between different kinds of monetary instruments.

First, concerning the quantity of assets, its rate of growth depends on factors specific to each asset but, in all cases, expectations about the future play an important role. If one considers machines, the investment level is what matters and the latter depends on the expectations of future profits by banks and entrepreneurs, and on the liquidity of financial positions (Minsky 1975a; Keynes 1936a). For homes, the rate of home construction depends on the expectation of income by households and banks, on the liquidity of financial positions, on the cost and availability of resources to build homes, as well as the mortgage rate. For financial assets, the change in their quantity depends on the level of net investment, and also on purely financial operations like mergers, or the refinancing of debts (Toporowski 2000). In the former case, the additional quantity of securities is equal to (Davidson 1978: 252, 302):

$$\Delta A_F = (1 - h)eP_{Is}Q_{In}/P_F.$$

with e the fraction of investment funded externally, h the proportion of long-term external funding granted by banks, P_{Is} the offer price of new capital assets, and P_F the current price of existing securities. Thus, given the nominal amount of net investment that needs to be funded through financial markets, the lower the prices of securities, the higher the quantity of new securities to be floated (Davidson 1978: 275). When securities are issued for refinancing operations, an equal nominal value of financial assets is created and destroyed but the quantity of assets destroyed does not need to be the same depending on the relative par price of redeemed financial assets and the success of the new issue (floated at a discount, a premium, or at par) compared to the one of the asset(s) redeemed. More formally, assuming that new titles are issued at the prevailing market price, and that the maturity value of both old and new securities is the same,

$$P_F \Delta_I A_F - M_F \Delta_R A_F = 0,$$

with $\Delta_I A_F$ the quantity of new titles issued, $\Delta_R A_F$ the quantity of old titles redeemed, and M_F the maturity value of the titles. If one defines the net increase in securities for refinancing as $\Delta_{n\mathrm{REF}} A_F \equiv \Delta_I A_F - \Delta_R A_F$, then $\Delta_{n\mathrm{REF}} A_F = (M_F/P_F - 1)\Delta_R A_F$, which has to be added to ΔA_F.

Second, the preference ratios also "are in part determined by future expectations" (Boulding 1944: 63). They introduce more directly than other variables "all the forces operating from the side of the future" (Boulding 1944: 63) through the impact of perceived uncertainty on the preference for liquid assets. The preference ratios change with "anticipated changes in prices" but are "independent of the absolute level of the price [...]" (Boulding 1944: 58). As developed further in chapter 2 and the next chapter, this dependence on the expected changes in prices was well understood by Keynes:

$$\bar{\alpha} = \bar{\alpha}(q, r, c, l, a).$$

One of the main consequences of this is that positive feedback loops can develop between price and price expectations (Robinson 1951: 103). In addition, because those ratios depend on what happens in other asset markets, a crisis or boom in one market can be transferred to other assets. More generally, Davidson (1978: 255–257) shows that the demand for securities depends on several factors, like expectations of capital gains, capital and income risk aversions, wealth, length of expectations, and confidence in expectations.

Concerning money, the preceding chapter shows that, in the Post-Keynesian literature, the endogeneity of money is an essential characteristic. Wray (1992b), following Kahn (1954), introduces in Boulding's model the endogeneity of money and the possibility of having different kinds of monetary instruments. In this case, M includes, in addition to the central bank liabilities, bank and non-bank liabilities. When banks are included in the analysis, the distinction between quantity-determining factors and price-determining factors is not as clear because banks affect both the level of transactions and the quantity of money (Kahn 1954; Wray 1992b: 73). The liquidity preference of banks becomes an important factor in the determination of the prices of assets because, when banks have a higher liquidity preference, they ration more easily and they charge a higher interest rate, which tends to push down asset prices (Dow 1996; Minsky 1975a; Wray 1990).

Finally, there is a different α_M for each type of monetary instrument. From this, two important conclusions follow. First, not only does the level $\bar{\alpha}_M$ matter, but its structure does too:

> Thus, even if the total liquidity ratio [...] did not rise, an attempt to shift out of illiquid forms of money and into liquid forms still might affect asset prices, generally.
>
> (Wray 1992b: 78)

A second important conclusion is that an increase in bank money will not necessarily affect asset prices, "this will affect the prices of all assets to the extent that preference ratios for these types of money enter into the determination of asset prices" (Wray 1992b: 78).

Overall, therefore, the theory of asset prices for second-hand assets is very complex and puts forward the central role of the liquidity preference of financial market participants. In this theory, there is no fundamental value, the only points of reference that individuals have are their null price, the market price, and the normal market price given by the convention.

The price level and level of transactions in the primary market

Davidson (1978, 1994, 2002) and Dalziel (1996, 1999, 2001) have completed the preceding model by showing how the flow prices of financial and capital assets are determined. Davidson focuses his analysis on financial assets, while Dalziel, extending Davidson, is mainly concerned with capital assets. First, concerning financial assets, Davidson simplifies the matter by assuming that the stock price P_F and the flow price are the same (Davidson 1978: 252), and then shows how the price of old financial assets is affected by flows of supply and demand, given "the normal factors affecting liquidity preference, e.g. expectations of future spot prices of securities, risk aversion, etc. [...] so [that] only the minor increments in wealth affect the market price of securities" (Davidson 1978: 325–326, n. 3). Assuming that securities are issued only to fund investment, the excess flow demand for securities is

$$z = xs_h W - eI.$$

This represents the net additional demand for securities, with eI the proportion of nominal investment that entrepreneurs want to fund externally on financial markets, and $xs_h W$ the proportion of households' saving allocated to the purchase of securities; x being the propensity to demand securities out of saving. If one supposes that the equilibrium between the stock of assets and the demand for this stock already has been reached, z will be the main determinant of financial asset prices. Then, if $z > 0$, that is to say, if firms do not supply enough new securities to match the demand for additional securities, given the stock equilibrium, the price of securities will go up. If $z < 0$, there is an undesired quantity of new financial assets owned by investment banks and other underwriters who arrange the floatation of the new securities. To maintain an orderly financial market, this holding must be financed. By supplying funds to underwriters, banks allow to close the gap between demand and supply of new securities and limit the decline in prices.

Dalziel also provides an explanation of the demand price of capital assets by flow variables. "Assuming [stock] equilibrium at the beginning of the period" (Dalziel 1999: 238), the growth of the price of old capital assets depends on the rate of growth of capital assets, on the propensity of enterprises to fund their investment externally, the propensity of households to hoard their wealth, and the inflation in the equity market.

These two explanations of flow prices complement, but in no way replace, the stock theory because flows do not reflect the main forces that drive both capital and financial assets prices:

> Placement market activity is, for the most part, independent of both investment activity and the rate at which new securities are being floated, i.e. [transactions resulting in new issues are] likely to be exceedingly small relative to the total number of transactions occurring in the securities market.
>
> (Davidson 1978: 265)

In addition, both previous flow theories assume that financial markets are mainly used to fund investment which may not be the case, either because enterprises may not, as a whole, issue a net positive amount of shares (Mayer 1988; Aglietta 2001), or because financial markets are used mainly for purely financial operations (Toporowski 2000).

Conclusion

Glickman (1994: 334) notes that some authors are afraid that the rejection of the framework used by the rational and irrational approaches would leave economists without a systematic theory of asset prices. The preceding shows that there is a systematic alternative to the orthodox approach to asset prices. This alternative rests on a theoretical framework that recognizes that the future is uncertain, that economic actors care about nominal values and prefer liquid assets, and that assumes that the main role of financial markets is not to allocate physical resources. This theory shows that a fundamental value is not a necessary theoretical tool to explain how stability can emerge in financial markets; all that is necessary is a diversity of opinions around a convention that provides an anchor. The notion of convention is "a *sine qua non* of Keynesian macrotheory" (Crotty 1994: 120). This theory also has some implications in terms of portfolio strategy, as shown by Thompson *et al.* (2003). Finally, in all the preceding approaches, authors are concerned with the equilibrium value of asset prices. Toporowski (2000) provides an explanation of how asset prices move out of equilibrium.

Implications in terms of central bank policy

The preceding theory of asset prices has several implications in terms of central banking. The first one is that assets that are prone to speculation should be carefully monitored by central banks because of their potential destabilizing effects on *all* asset prices and economic activity. The problem becomes to know how to check for those potential destabilizing effects. One of the main responses that comes out of the convention approach is that checking for the asset-price level or growth is not a good way to judge financial sustainability, because the appropriate level/growth always changes with expectations of the future and with the convention given to justify them. A better way to judge if an asset-price pattern is unsustainable is by noting that speculation changes the way economic actors behave. The main way this translates into economic terms is through the changes in the balance-sheet structure of economic actors. Their balance sheets become less liquid and more leveraged, and so more sensitive to changes in asset prices (Toporowski 2000; Minsky 1986a). This method of judging the sustainability of asset prices is more reliable and less subject to controversies because it can be observed, and because it is possible to simulate, at least in theory, the impact of asset-price variations on balance sheets with different levels of fragility.

Second, the role of the central bank is to maintain the liquidity of the financial system when its intrinsic macroeconomic illiquidity is revealed by the uniformity of opinions (Minsky 1975a, 1986a; Davidson 1978, 1998, 2002; Wray 1992a, 1992d; Kregel 1992a; Keynes 1930, 1936a). This, however, should be done in a way that does not encourage too much optimism by financial actors by making them believe that gains are guaranteed. Otherwise moral hazard will occur. As Martin Mayer notes:

> Both the fixed-income markets and the stock markets have come to rely to an unprecedented degree on a safety net from the Federal Reserve. The head of one of the largest hedge funds in the world said to me shortly after the rescue of Long Term Capital Management that the episode had carried a clear message for him: "If I get in big trouble, the Fed will come and save me." I told him that if Alan Greenspan could hear him he would turn white as a sheet and resign. But he was sure he was right.
>
> (Mayer 2001: 138–139)

One way to do so is to promote the financial moderation of the main economic actors by supervision and regulation. However, this supervision would be of a different nature than current supervision because of a different conception of human behavior: behavior is mainly socially and institutionally driven. Another way is to use moral suasion by using the fragility of financial positions (in terms of balance sheet, cash flows, and position-making channels), rather than overvaluation, as a justification. Finally, the central bank may announce that it will intervene only after asset prices dropped "enough," which depends on the sensitivity of financial positions to asset-price changes. Thus, the appropriate floor to put on asset prices (i.e. the appropriate accommodation of excess bearishness) depends on the financial fragility of the economic system. A strong system is able to absorb large decreases in asset prices so that the floor can be put lower, and a central bank should have an idea of how much decline a system is able to absorb. An appropriate floor will promote financial prudence and financial stability, not only by giving some certainty to the private sector that the central bank will intervene, but also by leaving some uncertainty about the level of the floor.

Conclusion

This chapter has shown that different theories of asset prices lead to different propositions in terms of management of asset prices by a central bank. The rational approach concludes that a central bank has no direct role because the market price is most of the time at its optimal level. The central bank should only promote indirectly fundamental valuation. The irrational approach also recognizes the same role for the central bank, which can help financial actors to become more rational by educating them. The convention approach shows that the role of the central bank is to influence the convention prevailing in financial markets by exposing the fragility of the financial positions of economic sectors. This last approach also shows that the concept of "bubble" is not relevant for central banking. Indeed, by claiming that financial market participants are irrational, the central bank will create social discontent and point at the wrong problem. It will create social discontent and disbelief because it is always possible to justify *ex post* any level of asset price. This sense of rationalization and denial may be especially strong for those who are heavily involved in the segments of the financial market where the pace of growth seems unsustainable according to the central bank. The latter will point at the wrong problem and will provide wrong guidance because, even if prices are believed by everybody, including the central bank and the most conservative financial analysts, to be at their appropriate level, financial disruptions can still occur. This goes through the sensitivity of balance-sheet positions, cash-flow positions and sources of position-making activities, to a change in asset prices. Very small changes in asset prices may lead to large problems, independently of the state of financial markets, if the economic system is financially fragile. In the end, therefore, central banks have a role in the management of asset prices but not by directly commenting on the correctness of the asset-price valuation. Their role is to promote financial stability and they should concentrate on the sensitivity of financial positions to asset-price changes.

The chapter also shows that to put the blame on financial market participants and their "irrationality" is not a good way to understand the core of the problem. Financial market participants adapt to their environment (so they are rational), and if policy makers want to change the behaviors of the previous individuals, it is necessary to change the institutional framework in which financial market participants intervene. Better supervisory and lender of last resort policies would work in this sense. However, there are other institutional factors, like too high competition among pension funds or mutual funds, or marking-to-market, and reward mechanisms based on short-term relative performances that promote short-termism.

There are, however, limits to what central banks are willing to do in terms of stabilization of expectations and direct intervention in troubled asset markets, in this case, other government institutions may be necessary. First, a floor policy will be effective only as long as a liquidity crisis occurs in markets in which the central bank is willing to intervene. A central bank may be reluctant, or may refuse, to take some assets as collateral or to buy assets with a low liquidity and a low probability of repayment ("junk" assets). It may also be reluctant to discount titles representing ownership of private businesses. History shows that central bankers can be very flexible in terms of the collateral they accept, especially in times of strong instability and when the law leaves them some flexibility regarding the structure of their balance sheet. For example, since 1932, sections 10b and 13 of the Federal Reserve Act allow a Federal Reserve Bank to accept anything it wants as collateral, provided that it is "secured to the satisfaction of such Federal Reserve Bank." The latter may also grant advances to non-bank private sectors if necessary (Small and Clouse 2005).

Second, if the crisis is not a liquidity crisis but a solvency crisis in which expectations of all private market participants (including market makers) are shifted downward, the floor policy of the central bank will work only if it intervenes directly (and not through market markers) in the market to buy assets in order to restore the liquidity and capital of the financial institutions in trouble. However, given that solvency crisis implies a large increase in the amount of junk assets, the central bank may be unwilling to enter troubled markets. In this case, a complementary institution like a government investment bank may be necessary. This should be complemented by a restructuring of companies in trouble, and the public institution involved in the injection of funds should be involved in the restructuration process.

4 Against the instrumental use of interest rates

Modern central banks constantly manipulate interest rates in order to fine tune economic activity and maintain a low level of inflation. As illustrated more clearly in chapter 6, the way central bankers set policy rates depends on their theoretical framework and political considerations but, overall, two categories of behavior can be distinguished. One type of behavior involves moving nominal interest rates up and down until the interest rates affect the economy to the satisfaction of central bankers. Another type involves targeting a specific real interest rate that is assumed to be the "neutral" rate.

In this chapter, a critique of these two behaviors is developed and used to draw some implications about the appropriate interest-rate policy for a central bank. First, following Fisher, many, including some Post-Keynesians, have argued that the concept of real rate of interest is useful to understand and to manage a capitalist economic system. It will be argued that the notion of real interest rate is not useful for economic analysis; therefore, using it for monetary policy purpose is not recommended. Second, other authors may put forward the manipulation of nominal interest rates for policy purposes. This is critiqued by showing that the traditional demand curve for money does not hold. This will show the importance of taking into account the setting of financial markets before using interest rates. In some settings, using this instrument creates volatility rather than stability. Therefore, neither nominal nor real interest rates are good instruments to manipulate. All this can be used to discuss the position taken by some Post-Keynesians regarding active interest-rate policies in the fine-tuning of the economy or the distribution of output. All these points will be based in part on the notion of breakeven point and its corollary, the notion of duration; therefore, these two notions will be presented first.

The importance of the notion of breakeven point:
A Post-Keynesian view

Modern portfolio management includes many different tools to try to deal with different risks; among those the notions of duration and breakeven point deal with interest-rate risk. To understand the importance of the notion of breakeven point for economic theory, it is first necessary to present briefly some basic concepts of financial theory (Fabozzi 1993). As shown below, these notions already were present in Keynes's *General Theory*.

Basic financial management concepts

Yield to maturity

A bond provides a total rate of return $\tilde{i}$ that is a function of the coupons, the interest income on the coupons (or "reinvestment income"), and the resale value of the bond relative to the price paid for it (capital gain or loss). The fair price V of a fix-rate bond T periods of time before maturity is

$$V \equiv \sum_{t=1}^{T} \frac{C}{(1+\bar{i})^t} + \frac{M}{(1+\bar{i})^T},$$

with C the periodic coupon payment, $\bar{i}$ a given periodic market rate, M the par value (or value at maturity), and T the number of coupon-payment periods before maturity. $\bar{i}$ is called the "yield to maturity," which, because of arbitrages, is assumed to be equal to the market yield at the time of purchase and represents the yield that can be obtained at maturity if all coupons are placed (i.e. "reinvested") at this rate.

The actual reinvestment yield will not be necessarily $\bar{i}$ during the holding period if the required market rate for the same class of risk changes in time. In addition, if one sells a bond before maturity, the resale price is not known and it will depend on the market yield at that time. The actual yield $\tilde{i}$ may be either higher or lower than $\bar{i}$. Therefore, individuals may want to protect themselves against the possibility that $\tilde{i} < \bar{i}$. To do so, they need to know how the actual yield will vary for a given change in i, which is done by checking the sensitivity of bond price and of reinvestment income to changes in i. Indeed, when the prevailing interest rate varies, the reinvestment income earned on coupons and the fair price change in opposite direction. Given this dilemma, an individual may be interested in two kinds of related questions. A first set of questions is related to a short-term strategy: What is the sensitivity of the fair price to a change in the rate of interest? Below what level of volatility of interest rate is it profitable to buy a bond in the short term? A second type of question is more related to a long-term strategy: How long will it take to be sure to get the yield to maturity, or any other targeted yield, whatever the changes in interest rate? To answer these questions, the notions of breakeven point and duration are very important.

Duration and breakeven point

The breakeven point reflects the absolute or relative variation in interest rate for which the capital loss (gain) is exactly compensated by the total gain (loss) from reinvestment income. This breakeven point can be calculated for different periods of time.

The calculation of the sensitivity of the fair price to the rate of interest requires to determine the duration of the bond,[1] and to deduce the modified duration. The duration of a bond is equal to

$$D = \frac{C}{Vi}\left(\frac{1-(1+i)^{-T}}{1-(1+i)^{-1}} - \frac{T}{(1+i)^{T}}\right) + \frac{M}{V}\frac{T}{(1+i)^{T}}.$$

If the coupon is paid yearly, this gives a measure in terms of years, and, for all bonds except zero-coupon bonds, the duration is always inferior to the time to maturity T. The duration is the time necessary to reach the breakeven point, i.e. the time necessary for a capital gain (loss) to be exactly compensated by a reinvestment income loss (gain) so that the actual rate of return is at least equal to a targeted total rate of return.

For perpetual bonds ($T \rightarrow \infty$), the duration is given by $D_P = (1+i)/i$ and the modified duration is $MD_P \equiv D_P/(1+i) = 1/i$. Knowing that the fair price of a consol is given by $V_P = C/i$, and knowing that $dV/V = -MD \cdot di$, for a given variation in the market yield, one has

$$\Delta V_P \approx -(C/i^2) \cdot \Delta i.$$

Of course, for consols, the first derivative of the price gives the same result and it is not necessary to find the duration. But, for more complex bonds, the result is not straightforward and the duration provides a convenient way to approximate the interest-rate elasticity of a bond price.

In addition, the calculation of duration allows implementing what is called in portfolio management an "immunization strategy." Indeed, one portfolio strategy is to target a yield rate $\bar{i}$ (and so a certain sum of money) for a given holding period, and to buy bonds that have a duration equal to the holding period for the targeted interest rate. This will guarantee that reinvestment income and capital gain at least will compensate for each other so that the actual yield obtained will be equal to or higher than the targeted rate. More formally, we know that the reinvestment income obtained at the time a bond is sold is (with h the holding period)

$$RI = C\left[\frac{(1+i)^{h} - 1}{i}\right] - hC.$$

Therefore,

$$\Delta RI \approx (C/i^2)[1 + hi(1+i)^{h-1} - (1+i)^{h}] \cdot \Delta i$$

and so for $h = D_P$, $\Delta RI_P \approx -\Delta V_P \approx (C/i^2) \cdot \Delta i$. Thus, one can conclude that, if the rate of interest goes below (above) a targeted yield, capital gains (losses) will be realized and *more* (*less*) than offset the reinvestment income losses (gains) so that the actual yield $\check{i}$ will be superior to $\bar{i}$. If i stays the same, then the yield obtained will be $\check{i} = \bar{i}$ (see Appendix 3).

The notions of breakeven point and duration are, thus, important to try to cope with liquidity risks induced by unforeseen changes in interest rates, and their adverse impacts on fair prices and reinvestment incomes. This can be applied usefully to balance-sheet structures in order to match the cash flows from assets and liabilities. Keynes was the first to show the importance of these notions for economic theory.

The breakeven point in the General Theory

The notion of breakeven point is essential to the understanding of the *General Theory*, and was presented in the following way by Keynes:

> [E]very fall in [*i*] reduces the current earnings from illiquidity, which are available as a sort of insurance premium to offset the risk of loss on capital account, by an amount equal to the difference between the *squares* of the old rate of interest and the new. For example, if the rate of interest on a long-term debt is 4 percent, it is preferable to sacrifice liquidity unless on a balance of probabilities it is feared that the long-term rate of interest may rise faster than by 4 percent of itself per annum, i.e. by an amount greater than 0.16 percent. per annum.
>
> (Keynes 1936a: 202)

The "square rule" (Kregel 1985, 1998a) implies that a person who expects the level of the rate of interest to go up by more than its square in absolute terms should increase his preference for money. Indeed, say that an individual bought a perpetual bond and decided to sell it after one coupon period. The nominal return obtained is

$$R = C + \Delta V,$$

which is approximately equal to

$$R \approx C - (C/i^2) \cdot di.$$

Consistent with Keynes's liquidity preference theory in which money "rules the roost," one placement strategy involves determining what change in the nominal market rate is expected to lead to a nil nominal return ($E(R) = 0$):

$$C - (C/i^2)E(di) = 0 \Rightarrow E(di) = i^2.$$

Thus, for a consol, the short-term breakeven point (corresponding to one coupon period) is reached when the level of the rate of interest varies by its square (i.e. when it grows at the level of itself). Therefore, if *i* is expected to increase and $E(\Delta i) < i^2$, the short-term holding a bond provides a net gain. The capital loss is expected to be inferior to the income gain.

Keynes called the case $E(\Delta i) > i^2$ a liquidity trap, i.e. a situation at which the central bank loses its capacity to influence nominal long-term rates, and stated that this kind of condition is rare, if ever observed (Keynes 1936a: 207; Kregel 2003). However, the previous condition was obtained by assuming that the targeted money return over the period was zero and by only looking at placement strategies over one coupon period. If one of these strict conditions is removed, the liquidity trap has much more chance to appear. First, it is highly probable that financial market participants have a positive rate of return in mind that makes them indifferent. At minimum, this positive return will be related to the rate they could get on saving deposits but stakeholders will be more demanding. Let us say that a person, at time 0, could sell a bond he holds for a sum of money S_0. In addition, let us assume that this person has a targeted nominal sum of money, S_T, that he would like to receive after one coupon period. His targeted yield over the coupon period is $\bar{i} = S_T/S_0 - 1$, which generates a targeted nominal return of $\bar{i} S_0$ over the coupon period. A time 0, a person, therefore, will be indifferent between bond and money if

$$C - (C/i^2) \cdot E(di) = \bar{i} S_0.$$

Thus, the expected change in the market rate that leaves the person indifferent is

$$E(di) = i^2 (1 - \bar{i} S_0 / C)$$

The higher the targeted sum at the end of the coupon period, the smaller the change in interest rates tolerated will be before parting with bonds. Given that S_0 is the current fair price V and that M is the par value of a bond so that $C = cM$, and c is the coupon rate, we have the following indifference condition for consols ($v = V/M$):

$$E(di) = i^2 \times \left(1 - \frac{\bar{i}}{c} v\right).$$

This generalized square rule shows that the higher the targeted return relative to the coupon rate, and the higher the fair price relative to its par value, the smaller the change in interest rate tolerated by actual and potential financial market participants, and the more the liquidity trap has a chance to emerge. For a high enough targeted yield, an expected decline in the interest rate is necessary not to affect adversely financial positions. All this helps to understand why gradualism and transparency is crucial when a central bank wants to use interest rates to manage the economy, and why it is easier to lower interest rates at a faster pace.

The second strict condition of the square rule is that the holding period is limited to the coupon period. For longer placement horizons, no generalization can be made about the indifferent condition because it depends on the long-term placement strategy followed. Under some very strict conditions, the long-term indifference condition may be equal to the square rule. Under other conditions, the indifference condition may be more or less sensitive to changes in interest rate, depending on the reliance on capital gains to obtain a targeted nominal return, and depending on the hedging technique. The higher the dependence on a bonanza, the higher sensitivity to changes in interest rates, and so the smaller the change in interest rate that would make individuals indifferent between holding bonds versus money.

Theoretical implications

As shown in chapter 2, Fisher's framework has direct implications in terms of goals for a central bank. The latter should be concerned with managing inflation expectations and interest rates in order to keep real interest rates at a stable level that promotes saving and investment. Some Post-Keynesians have also promoted the use of real interest rate, even though they claim that they only use it as a definition that does not have anything to do with Fisher's view. The following goes further in arguing against the use of such a concept and shows that using interest rates to manage the economy may be hazardous, depending on the configuration of financial markets.

A critique of the concept of real rate of interest

Chapter 2 shows that the concept of "real" is not appropriate when dealing with financial problems. What matters primarily is the liquidity of a financial position, not its purchasing power, and this will be illustrated again in this chapter. Below, five critiques of the concept of real rate of interest, from Fisher's point of view or as a definition, are provided.

Anticipated inflation does not affect nominal interest rates

The first critique of Fisher's theory was provided by Keynes in the *General Theory* (Keynes 1936a: 141–144). This critique was restated and developed by Harrod (1971) and Davidson (1974, 1986a). At the aggregate level, the Fisherian analysis yields the equality $i = r^* + E(\pi)$, i.e. given r^*, the required real rate determined in the loanable funds market, any expected increase (decrease) in inflation will lead to an increase (decrease) in the nominal rate of interest via arbitrages between future and present aggregate enjoyable income.

Keynes was among the first to be skeptic about this explanation of the business cycle and interest rates. One of the central reasons why Keynes rejected Fisher's theory is because the latter rests on the gross substitution axiom (Davidson 1974). This axiom assumes that all assets are highly substitutable so that the relevant transmission mechanisms of a monetary shock go beyond the portfolio adjustments in terms of financial assets to include also "such assets as durable and semi-durable consumer goods, structures and other real property" like "houses, automobiles, [...] furniture, household appliances, clothes and so on" (Friedman 1974: 28–29; Sargent 1972: 213). However, if it is true that there is a high substitutability among monetary assets, and between monetary assets and liquid non-monetary assets, Keynes argued that non-monetary assets are not usually a good substitute for monetary assets as a store of value. Thus, "so long as it is open to the individual to employ his wealth in hoarding or lending *money*, the alternative of purchasing actual capital assets cannot be rendered sufficiently attractive (especially to the man who does not manage the capital assets and knows very little about them), except by organising markets wherein these assets can be easily realised for money" (Keynes 1936a: 160). Usually, non-monetary assets are illiquid so they cannot be resold at all, or only can be resold by recording large capital losses. Thus, contrary to Fisher and Monetarists, illiquid assets are "not [...] a hedge against inflation and hence will be shunned by savers" (Davidson 1986a (1991): 350).

A second reason, related to the former, concerns the adjustment mechanism of Fisher's theory, which is delivered in the following way (Keynes 1933c (1979): 82–83):

> There is no escape from the dilemma that, if it is not foreseen, there will be no effect on current affairs; whilst, if it is foreseen, the prices of existing goods will be forthwith so adjusted that the advantages of holding money and of holding goods are again equalised, and it will be too late for holders of money to gain or to suffer a change in the rate of interest which will offset the prospective change during a period of the loan in the value of the money lent. For the dilemma is not successfully escaped by Professor Pigou's expedient of supposing that the prospective change in the value of money is foreseen by one set of people but not foreseen by another.
>
> (Keynes 1936a: 142)

Thus, in any case, in the context of Fisher's theory, the money holders (the lenders) will never be able to adjust the interest rate before inflation occurs. And, after inflation occurred, money holders will not have any incentive to do any arbitrage because all money rates will be equal again. To understand why, it is, first, necessary to understand how the rate of interest could go up because of perfectly expected inflation. This would not result from an arbitrage between money and bonds because both are monetary assets and so both are affected exactly in the same way by inflation:

> Bonds and cash are two forms of asset denominated in money. Neither has a hedge against inflation. [...] The rate of interest represents the rate at which bonds can be exchanged for cash. Since neither contains a hedge against inflation the new-found expectation that inflation will occur cannot change their relative values or therefore the rate of interest. [...] The idea that a new-found expectation can alter the relative value of two money-denominated assets, is logically impossible, and must not be accepted into the corpus of economic theory. [...]
>
> (Harrod 1971: 61–62)

The only reason why the interest rate would go up because of expected inflation is because individuals would like to move their portfolio out of monetary assets (bond and money) and into liquid non-monetary assets (shares and others). The problem becomes to know if they actually can do this arbitrage based on inflation expected perfectly with full confidence. Keynes's answer is no. Indeed, at time 1, if inflation is foreseen perfectly with total confidence then $\pi_1 = E_1(\pi_2)$. The price of non-monetary assets adjusts instantaneously by the expected amount as everybody rushes to try to buy them. The interest rate has no time to adjust and a loss in purchasing power is recorded by money holders, whereas a potential capital gain is recorded by holders of non-monetary assets. Then, at time 2, assuming that no inflation is expected and knowing that the growth of the money supply by m_2 has already been included in decisions in time 1, $i_0 = r^*$, again without any arbitrage to smooth consumption having been completed. Therefore,

> The monetarist theory of a real versus nominal interest rate is mired in its own logical mudhole. If expectations of inflation [...] which create the difference between the real and nominal interest rates do 'fully anticipate' the future so that, in Fisher's term, inflation is 'foreseen' [...], then the existing stock of real durables can never be a better *ex ante* inflation hedge than before the change in expectations occurred.
>
> (Davidson 1986a (1991): 351)

Only uncertainty about future inflation can influence the interest rate:

> The occurrence of a new-found belief firmly held, that a certain rate of inflation will occur, cannot affect the rate of interest. But the growth of *uncertainty* about what rate of inflation, if any, is in prospect, can send up the rate of interest [...] by making a larger number of people want to remain liquid in respect of a larger proportion of their assets for the time being.
>
> (Harrod 1971: 62–63)

Keynes proposed an alternative adjustment mechanism in which, rather than influencing the marginal efficiency on money (the interest rate), expected inflation impacts directly the marginal efficiency of capital. Inflation raises the monetary profit expectations of entrepreneurs, given the level of consumers' spending.

One of the main responses provided by Fisher's supporters is that Keynes had a "curious misunderstanding of Professor Fisher's celebrated proposition" (Roberston 1940: 21). The misunderstanding is that, theoretically, an expected inflation will lead to an instantaneous increase in i to compensate for the expected real loss but

> In actual practice, for the very lack of this perfect theoretical adjustment, the appreciation or depreciation of the monetary standard does produce a real effect on the rate of interest [...]. [...] This effect is due to the fact that the money rate of interest [...] does not usually change enough to fully compensate for the appreciation or depreciation. The inadequacy in the adjustment of the

rate of interest results in an unforeseen loss of the debtor, and an unforeseen gain to the creditor, [...].

(Fisher 1930: 493–494)

Expected inflation is modified after a lag and so is incorporated only progressively into the nominal rates of interest proposed by lenders, so when the central bank increases the money supply, $i_2 - \pi_2 < r^*$, i.e. the real yield on physical assets becomes superior to the real yield on money. This gives some incentive to borrow money until the equilibrium is restored. Assuming that inflation stays the same after time 2, this means that the equilibrium is restored when $i_3 - \pi_2 = r^*$ with $i_3 > i_0$. In the end, money holders have recorded a loss during the adjustment process because statistics show that "there is very little direct and conscious adjustment through foresight" (Fisher 1930: 494). Therefore, there is a possible stimulating effect of inflation from the discrepancy between "the marginal productivity of investable funds *to the user* and the rate of interest 'in the strict sense' which he is compelled to pay in the market" (Roberston 1940: 21). Money is not neutral in the short run.

This kind of counter critique is, however, very *ad hoc* and goes against the arbitrage principle that Fisher proposed, namely that expected inflation matters, not actual inflation. People want to avoid purchasing power loss, not to compensate for the loss. Forward/spot market transactions are involved (Fisher 1930: 69). This arbitrage process is essential for Fisher's theory because it leads directly to the notion of real rate of interest.

Several economists have provided an explanation of why interest rates do not fully adjust to inflation. Fisher argued that it is because inflation expectations contain lags, but he and others recognize that this explanation is unrealistic because of the very long lags necessary to make this explanation relevant (Sargent 1976). Another argument by Gordon (1973) is that given the nature of the monetary system during the prewar period, people tended to expect price stability on average. Price instability mainly resulted from the particular circumstances generated by First World War, which flooded the economy with money (and so kept interest rates low), left few commodities in the economy that could be used as hedging instruments, and made people believe that price instability was only temporary (and so was not included in expectations). Summers (1983) provides two counterarguments to this position. Other economists, like Fama (1975), have relied on statistical explanations by arguing that "the price level is mismeasured during the control period" (Summers 1983: 240) or that there is "some unmeasurable variable correlated with inflation that affects required real returns" (Summers 1983: 227). Mundell (1963), Tobin (1965), and Sargent (1972) provide a theoretical explanation of why the nominal interest rate will rise by a lower amount than expected inflation, by combining a Wicksell effect and a Pigou effect, as well as for Sargent, the effects of price and income lags. Assuming that the economy was previously at a non-inflationary equilibrium ($i = r^*$), expected inflation raises the nominal return on investment ($i < r^* + E(\pi)$), which raises investment relative to saving and so creates an inflationary gap. Following the loanable funds approach, the equilibrium is restored by raising the nominal interest rate by the expected inflation rate. However, expected inflation also reduces the expected stock of real money balance relative to its desired stock, which, given interest rate, also "stimulates increased saving" (Mundell 1963: 283) and so nominal interest rates do not have to rise as much as inflation to restore the equilibrium in the loanable funds market. This Mundell–Tobin effect can be critiqued on similar grounds as the Wicksell and Pigou effects. Rogers (1989) and Davidson (1994: 193–195) provide a good overview of the theoretical problems surrounding those effects and other characteristics of those models. Overall, the problem is, again, that it is assumed that capitalist economies are similar to barter economy patched with money.

Cottrell (1994), while rejecting the "vulgar" Fisherian view for the reasons advanced by Post-Keynesians (Cottrell 1997), provides another counter critique of Davidson and Harrod by stating that their points of view rely on partial equilibrium. For Cottrell, the two preceding authors do not take into account the fact that an increase in the marginal efficiency of capital induced by higher expected inflation must generate, indirectly via an IS/LM-type financial feedback, higher interest rates. That is, higher investment will generate higher income, and so higher demand for money for transactions, and therefore, *ceteris paribus*, higher interest rates. This counter critique, however, leaves aside the remark that Keynes made to Hicks. Contrary to the loanable funds theory and IS-LM, an increase in investment does not need to increase interest rates (Keynes 1937e (1973): 80). Therefore, Harrod and Davidson do not reason in terms of partial equilibrium. What they argue is that there is no automatic pressure on the rate of interest; it will depend, as Harrod said, on the effect of uncertainty on liquidity preference and on the way the money supply is affected by higher aggregate spending and monetary policy: IS and LM curves are not independent (Davidson 1978). As Cottrell notes, the decision of the central bank to accommodate liquidity needs at an unchanged interest rate is one condition for not producing a result similar to Fisher's (Cottrell 1997).

In conclusion, the idea that interest rates on monetary assets are driven mainly by expected future inflation has been refuted many times on both empirical and theoretical grounds. Another explanation is required, and Keynes provided one via the notions of liquidity preference and marginal efficiency of capital (the *money* rate of return on non-monetary assets). The only direct effect of inflation is to increase the marginal efficiency of capital (by raising expected nominal profits), i.e. contrary to Fisher, it is the monetary rate of return on non-monetary assets that adjusts for inflation (Keynes 1936a: 142–143; Kaldor 1982: 97; Kregel 1998a).

Fisher's condition of indifference is not the relevant one

This second critique of Fisher's real rate was also provided by Keynes in the *General Theory* even if he did not relate it to Fisher's theory. This critique was developed also by Kahn (1954) and by Kregel (1998a, 1999), and is directly related to the notion of breakeven point presented previously.

In Fisher's theory, the condition of indifference is given by $r^* + E(\pi) + r^* \cdot E(\pi) = i$, meaning that individuals are indifferent between lending and borrowing money in order to smooth their purchasing power overtime. In Fisher's terms, this would imply that the best way to protect the purchasing power of money, if inflation is expected, is to raise the interest rate on monetary assets. However, this completely eludes the impact of rising interest rates on the price of those assets. The income portion will have its purchasing power preserved, but this will also lead to a potential capital loss, which has several consequences. First, if one sells the income-providing assets, the capital loss may be so high that the purchasing power gain is completely wiped out. Second, even if the asset is kept in portfolio, the potential capital loss is reflected in net wealth and also in the creditworthiness of asset holders, and so ultimately on their capacity to get loans, which also affects purchasing power and the capacity to smooth income over time. Overall, therefore, increases in interest rates to adjust for expected inflation may be counterproductive.

A more inclusive condition of indifference is the one given by the breakeven point. For consols, the simplest short-term condition of indifference is $E(di) = i^2$. This condition of indifference (or any other similar arbitrage conditions that try to protect the liquidity of a position) is perfectly compatible with a portfolio strategy that aims at targeting a certain after-tax inflation-adjusted rate of return. The primacy of the solvency and liquidity concerns does not mean that economic agents are indifferent to purchasing power concerns; however, the latter are included in the broader scope of the former two. In a monetary economy, if one wants to hedge against purchasing power losses, one must care first about hedging against illiquidity and insolvency. This is done by taking into account potential capital gains and losses within the arbitrage condition.

The transfer of real income over time

Fisher assumes that the arbitrage that goes on at the microlevel between present and future enjoyable income can be applied at the macroeconomic level. This, again, has been critiqued by Keynes (Keynes 1936a: 210):

> Aggregate demand can be derived only from present consumption or from present provision for future consumption. The consumption for which we can profitably provide in advance cannot be pushed indefinitely into the future. *We cannot, as a community, provide for future consumption by financial expedients but only by current physical output.* In so far as our social and business organisation separates financial provision for the future from physical provision for the future so that efforts to secure the former do not necessarily carry the latter with them, financial prudence will be liable to diminish aggregate demand and thus impair well-being, as there are many examples to testify.
>
> (Keynes 1936a: 104–105. Italics added)

Thus, not only is Fisher's condition of indifference inappropriate at the microlevel, it is also impossible to implement at the aggregate level. In the former case, it does not necessarily protect individuals against purchasing power loss, and in the second case, arbitrage is impossible because there are no spot and forward markets for a "commodity" called "aggregate enjoyable income." Therefore, saving can only come in monetary terms, not in real terms. However, saving in financial terms today does not lead automatically to production, or provision for the production, of future goods and services. The only way to provide for the future in real terms is to invest today (i.e. increase capacities of production), and investment (physical accumulation)[2] has nothing to do with, and is not promoted by, saving (financial accumulation). On the contrary, higher saving today may discourage investment and contribute to the idleness of resources, by reducing current sales and so, over time, the monetary profit expectations of entrepreneurs.

Actually, in his own terms, Fisher is aware of all this. He recognizes that a person can change his/her real income streams in two ways (Fisher 1930: 128ff., 183): via impatience (borrowing and lending) and via investment. However, at the aggregate level, the first solution is not possible:

> Borrowing and lending, the narrower method of modifying income streams, cannot be applied to society as a whole, since there is no one outside to trade with; and yet society does have opportunities radically to change the character of its income stream by changing the employment of its capital.
>
> (Fisher 1930: 129)

Stated alternatively, the arbitrage process that leads to the condition of indifference cannot be applied at the aggregate level.

The theory of rate of interest and marginal efficiency

This critique has already been developed partly in chapter 2 and concerns two points: one regarding the monetary explanation of interest rates and another regarding the existence of a natural rate of interest. Fisher assumes that r^* is a physical return given by technology and tastes. However, in his analysis, Fisher recognizes that r^* is actually calculated in money terms and that price expectations matter for the decision. The rate of return over cost is the monetary expression of r^* and is the essential variable for investment (Fisher 1930: 150ff.). Later, Keynes explicitly stated that the marginal efficiency of capital and the rate of return over cost are identical concepts (Keynes 1937a (1973): 101, n. 2). One, then, could wonder if it is justified to critique Fisher's analysis for not taking into account the importance of money and monetary expectations.

In fact, in Fisher's theory money is a veil, and Keynes should not have confounded marginal efficiency of capital with marginal rate of return over cost as depicted by Fisher. The rate of return over cost is a monetary expression of the physical gain generated within the production process, whereas the marginal efficiency of capital reflects the profit obtained from the sale of production. This should be clear if one reads the following quote:

> In the real world our options are such that if present income is sacrificed for the sake of future income, the amount of future income secured thereby is greater than the present income sacrificed. [...] Man can obtain from the forest or the farm more by waiting than by premature cutting of trees or by exhausting the soil. [...] Nature offers man many opportunities for future abundance at trifling present cost. So also human technique and invention tend to produce big returns over cost.
>
> (Fisher 1930: 192–193)

Thus, the rate of return is just a monetary expression of the "primitive cost and return typified by labor and satisfaction" (Fisher 1930: 180). On the other side, Keynes was very careful to state that the marginal efficiency of capital does not rest directly on technical concepts (Kregel 1988b: 63; Kahn 1984: 146–147): "If capital becomes less scarce, the excess yield will diminish, without its having become less productive – at least in the physical sense" (Keynes 1936a: 213). Marginal productivity and marginal efficiency are two different concepts.

Regarding the existence of a natural rate of interest, the capital controversy has shown that it is logically impossible "*to define the natural rate of interest outside of a one-commodity model*" (Rogers 1989: 32), and that the dynamics of the Neoclassical growth model are non-linear and generate unstable equilibria (Kregel 1971; Harcourt 1972). This problem can be solved by using the Walrasian apparatus but this comes at a high cost because there is no role for money in this framework of analysis (Arrow and Hahn 1971; Rogers 1989).

The Fisher indifference condition as a definition

Some Post-Keynesian authors (e.g. Smithin (2003) or Cottrell (1994)), even though they reject the notion of natural interest rate, agree that the notion of real rate of interest is a useful concept in terms of definition:

> Interest rates are determined in the financial sector proximately by the decision of the ultimate provider of credit, in other words the central bank. This institution also sets the pace for real interest rates, and not just for nominal rates. The real interest rate (on Fisher's definition) is just the nominal rate minus expected inflation. Hence the central bank can set the real rate, if it wishes, simply by adjusting the settings of the nominal rate to offset changes in expectation of inflation.
>
> (Smithin 2003: 126)

This position is, however, quite problematic for several reasons. First, the financial power of money is more important than the purchasing power of money. For example, Pigeon notes that unionized workers in Canada have wage demands that "are anchored on expected inflation and interest rates" (Pigeon 2004: 118). In itself, the real wage is an inefficient way to protect the purchasing power of wage; the whole range of cash outflows should be included. It is the same with financial-income earners whose consumption outflow may be less important than cash outflows due to financial commitments like interest, margin calls, or other off-balance-sheet commitments. In this case, raising interest rates may be bad for them. It is the relation between nominal cash inflows and nominal cash outflows that matters.

Second, the idea that Fisher's real rate of interest is "just" a definition is not what Fisher has in mind. Fisher's indifference condition reflects a hypothesis about the behavior of individuals and their way of selecting assets. It also reflects a particular conception of income (Kregel 1999; Veblen 1908, 1909). However, as shown above, this indifference condition is problematic for several reasons. In addition, if one assumes that the real rate of interest is just a definition, one must assume that there is a clear correlation between inflation and nominal interest rates. However, many empirical studies, including Fisher's, have shown that the Fisher effect does not hold. Cooray (2002) provides a good review of the enormous empirical literature and additional references can be found in Stock and Watson (2003), Ghazali and Ramlee (2003), Koustas and Serletis (1999), Sargent (1976), and Haliassos and Tobin (1990).

Figure 4.1 shows that, in the US, there is no relation between inflation measured by the CPI and interest rates, whatever the maturity, until the mid-1950s.

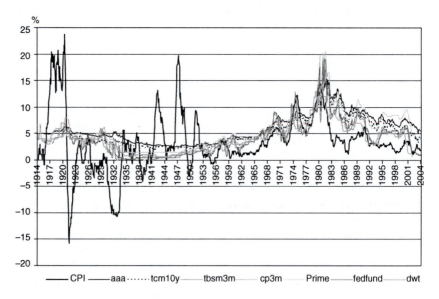

Figure 4.1 Nominal interest rates and inflation: Jan 1914–Feb 2004.
Source: Federal Reserve Bank of New York, NBER, and BLS.

Note: aaa, AAA Corporate bonds; tcm10y, T-Bonds 10 years; tbsm3m, T-Bills 3 months; cp3m, Commercial papers 3 months; fedfund, fed funds rate.

After that period, interest rates are more closely related to inflation. One may wonder why suddenly the relation changed, as if individuals could suddenly better account for changes in the price level. Friedman and Schwartz (1976) and Summers (1983) have also noted this change in time pattern and argue that, perhaps, financial market participants have "learned their Fisher." However, Table 4.1 suggests a different explanation of the break in the relationship between interest rates and inflation. Before 1953, the correlation is around 0 or negative but after 1953, the correlation is moderately high, between 0.65 and 0.79, especially for short-term papers.[3] On the other side, the close correlation between interest rates and policy rates has always been extremely high, between 0.83 and 0.99.

The break date can be explained by the change in monetary policy following the Treasury Accord of 1951, after which the Federal Reserve progressively changed its operating procedures. By 1953, with its "bills only" policy, the Fed had freed itself completely from any obligations toward ensuring the perfect liquidity of Treasuries (Beard 1964). Following this operational change, and given the growing concerns about inflation and the renewal of Monetarist ideas, the central bank oriented its policy toward "fighting inflation" by raising or lowering its interest rates with changes in the consumer-price index (or other price indexes) (Seccareccia 1998; Clarida *et al.* 2000; Orphanides 2004).

One of the immediate implications is that the other rates also became more correlated to the rate of inflation. Therefore, the higher correlations after 1953 do not reflect the fact that people suddenly became more preoccupied with inflation. On the contrary, it reflects the continuity of economic behaviors: the primacy of liquidity concerns. Changes in short-term rates create instability by generating disturbing fluctuations in prices and reinvestment incomes in the long-term range, and by affecting the profitability of borrowing short-term for speculation. As shown in chapter 6, the number of strong corrections in the long-term and short-term security markets has increased dramatically after 1953. To hedge their positions and to profit from arbitrage opportunities, financial market participants constantly anticipate changes in policy rates.

One can further confirm those results and obtain more insights by doing a more systematic econometric analysis. Several authors have already studied the influence of the interest rates set by the central bank on other interest rates. Heffernan (1997) focuses on administrative interest rates set in the UK between 1986 and 1993 by banks and building societies. He shows that retail interest rates react positively to changes in policy rates but they do so with a lag and more or less fully. Biefang-Frisancho Mariscal and Howells (2002) study the reaction of some UK market and administrative rates for the period 1975 to 2001 and find results similar to Heffernan's. Cook and Hahn (1989) focus on US bill and bond rates between 1974 and 1979 and show that the reaction of market rates to changes in the federal funds rate target is positive and strongly significant. The reaction is the stronger the shorter the maturity is and right after the change as "it took market participants at least a day following the initial Fed action signaling a target change to be completely sure that a change had occurred" (Cook and Hahn 1989: 341).

Table 4.1 Yield rates, inflation, and monetary policy: Jan 1914–Feb 2004

Monthly rates	Corporate bonds AAA	T-bonds (10 years)	T-bills (3 months)	Commercial papers (3 months)	Prime	Fed funds	Discount window
Correlation between CPI inflation and interest rates							
1914–2004	0.250	0.338	0.326	0.381	0.381	0.352	0.287
1914–1952	-0.070	-0.125	0.076	-0.104	-0.464	0.077	-0.044
1953–2004	0.652	0.677	0.777	0.761	0.738	0.779	0.798
Correlation between discount rate and interest rates							
1914–2002	0.902	0.916	0.975	0.975	0.966	0.973	1.000
1914–1952	0.902	0.907	0.954	0.943	0.884	0.954	1.000
1953–2002	0.871	0.908	0.970	0.976	0.950	0.968	1.000
Correlation between fed funds rate and interest rates							
1914–2004	0.891	0.913	0.990	0.990	0.969	1.000	0.973
1914–1952	0.831	0.857	0.985	0.991	0.862	1.000	0.954
1953–2004	0.845	0.885	0.993	0.987	0.951	1.000	0.968

Source: BLS, NBER, Federal Reserve Bank of New York (ftp website), www.wrenresearch.com.au.

They also find that the expected level of the fed funds rate target strongly influences market rates before the target is changed. Atesoglu (2003, 2005) confirms those results for the US from 1987 to the early 2000s by finding a unidirectional Granger causality from fed funds rate to prime rate and to the long-term rates after the Federal Reserve started to announce changes in its targeted rate in 1994. Before 1994, he finds a bidirectional causality between the fed funds rate and the prime rate. Overall, however, Atesoglu argues that the central bank does not have much influence on long-term rates in the short run.

A very interesting study by Roley and Sellon (1995) focuses on the impact of expected future monetary policy following a change in policy rate. A move in policy rate that is expected to be permanent or to be pursued further (e.g. an increase in the targeted rate is expected to be followed by further increases) should have a stronger impact on interest rates of all maturities. Through this methodology, they find a stronger positive impact of monetary policy on long-term rates than most previous studies, even though it is still relatively small. Finally, they show that, between 1987 and 1995, market participants tended to view monetary policy as persistent over a one-to-three year horizon, but they did not expect policy changes to be permanent.

One can perform a VAR analysis on all variables and check the Granger causality. A non-rejection of the preceding conclusions would show that one cannot reject the hypothesis that changes in policy rates of the Federal Reserve Granger cause changes in all the other rates, while changes in market rates do not Granger cause changes in policy rates. In addition, the policy rates should be Granger caused by inflation and its expected value. It will be assumed that the federal funds rate is the policy rate of the Federal Reserve. In addition, theory tells us that market rates depend partly on expected policy rates. Below expectations of fed funds rate are determined by assuming that financial market participants make perfect expectations of next month fed funds rate: $E_t(i_{FFRt+1}) = i_{FFRt+1}$.

Before going further, a few words of caution are in order. Indeed, one central problem of the Granger causality procedure is that it is very sensitive to the preliminary tests necessary to perform the causality test. The preliminary tests concern the lag structure of the VAR and the stationarity of variables (orders of integration and cointegration). Recent developments in the econometrics of time series have tried to provide several solutions but there is still large room for future developments and improvements (Clarke and Mirza 2006). In addition, Granger causality is different from theoretical causality; if a variable X Granger causes a variable Y, it means that X helps to predict future values of Y, stated alternatively, X precedes Y in time (Sims *et al.* 1990; Kónya and Singh 2006). However, predictive power, or precedence, do not imply causation. Finally, the following is only a rapid econometric analysis, for example, we did not do important tests regarding the normality and white-noise properties of residuals, we did not check for structural breaks in the database, and we did not add any dummy variables to account for wars, oil shocks and any other specific events. The following tests are sensitive to the previous points. The idea is to suggest possible future directions for more rigorous econometric analyses.

The Dickey-Fuller tests show that interest rates and expected inflation are I(1) variables; the inflation rate is a stationary variable. Leaving aside potential cointegration relationships, a VAR analysis on variations of interest rates is first performed. Absolute variations of interest rates are I(0). The first step is to determine what lag length is relevant. The most common way to do that is to estimate a VAR in levels (Enders 2004: 363). All the following results are presented in detail in Appendix 4. Table A4.1 shows that, following the Schwartz criteria (which is the most consistent criteria and the one preferred for large samples (Enders 2004)), a 3-month lag structure is appropriate. Taking as reference what the FOMC has done since 1981 – meeting every five to eight weeks – this three-month lag is not unreasonable. A VAR in first difference generates a lag of two months from the Schwartz criteria. Table A4.2 shows the results of a Granger test for all the changes in market rates. One cannot reject the hypothesis that changes in expected fed funds rate Granger cause all other changes in market rates, whereas none of the changes in other rates Granger cause changes in the expected federal funds rate at a 5 percent confidence level. This unidirectional Granger causality holds for lags from one month to four months, even though it concerns only long-term rates for a one-month lag. For other lags, there is no unidirectional Granger causality.

The next step is to see if the relationship between the central-bank rate and inflation (expected or actual) follows any Granger causality. Looking at inflation first, between 1914 and 1952, Table A4.3 shows that there is no apparent Granger causality between changes in fed funds rate and inflation. This result holds whatever the lag structure used. From 1953, however, Table A4.4 shows that changes in fed funds rate Granger cause changes in inflation. Thus, even though the Federal Reserve claims to fight inflation by trying to manage economic activity via its interest-rate policy, it seems that the opposite result holds, i.e. the central bank interest-rate policy contributes to inflation; this is true for any lag structure. There is nothing surprising with this result if, as Post-Keynesians have claimed for a long-time, interest rates have a significant impact on costs. Recent empirical work in the New Keynesian literature also supports the non-rejection of this hypothesis (Tillmann 2007).

If one considers expected inflation (measured by the survey of consumers of the University of Michigan) rather than inflation, then here again the results would be counterintuitive to most economists. Only for a lag of three months or more can we assume that changes in expected inflation Granger cause changes in federal funds rate, but the causality also runs the other way. For smaller lags, only the reverse causality cannot be rejected: changes in fed funds rate Granger cause changes in expected inflation. Table A4.5 shows the result of the Granger test. According to the Schwartz criteria obtained from the VAR in levels, Table A4.6 shows that a lag of three months is optimal and so it seems that results from the two-month lag structure should not be trusted.

In conclusion, it seems that there is little reason to believe that interest rates and inflation are related to each other as long as the central bank does not become highly preoccupied with inflation. This close relationship between inflation and interest rates exists either because the central bank responds to inflation by increasing its interest rates, or because inflation results from a tightening of monetary policy.

The previous conclusion helps in not rejecting the conclusion reached previously: the period 1953–2004 does not see financial market participants become Fisherian, the Federal Reserve did. However, the results on unrestricted VAR in first differences are not reliable when cointegration exists. The only reliable results concern the relationship between inflation and changes in fed funds rates, which does not need more careful study. Some econometricians like Sims *et al.* (1990) argue that, in most cases, there is no need to be parsimonious and to make variables stationary by detrending or differencing. This does not seem to be the consensus among econometricians however. To deal with cointegration and non-stationarity, several solutions have been proposed (Clarke and Mirza 2006; Kónya and Singh 2006). In what follows, only the so-called "indirect" approach is used to estimate a VECM.

The first step in a VECM estimation is to check the number of cointegrations. This will give us a first indication of the presence of a Granger causality because if two variables are cointegrated, there is a Granger causality in at least one direction (Granger 1988). To check for cointegrations, one first needs to determine the appropriate lag by looking at the VAR in levels. We already have found a lag of three months according to the Schwartz criteria. Table A4.7 shows that Johansen's cointegration test suggests three cointegrations at 1 percent of confidence. This result holds for lag structures of two to seven months. The cointegration between the policy rate and expected inflation was checked in the same way. The following presents the cointegration results for the optimal lag structure determined by the Schwartz criteria. Table A4.8 shows one cointegration between the fed funds rate and expected inflation. This result is sensitive to the lag structure chosen. The cointegration between inflation and the federal funds rate does not need to be tested because the two variables are integrated of different orders and so they cannot be cointegrated.

In the VECM approach, variables I(1) are made stationary by expressing the absolute change of each variable relative to changes in its own lags and lagged changes of other variables (which is similar to the previous VAR analysis), but in addition, the change in each variable is a function of one or several cointegration equation(s), which is (are) stationary linear combination(s) of I(1) variables. More formally, given a condition regarding matrix rank, we have

$$\Delta X_t = BAX_{t-1} + \Sigma_i C_i \Delta X_{t-i} + \varepsilon_t,$$

where X is a vector of I(1) variables, AX is a stationary linear combination of those variables (the cointegration equation(s)), B is the vector of coefficients attached to each cointegration equation (the speed of adjustment parameters), and C_i are the responses to lagged changes in all variables. Thus, if one wants to test that expected fed funds rate is not Granger caused by any other variables, one has to make sure that the equation for Δ EXPFEDFUNDS does not have any *BA* coefficients significantly different from zero (which is tested by a test of $B = 0$), and that $C_i = 0$ altogether for the lagged changes of all other rates than expected fed funds rate. Kónya and Singh (2006) do a *t*-test on $B = 0$ and a block exogeneity test on $C_i = 0$. We followed the same procedure even though a Wald test on the joint hypothesis $B = C_i = 0$ may be more appropriate (Clarke and Mirza 2006; Rambaldi 1997).

Starting first with interest rates, we know that the optimal lag structure is three months and that there are three cointegration equations. Below we show the result for different lag structures. First, concerning the significance of the *B* parameters, we obtained the results shown in Table A4.9. The coefficients for the first equation are not significant in the equation representing changes in federal funds rate, they are significant at 1–10 percent depending on the lag in the second equation, and they are significant at least at 5 percent in the third cointegration equation, whatever the lag is. One may conclude that there is a long-term bidirectional causality between interest rates. Let us look at the short-term causality that is given in Table A4.10. The results show a weak support for the idea that the federal funds rate can be treated as an independent variable. Changes in the three-month T-bill and the ten-year T-bond are the most able to precede the fed funds rate in the short-term. Overall, therefore, the previous VECM partially suggests a unidirectional causality from expected fed funds rate to other market rates but it is weak. The strongest results are obtained by excluding the T-bill rate and for a lag structure of two months, which are shown in Tables A4.11 and A4.12 (cointegration tests stated that there are three cointegration equations at 5 percent and 1 percent level). In this case, within the 99 percent interval of confidence, one cannot reject that the fed funds rate Granger causes all the other rates both in the short-term and the long run.

Looking at the relationship between the federal funds rate and expected inflation, Tables A4.13 and A4.14 confirm the analysis that was made previously. There is a Granger causality that is bidirectional in the short run (except for a two-month lag). However, in the long run, the causality is unidirectional and runs from expected inflation to fed funds rate, i.e. one cannot reject that the federal funds rate behavior was Granger caused by expected inflation.

Summers notes that all these empirical results are a strong blow to the Fisherian theory, especially during the pre-Second World War period when conditions were ideal for its implementation:

> The strong evidence against the Fisher proposition [...] for the prewar period is particularly striking because of the laissez-faire character of the economy. Nominal rigidities caused by deposit ceilings, wage contracts, pension arrangements, or long-term wage contracts were virtually nonexistent. Taxes were also negligible.
>
> (Summers 1983: 222)

He suggests that "the failure of interest rates to fully incorporate inflation premiums reflects something more fundamental than the effect of institutional nonneutralities" (Summers 1983: 222). It has been argued that the fundamental element missing in the Fisherian analysis is an understanding of the nature of a capitalist system. The latter is a monetary production economy, not a barter economy with money merely used as a medium of exchange. In a monetary production economy, money is the end goal and the relevance of any economic activity is measured by its monetary profitability, not its physical productivity. In this type of economy, purchasing power concerns, even though relevant, are outweighed by liquidity and solvency concerns.

Keynes's theory of liquidity preference, capital gains, and uncertainty

Now that the notion of real interest rate has been criticized, the following develops an argument based on Keynes's theory of money demand to show that the manipulation of nominal interest rates may be hazardous and may create financial instability. Traditionally, the demand for money is assumed to be inversely related to the rate of interest, and for the sake of simplification, Keynes did argue that one can assume a "smooth curve" that is downward sloped. However, he was also aware that this is a simplification, and that portfolio arbitrages imply a complex relationship between the rate of interest, its expected variations, and the demand for money. As Kahn (1954), Robinson (1951), and Kregel (1998a) noted, a rigorous analysis of this relationship implies taking into the notions of duration and breakeven point, as well as the type of financial market participants. If these are taken seriously, there is no reason to think that there is a straightforward relationship between the demand for money and the current interest rate, given expectations of the latter. An upward sloping curve is as conceivable as a downward or a flat curve. All this gives some insights about the role of financial market configuration for monetary intervention via interest rates.

The traditional speculative demand for money

The traditional argument that justifies the downward sloping curve of money demand goes as follows. Suppose that there is an increase in the money supply, given the normal rate of interest (i_n), this generates an excess money supply that pushes some individuals to switch to bonds. As the bond price goes up, the difference between i_n and i grows so that some bullish or indifferent agents become[4] bearish and increase their demand for money (L). Progressively, the bond price (and L) goes up but at a decelerating rate so that "the market price will be fixed at the point at which the sales of the 'bears' and the purchases of the 'bulls' are balanced" (Keynes 1936a: 170). This arbitrage process is smooth and more or less fast, depending on the elasticity of L relative to i.

From the previous explanation, Keynes argues that "[a]s a rule, we can suppose that the schedule of liquidity-preference relating the quantity of money to the rate of interest is given by a smooth curve which shows the rate of interest falling as the quantity of money is increased" (Keynes 1936a: 171). Further, he qualifies "in any given state of expectation a fall in [i] will be associated with an increase in M_2" (Keynes 1936a: 202) and "M_2 may tend to increase almost without limit in response to a reduction of [i] below a certain figure" (Keynes 1936a: 203). Thus, for Keynes, a downward sloping curve can be justified because, given expectations of future interest rate, as interest rate falls, the risk of illiquidity increases (the bearishness of the financial community increases and so its propensity to hoard), whereas the reward for being illiquid diminishes (which decreases the incentive to become or to stay illiquid) (Keynes 1936a: 202). However, this is a very rough simplification of the role of given expectations. Keynes was aware of this and recognized that "a given M_2 will not have a definite quantitative relation to a given rate of interest" (Keynes 1936a: 201). To understand why, it is necessary to look at the way individuals form their expectations; this implies looking first at the difference between the current, the expected, and the normal interest rate.

Normal rate of interest, expectations, and current rate of interest

Because the economic situation is uncertain, individuals rely on past experiences and consider the current predominant view regarding the economic situation as the relevant one. In the bond market, this leads to the establishment of a convention that determines the "normal" or "safe" rate of interest. This normal rate of interest is a function of the expectations about future monetary policies and about the future levels of long-term interest rates (Keynes 1936a: 202–203).[5] Therefore, there is a functional relationship between the rate of interest i, the expected rate $E(i)$, and the normal rate (Chick 1983):

$$E(i) - i = f(i_n - i) \text{ or } E(\Delta i) = f(i_n - i)$$

The expectation regarding the rate of interest, and more importantly its expected variation, is a function of the spread between the normal rate and the current rate of interest. If the rate of interest is below the safe rate, an individual who agrees with the convention prevailing in the market will anticipate an increase of the rate of interest ($E(i) > i$) toward the normal rate.[6] If an individual expects the rate of interest to go up, it seems relevant for him to increase his speculative stock of money because of expected capital losses. Thus, there is a positive relationship between the demand for money and the expected rate of interest, whereas the relationship is negative when the current rate of interest is considered. The question becomes what will be the impact on the demand for money if the current rate of interest goes up but is expected to go down in the short term? Will the speculative demand for money go up or down? In order to respond, Keynes introduces the notion of breakeven point.

Implications for the speculative demand for money

In the following, it will be assumed that the horizon of expectations is equal to the coupon period; therefore, bond-market participants compare the change in fair price (ΔV) to the periodic coupon income (C) and the total return is $R = C + \Delta V$. In addition, all the reasoning is done from the point of view of a bond holder (or a potential buyer) who checks the net benefit of keeping (buying) a bond today and gaining some interest income and potential capital gains, but also of having to record some potential capital losses.[7]

A current rise (decrease) in interest rates does not imply that an individual will buy (sell) bonds because this change may not be permanent. One, thus, needs to take into account the expectations for future interest rates before buying a bond to be reassured that the future nominal total return will be positive. As shown earlier, an individual is indifferent between bonds and money when he expects that $E(\Delta i) = i^2$. From the point of view of a bondholder (or potential buyer), Figure 4.2 shows that there are five possible expectational states following a current increase in the rate of interest.

Thus, a bear will *hold* (*buy*) some consols today unless he expects a net loss in the short-term: $-\Delta V > C$ (case 1). Only case 1 leads to an increase in the demand for money today. As interest rate increases, the bearishness of individuals decreases (as large increase in i become less probable) and their bullishness may start to take over, i.e. more individuals are in cases 3 or 2. For sufficiently high interest rates, bullishness prevails and is strengthened, i.e. more and more people are in case 4. Thus, it is fair to assume, as a first approximation, that, following an increase in the rate of interest, L will decrease because the net gain from holding a bond is positive.

The prevalence of a negative relationship between the interest rate and the speculative demand for money can be further justified by stating that the liquidity trap is a rare case. One limit to this conclusion, however, is that it ignores the case of low interest rates; "low" depends on the type of bond involved and can actually be quite high (Kregel 1998a: 130). In this situation, cases 1 and 4 have a higher chance to occur, simply because an absolute variation of the interest rate by more than the square of itself is easier to get for a low interest rate. The previous reasoning also assumes a breakeven point at zero dollars. Different placement strategies may make financial market participants more sensitive to changes in interest rates and may raise the possibility of occurrence of a liquidity trap. In the end, the demand for money (bond) can be quite unstable, depending on who is in the financial market and at what level the interest rate is.

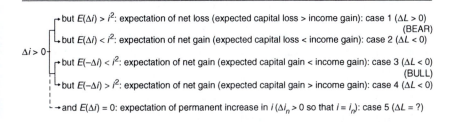

$\Delta i > 0$

- but $E(\Delta i) > i^2$: expectation of net loss (expected capital loss > income gain): case 1 ($\Delta L > 0$) (BEAR)
- but $E(\Delta i) < i^2$: expectation of net gain (expected capital loss < income gain): case 2 ($\Delta L < 0$)
- but $E(-\Delta i) < i^2$: expectation of net gain (expected capital gain < income gain): case 3 ($\Delta L < 0$) (BULL)
- but $E(-\Delta i) > i^2$: expectation of net gain (expected capital gain > income gain): case 4 ($\Delta L < 0$)
- and $E(\Delta i) = 0$: expectation of permanent increase in i ($\Delta i_n > 0$ so that $i = i_n$): case 5 ($\Delta L = ?$)

Figure 4.2 Possible financial positions of an individual (excluding indifference).

In case 5, for which the normal rate adjusts totally to the change in i, the effect on the demand for money will depend on the interest- and capital-risk sensitivity of bondholders as shown below. Gentlemen, as defined in chapter 3, will be pleased as long as the decrease in their net wealth is not too affected; even in the latter case they will stay in bonds because they cannot do anything about the loss of wealth. Fund managers will prefer to switch to money and find more active assets, at least as long as the potential losses resulting from the permanent increase in i are not too high, in which case they are stuck with bonds; in any case, their preference for money increases (Chick 1983: 207).

Thus, by taking into account the short-term breakeven point, one can see how the current rate of interest and the normal rate of interest interact to determine the speculative demand for money. The idea that the speculative demand for money is necessarily, or usually, a decreasing function of money is not true, even if expectations are given. This indeterminacy of the curve is even more evident when one includes the role of the precautionary motive in the demand for money as a store of wealth. Indeed, for example, one may wonder how an indifferent person will allocate his portfolio. When one tries to answer this question, the nice "smooth curve" totally disappears.

Income risk, capital risk, and demand for money

Keynes recognizes in the *General Theory* that, for an individual, "the transaction-motive and the precautionary-motive [are] not entirely independent of what he is holding to satisfy the speculative-motive" (Keynes 1936a: 199). Kahn (1954) is the first to take this remark seriously and what follows relies on his work. Drawing on Robinson (1951), he redefines the precautionary and the speculative motives to provide a better explanation of liquidity preference, and of the way individuals allocate their portfolio between liquid and illiquid assets.

MICROECONOMIC IMPLICATIONS

A person holds monetary assets for precautionary motive because he thinks that the interest rate will move but he does not know how, when, and the degree of conviction in his expectation about $E(\Delta i)$ is low. This precautionary motive implies making a distinction between income-risk sensitivity and capital-risk sensitivity, as presented in chapter 3. It is only if the interest rate goes down steeply, or is already at a very low level relative to the normal rate, that a gentleman prefers to hold money. On the contrary, the precaution of fund managers pushes them to stay liquid because "the fear of capital loss more than offsets a mild chance of capital gain" (Kahn 1954 (1972): 83).

Thus, the precautionary motive works differently for persons who are concerned about income changes (gentlemen) compared to persons who are concerned about capital-value changes (fund managers). This also has an effect on the speculative motive. For example, a fund manager will not place in bonds unless expectations of capital gains are strong enough (case 4), that is to say, until i is high enough and is expected to go down steeply during the coupon period. Inversely, a gentleman will not sell his bonds until the income gain is more than compensated by an expected capital loss (case 1). If the expected capital loss is small (case 2), a gentleman will stay in bonds, whereas a fund manager will switch to money.

Of course, the intensity with which the speculative and the precautionary motives affect portfolio arbitrages depends on the degree of conviction with which an individual holds his expectations. The higher the weight of argument, the more an individual has the courage to act upon the argumentation that sustained his expectation of the future. Thus, for a given degree of conviction, and following an increase in interest rate ($\Delta i > 0$), one gets Figure 4.3.

One can see that the net effect of a variation of the interest rate on the demand for money as a store of wealth depends on the interplay between the precautionary motive and the speculative motive. The total effect can be opposite to the traditional case. This latter relation is verified only in one case and is completely reversed in another case.

This consideration is reinforced if one takes into account the relative income-risk sensitivity (income-risk relative to capital-risk sensitivity: IR/CR) and the role of the degree of conviction. The lower IR/CR, the higher the capacity of the speculative motive to be operative for an individual is. The higher the degree of conviction, the lower the role of the precautionary motive (risk-sensitiveness decreases), and so the higher the responsiveness of money demand to the interest rate if the gentleman-side does not completely dominate (otherwise the speculative motive does not operate[8]). In the end, there is no straightforward relation between the rate of interest and the demand for money at the individual level.

MACROECONOMIC IMPLICATIONS

At the macroeconomic level, when the variety of opinions and the proportion of gentlemen relative to fund managers are taken into account, in addition to the degree of conviction and the relative income-risk sensitivity (for example some fund managers may be more capital-risk sensitive than others: hedge funds versus pension funds), the straightforward relation is even more doubtful. Indeed, even if the market is mainly bullish (bearish), the demand for money can still go up (down), following an increase in the rate of interest. Assuming that there are mainly gentlemen, given the results of Figure 4.3, Figure 4.4 shows the different possible cases. Figure 4.5 does the same thing for a financial market dominated by fund managers.

Thus, bulls can contribute to the depressive effect on the market price if the expected rise in price is not high enough, and if the majority of the financial community is composed of fund managers. Accordingly, bears can contribute to the boom in financial markets if the financial community is mainly composed of gentlemen. In total, bears and bulls do not need to balance each other and they may complement each other. In both types of markets, when bulls and bears compensate for each other, the ultimate effect on the willingness to hoard is undetermined even

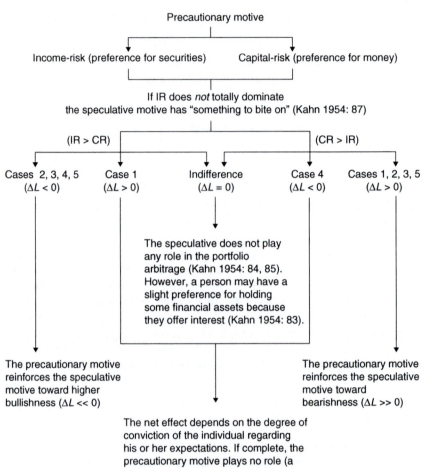

Precautionary motive

Income-risk (preference for securities)   Capital-risk (preference for money)

If IR does *not* totally dominate
the speculative motive has "something to bite on" (Kahn 1954: 87)

(IR > CR)   (CR > IR)

| Cases 2, 3, 4, 5 | Case 1 | Indifference | Case 4 | Cases 1, 2, 3, 5 |
| ($\Delta L < 0$) | ($\Delta L > 0$) | ($\Delta L = 0$) | ($\Delta L < 0$) | ($\Delta L > 0$) |

The speculative does not play
any role in the portfolio
arbitrage (Kahn 1954: 84, 85).
However, a person may have a
slight preference for holding
some financial assets because
they offer interest (Kahn 1954: 83).

The precautionary motive
reinforces the speculative
motive toward higher
bullishness ($\Delta L \ll 0$)

The precautionary motive
reinforces the speculative
motive toward
bearishness ($\Delta L \gg 0$)

The net effect depends on the degree of
conviction of the individual regarding
his or her expectations. If complete, the
precautionary motive plays no role (a
bear only holds securities and a bull
only holds money as wealth). (Kahn 1954: 83, 87).
If complete uncertainty or low
confidence, the precautionary motive
dominates (Kahn 1954: 84).

Figure 4.3 Microeconomic impacts an increase in *i* on the demand for money.

if finite. The ultimate effect will depend on the degree of confidence with which bears and bulls hold their expectations and their relative income-risk sensitivity. Two bulls who expect the same change in *i*, but who have different degrees of conviction and different relative risk-income sensitivity, will have different commitments in financial markets. The volatility of the market will be higher when the market is composed mainly of fund managers.

The aggregate demand for money has, thus, an elasticity that depends on the degree of conviction of market participants, the degree of heterogeneity in the

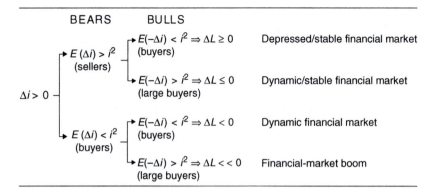

Figure 4.4 Financial market configurations with a majority of gentlemen.

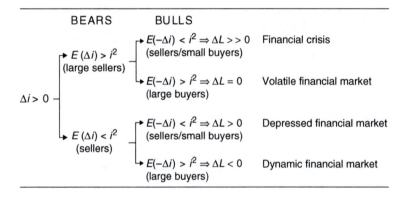

Figure 4.5 Financial market configurations with a majority of fund managers.

market (the financial power of bears relative to the financial power of bulls), and also the relative income-risk sensitivity (as it operates on the precautionary motives of each individual), as well as the strength of expectations reflected by the level of $E(\Delta i)$. If financial actors have a strong income-risk sensitivity, most of them are buyers when interest rates increase, except in one case, which depends on the strength of expectations and the relative financial power of bulls and bears. If there is a majority of fund managers in the market, an increase in the rate of interest may have a negative impact on the market (the ultimate effect depending on the relative income-risk sensitivity of fund managers).

Ultimately, one cannot have clear-cut results for the impact of the long-term rate on the demand for money. However, the preceding allows knowing in which financial-market configuration a particular elasticity is more probably true. If the financial actors are mainly fund managers, the liquidity function has much more chance to be positively related to the long-term interest rate. In addition, variability of interest rates will be highly unwelcome by fund managers unless they are very small and highly predictable; but, even in the latter case, fund managers who have a preference for bonds will not like interest-rate variability. This helps to understand why the Federal Reserve moved to a policy of gradualism and transparency in order make sure that financial market participants read well the intentions of the Federal Open Market Committee, and hedge their positions so that disruptions similar to the one in early 1994 are avoided.

Monetary policy in the Post-Keynesian framework

All the preceding has several implications in terms of monetary policy. It confirms that interest-rate instability, expected or not, can be a source of financial instability (Papadimitriou and Wray 1994: 46; Hannsgen 2005, 2006a; Wray 1996c); therefore, the central bank should avoid moving its interest rates frequently, or even at all, so that i_n is more stable and the relation between i and i_n is also more stable. The preceding sections also show the importance for a central bank to be aware of the institutional context and so of the most probable channels of transmission of its monetary policy. It is now a good place to review the different Post-Keynesian views concerning monetary policy.

Manipulating interest rates to manage the economy

The way the central bank should use interest rates to manage the economy varies in the Post-Keynesian analysis in terms of goals and implementation. Some authors have proposed to use interest rates to manage economic activity and inflation (Dalziel 1999, 2002; Palacio-Vera 2005; Fontana and Palacio-Vera 2003, 2007; Arestis and Sawyer 2004a, 2004b, 2006; Palley 2006; Setterfield 2006; Atesoglu 2007):

> The central bank might seek to encourage growth (expansionism) by reducing its base interest rate, while at the same time announcing a strict commitment to raising interest rates again if inflationary pressures should emerge (*cautious expansionism*).
>
> (Dalziel 2001: 121)

By decreasing (increasing) interest rates, a central bank should be able to promote (to reduce) economic activity because there is an inverse relationship between interest rate and loan demand. For those authors, the main influence of monetary policy is not on inflation but economic growth, and so the weight of inflation in the reaction function should be relatively low and the central bank should have a targeted range of inflation rather than a specific number. Too high inflation weight leads to disruptions in the economy via increased output and nominal interest-rate variability (Alonso-González and Palacio-Vera 2002; Fair 2005). By putting more weight on the output gap and making sure "to keep real interest rate [stable] as long as inflation remains below a certain upper threshold" (Palacio-Vera 2005: 764), the central bank will be able to affect current economic activity. By doing so, the central bank will be able to affect potential output indirectly because, as stated in chapter 2, potential output (the supply side) is not independent from current economic activity (the demand side). By not raising interest rates immediately with inflation, and by actually lowering interest rates, even when inflation is on target (Fontana and Palacio-Vera 2007: 291), the central bank will allow expansion to continue and so will allow time for potential output to rise, which will indirectly decrease inflationary pressures.

Other authors, by focusing on the distributive consequences of interest-rate policy, have proposed to have a policy rule based on the "fair" rate (Pasinetti 1981: 166–168; Lavoie 1996a, 1997b; Seccareccia and Lavoie 1989; Lavoie and Seccareccia 1999; Kriesler and Lavoie 2007), or on a given small positive real rate of interest (Smithin 2003, 2004, 2007). This is in the best interests of both workers and entrepreneurs (Lavoie 1999).

Interest rates and demand for loans, and economic growth

The Horizontalist approach, initiated by Moore (1988) and Kaldor (1982), is a dominant theoretical framework in the Post-Keynesian school of thought. Its main contribution is to show that the central bank does not have any quantitative control over the supply of reserves, and to take seriously into account the fact that loans create deposits, which in turn creates a need for reserves (Lavoie 1984, 1992). However, the Horizontalist approach also assumes that, *ceteris paribus*, the demand for loans is downward relative to interest rates. Depending on the elasticity of demand for loans,[9] the absolute effect is more or less high, but even if the elasticity is low, a large enough decrease in interest rates should be able to promote economic activity.

This downward relationship is, however, problematic from three points of view. First, by emphasizing the inverse relationship, economists may focus on the wrong variable to influence and put too much faith into the effectiveness of monetary policy. As Figure 4.6 shows, the recent Japanese experience provides a good example of this point. From 1991 to 2003, nominal and real interest rates mainly had been decreasing below 3 percent. However, despite very low interest rates, the central bank failed to promote robust economic expansion, and the rate of growth of loans has been negative since 1998. Unemployment continuously grew after 1991 from 2.1 percent to 5.4 percent in 2003 and the GDP oscillated between positive and negative growth. In 2004, banks were filled with excess reserves[10] and government bonds, but bank loans were low because there was no demand for loans. The problem is not a problem of demand elasticity; there were no bank loans because there were no profitable activities to implement. This positive relationship between interest rate and credit growth is due to the fact that the *ceteris paribus* condition did not apply in Japan during this period. The decline in the state of expectation dominated the effect of lower interest rate on the demand for loans.

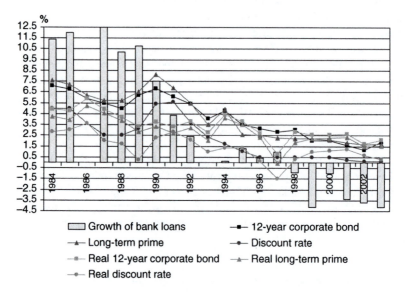

Figure 4.6 Real and nominal interest rates and growth of bank loans in Japan: 1984–2003.
Source: Bank of Japan.

Note: Real rates of interest are calculated by subtracting by the CPI inflation. Data for bank loans by
domestically licensed banks are not available for 1986 and 1993.

Another problem with the *ceteris paribus* condition is that it downplays the
implications of the financing and refinancing processes:

> Thus when an investment boom takes place in the context of an enlarged need
> to refinance maturing debt, the demand "curve" for short-term debt increases
> (shifts to the right) and becomes steeper (less elastic).
>
> (Minsky 1982b: 10)

Firms have to meet their financial commitments, whatever the level of interest
rates, in order to avoid default and its consequences (higher risk category, loss
of reputation, and ultimately bankruptcy). In addition, besides shifting the curve,
financial commitments may create a positive relationship between interest rates
and the demand for loans. Indeed, higher interest rates mean higher financial
commitments, which creates a potential need to borrow more money to meet those
commitments (Wray 1993; Hannsgen 2006a: 217).

   Third, if one is interested in capital-market inflation, Galbraith (1961), Rousseas
(1994), and Toporowski (2000) have shown that a central bank may be ineffective
in managing this type of inflation because it must compensate for high expectations
of capital gains. Therefore, the central bank may have to increase its interest rates
to levels that are harmful for economic activity, which is not an effective way
to break speculation. Moore suggested to set the central bank rate at a low but

positive interest rate in order to minimize the effect on the real economy and to constrain speculation:

$$i_{cb} = b > 0.$$

However, as stated in chapter 3, low interest rates are not necessarily a cause of financial speculation (Japan, again, is the most recent counterexample). In addition, even if the central-bank rate is low, other rates are higher and already discourage the emergence of speculative behaviors. More generally, a positive yield curve (starting at zero percent or above) is not by itself a source of massive speculation and infinite borrowing because placing in positive-return assets entails risks. Loosening risk perception is the main source of speculation.

In all the previous cases, emphasizing the inverse relationship between interest rate and loan demand will give too much credit to the efficiency of monetary policy. Most economists like to draw on this relationship because it gives some importance to interest-rate policy, which is assumed to be the main countercyclical management tool that a central bank has. Unfortunately, interest-rate policies are rather ineffective and uncertain in their effects, and there are more direct and effective ways to intervene in the long-term affairs of the economic system by directly influencing the financial position of economic agents.

Interest rate, inflation, and distribution

Interest-rate changes also have some inflationary and redistributive effects that are usually ignored or played down in the New Neoclassical Synthesis literature but have been analyzed by economists like Graziani (1990, 2003a), Arestis and Howells (1992, 1994), Niggle (1989a), Moore (1989), Lavoie (1996a), Sawyer (2002), Fontana and Palacio-Vera (2002), Smithin (2003), Argitis and Pitelis (2001), and Seccareccia and Lavoie (1989).

Indeed, interest payments are a cost for firms that need to borrow to maintain their activities; therefore, they may just pass their financial cost onto their prices depending on "the magnitude and the expected permanence of interest rate changes" (Moore 1989: 26). Thus, rising interest rates may promote inflation, especially when firms are heavily indebted. Minsky (1975a) stated that a fragile financial system tends to be inflationary, and as shown in chapter 6, the early 1980s provides an example of this phenomenon.

The other direct effect of tighter monetary policy is to increase the income received by the financial sector at the expense of the indebted sector. This distributive effect "raise[s] moral questions of equity as well as technical questions about the effectiveness of monetary policy in influencing aggregate demand" (Arestis and Howells 1994: 64). Higher interest rates may stimulate economic activity if consumption out of interest income is high and investment is not sensitive to interest rates (Lavoie 1995; Tauheed and Wray 2006; Kelton and Wray 2006). To limit redistributive effects, some Post-Keynesian economists have proposed that the central bank rate be fixed at a level that is neutral in terms of distribution.

However, those authors do not agree on what neutrality implies. For Smithin, the central bank rate should be fixed at a level that is consistent with inflation expectations so that a small positive expected real rate of interest is set (and optimally this expected rate should be zero) (Smithin 2004: 64–65):

$$i_{cb} \approx E(\pi) \text{ with } i_{cb} \geq E(\pi).$$

By following this rule, a central bank would preserve the purchasing power of interest-income earners. Lavoie, Seccareccia, and others prefer to follow Pasinetti and have an interest-rate rule that is related to the fair rate. Following Pasinetti (1981: 167), Lavoie (1996a, 1997b) states that the central bank rate should be fixed so that

$$i_{cb} = g_{AP} + E(\pi),$$

with g_{AP} the rate of growth of average multifactor productivity. By doing so, the central bank will provide a fair reward to credit suppliers, who are essential to the economic process, while preventing the real interest rate going too high relative to zero (Smithin 2006) or relative to labor productivity growth (Lavoie and Seccareccia 1988; Lavoie 1999) because these situations are major causes of recessions.

There are, however, several problems with any of those real-interest-rate-target rules. The most obvious is that interest rates and inflation are not independent variables, and so a positive feedback effect may emerge from these types of policy rules, which may lead to destabilizing effects. This is all the more the case that a lot of weight is put on inflation by the central bank (Hannsgen 2004, 2006b). Second, these types of policy have to determine the relevant time frame that should be used for inflation expectations. As shown in chapter 6, this may lead central bankers to become paranoid about the possible emergence of inflation, and to try to justify an increase in interest rates when there is actually no sign of any potential increase in price. Greenspan's policy of preemptively raising the policy rates is a perfect example of this, and a perfect example of how this promotes low growth and unstable financial markets (Papadimitriou and Wray 1994; Wray 1997b). The time frame is also problematic in terms of determining which maturity should be followed. For example, Lavoie and others state that the central bank should fix "the" interest rate to the fair rate, but do not specify clearly what "the" means. In their empirical study, Seccareccia and Lavoie (1999) use long-term government rates, but then rentiers that only hold short or medium securities (or securities for which the interest rate is not fixed at the fair rate) are treated "unfairly" (too high or too low yield). Third, the preceding rules assume a relatively stable rate of inflation and rate of growth of productivity over time. If this is not the case, a central bank may have to move its interest rates widely, promoting financial instability in financial markets and the indebted economic sectors.

The fourth problem is that it ignores the capital side of rentiers' financial positions. No rentier only cares about the interest income and the real interest rate gives a poor measure of the financial power of rentiers. As stated previously, what is usually more important is the total rate of return from a placement, their marginal efficiency. In this case, rentiers may be against a policy that constantly moves nominal interest rates to preserve the real interest income. If they are not prepared for it, rentiers want stability or predictability in terms of nominal interest rate, not real interest rate; this is all the more the case if they are fund-manager rentiers and that gentlemen-rentiers represent a small portion of financial markets.[11]

Finally, maintaining a certain level of real interest rate may lead to a Ponzi-financing situation if the cash inflow of borrowers cannot be adjusted to the required nominal interest rate. Indeed, it is the nominal interest rates that matter for the compounding process, not the real rate. Thus maintaining a low real rate of interest promotes financial instability if high, or even moderate, nominal interest rates have to be maintained. As stated in chapter 2, real gain and loss are financially irrelevant for capitalist economic systems. In addition, as Gale shows, Ponzi situation will emerge for firms, even if inflation is perfectly anticipated by them and is included immediately in the price of their output. Indeed, because of the $rE(\pi)$ component of the Fisherian condition of indifference, the interest rate must adjust by more than inflation in order to maintain a certain real interest rate, and firms need to borrow to pay the additional interest servicing (Gale 1982: 153–158). Ultimately, this also goes against the interests of rentiers because bankruptcies reduce the amount of income payment they receive.

In the end, therefore, real-interest-rate rules are bad rules because they create instability in terms of nominal interest rates and because they focus on the wrong method to assess if an interest-rate level is tight. Economic agents care about nominal values in terms of total return and net cash flow, and instability in the latter two creates financial instability. In addition, nominal interest rates, when compared to the marginal efficiencies of assets, provide a better measure of tightness than the real interest rate alone. Stated alternatively, monetary-policy tightness can be checked by looking at the inflow effects (for lenders) and outflow effects (for borrowers) of interest rates compared to their respective effects on outflows and inflows.

Arguments for a permanent zero central bank rate

Mosler and Forstater (2004) and Wray (2004c, 2007b) have proposed that the central bank sets permanently at zero the overnight rates on its advances. Recent reviews by Rochon and Setterfield (2007b), Palley (2007), and Smithin (2007) argue that such a policy would lead to instability because destabilizing inflationary forces would be allowed to "continue forever, and at an accelerating rate" (Smithin 2007: 109). Other arguments against a zero policy rate might be that it would generate speculation in the financial markets (asset-price inflation rather than output-price inflation), or that it would be unfair to the rentier class.

Several counter critiques to those positions can be brought forward. First, one should note that a zero overnight policy rate does not mean that all other rates would be zero. Private agents would still set retail and wholesale rates based on their expectations of the future regarding default risk, uncertainty, interest rates, inflation, and any other factors that they wish to take into consideration while setting interest rates. The free lunch granted by a positive central bank rate, however, would be removed. A positive central bank rate adds a premium to the yield curve that does not reward competence or risk. If authorities are not satisfied with the way long-term rates behave, the zero-policy-rate policy could be complemented by a slightly positive targeted rate on long-term Treasuries to reward market risk, so that the government provides an anchor for, but in no way fully determines, the whole interest-rate structure.

Second, a zero policy rate in no way promotes accelerating inflation in output or asset markets, whereas fluctuations in interest rates may create price instability through cost-push effect and financial instability through speculative incentives. As already noted, both inflationary processes do not have only, or even mainly, monetary origins and are not managed effectively through an interest-rate policy. To manage inflationary forces, other structural permanent institutions should be created. Permanent (and not temporary like in the 1970s) income policies should be put in place to fight output-price inflation. These policies would take into account distributional issues related to rentiers and would be much more effective in dealing with them than the indirect and remote influence of short-term policy rate. As Kaldor noted:

> The essential prerequisite of a successful wage policy lies in the recognition of the fact that while wages *in general* should increase in proportion to the rise in productivity *in general*, this does not mean that the changes in wage-rates in particular industries should be governed by the rise in productivity in those industries. Increases in productivity in particular industries which are not the result of a more intense effort by the workers but of new techniques or more efficient management should, in general, be passed on to the community as a whole in the form of lower prices rather than retained by those in the industry in the form of higher wages and profits. Such price reductions are an essential component of a successful full employment policy.
>
> (Kaldor 1950 (1964): 114–115)

Income policies should be complemented with buffer stock policies and an employer of last resort policy. In terms of financial inflation, it has been argued also that a better way to manage it is by an analysis of the financial positions of financial market participants. Ultimately, a zero-rate policy alone is not what would be optimal, a complete institutional reform would be necessary to make it work best.

Third, arguments about active monetary policies are always made in compact models in which the financial side is extremely poorly developed or even absent.[12] As Goodhart and Tsomocos noted:

> Most mainstream macro and monetary analysis makes the assumption that no economic agent ever defaults.
>
> (Goodhart and Tsomocos 2007: 19)

The same critique applies to many Post-Keynesian models. The importance of liquidity and solvency for individuals is thought to be secondary and much more emphasis is put on purchasing power. As argued previously, in a monetary economy, the primary concerns are liquidity and solvency, not purchasing power. Fazzari and Caskey (1989) provide a straightforward illustration of how dramatically different macroeconomic effects are when considerations about liquidity and solvency are added to a simple AS-AD model. Fluctuations in interest rates create financial instability by negatively affecting liquidity and solvency through the impact on nominal cash commitments and asset prices.

However, fluctuations in interest rates create financial instability in deeper and more dangerous ways (Kaldor 1958 (1964): 135–137). A first way is by making it dangerous and costly for financial institutions to hold assets that pay a regular fixed income. This creates a disincentive for financial institutions to play their role of loan officer, and increases the opaqueness of the financial system by limiting the incentive to keep on balance sheet long-term commitments that are interest-rate sensitive. The switch from a "commitment" model of banking to an "originate and distribute" model, which will be presented in more details in the next chapter, can be explained by the growing use of interest rates by the central bank since the 1950s and by the increased interest-rate variability that followed. This led financial institutions to protect themselves against such variability by more and more sophisticated means, and the deregulation of the 1980s led to the emergence of full fledged risk-management strategies and a promotion of their use by regulatory bodies at the end of the 1980s.

The second way, through which financial instability is promoted by interest-rate manipulations, is the promotion of speculative behaviors by financial institutions. The risk-management tools and derivative instruments developed to hedge against interest-rate fluctuations have allowed an enormous increase in financial gambling. Today financial market participants have integrated interest-rate variability in their portfolio strategies and thrive upon it. A large amount of financial resources, brainpower, and time is diverted toward anticipating, interpreting, and analyzing every comment, policy move, and speech of central bankers. Thus, not only do wide policy-rate fluctuations create a disincentive to perform loan officer tasks, but also they create an incentive to concentrate on speculative activities.

The central bank operations primarily affect the financial side of the economy, not the production side. Thus, central banks should focus on the former and leave the management of the latter to other structural institutions that are better able to cope directly with questions of output-price inflation, economic growth, and income distribution.

Conclusion

An active use of interest rates is not recommended, either because its effect on inflation and output is highly uncertain and weak, and can be the reverse to the one intended, or because active interest-rate policy can promote financial instability.

In terms of their effects of the production side of the economy, constant manipulations of interest rates may generate price instability through the impact on cost and demand, and may not have any or only limited influence on spending if the change is not permanent and if economic decisions are not very sensitive to long-term rates. In any of those cases, interest rate manipulation will have perverse effects or be ineffective.

Regarding financial stability, rules based on a real interest rate are more hurtful than those based on nominal interest rate because the former tend to require larger fluctuations in central bank policy rates. These large fluctuations create disruptions in financial markets and in the rest of the economic system by increasing the potential reliance on Ponzi financing. Thus, one can understand why nominal interest rates have failed to account for expected inflation over the past century. It is not in the interest of anybody, including rentiers, to demand a constant real rate of interest because the negative financial implications of such a demand outweigh the positive purchasing power gains of such a demand. This is all the more the case that, today, most rentiers are capital-risk sensitive.

A permanent zero overnight rate would go in the direction of providing a more stable and credible anchor for the normal long-term rate, which could still be affected by expectations of long-term rates and other considerations, leading to positive nominal long-term rates. By fixing the policy rate permanently at zero, beneficial effects on financial stability would go beyond smoothing the impact on cash commitments and the price of assets, and limiting the compounding process by only rewarding risk and skill. The central bank would reduce the uncertainty about future profitability of loans and so would give an incentive to financial institutions to keep long-term commitments on their balance sheet. This would give them an incentive to think more carefully about the creditworthiness of their clients and so would promote financial stability. Finally, a stable short-term rate would decrease speculation in financial markets and would reorient the activities of financial institutions toward more socially beneficial activities.

5 An analysis of financial fragility in the Minskian tradition

Hyman P. Minsky was an early proponent of the integration of the central bank into a policy strategy oriented toward achieving stable full employment. He conceptualized capitalism as a dynamic but unstable economic system, and he called the dynamics at the heart of this system the Financial Instability Hypothesis. The latter provides a view of the capitalist economic system that turns out to be very useful to understand the role that should be given to a central bank. The previous chapters of this book have argued that financial considerations should be the main preoccupation of a central bank. The latter should foster prudent financial behaviors, should manage aggregate financial stability, and should intervene to prevent the spreading of liquidity crises. What follows combines the Minskian framework with some of the hypotheses laid out in chapters 2 and 3, in order to reinforce the conclusions that have been reached regarding the role of a central bank. This is done first by reviewing the framework developed by Minsky and its critiques and extensions by different authors. It will be shown that any good formalization or empirical testing of the Minskian framework must be aware of several important hypotheses and dynamics. In a second part of the chapter, a stock-flow consistent model (Godley and Lavoie 2007; Dos Santos 2005; Godley and Shaikh 1998) is combined with System Dynamics (Sterman 2000) in order to capture some elements of the Minskian framework, and in order to draw some conclusions about the role of the central bank in the management of the economic system.

The fundamental hypotheses and dynamics of the Minskian analysis

Main important points

Some authors have argued that Minsky's theory rests on irrational behaviors and euphoria (Bernanke 1983: 258; Mullineux 1990: 100; Benston and Kaufman 1995; Davis 1995), on the loanable funds theory or on fallacies of composition (Lavoie 1983, 1986, 1996b, 1997a; Brossard 1998, 2001; Lavoie and Seccareccia 2001; Parguez 2003; Rochon 2003b), or on a reserve-multiplier process (Rochon 2003a), or that asymmetric information is essential for the analysis (Fazzari 1992).

Less friendly authors have simply stated that Minsky's theory is "noninformative," "obscure," "vague," or, more colorfully, full of "empty boxes" "which he filled with carrots, chickens, eggs, milk, cream, and the like" (Meiselman 1967: 329, n. 23). Therefore, some clarifications seem necessary, not about what Minsky "really meant," but more basically, about the way his theory developed and about the causes of financial instability. The following shows that the main organizing principles of Minsky's theory can be regrouped into eleven different points going from the nature of capitalism to the role of public authorities in the management of the economic system. All Minskian modeling optimally should contain these points.

The nature of the capitalist system: a monetary production economy

Minsky's center of attention is the capitalist economic system (Ferri and Minsky 1989). As he recognizes, there are different forms of capitalist system (Minsky 1989a, 1990b, 1990d, 1993a; Whalen 1997; Papadimitriou and Wray 1997) but all these forms have similar characteristics:

> A capitalist economy [...] [is] an integrated production, trading, and wealth owning system, with a structure of financial claims and commitments, [that] operates through real world and irreversible time.
>
> (Minsky 1983b: 106)

This definition shows that a capitalist economy is, first and foremost, a monetary production economy. It is a monetary economy, not because money is used, but because money is at the center of economic decisions both at the beginning and at the end of the economic process. "Only that which is financed can happen" (Minsky 1990d: 66), and the aim of any economic activity is to make a net monetary gain in order to stay liquid and solvent. This implies that the financial frame is an essential component of the capitalist system and that, as shown later, it is a central cause of flexibility and instability. Second, competition is an essential ingredient of capitalism to take into account in order to understand its dynamics (Goldstein 1995; Davis 1995; Guttentag and Herring 1988; Herring 1999; Vercelli 2001). The agents involved in this economic system are always trying to guess the uncertain future in order to obtain a bigger monetary profit relative to their competitors. Competition is an essential ingredient in the formation of conventions and their wide use by economic agents as anchors for economic decisions. Competition pushes economic units to follow those who perform best (the gurus or leaders), and to ignore information that is too costly to be obtained or could threaten competitive positions (independently of the cost of obtaining it). As Wojnilower notes about bankers,

> In the 1960s, commercial bank clients frequently inquired how far they could prudently go in breaching traditional standards of liquidity and capitalization that were clearly obsolescent. My advice was always the same – to stick with

the majority. Anyone out front risked drawing the lightning of the Federal Reserve or other regulatory retribution. Anyone who lagged behind would lose their market share. But those in the middle had safety in numbers; they could not all be punished, for fear of the repercussion of the economy as a whole. [...] And if the problem grew too big for the Federal Reserve and the banking system were swamped, well then the world would be at an end anyhow and even the most cautious of banks would likely be dragged down with the rest.

(Wojnilower 1977: 235–236)

Regarding the financial troubles involving the hedge fund Long-Term Capital Management (LTCM), Shinasi notes that

Although it is easy in retrospect to question why LTCM's counterparties did not demand more information, in a competitive environment, cost considerations must have weighed heavily. Clearly, LTCM's counterparties thought the cost of more information was too high, and walking away from deals was not in their interests.

(Schinasi 2006: 221)

More recently, the same type of behavior was observed in the mortgage industry, even though the IRS made it very easy to verify the income claimed by borrowers:

Almost all mortgage applicants had to sign a document allowing lenders to verify their incomes with the Internal Revenue Service. At least 90 percent of borrowers had to sign, seal and deliver this form, known as a 4506T, industry experts say. This includes the so-called stated income mortgages, affectionately known as "liar loans." So while borrowers may have misrepresented their incomes, either on their own or at the urging of their mortgage brokers, lenders had the tools to identify these fibs before making the loans. All they had to do was ask the I.R.S. The fact that in most cases they apparently didn't do puts the lie to the idea that cagey borrowers duped unsuspecting lenders [...] "My estimate was between 3 and 5 percent of all the loans that were funded in 2006 were executed with a 4506," Mr. Summers said. "They just turned a blind eye, saying, 'Everything is going to be fine.'"

(Morgenson 2008b)

Thus, the competitive race to anticipate the future is at the source of the productivity of the capitalist system but also at the source of its instability. Finally, the future is uncertain and time is not reversible. This is, again, a source of both dynamism and instability, because if investment depended on "nothing but a mathematical expectation, enterprise [would] fade and die" (Keynes 1936a: 162). Uncertainty leaves the future open to the imagination of entrepreneurs.

This recognition of the dynamic and unstable aspects of the capitalist system is integral to Minsky's theory. For him, this dialectical aspect of capitalist is reflected especially in the "constitutional" or "inherent" flaw of the financial structure, which is the need to "make position" (i.e. to refinance or to liquidate a position) induced by the normal functioning of the capitalist system (Minsky 1989b: 23). In a complex financial system, this need may lead to financial fragility, rising inflation, unemployment, and poverty (Minsky 1986a).

This flaw is related to the existence of long-term capital assets, which are a fundamental source of uncertainty (Keynes 1936a: 146). However, if the uncertainty of the future, and so the non-realization of expectations, matters to explain instability (Minsky 1980a (1982): 21), it is not specific to the capitalist economic system. For the latter, the flaw rests more deeply on the financing and funding methods of capital equipment (Minsky 1975a: 57, 1977a: 21). Indeed, because the latter are very expensive and have a long gestation period (determined by their construction, installment, and testing periods over which they do not generate any cash inflows (Minsky 1977c, 1986a)), and because the financing of their production and the funding of their acquisition are usually done with loans that have a maturity shorter than the gestation period, there is a maturity mismatch between assets and liabilities on the balance sheet of enterprises and banks. This mismatch creates a dependence on future availability of affordable external funds, and so generates a "speculative" financial structure. This need to make positions is at the origins of "the emergence of financial relations that can lead to snowballing instability" (Fazzari and Minsky 1984: 109).

This financial mismatch not only concerns the production and acquisition of capital assets but also concerns all kinds of economic activities from consumption to speculation on financial assets (Minsky 1984b, 1995). Even if the dependence on investment were reduced greatly, this would not do the trick if consumption or other major economic activities were financed and funded in the same way. Thus, the fundamental flaw of the capitalist system really lies in the financial system, not in the entrepreneurial system:

> Because of the nature of the financial structures necessary for a successful capitalism, capitalism remains a flawed economic structure [...].
>
> (Minsky 1995: 206)

Isenberg (1988, 1994) and Stanfield and Phillips (1991) assume that "the problem of instability is rooted in the nature of capitalist commodity production" (Stanfield and Phillips 1991: 348), but this is a narrow view of Minsky's theory.

A formal model of the Minskian framework requires, therefore, that the financing and the funding methods of all economic activities, as well as nominal cash-flow relationships, be stated explicitly for all economic sectors. In addition, taking into account the financial activities, i.e. refinancing loans, that emerge as a by-product of the routine financing and funding of production-related activities is central to the Minskian system.

Agents are rational: over-optimism and conventions

In Minsky's theoretical framework, the Wall-Street view, agents make arbitrages between all assets (physical and financial) based on their expected rate of return from income and capital gains (Minsky 1972a (1982): 203–204, 1975a, 1986a). The "fundamental speculative decision" is to decide which assets to acquire and how to fund the position in those assets (Minsky 1975a: 86, 89).

Because of the nature of the system that Minsky studies, the previous decisions are based on conventions. As stated in chapters 2 and 3, this kind of behavior is rational (Minsky 1989c, 1993b; Goldstein 1995; Crotty 1994). Indeed, in order to make any decision, individuals construct mental explanations (or "models") of how they think the economic system works and will work in the future. They know, however, that these explanations do not replicate any true model of the economic system, but are just representations that have been agreed upon by a group of economic units. Therefore, economic agents know that they can be systematically wrong; that is, they know that their views of the future may be totally inadequate and that the decisions based on these views may turn out to be inappropriate, in the sense that they may not lead to the expected results. These errors are not based on the existence of asymmetric information, or bounded rationality, but on the uncertainty of the economic system (Dunn 2001). Asymmetries of information can be added to the explanation to provide additional insights, but they are not essential to understand the behaviors of entrepreneurs and bankers (Minsky 1989c: 177, 1993b; Dymski 1994; Kregel 1992a: 87).

Conventions play a central role in Minsky's analysis. Usually, there is always a "consensus" (Minsky 1972a (1982): 214) that exists and stabilizes the decision-making process by playing the role of "certainty equivalent" (Minsky 1975a: 66). Those conventions do not need to rest on any predefined criteria, but may rest on the "prevailing mood of bankers, the users of their liabilities, and the regulatory authorities as to the safety of various types of assets" and methods of financing and funding (Minsky 1975b: 334). These conventions are used to determine the acceptable criteria that borrowers must meet in order to be granted advances. As shown below both borrowers and lenders are actively involved in this process of selection and there is no a priori supposition that bankers are in an inferior position. When the consensus is broken, there is no point of reference anymore, and economic decisions are frozen as perceived uncertainty increases. Entrepreneurs stop investing and loan officers become more conservative in their lending practices. If uncertainty is very high, no margins of safety, no matter how good they are, will help to stimulate borrowers and lenders.

The prevailing convention about the way the economic system works determines the state of long-term expectations, i.e. the expected profitability and liquidity of assets. This state of expectations is used to determine the level of economic activity as well as the normal margins of safety (Minsky 1975a: 109). The causality runs as follows:

Convention → State of expectations → Normal margins of safety.

One of the central points of the modeling is, thus, to specify how the convention, and so the normal margins of safety, change over time:

> The fundamental instability is the way in which a period of steady growth evolves into a speculative boom. Central to this evolution is the endogenous determination of the accepted or desired liability structure of not only ordinary business firms (corporations) but also banks.
>
> (Minsky 1974: 267)

In Minsky's theory, the normal margins of safety always loosen during a period of prolonged economic growth, as the convention sustaining these margins seems to represent well what is going on, or as unexpected events can be explained by the convention.[1] This reflects a change in the state of expectation that represents more confidence in a given set of expected monetary cash flows Π; borrower's and lender's risks are relaxed given $E(\Pi)$. Economic actors become more daring (Minsky 1975a: 127). At the same time, $E(\Pi)$ may be revised upward and, ultimately, the possibility of failure (negative or too low Π) may become progressively inconceivable. This is what Minsky called a period of euphoria: "gross profits in the present-value calculations that had reflected expected recessions are replaced by those that reflect continuing expansion. Simultaneously, there is less uncertainty about the future behavior of the economy" (Minsky 1972b: 100). Thus, a euphoric period assumes that cycles are "a thing of the past" ($E(\Pi)$ always positive and high) (Minsky 1975a: 140) and the confidence in the explanation sustaining this belief (the "new era" convention) is high. More formally, one may define $Q \equiv E(\Pi) \pm \theta \sigma_\Pi$, with σ_Π the standard deviation of expectations and θ a multiplicative factor attached to the standard deviation. The more confident individuals are, the lower θ will be, i.e. there will be less room for error of expectations. Thus, both $\Delta E(\Pi) > 0$ and $\Delta \theta < 0$ lead to $\Delta Q > 0$ but via different channels.

Note that euphoria is not defined in relation to past economic trends, i.e. the idea that, for example, the economy grew at 3 percent over the last century and so it is over-optimistic to believe it will grow at 4 percent for a long time in the future. Euphoria is defined in relation to thinning margins of safety, as defined more precisely below, and to the idea that crises can never occur. Growing financial fragility and new-era convention defined euphoria, not invariable a priori "fundamentals" about the economy. Conventions, by sustaining certain behaviors, may promote a much more dynamic economy than in the past and may create the reality that the convention sustains.

However, euphoria, also called over-optimism, is not necessary to explain why the acceptable margins of safety loosen. Indeed, the notion of "over" implies that there is an explicit a priori norm of judgment where in fact there is none. What is considered "over-optimistic" at the beginning of a cycle may become part of the newly established convention and what was previously "normal" is now "pessimistic." The only thing necessary to explain the loosening of normal margins of safety is an understanding of the dynamics of conventions over time. Prolonged expansion means a history of successes, and so more favorable data inputted in the decision process, and so a rational increase in optimism and expected future monetary gains (Kregel 1997, 2008):

> As we tend to learn from the past and as horizons are short, a run of success or failure will feed back quickly into the evaluation of risks.
>
> (Minsky 1967a: 293)

> The determination of the cash to be expected by the borrower depends upon the loan officer's views of what business conditions over the time of the contract will be; these views, even in an era where loan officers use forecasts of the economy, are seriously affected by the performance on outstanding loans.
>
> (Minsky 1984b: 238)

Today, this is illustrated by the heavy use of the HS methodology to estimate VARs, which assumes that the recent past provides a good guide of future price volatility (International Monetary Fund 2007: 56, 64). Thus, in addition to economic prosperity, the rise in optimism is due to the socio-psychological factors discussed in chapter 3. Guttentag and Herring (1984) have shown how heuristic biases may lead people to underestimate the probability of disaster even though there is no euphoria. Euphoria cannot explain the progressive weakening of the economy because "the euphoric period has a short lifespan" (Minsky 1972b: 102). Therefore, "over-optimism" may only enter late into the analysis and only helps to precipitate the turning point of a business cycle. As Taylor and O'Connel (1985), and Franke and Semmler (1989) note, bubbles are not central to explain the emergence of a crisis in Minsky's framework (Minsky 1972b: 118).

Financial innovations

Minsky's dialectical view of capitalism also exists at the level of financial innovations because the latter play an essential role in the long-term financial weakening of the economic system, but they also improve its flexibility. Following the logic of monetary economies, financial innovations are not driven by welfare considerations but by competitive pressures to make profit (Minsky 1957a, 1969a: 227, 1986a: 197–198; Carter 1989; Wojnilower 1991). They allow financial institutions to overcome the "erosion of traditional bases of profitability in heretofore protected markets" (Carter 1989: 787), and are first experienced by giant banks and enterprises, and then diffused to the rest of the economy (Minsky 1983a). Indeed, bankers and entrepreneurs are profit-seeking agents and so they always try to innovate financially in order to bypass the barriers imposed on monetary accumulation by the regulatory system, or to adapt the financing and funding mechanisms to the needs of more economic activities (Dow 2006). In the latter case, financial innovations are a welcome counterpart to technological innovations and should be promoted by regulatory authorities as long as they are safe (Minsky 1967b: 51, 1969b, 1972b: 117).

One essential difference between technological innovations and financial innovations is that the latter have no natural limit:

> The rate of increase of financial variables is limited only by ingenuity and acceptability. In a world with layering, the rate of change of financial variables really has no bounds. The ability of financial layering to increase the burden on the payments mechanism is one way in which the conditions necessary for financial instability can be generated.
>
> (Minsky 1967a: 270)

This unlimited a priori constraint on financial innovations is a potential source of instability (Minsky 1984a; Spotton 1997). Indeed, more layering of IOUs leads to an increasing interdependence of economic agents for their money inflows and outflows, and so increasing dependence on economic conditions over which they do not have any control. Recent developments in the financial system illustrate that well with securitization and re-securitization. Financial instruments have become so complex that nobody knows, even their creators, what the full cash-flow implications are. Finally, financial innovations can have several perverse effects, from the illusion of safety that gives the incentive to reduce margins of safety, to the allocation of risks toward the financial entities the least able to cope with them efficiently (Galbraith 1961; Carter 1989).

Financing and funding of the economic process

All economic activities can be classified into two different categories (Minsky 1983a: 270, 1984a: 31): the production of assets and the carrying of assets. The second category includes the acquisition and maintenance of positions in existing financial and physical assets. All these economic activities are supported by a financing and funding process, so the financial and the production sides of a model must be developed explicitly simultaneously:

> It is impossible to draw a meaningful investment demand function without simultaneously specifying the liabilities that will be emitted.
>
> (Minsky 1967b: 47)

> A commandment for creating economic theory that is relevant for capitalist economies is: 'Thou shalt not dichotomize' between the presumably real and the financial spheres of the economy.
>
> (Minsky 1990b: 212)

Minsky contended that "Any economic unit can emit liabilities; the only problem is to secure general acceptance for them." (Minsky 1972c: 39). Banks and other financial institutions accept IOUs of private non-banks agents in exchange for their own IOUs that are transferable means of payments. This transferability, or payment capacity, is hierarchically determined with the central bank liabilities at the top

(Minsky 1967a: 267–268, 1985a; Innes 1914: 154; Bell 2001).[2] As the process of growth proceeds and financial innovations emerge, "a hierarchy of liquid assets comes into being" (Minsky 1986a: 219) and so there is a deepening in the layering of financial relationships.

ACCEPTANCE OF LIABILITY, REFLUX MECHANISMS, AND INFLATION

The acceptance by banks of the IOUs of non-bank private agents rests on the expected capacity "to force a net flow of cash in its favor", i.e. creditworthiness (Minsky 1986a: 71; Innes 1913, 1914). The actual capacity to acquire cash flows affects the value of circulating financial instruments through its impacts on creditworthiness. Indeed, acknowledgements of debt must be able to come back to their issuers when needed so that their value is preserved, i.e. the creditworthiness of the issuer is confirmed. For commercial banks, the value of their IOUs depends on their capacity to deliver central bank IOUs on demand. For central bank IOUs and Treasury IOUs, their value depends on the capacity of the government to collect taxes or other compulsory payments it imposes on others, as well as on the fulfillment of self-imposed obligations (maintaining a fixed exchange rate, repaying foreign-denominated debts, or other financial obligations).

Therefore, in total, the value of money "is maintained because of the need to make payments to banks and Treasuries by debtors and taxpayers" (Minsky 1985b: 4, 1985a: 16, 1979: 107). The role of the reflux mechanism (and so destruction of money) is, therefore, very important and directly related to the weakening process of the financial structure. IOUs must be able to come back to their issuers when needed. If there is no reflux, there is a refinancing process that leads, at the macroeconomic level, to inflation, or, at the international level, to a depreciation of the currency (Minsky 1979, 1986b). Speculative and Ponzi financial structures are prone to inflationary pressures because the reflux is either partial or nil. The reflux mechanisms, therefore, must be modeled carefully when financial relationships are studied.

EXOGENOUS MONEY, ENDOGENOUS MONEY, AND FINANCIAL INNOVATIONS

Questions about the endogeneity of the money supply were not developed in Minsky's approach before the mid-1960s when they became of greater interest with the emergence of Monetarism. In 1967, he critiqued the idea that a central bank can control the amount of its IOUs in circulation:

> It cannot be assumed that the amount and the rate of change of reserve money is either exogenously determined or the result of a policy decision.
>
> (Minsky 1967a: 266)

Later, he constantly repeated that the supply of financial instruments changes with the financial needs of the economic system (Minsky 1984a: 31–32, 1985a: 13).

An agent who creates an IOU today leverages his position because, today, he is short in the thing he promises to deliver. In this context, "leveraging" does not mean "multiplying" on borrowed funds, it means "promising to pay/deliver." Thus

> A bank is not a money lender that first acquires and then places funds. [...]
> [A] bank first lends or invests and then "finds" the cash to cover whatever cash drains arise.
>
> (Minsky 1975c: 154)

Therefore, the monetary-creation process has no technical limits like a multiplier. A shortage of reserves does not restrain lending unless getting them is harmful for the profitability and solvency of banks (Minsky 1986a: 70–71). Thus, the capability to get reserves at a relatively cheap cost will define the profitability limit for the issuance of bank IOUs. Financial innovations are a way for banks to relax this profitability limit by allowing a refinancing of reserve positions at a lower interest rate relative to existing sources of reserves, or by creating new lucrative ways to diversify their portfolio of assets. Thus, financial innovations are not a cause of endogeneity of money (which it is by nature) but a way to increase the profitability of monetary creation. Only profitability and conventions determine the structure of the balance sheets of banks (Minsky 1979: 107).

The fact that bank money is endogenous does not preclude that a part of the money supply and of reserves is injected exogenously by the transactions of the Treasury: "the money supply is in part endogenous and in part exogenous" (Minsky 1991a: 208). Contrary to Moore (1996) or Chick (1986), however, this is not due to historical or institutional characteristics but due to different procedures of injection of IOUs between the private sector and the public sector. Banks' IOUs are mostly created at the initiative of the needs of creditworthy economic agents (if banks buy goods and services there is a vertical injection of bank money), whereas Treasury transactions mostly add (and remove) funds independently of the request of private economic units. This latter injection of funds is "vertical" even though the government may have to pay interest on them to keep overnight rates above zero (Wray 1998a: 111ff.), and this "second meaning of exogeneity requires that profit seeking activity be removed from financial markets and institutions" (Minsky 1991a: 212). Today, this injection of funds by the Treasury goes mainly through the banking system, and is offset constantly by the central bank, in coordination with the Treasury department, in order to keep policy rates on target (Meulendyke 1998: 156–157; Bell 2000; Wray 1998a, 2003a, 2003c). Indeed, Treasury spending creates an excess amount of reserves, which bring down short-term rates, while taxes create a shortage of reserves, which pushes interest rates upward.

The role of bankers

As stated earlier, asymmetric information is not essential to the Minskian approach and so the theory does not depend on "borrowers being smart and bankers being dumb" (Minsky 1993b: 79). On the contrary, bankers are an essential component of the system at all stages of the economic process in order for the economy to grow properly. However, bankers also contribute to the destabilization of the economic system and so need to be supervised (Minsky 1980b: 520).

This dialectical conclusion is due to the structural organization of banks; the latter being defined in a broad sense as "the various classes of dealers (position-takers) and brokers that intermediate and facilitate financing" (Minsky 1984a: 41, n. 16). In any bank, there are two essential "operators" (Minsky 1984b: 237ff.): the loan officer and the position-making desk. One central role of the banking system is to evaluate the creditworthiness of borrowers (Minsky 1986a: 188, 229):

> Bankers are "specialists" in "determining" the likelihood of success of money-making business schemes that require external finance.
>
> (Minsky 1984b: 236)

> Loan officers of banks are professionals, skilled in the evaluation of privately submitted and often confidential information about the operations of businesses, households, and government units that require financing.
>
> (Minsky 1994: 9)

Loans officers represent the conservative side of a bank and examine each project presented to them in great details to "transform the optimistic views of profit expectations put forth by potential borrowers into realist expectations" (Minsky 1994: 9). They are the "designated skeptics" (Minsky 1994: 10) in the game of guessing the future, and help to contain the potential fragility of the economy (Minsky 1986a: 212; Kregel 1997).[3] Loan officers are, thus, essential to the stability of the capitalist system, even though their skepticism may be eroded over a prolonged expansion.

The conservative side of banks is completed by its opposite. Indeed, bankers "are sceptics as 'underwriters' and enthusiasts as 'sellers'" (Minsky 1996: 76), that is, bankers assume that they will usually be able to refinance their positions at a cost low enough not to compromise the profitability of granting advances, or that they will be able to transfer the financial cost on their cash-inflow-generating activities to their customers (increase in interest rates, fees, and other sources of funds). Banks are "profit maximizing, highly levered, speculative enterprises" (Minsky 1975b: 330) because the maturity of their debts is far shorter than the maturity of their assets and so there is a refinancing cost upon which they have to "speculate" (Minsky 1977a: 19–20).

Furthermore, in addition to being intrinsic speculative economic agents, banks promote speculative financing:

> Not only do banks engage in speculative finance, but they are the transmission belt toward speculative financing by others.
>
> (Minsky 1977a: 20)

All this can be best understood by decomposing the net profit rate of banks (Minsky 1975b, 1977a, 1986a: 234–238):

$$\frac{\Pi_n}{E} = \frac{\Pi_n}{A} \times \frac{A}{E}.$$

The net profit ratio of bank before distribution relative to equity is equal to the net return on assets multiplied by asset-to-equity ratio. Retained earnings lead to an increase in equity and so, following arithmetic, a decline in the net profit rate of banks. If, due to competitive pressures and demand from shareholders, banks have to meet a given targeted net profit rate, they respond to the decline in net profit rate in two ways.

The first method is to increase the net return on assets, which is done, given operating costs and the size total assets in portfolio, by finding cheaper sources of funds (liability management) or by switching toward more profitable assets (asset management). In the former case, this usually means finding shorter-term source of funds that provide more guarantees to the lender. In the latter case, this usually means courting more risky borrowers and providing longer-term loans. In both cases, financial innovations are a crucial component. In addition, in both cases, financial fragility increases as the maturity mismatch increases, and as the riskiness of the projects funded increases from the point of view of banks (either because they are intrinsically more risky or because banks have to commit for a longer period of time).

The second way to raise the net profit rate is to increase the asset-to-equity ratio. This method increases the leveraging of banks and contributes to the spreading of the maturity mismatch to the rest of the economy. Indeed, in order to limit maturity mismatch on their balance sheet and due to competitive pressures, banks usually provide loans with a shorter maturity than the maturity of the positions that need to be externally funded (Minsky 1977a: 20), and banks have an incentive to encourage borrowers to substitute long-term debts for short-term debts (Minsky 1982a: 26).

Of course, the same analysis of the net profit rate relative to its targeted value can be applied to any company that is under strong competitive pressures and that needs to meet demands imposed by stakeholders. However, banks are a central element because they allow all these dynamics to operate by defining what is financially acceptable. Overall, the banking system is again a good representation of the dialectic that Minsky finds in the capitalist economic system. Banks may promote the implementation of less risky projects as long as competitive pressures and long-term stability do not erode the acceptable margins of safety set by bankers, but they may also promote risky external financing and funding by granting loans with a shorter maturity than the maturity of the projects funded. In this case, even strong projects have a greater chance of failure as multiple refinancing operations increase the dependence on future market conditions in goods and financial markets.

Developments in the financial sector after 1980 have accentuated the destabilizing effects of bank operations by shifting most of the profit-making activities toward the position-making desk and giving only a marginal role to the loan-officer desk. The latter no longer has a long-term individualized relationship with each borrower. The relation is impersonal and judged in minutes through a credit-scoring method based on a comparison of the credit history of a borrower relative to the credit history of other borrowers with similar credit history (Kregel 2008). We have moved from a "commitment" banking model to an "originate and distribute" model, in which banks make most of their profits from fees obtained from selling and servicing structured financial instruments (mortgage-backed securities, collateralized debt obligations, etc.) rather than from interest-rate spreads.

In this new financial system, risk-management has become a central concept that has been embraced by the Basel Accord (Gallati 2003). Each type of identified risk – market risk, credit risk, and operational risk – is determined separately and then integrated into a global framework to determine the total risk. Coupled with securitization, the focus is now on the credit risk of securities that bundle lots of underlying debt instruments that may have different types of creditworthy borrowers. Judging the "creditworthiness" of a security, i.e. the probability of payment, rather than the creditworthiness of a person has become a central task of the new financial system. Thus, assets and liabilities are picked in order to mimic a preferred expected loss pattern, regardless of the risk of each item on the balance sheet:

> Financial institutions now manage their liabilities and assets in a holistic way. They do not simply approach the market to fund a given portfolio of assets. Rather, they confront changing market conditions using risk management techniques that involve a combination of asset sales, liability issuance and derivative transactions, aimed at achieving the optimum risk profile, given their assessment of the risks and returns from alternative portfolios.
>
> (Crockett 2008: 14–15)

> Risk management seeks to maximize risk-adjusted rates of return on equity; often, in the process, underused capital is considered "waste." Gone are the days when banks prided themselves on triple-A ratings and sometimes hinted at hidden balance-sheet reserves (often true) that conveyed an aura of invulnerability. Today, or at least prior to August 9 2007, the assets and capital that define triple-A status, or seemed to, entailed too high a competitive cost.
>
> (Greenspan 2008)

Minsky deplored that developments in the financial sector over the past 30 years have promoted financial institutions that are "banks without loan officers" (Minsky 1981: 15).

This promotion of risk-management strategies, however, has limits because it puts a lot of emphasis on the number generated by a computer and because it loses sight of the overall context that produced the default probability:

> Today's obsession with risk management focuses too intently on the instru-ments of the management and measurement of risk. The more we stare at

the jumble of equations and models the more we lose sight of the mystery of life. [...] In the end, what matters is the quality of our decision in the face of uncertainty.

(Bernstein 2000: 42)

Our heedless dependence on measures of central tendency persuades us to base our decisions on averages, trends, coefficients of correlation, and almost-normal distributions [...]. The trick in risk management, in fact, is in recognizing that "normal" is not a state of nature but a state of transition, and trend is not destiny [...].

(Bernstein 1997b: 3)

In addition, one may wonder if past information is reliable to forecast the future. As many Post-Keynesians (Lawson 1988; Dow 1995; Kregel 1987, 2008; Kregel and Nasica 1999; Lavoie 1985; Runde 1995), following Keynes (1921, 1936a, 1937b), Davidson (1978, 1982, 1988a, 1991, 1995), and Shackle (1974, 1955), have argued, a probabilistic assessment of the future based on past statistics is either impossible or not necessarily "useful" (Davidson 1982 (1991): 129). Each new economic situation brings with it a new institutional context that may dramatically affect the relevance of a frequency distribution obtained from past experiences. This is all the more the case that financial innovations alter the structure of the economy, and create additional opportunities for the emergence of low-frequency events that are difficult or impossible to catch by probabilistic assessments:

Low-probability shocks are much more troublesome because they tend to be unpredictable. The infrequency of incidents relative to changes in the underlying economic structure prevents any reliable empirical basis for estimating probabilities. [...] Financial innovations are particularly worrisome in this regard because of the absence of experience regarding how new activities and instruments will respond to cyclical variations in the economic environment.

(Guttentag and Herring 1988: 613–614)

The pace of financial innovation raises serious questions about whether economic behaviour has been stable over a long span of historical data. [...] Unfortunately, the pace of financial innovation leaves the i.i.d. assumption open to question.

(Herring 1999: 68–69, n. 13)

Overreliance on probabilities will give a false sense of safety and market efficiency. For example, recently, AAA-rated securities have been issued on the basis of a bundle of subprime mortgages or other loans made to borrowers with poor creditworthiness, by using subordination and other credit enhancement techniques that allow to reproduce the default probability of AAA-rated borrowers (Herring 1999; Norris 2007; Adelson 2006).

Finally, the task of judging credit risk has been put in the hands of credit-rating agencies that do not have a long-term relationship with their clients. Combined with competitive pressures and with a rewarding structure in which credit-rating agencies "are paid by the very issuers they are supposed to be rating" (Kanter 2007) and independently of their capacity to measure credit risk correctly, this lack of commitment makes these new loan officers prone to optimism and complaisance, and it disconnects loan originators and ultimately the holders of structured obligations from the economic realities that borrowers must confront (Guttentag and Herring 1984; Minsky 1994, 1986b; Davis 1995; Shiller 2000; Schinasi 2006; Kregel 2008):

> From a structural point of view, the economic incentive for a thorough credit analysis of each and every loan by the originating institution is clearly diluted by the knowledge that that institution will only have the loan on its books for a few weeks or months. And once a loan has been packaged along with hundreds or thousands of other loans [...], its individual characteristics, including default risk, become completely opaque.
>
> (Carter 1989: 789)

Recent developments in the US mortgage market with the emergence of stated-income loans (for which only a verbal statement of income is necessary) and speculative loans such as NINJA loans (No Income, No Job, No Assets declared) clearly illustrate the dangers of lack of commitments between loan originators and their clients (Pearlstein 2007). As shown later, all this has important implications for the dynamics of the system and the pre-deregulation channels of financial weakening have been modified (Kregel 2008).

The cost of external funds

One important point to take into account for the modeling of Minsky's theory is the total cost of external funds. Indeed, in the expansionary phase, the change in the relationship between the amount of cash outflows and the amount of cash inflows is central to the Financial Instability Hypothesis.

In the most abstract terms, the carrying cost of assets is what should be used to determine the cost of producing and holding assets (Minsky 1975a: 84–85). To simplify, only the financial cost may be taken into account, but this still includes debt services, the rental cost for storage, the insurance cost, as well as all other cash outflows generated by contractual obligations. To simplify even more, only the interest payment of debt services may be taken into account, but, as Minsky recognizes, this is not a good approximation of the financial cost when debts have a shorter maturity because the amortization of the principal becomes important (Caskey and Fazzari 1986):

> In fact, if the financial contracts are sufficiently short, then the cash payments on financial contracts can exceed the total quasi-rents.
>
> (Minsky 1975a: 84)

The interest rate is only a "shorthand" description of the cost of external funds, and what really matters are the terms of financial contracts including the maturity term and "various protections desired by producers and lenders" (Minsky 1980a (1982): 37). An increase in the cost of external funds is represented by higher interest rates, lower maturity terms, higher collateral demands, and more covenants and codicils (Minsky 1986a: 192).

Therefore, an increase in cash commitments may not be due to an increase in interest rates and, for a given amount borrowed, an increase in the required speed of amortization is enough.[4] Thus, a modeling and testing Minsky's theory cannot be based only on analyzing interest payments. At minimum, one should check the amortization process by looking at the maturity-characteristics of debts:

> In a fully amortized contract a series of payments is specified and at the end of the time the contract is fully paid. In a partially amortized contract there is a payment due at the end of the contract which is a portion of the original principal. An unamortized contract has the full original principal due at its end.
>
> (Minsky 1980a (1982): 30)

Maturity considerations are important not only because, as shown later, they are central to the dynamics of the Financial Instability Hypothesis, but also because they have practical consequences. Indeed, if maturity terms increase, an increase in the debt-to-equity may not reflect a higher fragility of the economy:

> Inasmuch as the nature of mortgage debt changed markedly between 1929 and 1962, the larger household debt-income ratio in 1962 may not indicate a greater sensitivity to a shock.
>
> (Minsky 1963a (1982): 10)

The emergence of fully amortized mortgages decreased the cash-flow impact of the stock of debts by increasing the maturity matching of outflows and inflows of funds.

The cash box condition and margins of safety

Because money is at the center of economic decisions, one central component of the Minskian framework is the cash-flow analysis. In his first extensive study about the Financial Instability Hypothesis, published in 1964, Minsky introduced what he called the "cash box condition":

> A key to understanding the behavior of a capitalist economy is the precise statement of the payments required by the liability structure and how the cash to meet such commitments is generated.
>
> (Minsky 1982a: 19)

An economic unit (or the economy) has to be sure to generate enough cash inflows (CIF), or to have enough idle cash balance (IB), in order to meet its cash outflows (COF):

$$IB + CIF \geq COF,$$

$$IB + NCF \geq 0.$$

If the net cash inflow (NCF) is negative, and no idle cash balance is available, an economic unit will be considered illiquid. If it is expected that the previous situation will continue to prevail in the foreseeable future, an economic unit will be considered insolvent. The cash box condition, therefore, provides good insights on how an economic unit could get into trouble and what its margins of safety are.

CASH BOX CONDITION, POSITION MAKING, AND FINANCIAL FRAGILITY

Following accounting principles, all sources and uses of cash can be classified into three different categories: income transactions, balance-sheet transactions, and portfolio transactions (Minsky 1962, 1964a, 1972b: 121, n. 37):

> An ultimate reality in a capitalist economy is the set of interrelated balance sheets among the various units. Items in the balance sheets set up cash flows. Cash flows are the result of (1) the income-producing system, which includes wages, taxes, and nonfinancial corporate gross profits after taxes, (2) the financial structure, which is composed of as interest, dividends, rents, and repayments on loans, and (3) the dealing or trading in capital assets and financial instruments.
>
> (Minsky 1975a: 118)

The cash outflows induced by balance-sheet operations are numerous and do not correspond only to debt servicing (Minsky 1978). They contain all cash-flow commitments determined by the dated (due at a specific date or time schedule), demand (honored at the will of the creditor), and contingent (due if specific events are realized) liabilities: Dividends, leases, rents, insurance premiums, and margin calls are among them (Minsky 1962: 258, n. 2, 1964a: 230, 1964b: 330–331, 1972a (1982): 203). In addition, the term "liabilities" (and "balance sheet") is taken in a broad sense to include all off-balance-sheet contractual obligations. For example, dated off-balance-sheet items are insurance and lease contracts (Minsky 1964a: 231), demand off-balance-sheet items are contractual credit lines (rather than informal credit lines) (Minsky 1969b (1982): 183), and contingent off-balance-sheet items are derivative contracts.

There are different sources and uses of funds for each economic activity, and, depending on the main economic activity of a unit, some of them will be more important than others. For example, some economic units, like security dealers and mutual funds, have their core net cash inflow that depends on routinely performed portfolio transactions, but most economic units get a positive net cash inflow, mainly from income and balance-sheet operations. Also, depending on the level of analysis (individual, sector, or economy), the possible sources of funds and normal net cash inflows are different. For example, if at the individual level the choice between refinancing and liquidation is a matter of relative cost, at the aggregate level the latter portfolio operation is impossible and so it is an abnormal source of cash inflows (Minsky 1962):

> As an empirical generalization, almost all financial commitments are met from two normal sources of cash: income flows and refinancing of positions. For most units – especially those that have real capital goods at their assets – the selling out of their position is not feasible (no market exists for a quick sale); for others, aside from marginal adjustments by way of special money markets, it is an unusual source of cash. [...] Financial instability occurs whenever a large number of units resort to extraordinary sources for cash.
>
> (Minsky 1972b: 105)

Financial fragility can be measured at the aggregate level by looking at the proportion of income transactions relative to balance-sheet transactions and portfolio transactions (Minsky 1962, 1964a, 1986a: 203–204). This gives an approximation of the dependence upon the need to "make position," i.e. to meet balance-sheet commitments with portfolio transactions. The more an economy is involved in position-making activities, the more it is dependent upon the short-term financial conditions in financial markets because of the dependence on the "cash available from selling out or refinancing the position" (Minsky 1984b: 248).

The previous measure is, however, only an approximation because not all portfolio transactions are a sign of fragility. Indeed, if an economic unit has a large amount of idle cash and liquid superfluous assets, it does not need to enter into any position-making activities that are subject to uncertainty concerning their liquidity or their cost. In addition, a certain amount of portfolio transactions (borrowing, dishoarding, liquidation) is necessary to complete normal economic operations, and, as stated above, some economic units routinely use portfolio transactions to generate a positive net cash inflow. A better approximation can be obtained by classifying portfolio operations between position-making operations and strategic/routine portfolio operations (Minsky 1969b, 1972b). The former sources of net cash flow (NCF_{PM}) can be considered as abnormal because an economic unit has to enter financial markets no matter how adverse conditions are. The higher the dependence on position-making operations to generate a positive net cash flow, the higher the fragility of an economic unit is.

The cash box condition shows that there are several margins of safety for economic units that can prevent them from entering position-making operations. These margins are essential for the working of capitalist economies because

> The system of financing in a capitalist economy is based upon margins of safety embodied in anticipated excesses of cash receipts over payment commitments and of asset values over capitalized payment commitments. Whenever, for whatever reasons, the margins of safety in existing contracts are compromised then the ability and willingness of bankers and business to finance new expenditures and to enter into debt contracts to finance holdings of capital assets are compromised.
>
> (Minsky 1984b: 241)

If one excludes strategic portfolio operations from the normal sources of cash, there are three margins of safety: the expected positive net cash inflow on income and balance-sheet operations, or cash-flow margin ($E(NCF_O) > 0$); the existence of a comfortable idle amount of cash and superfluous liquid assets, or cash margin ($IB > 0$), that limits the expected need to liquidate strategic positions or to enter other adverse portfolio operations; and the portfolio margin or net-worth margin (present value of strategic assets (P_A)> present value of liabilities (P_L)) (Minsky 1986a: 339). If $E(NCF_O) > 0$ a unit is considered liquid in normal time; if $P_A > P_L$ a unit is considered solvent (it is expected to be liquid for the whole period of its existence). Finally, the structure of assets and liabilities (quality, maturity, liquidity, proportion) affects the solvency and the liquidity of a unit (Minsky 1975c; Kindleberger 1992).

Minsky characterized these margins for three financial structures: hedge, speculative, and Ponzi (Minsky 1974). Table 5.1 shows these different financial positions (Minsky 1972b: 118–119, 1977a, 1980a, 1986a: 335–341). In a hedge situation, there is no expectation, even with conservative expectations of cash inflows (Minsky 1980a (1982): 25), that the cash inflows from production and distribution will be less than the cash outflows on liability commitments ($E(NCF_{Ot}) > 0 \forall t$); therefore, there is no expectation that one will have to enter position-making operations. This is so for most of the considered possible variations in cash inflows, interest rates, maturity terms, and other cash-outflow-related characteristics of liability contracts. However, some idle cash and superfluous liquid assets are kept aside to meet possible disappointments in expectations (Minsky 1975b: 323). In addition, if some cash commitments are denominated in other units of account than the main cash inflows, some cash and liquid assets denominated in these currencies are kept idle (Minsky 1980a (1982): 26). Finally, the external funding sources of a hedge unit are very reliable and based on long-term commitments with bankers. In the end, therefore, a hedge unit is expected to be very liquid now and in the future. All this leads to a strong

Table 5.1 Hedge, speculative, Ponzi financial positions

	Hedge	Speculative	Ponzi
Cash-flow margin (Liquidity)	$E(NCF_{Ot}) > 0 \forall t$	$E(NCF_{Ot}) < 0 t$ small and necessity to make position for the capital component: $E(NCF_{PM}) = E(aL_t) > 0$	$E(NCF_{Ot}) < 0 \forall t < n$ and necessity to make position for: $E(NCF_{PM}) = E((i+a)L_t) > 0$
Net worth: portfolio margin (Solvency)	$P_A > P_L \forall i, g, E(\Delta P_A)$	$P_A > P_L$ for some $i, g, E(\Delta P_A)$	$P_A > P_L$ for some $i, g, E(\Delta P_A)$
Balance-sheet: cash margin (Liquidity/Solvency)	Assets: Some cash and cash kickers. Liabilities: Debts are mainly long-term debts. Long-term debts with sinking funds arrangements. Low proportion of contingent and demand liabilities. No or insignificant proportion debts with floating rates. Maturity: No or few mismatches between assets and liabilities.	Assets: Cash kickers in high proportion, cash. Liabilities: Long-term debts. Demand and contingent short-term debts. High proportion of floating rate debts. Maturity: Some large mismatches between assets and liabilities. Off-balance sheet: Credit lines. Rapid access to markets is available.	Assets: Cash kickers in low proportion, few cash. Liabilities: Short-term debts in high proportion. No reliable source of funds. Maturity: Large mismatches between assets and liabilities.

balance-sheet position in which the market value of assets is superior to the market value of debts, even for very large changes in interest rates, expectations of income growth (g), and in asset prices ($E(\Delta P_A)$). Thus, hedge units are only vulnerable to problems affecting the demands for their product, or to dependence on "unrealistic euphoric expectations with respect to markets and their growth" (Minsky 1977c: 144).

For a speculative economic unit, it is expected that cash inflows from the main economic activity will not cover the capital component of cash commitments (e.g. amortization of debts), even though all income commitments can be paid (rent payments, dividend payments, insurance premium, and others). Therefore, a refinancing (or liquidation) is expected, but only for the capital component of cash commitments (aL) so that there is no expected increase in liabilities. This refinancing need is, however, a flaw in the financial structure of the unit because

> Whereas a hedge-financing unit is dependent only upon the normal functioning of product and factor markets (or, for a financial unit, upon the fulfillment of contracts), a speculative unit is dependent upon the normal functioning of product, factor, and money markets.
>
> (Minsky 1986a: 337–338)

A speculative position may get into troubles more easily and by more channels than a hedge position, and will be more sensitive to changes in interest rates for its flow and stock variables. Finally, for a speculative unit, the cash margin is lower in size and less liquid in its structure. Typically, it will depend more on liquid assets and on quick access to short-term external sources of cash. This lower protection from the possible disappointments of the expectations of normal net cash inflows leads to a higher sensitivity to changes in income growth and in asset-prices. Hedge financing with a high proportion of floating-rates liabilities is considered speculative because of the dependence on changes in financial conditions (Minsky 1986a: 208, n. 11).

Ponzi finance is similar to speculative finance, except that the cash-flow, portfolio, and cash margins are thinner, and the position-making channels come from more "volatile" and "exotic" sources (Minsky 1980a (1982): 51, 1975d: 8). The Ponzi situation is a special speculative situation in which refinancing operations leads to a decrease in net worth:

> With speculative finance, net worth and liquidity can increase even as debt is refinanced, whereas for a Ponzi unit net worth and liquidity necessarily decrease.
>
> (Minsky 1986a: 340)

Indeed, the refinancing need concerns not only the capital components of financial commitments but also their income components (iL). However, a Ponzi finance situation does not lead necessarily to an increase in debt if the liquidation of assets and the running down of idle cash are preferred alternatives (Minsky 1977a: 19).

In addition, in the case of Ponzi finance, the expected net worth of a project is negative for "any honest computation of present value," even though the overall net worth of an economic unit engaging in Ponzi financing may be positive (Minsky 1977c: 143). However, there is still a hope that the net worth on the project externally funded will turn positive in the future, otherwise the unit could never issue new debts. If, for example, Ponzi finance is used for the production of investment goods, then there is a potential future increase in the cash-flow generating power. However, only when a finished new capital good is involved in the productive process does it have any value (Minsky 1986a: 194). If Ponzi finance is provided through collateral-oriented loans then, in this case, only an increase in the price of the assets pledged can lead to a positive net worth in the future (Minsky 1986a: 233).

A Ponzi position, therefore, does not mean that an economic unit is involved in fraudulent economic activities. In addition, it can take many forms more or less interesting for the study of financial instability. An example of "uninteresting" Ponzi situation is when the seasonal gross profit may not be sufficient to pay fixed quarterly dividend payments (Minsky 1986a: 340). Examples of interesting Ponzi activities are the following (Minsky 1980a (1982): 28, 1984b: 247ff.): borrowing funds to buy securities, for which income will never cover debt-service payments (only capital gains can make the operation profitable); the acquisition of expensive capital assets with a long maturity; and any other project for which the income generated by the holding of an asset is persistently expected to be lower than the total (i.e. income and capital parts of the) carrying cost of this asset. Finally, Ponzi situations can be hard to detect because they can be hidden by creative accounting practices (Minsky 1989c: 180).

In a period of euphoria, Ponzi finance can be sustained because of the convention in place or because of the amount of money at stake:

> Ponzi units can be sustained either because of Micawber sentiments – something will turn up – or because no one is willing to announce that "the Emperor has no clothes."
>
> (Minsky 1975c: 153)

As stated in chapter 3, it is not in the interest of the persons involved in a Ponzi process to recognize that the whole operation may be based on highly doubtful economic activities.

One important characteristic of both speculative situations is that they maintain or increase the liability side of a balance sheet without increasing the cash-flow generating power of the asset side (Minsky 1991c: 15). It will be shown later that "there are both rational reasons and market processes which lead firms, households, and financial institutions into speculative finance" (Minsky 1975b: 317).

Accumulation process

Accumulation is the driving force of capitalist economic systems, and, at the aggregate level, physical accumulation is a central determinant of monetary accumulation, and the latter affects the former. In this section, an explanation of monetary accumulation process is provided first and is followed by the determination of the level of investment.

THE DETERMINATION OF AGGREGATE MONETARY PROFIT

From 1977, Minsky (1977b, 1978, 1986a, 1991b) preferred to use Kalecki's equation of aggregate profit rather than Kahn's multiplier to explain the determination of aggregate income. One central point of the Kalecki equation, presented in chapter 2, is to show that there are two leading variables in the economic system: private domestic investment and government expenditure (Minsky 1986a: 164–165). These two variables are not primarily determined by the current level of aggregate income, and aggregate public expenditures can be used to stabilize the adverse effect of a decline in private and foreign aggregate spending on aggregate monetary profit. Another important point is that the latter is determined independently of the mark-up that firms set. It is the structure of aggregate demand that determines the aggregate mark-up (Minsky 1982a: 26–30; Kalecki 1971a):

> This framework yields a macroeconomic theory of profits in which profits exist not because capital is productive but because investment demand makes consumption output scarce. [...] Profits arising in the production of consumer goods are due to spending on consumer goods in excess of the wage bill generated by the production of consumer goods.
>
> (Minsky 1986b: 11–12)

The microeconomic decisions over the mark-up included in prices only influence the distribution of aggregate profit (Minsky 1986a: 163).

THE DETERMINATION OF THE INVESTMENT LEVEL

The determination of the level of investment is based on a Marshallian supply and demand analysis augmented with Kalecki's principle of increasing risk (Minsky 1967b, 1975a, 1986a, 1989d; Kalecki 1971b). At the aggregate level, Kalecki's equation of profit is added and output prices are explained by using Weintraub's output-price equations.

The profit equation and the principle of increasing risk express the importance of financial factors in the determination of investment. The principle of increasing risk states that, as expected external funding increases, there is an expected increase in the debt–equity ratio that affects the perceived risk of engaging in an economic activity. This perceived risk may be completely unfounded, and as Minsky (1963b: 412; 1986a: 211–213), Lavoie (1995, 1996b, 1997a, 2006), and Steindl (1952: 107ff.) note, there are macroeconomic forces that may lead to a decrease in the debt-to-equity ratio as economic agents increasingly rely on external funds. However, the preceding does not question the relevance of principle of increasing risk at the micro or macro level as long as one stays in the realm of expectations, and as long as one recognizes that individuals do not take into account macroeconomic mechanisms when forming their expectations.

The modeling of the investment decision changed over time, starting with a loanable funds framework (Minsky 1957b, 1959, 1964a, 1965a) and ending with a framework based on chapter 17 of Keynes's *General Theory* (Minsky 1975a, 1986a) in which relative prices, financial structure, and uncertainty are central.

At the level of a firm, investment is determined as shown in Figure 5.1. An entrepreneur compares the demand price (P_{Id}), which is the price he is ready to pay for a certain type of investment good, to the supply price of the investment good (P_{Is}).

The demand price represents the view of an entrepreneur regarding the discounted expected gross quasi rents over the life of the investment good. The discount factor depends on the entrepreneur's risk (or borrower's risk if investment is externally funded), which in turn depends on the confidence of an entrepreneur in the future. As the level of investment increases, the entrepreneur's risk increases, and this leads to a decline in the demand price. The decrease does not need to start when investment begins to be externally funded; it can happen before or, usually, after (Minsky 1975a: 109), because the entrepreneur's risk does not depend only on the level of external funding. Indeed, another major variable that affects the discount factor of the demand price is the marginal user cost of money, i.e. the implicit rate of return on money (Keynes 1936a; Kregel 1997). This is so because an entrepreneur can choose among many different types of assets, and the choice will depend on the relative profitability and liquidity of each of them. As Minsky states, capital assets can be "best thought of as a special type of financial instrument" (Minsky 1977c: 142) in the sense that they are expected to generate an income stream but their liquidity is nil or very low

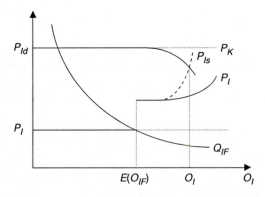

Figure 5.1 Microeconomic determination of investment demand.

(Minsky 1975a: 132). As an entrepreneur increases his investment in a specific sector of the economy, market saturation will set in and the quasi-rent from this investment will decline, leading to a decline in the demand price of those capital goods.

The "offer price" (Minsky 1982a: 29), or "delivered price" (Minsky 1978 (1985): 45), P_I represents the short-term side of the investment decision. It is a horizontal line because it is assumed that the buyer does not have any influence on the cost of production of the producer of the investment good. The offer price is determined by a mark-up over the marginal cost of production. The mark-up depends in part on the user cost of capital equipment, that is, short-term profit expectations relative to current expected profit (Minsky 1971). More precisely, the marginal user cost of capital equipment determines the minimum mark-up necessary to give the producer the incentive to produce now relative to the future (Keynes 1936a: 66ff.). The mark-up depends also on the short-term cost of financing production and on the market power of a firm (Minsky 1978, 1986a). In addition, a producer may be forced to produce even if the price is below its minimum desired level because he may have to meet financial commitments (Minsky 1975a: 138, 1971).

The desired structure of investment funding is composed of the expected amount of net quasi-rent allocated to investment (Q_{IF}) and the desired/expected external funding of investment ($E(\Delta L_I)$). The expected "internal financing constraint" (Minsky 1975a: 107) is $Q_{IF} = P_I \cdot E(O_{IF})$, which gives the expected quantity of investment goods that can be bought with expected internal funds: $E(O_{IF}) = Q_{IF}/P_I$. The difference $O_I - E(O_{IF})$ represents the expected quantity of investment goods that will be bought by requesting external funds. This is expected to raise cash commitments ($E(\Delta CC) > 0$). If part of the investment has to be externally funded, the offer price is not, from the buyer's point of view, the relevant cost of new capital goods. Indeed, it is also necessary to include the cost of the external funds. The supply price of capital is equal to the sum of the offer price plus the discounted value of the expected cash-flow commitments induced by the investment level (Minsky 1975a: 110). The supply price is an increasing function of the level of investment because of the lender's risk, which reflects bankers' vision of the future. This vision sets some acceptable margins of safety to meet and so what bankers see as an appropriate or "optimal" financial structure. As investment expenditure increases, the expected increase in debt relative to equity leads to an increase in the perceived risk of the investment operation. The strength of this risk (the curvature of the supply price) depends on how loose the bankers' convention is. Finally, if an entrepreneur was previously indebted, there is an additional cost to add, induced by the refinancing of existing positions, what Minsky called the "marginal lender's risk" (Minsky 1975a: 110). This leads to the supply price curve P_{Is}. In what follows, no difference is made between lender's risk and marginal lender's risk.

In the microeconomic approach, "all prices and prospective yields are independent of the firm's own scale of operation" (Minsky 1975a: 109). At the macroeconomic level, this does not stand anymore for several reasons. First, at the macroeconomic level, it is necessary to distinguish between two price systems with two sets of prices (Kregel 1992a; Minsky 1969a, 1969c, 1975a, 1977b, 1978, 1986a, 1996). The first price system is the flow-price system (or output-price system) P_O, which is the "carrier of profits" (Minsky 1986a: 141–142). It contains two sets of prices, one concerning consumption goods (P_C) and another one concerning investment goods (P_I), and both are necessary to determine the profit level in each sector. The second price system is the stock-price system (or asset-price system) P_A (Minsky 1977b (1977): 21). The latter contains the price of liabilities (financial assets), P_L, and the price of capital assets (non-financial assets), P_K (Keynes 1936a: 173–174):

> There are two levels to the "two prices" approach: The first level, presented in the *Treatise*, distinguishes between the prices of current output and capital goods output; the second level, added in the *General Theory*, distinguishes the prices of new and existing capital assets from the prices of new and existing financial liabilities.
>
> (Kregel 1992a: 95)

Each of these price systems is influenced by the developments taking place in the economy.

As shown in chapter 2, the output price system depends on the level of aggregate demand via its impact on the average productivity of labor and the aggregate mark-up. As shown in chapter 3, the value of existing assets evolves around an anchor, the normal price. Economic prosperity leads to an increase in asset prices, which affects investment via the effect of the price of liabilities and the price of capital assets on the demand price for investment. This latter price has no concrete existence; it is an implicit variable that is approximated by the price of old capital assets, P_K, because it is assumed that firms would never buy new capital assets if there are cheaper capital assets available in secondary markets (Keynes 1936a: 151). P_K is determined by entrepreneurs' expectations but also by the expectations prevailing in financial markets. In fact, P_K is still an implicit price, and if one wants to give a concrete counterpart to this variable, the best approximation that we have is the price of marketable financial assets that is not determined by entrepreneurs (Minsky 1986a: 227):

> In a capitalist economy, an implicit price system of capital assets – the real capital of the economy – is determined in markets, just as is the price system of current output. This implicit price system is buried in the explicit price system of shares and bonds visible in financial markets and in the prices set in mergers and acquisitions. [...] The starting point for bids on existing firms is the market valuation of the equity and debt liabilities.
>
> (Minsky 1986c: 347–348)

This approximation is discounted by the entrepreneur's risk to give an approximation of the demand price of new capital goods. Minsky was careful to say that this series of approximations is not very satisfactory because the link between stock markets and investment is not well known (Minsky 1969a: 230, n. 13). However, sometimes he oversimplified the matter by blankly stating that both P_{Id} and stock-market prices are the same (Minsky 1996: 78).

The level of investment, therefore, is determined by a double arbitrage. One between non-monetary and monetary assets, which affect P_{Id}, and another between new and old capital assets, represented by the relative price P_{Id}/P_{Is}. This relative price is affected by the entrepreneur's risk and lender's risk that represent the confidence of both actors and so their required margins of safety:

> The 'margins of safety' were characterized by Keynes as borrowers' risk and lenders' risk; lenders' risk takes the form of premiums in financing terms, borrowers' risk is a 'subjective' valuation which, as the dependency on external funds varies, affects the maximum price that units are willing to pay for capital assets.
>
> (Minsky 1989d: 64)

Thus, contrary to the mainstream, monetary conditions influence relative prices by affecting both arbitrages (Minsky 1975a: 95–96, 1978, 1980a, 1993b). If considerations about the financial structure were not included, the level of investment would be limited only by the entrepreneur's risk. If, in addition, there were no risk and no uncertainty, the demand for investment would be unlimited for an entrepreneur (Minsky 1975a: 109–110), and would be limited by full employment at the level of the economy (at which $P_K = P_I$ would prevail).

Another important variable that affects investment, even if only indirectly and progressively, is the level of aggregate profit. It is very important to distinguish between expected gross profit (Q) and actual gross profit (Π) by looking at how they are determined and how they affect each other. First, Q is determined at the microeconomic level by the state of long-term expectations of entrepreneurs and bankers, whereas Π is macroeconomically determined. Second, Π is determined by aggregate nominal investment (I), and I is determined partly by Q. Therefore, the more entrepreneurs invest, the more they will be able to realize their expectations, and the more they realize their expectations, the more they will be willing to invest. There is the following positive feedback process going on at the aggregate level:

$$\text{Expectation about future} \rightarrow Q + \text{normal margins of safety} \rightarrow P_{Id}/P_{Is} \rightarrow I \rightarrow \Pi$$

This "peculiar circularity of a capitalist economy" (Minsky 1986a: 227) is part of its internal flaw. However, entrepreneurs have usually no knowledge of this process, or do not take it into account, which, as shown later, can lead to what can be called a paradox of leverage. This possible frustration of expectations because of macroeconomic forces that individuals do not know is essential for the dynamics of the Minskian system.

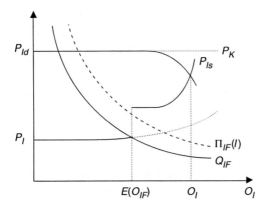

Figure 5.2 Macroeconomic determination of the level of investment.

Figure 5.2 explains the determination aggregate investment. Again, one should note that the structure of funding is an expected structure where Q_{IF} is used to determine $E(O_{IF})$.

The actual funding structure, determined by Π, will have important feedback effects on the behavior of individuals and their willingness to go into debt in order to invest. The main difference with the micro-determination is that the actual internal funding constraint becomes endogenously determined through its dependence on the level of investment: $\Pi_{IF}(P_I \cdot O_I) = P_I \cdot O_{IF}$ (Minsky 1975a: 113ff.). Minsky does not make a clear difference between Q and Π and assumes directly that $Q(P_I \cdot O_I)$. This is not acceptable if one stays in the Keynesian methodology of shifting equilibrium (Kregel 1976, 1986b). One must assume that the state of expectations is affected only progressively by investment (via the level of profit), which is actually what Minsky assumes. The difference between actual and desired financial structures (and so actual and desired cash commitments) will be analyzed.

Fragility, instability, and crisis

The concepts of "financial fragility," "financial instability," and "financial crisis" have been widely used by Minsky and sometimes he has been accused of not giving a precise definition of what he meant (Goldsmith 1982). However, as he developed his theory, the definition became more precise.

The simplest way to qualify financial fragility is to associate it with overindebtedness (Minsky 1992: 20; Fisher 1932, 1933). The concept of "overindebtedness" is related, however, to the idea of optimal financial structure that has already been rejected. There is no "true" or a priori optimal financial structure. It all depends on the conventions prevailing in the economic system, and these conventions may lead to the implementation of economic activities that may generate and sustain the acceptable liability structure as defined by the convention.

One, then, needs to be more precise on what is meant by "fragility." One way to do so would be to define it by its antonym, namely "robustness," and Minsky does do it this way sometimes:

> The place of an economy on a financial robustness-fragility scale is determined by 1) the weight of hedge, speculative, and Ponzi finance units in the economy; 2) the willingness and ability of the authorities to refinance units at concessionary terms when current market rates transform units into Ponzi units; and 3) the in-place power of the authorities to sustain aggregate profits (cash flows to business) and aggregate wages when current market rates turn a large number of units into Ponzi financing units and when the flow of profits and wages could slow down.
>
> (Minsky 1993b: 80)

The fragility/robustness of the economy depends on what Minsky called the "built-in stabilizers" (Minsky 1964a: 267ff.) – endogenous and exogenous factors that affect the domain of stability of the economy (Minsky 1972b: 118–119). The endogenous factors are related to the classification between hedge, speculative, and Ponzi finance. Thus, in a robust financial system, "it takes large changes and there are only a few channels by which financial instability can be induced" (Minsky 1975b: 317). The exogenous factors are related, not only to the lender of last resort intervention or countercyclical fiscal policy, but also to a whole range of financial institutions and practices that limit the financial weakening of the system (loan officers, amortized mortgages, government transfers and others) (Minsky 1963a, 1964a, 1981, 1984b, 1986a). In the end, therefore, fragility can be defined as the propensity of an economic system to generate financial instability. In a fragile financial system, even "a 'slight disturbance' in money flows" (Minsky 1964a: 251) can generate financial instability because of the high articulation between cash inflows and cash outflows.

The problem becomes to define financial instability, which links the effects of financial fragility to the non-financial side of the economy. The best way to comprehend this notion is to start with the definition of macroeconomic stability given by Minsky:

> Stability, in the macroeconomic sense, means that a close approximation to full employment at stable prices can be achieved and sustained by market processes.
>
> (Minsky 1981: 6)

Thus, an economic system is economically unstable when it cannot sustain full employment and price stability, and for Minsky, significant business cycles are mainly "due to financial attributes that are essential to capitalism" (Minsky 1986a: 173). One, then, can make a difference between "upward instability" and "downward instability," the former being the cause of the latter (Minsky 1969a: 228, 1980b: 512). Clearly, the more fragile the financial system is, the more prone to economic instability it becomes. In terms of upward instability, this is because a fragile financial system promotes inflation by increasing the cost of production, and by the incorporation of expectations of a higher level and growth of output price (Minsky 1975a: 140–141). The first cause of inflation can be cured by policy means, but the correction of expectations may be more difficult to achieve, both because it is harder to change people's mind and because these expectations may sustain a level of indebtedness. Therefore, a "fragile financial system is particularly conducive to accelerated inflation" (Minsky 1975a: 163). In terms of downward instability, a fragile system is unstable because it promotes the emergence of debt-deflation processes. The possibility of downward instability, therefore, depends on "the importance of the uninterrupted flow of receipts" (Minsky 1972b: 121, 123) and potential systemic risk.[5] This downward instability is promoted by several factors: the growth of short-term position-making instruments, a tighter central bank policy, a tighter fiscal policy, and the increase in financial layering and possible "domino effect" (Minsky 1986a: 87). Pollin and Dymski give a good definition of downward instability:

> Financial instability occurs when disturbances in an economy's financial structure – such as a stock-market crash, major bank failure, or nonpayment of foreign debt obligations – affect the level of real activity in that economy.
> (Pollin and Dymski 1994: 371, n. 2)

Thus, the financial instability of an economic system is related to the propensity of financial fragility to affect non-financial variables.

Finally, a financial crisis characterizes a situation of widespread financial distress in the economy (Minsky 1964a: 251). If this distress manifests itself by a liquidation of some assets, then there is a large drop in the price of those assets, with possible ripple effects on other markets.

The role of the boom period

The analysis of Minsky's theoretical framework would not be complete without referring to the boom period. The latter is a short-term phenomenon that "lives a precarious life" (Minsky 1975a: 115), during which a free-market economy is close to full employment and is led by "lenders (and borrowers too) [who] systematically underestimate the increase in risk as borrowers' leverage rises and as near-term debt payments balloon in relation to near-term expected income flows" (Carter 1989: 782). For Minsky, even if this period is short, it is essential:

> In this interpretation the boom is critical; it builds an ever-more-demanding liability structure on the base of a cash-flow foundation consisting of the prospective yields of capital assets, which are, because of technology and the

limited ability to squeeze workers' real wages, at best constrained ultimately to grow at a steady rate in real terms. The debt base, which grows at an accelerating rate during a boom, is not so constrained.

(Minsky 1975a: 142–143)

The idea behind the boom period is, therefore, that the sum of the net cash inflows from income operations and cash inflows from balance-sheet operations cannot grow as fast as the cash outflows from financial commitments without generating inflation (in output or asset markets). Therefore, at full employment, a free-market economy will be subject to an "inflation barrier" due to real constraints that can only be removed by technological progress, by a better training of workers, or by limiting the growth of nominal wages and other incomes. This inflationary pressure will be built up in financial contracts, and the economy will become more sensitive to the realization of price expectations, which will lead to a crisis when the expectations are not realized and refinancing needs cannot be met.

In an economy with a big government that applies an Employer of Last Resort program (Minsky (1986a); Wray (1997a, 1998a, 1998b); Mitchell (1998); Mitchell and Watts (2004); Fullwiler (2007)), an income policy, and follows a functional finance approach to fiscal policy (Lerner 1943, 1944), the inflationary pressures would be dampened. In this case, aggregate profit would increase only with improvements in the production capacity of the economy because additional total spending would be forthcoming only when it would not generate inflation. In an economy in which the preceding type of government does not exist, output-price inflation leads to a large tightening of fiscal and monetary policies,[6] which squeezes profits on both sides (demand and financial cost) and can precipitate a crisis.

The importance of real constraints and productivity in the determination of aggregate profit, therefore, is not related to a Neoclassical foundation of the nature of profit. It is related to the problem of "inflation barrier," which, if unchecked, leads to financial instability, and, if checked correctly, imposes a constraint on aggregate spending so that it grows only with the improvement in the capacity of production. On the other hand, the growth of financial commitments is potentially unlimited and, as shown earlier, banks may have an incentive to grow their assets rapidly in order to maintain a certain net profit rate. Thus, a constraint on the growth of bank assets must also be implemented to maintain a stable full-employment situation.

Another factor that enters into consideration during the boom is the widespread external funding of purely financial activities like "corporate maneuverings, takeovers, mergers and conglomerate expansions that characterize the boom" (Minsky 1975a: 89). Also, during this period, "households will become more willing to use more debt to own shares, bankers will be more willing to finance such 'margin' purchases of shares" (Minsky 1975a: 112). These kinds of activities increase the amount of cash commitments without financing or funding any potential increase in national income, they are based on collateral-oriented loans rather than cash-flow oriented loans. The capacity to meet cash commitments rests on an expected realization of capital gains. Thus, price speculation may spread to all sectors of the economy as both product markets and financial markets become more dependent on the realization of a bonanza via capital gains from asset-price and output-price increases.

Finally, the boom also matters because, as it proceeds, the pool of high quality borrowers shrinks and to maintain their market share bankers need to expand their business toward more risky loans. In addition, the boom makes hedge positions more fragile by making them more dependent on the realization of unreasonable expectations (Minsky 1977c: 144). For example, all investment projects may be highly profitable, may be expected to be highly profitable, and may be hedge-financed even late during the boom. However, if this profitability rests heavily on the continuation of output inflation (even moderate) rather than growth in customers, and if, for example, the Treasury starts to tighten its policies to fight inflation, some projects suddenly will become speculative or even Ponzi.

If the boom matters, however, it can only explain the acceleration of the financial weakening of financial positions but cannot explain the emergence of a progressive weakening of financial positions. As Minsky recognizes:

> Even though a prolonged expansion, *dominated by private demand*, will bring about a transformation of portfolios and changes in asset structures conducive to financial crises, the transformations in portfolios that take place under euphoric conditions sharply accentuate such trends. [...] Thus, the theory of financial stability takes into account two aspects of the behavior of capitalist economy. The first is the evolution of the financial structure over a prolonged expansion [...]. The second consists of the financial impacts over a short period due to the existence of highly optimistic, euphoric economy; the euphoric economy is a natural consequence of the economy doing well over a prolonged period.
>
> (Minsky 1972b: 119, italics added)

A monetary economy will become fragile in the first place because of the way borrowing and lending activities are conducted in an uncertain world. The boom, or euphoric period, only precipitates the turning point that would occur anyway, unless economic growth was driven by governmental expenditures (or, more generally, the economic unit issuing the top IOU). This last point is very important:

> During a protracted expansion dominated by household and business deficits the ratio of household and business financial commitments to income rises, whereas in an expansion dominated by government deficits the ratio of private commitments to income decreases.
>
> (Minsky 1963b: 412)

Economic growth, therefore, will not generate a weakening of the financial positions of private units if it is based on government programs that continuously inject safe assets in the balance sheets of private units (Minsky 1980b: 518;

Lavoie 1986). The long period of financial stability in the United States after Second World War is an example of the impact of highly liquid balance sheets due to large government spending (Minsky 1983a: 272).

Financial structure, inflation, employment, and policy

One last important point of Minsky's theory concerns the impact of all the preceding for inflation and employment. At the theoretical level, there are two important points. First, in the tradition of Keynes, full employment equilibrium (let alone stable full employment equilibrium) is not a natural outcome of a free-market capitalist economy. One of the main roles of the government is, thus, to promote stable full employment. A second point is that inflation does not necessarily have monetary origins:

> Monetary abundance and monetary growth are not, in and of themselves, sufficient cause of rapid inflation.
>
> (Minsky 1983b: 110)

Additional conditions are necessary and among them are a fragile financial structure, an inappropriate fiscal policy (e.g. too large deficits), and policy goals that are oriented toward growth rather than full employment (Minsky 1975a: 164–166, 1983b). This last cause is important because it shows that Minsky divorced the goal of full employment from the goal of economic growth. These goals should be pursued independently.

Given the structural flaws of the capitalist system, authorities can choose among three solutions (Minsky 1962): let the debt-deflation process go, stagflation, or full-employment policy. The last two prevent deflation, but growth-oriented policies promote stagflation and so are not ideal. Therefore, at the practical level the role of the government is not to promote maximum growth but stable full employment (growth should be encouraged but within the goal of increasing the standard of living of all, and not just for the sake of growing to make more profit without considerations for economic and environmental stability). In terms of central banking, the goal is to promote a strong financial structure (Minsky 1978 (1985): 27, 1986a) by discouraging the use of speculative finance through a flexible capital-requirement policy, which limits the growth of the leverage ratio (A/E) of banks; an asset-management policy that limits the growth of risky assets relative to safe assets and so the growth of Π_n/A; and other policies that control the growth of banks' equity and the liabilities (off and on balance sheet) that can be issued by banks (Minsky 1975b: 330ff., 1986a: 243, 318ff.). This central bank policy should be part of the broader strategy of maintaining stable full employment (in the sense of a zero percent unemployment rate).

Davidson (1978: 417–418) and Minsky (1986a: 328) note that the promotion of a hedge financial structure might not be good because it may decrease aggregate demand, and Pollin and Dymski (1994) have shown that a big-government era leads to smoother but slower economic growth.[7] Minsky is conscious of that, but he puts forward at least two reasons why this is the best policy. First, a strong financial structure increases the effectiveness of monetary and fiscal policy by limiting the moral hazard generated by the existence of a floor on profits and asset prices (Minsky 1972b, 1985). Indeed, with a strong financial structure, it is possible to have "a depression without a depression" (Minsky 1975b: 350, 1975d: 12), that is to say, the good financial effects of a depression (increase in prudence, increase in the liquidity of portfolios, decrease in leveraging) without the negative effects (widespread bankruptcies, high unemployment, wastage). On the contrary, with a fragile financial structure, the floors have to be put higher ("premature" lender of last resort intervention and countercyclical fiscal policy) and this may prevent the restoration of sound financial practices (Minsky 1963b: 411, 1972b: 132, 1977b (1977): 26, 1983b: 118). Second, inflation is far more difficult to deal with in a fragile environment because inflation expectations are incorporated into the expectations of cash inflows and so the normal financial structure (Minsky 1975a: 140–141).

A full-employment policy in a capitalist economy is the best way to fight poverty by providing a guaranteed access to a job (Minsky 1965b, 1965c, 1966, 1973; Davidson 1968c; Bell and Wray 2004).[8] In addition, a full-employment policy also helps to stabilize an economy by providing an income buffer to people laid off from the private sector. In the end, therefore, a stabilization policy that includes the containment of financial crisis and the guidance of the financial practices, as well as an employer of last resort program, an income policy,[9] and a socialization of investments, is the best policy package today (Minsky 1975a, 1983a, 1986a). The stabilization policy aims at constraining directly the growth of private and public expenditures to a level consistent with the growth of capacity of production, while guaranteeing access to a job independently of the state of the economy.

This stabilization policy, however, is limited in its effectiveness because a stabilization policy has "pitfalls" (Minsky 1983b). Indeed, successful policies change the responses to policy, big government generates inflationary pressures, and the stabilization of some variables destabilizes other dimensions. Here again, at the policy level, we find the dialectical approach that exists in Minsky's analysis (Pollin and Dymski 1994: 373). Thus, regulation always has to adapt; there are no definitive solutions or rules that guarantee stability (Minsky 1975a: 168, 1989b: 19):

> The only universal rule for Federal Reserve policy is that it cannot be dictated by any universal rule.
>
> (Minsky 1977c: 152)

Individual behaviors (psychological factors), social valuation (social factors), profit-seeking behaviors and competition for monetary accumulation (economic factors), fine-tuning and inadequate regulation and supervision (policy factors) will always have the tendency to promote instability in a capitalist economy, and the authorities have to take this into account (Papadimitriou and Wray 1997).

The dynamics of Minsky's framework: The financial instability hypothesis

On the basis of all the preceding points, Minsky established what he called the Financial Instability Hypothesis (Minsky 1977b, 1978, 1986a). Its earliest version dates from the early 1960s in the form of three hypotheses (Minsky 1964a: 175). First, the behavior of real variables depends on the financial structure of the economy, which reflects the past history of the economy. Second, the likelihood of a financial crisis also depends on the financial structure of the economy. Third, the financial structure becomes more and more unstable during an expansion.

The aim of this Financial Instability Hypothesis is to show that the normal functioning of "a capitalist economy endogenously generates a financial structure which is susceptible to financial crises" (Minsky 1977b (1977): 25). Thus, it is important to explain how the financial structure of the economy (or a sector) changes. This implies studying how it is affected by the prevailing convention regarding the appropriate balance-sheet and cash-flow structures, and by the developments in the production and financial sides of economy. Both the expectational and actual sides of the economy affect its financial structure.

The logic of this hypothesis is that during a prosperous economic period, there are forces that progressively lead the economy from conservative financial positions (hedge positions) to positions in which the articulation of cash flows is high and balance sheets are illiquid and highly leveraged (Minsky 1986a: 210–211):

> The logic of this theorem is twofold. First, within a financial structure that is dominated by hedge finance, there will be a plentiful supply of short-term funds, so that short-term financing is "cheaper" than long-term financing. Accordingly, firms will be tempted to engage in speculative finance. Second, over a period of good times, the financial markets will become less averse to risk. This leads to the proliferation of financing forms that involve closer coordination of cash flows out with cash flows in – that is, narrower safety margins and greater use of speculative and Ponzi financing.
>
> (Minsky 1986b: 5)

The economy, therefore, becomes more sensitive to changes in incomes, cash commitments, and asset prices, and depends more on the availability of refinancing sources. An interruption in the channels that usually provide refinancing sources generates a liquidation process, which, if it spreads and is not controlled by built-in stabilizers, leads to large decreases in asset prices. This generates feedback effects on economic activities related to production by affecting net wealth (and so collateral values), entrepreneur's risk, as well as the lender's risk. This effect on production in turn affects the financial system and leads to further downturns.

The essential conclusion of the hypothesis is that market mechanisms cannot lead to sustained full-employment with stable prices, which leads to two theorems: the anti-laissez faire theorem and the performance theorem (Ferri and

Minsky 1992: 87–89). The first theorem implies that a "big" government (that is, a government large enough to sustain aggregate profit in case non-government spending drops, and to put a floor on asset prices) is necessary to have an economy "where freedom to innovate and to finance is the rule" (Minsky 1993b: 81). Individual economic freedom and big government are complementary not conflicting elements. The second theorem means that not only does a free market economy not generate to full employment, but, in addition, it has a tendency to generate deep and long economic depressions: free-market capitalism is self-destructive.

There are two main dynamics in the Minskian analysis. One concerns the change in the acceptable and desired financial leverages, i.e. the expectational side, and the other concerns what happens actually in the economy, i.e. the actual side of the economy. For each side, it is the articulation between cash flows that drives the dynamics; therefore, it is the one that should be studied in detail. This is done, following Minsky, in the context of investment decisions by entrepreneurs. The analysis, however, could be done for all economic activities that need external funds (from consumption to speculation in financial markets).

Business cycle and convention: The expectational side of the economy

When making their "fundamental speculative decisions," individuals have to decide what the normal leveraging of expectations is. In terms of cash flows, this means that individuals have to decide what the normal relationship between expected cash commitments and expected cash inflows from gross operational income should be. For the firm sector, assuming to simplify that $Q = E(\Pi)$, with Π the gross profit, we have

$$cc_n \equiv E(CC)/E(\Pi).$$

This ratio is the normal leveraging ratio of profit, or normal flow-leveraging ratio. This ratio can be elaborated a little bit more. Indeed, one part of $E(CC)$ is certain and includes cash outflows induced by past financial commitments that depend on the characteristics of existing liabilities. The other part of cc_n is the expected additional cash commitments induced by the expected external funding of investment (Minsky 1975a: 110). Therefore,

$$E(CC) \equiv CC + E(\Delta CC).$$

Thus

$$cc_n \equiv CC/E(\Pi) + E(\Delta CC)/E(\Pi).$$

Depending on the type of activity, the economic units involved in the determination of the preceding ratio would change, but for investment funding and capital-asset-holding decisions, it is the entrepreneurs' and bankers' conventions that matter (Minsky 1975a: 112). More formally, expectations are bounded by what is considered to be reasonable/normal by the most pessimistic economic sector:

$$cc_n = \min(cc_d, cc_a),$$

where cc_d represents the desired flow-leveraging ratio (determined by the entrepreneurs' convention), and cc_a represents the acceptable flow-leveraging ratio (determined by the banking system). Thus, cc_n is a convention; it represents what economic units think is a normal way to fund externally economic activity, and so is a target that they try to reach either by decreasing or by increasing external funding. It is a concrete expression of risk aversion and perceived uncertainty.

All this leads to the determination of what economic actors consider to be the appropriate liability structure, and so a level of expected borrowing: "Acceptable liability structures are based upon some margin of safety" (Minsky 1977b (1977): 24). The expected change in CC is determined by the expected external funding of investment. If i represents the interest rate and a is the amortization rate we have

$$E(\Delta CC) = (i+a)E(\Delta L_I).$$

Therefore, knowing the definition of cc_n and of $E(\Delta CC)$

$$E(\Delta L_I) = \frac{E(\Delta CC)}{(i+a)} = \left(cc_n - \frac{CC}{E(\Pi)}\right) \cdot \frac{E(\Pi)}{(i+a)}.$$

So

$$E(\Delta L_I) = \left(cc_n - cc \cdot \frac{\Pi}{E(\Pi)}\right) \cdot \frac{E(\Pi)}{(i+a)}.$$

Thus, the expected external funding of investment depends on two factors. The first represents the borrowing power, that is, the difference between the normal flow-leveraging ratio and the current flow-leveraging ratio ($cc \equiv CC/\Pi$). The latter is adjusted by the ratio between current expectations of profit and current profit.[10] If $\Pi_t > E_t(\Pi)$, it means that entrepreneurs are bearish about future economic activity and so they wish to decrease their use of external funds. The second central element is the state of long-term expectations regarding quasi-rents discounted by the unit cost of external funds.

Flow-leveraging ratios and cash-flow margins are the same thing. One, however, should be aware of their inverse implications for economic activity. Indeed, a lower cc is equivalent to a higher actual cash-flow margin, which means that an economic unit is more liquid, which is good for investment. A lower cc_n represents a higher normal cash-flow margin, that is, bankers and

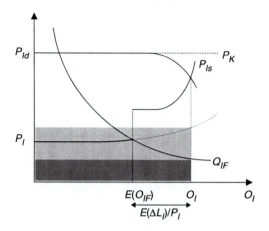

Figure 5.3 Determination of the level of expected external funding.

entrepreneurs have more conservative criteria of decision, which is bad for investment.

Now that this clarification has been made, the preceding can be represented graphically in Figure 5.3. The expected level of external funding will pay for part of the desired investment goods (light gray area), and entrepreneurs expect that a proportion of desired investment, determined by the dark gray area, will be paid for by internal funds.

As hinted above, and developed below, the previous formula should be used to determine the proportion of external funding, not the desired level of investment. The latter is explained independently of its desired funding structure by production considerations, given monetary profit expectations and given $P_K > P_I$. However, the desired funding structure may ration nominal investment below the desired nominal investment.

Minsky's view of the business cycle is presented in detail in *John Maynard Keynes* and is crucial to understand how cc_n changes. Figure 5.4 shows the essential points at each stage of the business cycle. The leading element is a convention about the appropriate use of leverage. Over a period of prolonged expansion, the normal flow-leveraging ratio always goes up, reflecting a loosening in the conventions concerning what can be considered as a "viable" economic project. This tendency is rooted in the psychological and social factors determining economic decisions, in the fact that expansion means a history of success and so a higher intrinsic creditworthiness of borrowers, as well as in the competitive nature of the capitalist economic system. The decline in the acceptable margins of safety is not related at all to irrationality; it is rooted in the dynamics generated by a period of expansion during which borrowers' projects perform well because of the dynamism of the economy.

Crisis: (Minsky 1975a: 124, 127, 143)
"A sharp change occurs when position making by refinancing breaks down."
$\Delta Y < 0$ (large or not) or change in the convention about leveraging: leveraging is
dangerous $\Rightarrow$ increase in the demand for money as a store of value.
↓

Debt-deflation: (Minsky 1975a: 126, 128)
Liquidation of assets and repayment of debts are the first priorities of economic units.
$\Delta Y << 0$ and $\Delta PA << 0$ (and so wealth and collateral decrease).
Convention: "the guiding wisdom is that debts are to be avoided, for debts lead to disaster."
↓

Stagnation: (Minsky 1975a: 126, 128)
Economic units are traumatized.
Convention: "the guiding wisdom is that debts are to be avoided, for debts lead to disaster."
↓

"As subjective repercussions of the debt-deflation wear off, as disinvestment occurs,
and as financial positions are rebuilt."
↓

Recovery: (Minsky 1975a: 127)
"Strong memory of the penalty" induced by past behaviors.
Liability structures are "purged of debt."
Convention: prudence/ "wise" use of the leverage.
↓

Expansion: (Minsky 1975a: 127)
"Over time the memory of the past disaster is eroded."
"Success breeds daring" and "more adventurous financing of investment pays off to the leaders."
This gives the incentive to those who used "wisely" the leverage to follow the previous units
who dared to challenge the convention.
Convention: the leverage is a convenient way to increase profit.
↓

The expansion "will, at an accelerating rate, feed into a boom."
↓

Boom: (Minsky 1975a: 128)
The economy is close to full employment.
The "current generation of economic soothsayers will proclaim that business cycle
has been banished from the land and a new era of permanent prosperity has been inaugurated."
+ "new policy instruments" + "great sophistication of the economic scientists advising on
policy " $\Rightarrow$ "crises and debt-deflations are now things of the past." $\Rightarrow$ "Debts can be taken on"
Convention: the leverage is not risky and provides automatically great monetary rewards.

DESTABILIZING

Figure 5.4 Business cycle and change in leveraging convention.

During a sustained expansion and the boom, cc_n increases as most economic
units, persuaded by "gurus" and other "experts" and pushed by competitive
pressures to conform, believe that the economy has reached a "new era:"

> Economic history is a useful guide in this respect. [...] In fact, each downturn
> was preceded by a period of non-inflationary growth exuberant enough to lead
> many commentators to suggest that a "new era" had arrived.
> (Bank of International Settlements 2007: 139)

This "new economy" convention leads one to believe that leveraging is safe and
always provides great returns. Only "stupid" people would think the contrary, and
the success of others seems to confirm the "stupidity" of skeptic individuals. In
a growing economy, therefore, the normal cash-flow margin of, first, the leading

economic sector, and then other economic sectors, will go down. On the contrary, when the "new era" convention is questioned and proved wrong, cc_n goes down and then stays low as nobody is ready to leverage highly, or at all, expectations of gross cash flows. This generates a more or less deep economic crisis, depending on the degree of leveraging and the impact on expectations. In terms of the equation presented above, if $E(\Delta L_I)/I$ is not significant, then changes in cc_n will not have a big impact on I, Π and so the liquidity of the firm sector.

Changes in cc_n change the borrowing power of an economic unit. If it decreases, this may have detrimental effects on the economy through several channels. First, the number of investment projects that can be implemented diminishes as it is expected[11] that some of them can only be implemented by requiring an "excessive" amount of external funds, which affects adversely aggregate investment and so aggregate profit via Kalecki's equation of profit. More generally, all activities that require external funding are affected adversely by a decline in cc_n. Second, refinancing possibilities also shrink, and when the economy has high refinancing needs, this generates a financial crisis as massive forced liquidations are necessary to meet cash commitments. Eventually, therefore, a decrease in the state of long-term expectations may have some dramatic consequences on production and employment if the financial positions of economic agents are fragile (Minsky 1975a, 1986a; Davidson 1993, 1994). Expectational side and actual side are intertwined.

As stated earlier, the mechanism through which this expectational side works has been modified now that we have moved to an "originate and distribute" banking model. A prolonged expansion still leads to a decline in the margins of safety but it does so with two additional novelties. First, the decline proceeds at an accelerated pace because of the incentives of banks and credit-rating agencies to emulate overestimation of creditworthiness in order to stimulate the distribution of structured financial instruments. Second, credit enhancement techniques like credit subordination, excess spread, and overcollateralization allow structured financial instruments like private-label mortgage-backed securities to have a tranche with AAA credit rating, even though the incomes received come from junk assets (Adelson 2006). Thus, a high proportion of Ponzi financing may exist from the very beginning of the expansion. Given this last point, a prolonged period of expansion may no longer be necessary to explain the dynamics of acceptable leveraging ratios. All that is necessary is a favorable trend of the prices of the assets underlying the Ponzi financing process. If prices stop growing fast enough to generate a positive net present value, there is an adverse change in price expectations. Recent developments in the housing market provide a clear example of this kind of dynamics (Kregel 2008).

The actual side of the economy

The expectational side may be the only one necessary to generate fragility, but it is also good to show that there is a higher articulation of actual cash flows so that refinancing needs increase. On the actual side, macroeconomic forces may make microeconomic desires self-defeating. The paradox of thrift is a famous example of this type of situation. Minsky was aware of this (Minsky 1975a: 107, 113, 1980b: 518, 1986a: 211–213), but he showed that macroeconomic processes are a central mechanism to explain the financial weakening of the economy. There are, moreover, additional forces that lead to a financial weakening of the economy. All those forces are presented below, starting with what can be called the paradox of leverage.

THE PARADOX OF LEVERAGE

This paradox has been put forward by Steindl (1952: 107ff.) and more recently by Lavoie (1995, 1996b, 1997a, 2006) and is present in Minsky's framework. At the aggregate level, profit is endogenously determined by the level of investment. This implies that higher investment spending leads to higher profit and so a lower dependence on external funds. Similarly, lower investment leads to lower profit and so higher dependence on external funds. Thus, the debt-to-equity ratio may not behave according to the will of entrepreneurs, e.g. a willingness to reduce the dependence on external funds may lead to lower investment and so lower profit, which increases the dependence on external funds. As a consequence, expectations may be "frustrated" (Minsky 1975a: 114, 1986a: 213) and during a period of economic growth, this leads to a decline in the lender's risk and entrepreneurs' risk, which "reinforces the willingness of firms and bankers to debt-finance further increases in investment" (Minsky 1975a: 114). Therefore, the following process is at work at the macroeconomic level:

1 Entrepreneurs expect flows of quasi-rent Q to be sufficient "after taxes, and after [their] required payments on [their] debts and [their] dividends to stockholders" (Minsky 1975a: 107) to fund $E(O_{IF})$: $Q_{IF} = Q - t_\Pi Q - CC$. This expected flow Q is largely independent of current gross profit.
2 To fund a desired level of investment, entrepreneurs have to determine a funding plan. They have a flow-leveraging ratio cc_d that reflects the willingness to debt-finance their activities. If $cc_d > 0$, entrepreneurs go to banks or financial markets. cc_d depends on past experience, uncertainty, and risk preference.
3 This cc_d is compared to cc and to the acceptable leverage ratio cc_a defined by the financial community (Minsky 1975a: 109–112). If $cc < cc_d < cc_a$, the desired external funding plan is "carried through" (Minsky 1975a: 114). If $cc < cc_a < cc_d$ there is some credit-rationing.
4 Entrepreneurs anticipate the cash-flow Q by investing today through an application of the funding plan that allows buying $P_I O_I$, which may be inferior or equal to $P_I O_{Id}$.
5 This generates an aggregate profit Π from which derives the Π_{IF}-curve.
6 If $\Pi_{IFt}(I) > Q_{IFt-1}$, the funding plan that entrepreneurs wanted to apply is "frustrated." A higher proportion of investment goods can be funded internally, and ΔCC, and so CC, is lower than expected.

7   This good surprise increases the willingness to fund externally a given level of investment expenditure (the desired proportion of external funding increases): $\Delta cc_d > 0$ and $\Delta cc_a > 0$, and therefore, $\Delta cc_n > 0$.

8   The unused leverage, $cc_n - cc$, can be used for future investments, and competition and incentives push managers to use this unused leverage as long as uncertainty is low, and as long as expected sales justify an increase in production capacity.

9   As cc_n grows, Π tends to grow less rapidly than I and CC (Minsky 1975a: 114). Thus, overtime, cc increases even though this may not happen during the whole expansion, especially at the beginning of the business cycle.

Therefore, there is what can be called a paradox of leverage because Q is determined at the micro-level, whereas Π is determined at the macro-level: the higher the willingness to fund investment externally, the lower the proportion of external funding of investment is. This paradox does not mean that all firms are affected but concerns the average financial situation of firms. This paradox is essential to understand why the boom can emerge, because if economic actors could understand the macroeconomic consequences of their decisions (if they had rational expectations in the mainstream sense of the term), then they would not be frustrated, and they would not have an incentive to become more daring (at least up to a point because psychologists have shown that just meeting expectations boosts confidence). In this case, there would not be any financial weakening on the actual side induced by the expectational side. This provides another illustration that Minsky's approach does not rely on asymmetry of information. The mechanism at work is a lack of understanding of macroeconomic forces by individuals. All individuals assume that their own isolated economic experiences (capacity to run a business and others) provide a good background to understand the behavior of the whole economy. However, they usually ignore in their analysis the role of macroeconomic interdependences, i.e. how the spending by some of them affects the incomes of others, which in turn affects them back through indirect and lagged feedback loops. The ignorance by individuals of the social implications of their personal decisions is at the core of the Minskian dynamics.

There is, however, a point that is left unexplained in the paradox of leverage. It has been shown why cc_n would go up during a prolonged expansion, but Point 9 did not show clearly how cc would grow over time, that is, why the growth rate of profit is lower than that of cash commitments after a prolonged economic growth, which is a central point of the Minskian analysis (Minsky 1995: 201, 1974: 270). To explain this, one needs to look at other forces that weaken the economy during the expansion.

INCOME GROWTH VERSUS CASH-COMMITMENT GROWTH

Other forces that operate at the actual level in the expansionary period can be separated into categories: those related to the decline in the rate of growth of aggregate gross income and those related to the increase in the rate of growth of cash commitments. Here again we will focus on the firm sector.

The decrease or deceleration of the gross profit after tax as the economy grows can be explained by looking at each element of the Kalecki profit equation. Following the same technique as chapter 2, the growth of gross profit after tax is (assuming to simplify that corporate taxes are based on gross profit):

$$g_\Pi = (g_I s_I - g_{Sw} s_{Sw} + g_G s_G - g_T s_T + g_X s_X - g_J s_J)/s_\Pi,$$

where s_i is the share of variable i in GDP. During a period of expansion, several things may happen to each growth rate. First, investment may grow at a slower path, or go down and the share of investment in the economy may decline. This is so either because the cost of external funds goes up through higher interest rates, lower maturities and other loan requirements, or because optimism cannot maintain its impact on the growth of profit expectations and the decrease in the perceived risk, or because markets saturate. Second, as income goes up, the saving of workers may accelerate. This second channel may not apply if consumption out of wealth is large enough and consumption is speculatively funded. For Minsky, consumption is usually hedge funded; however, with the development of credit cards and other forms of consumer loans, consumption has become more prone to speculative finance over the past thirty years (Minsky 1980a (1982): 32, 1995; Palley 1994). All this may lead to a negative growth rate of households' saving to the point where the share of saving in GDP became nil or even negative (Brown 2007; Tymoigne 2007a), which boosts aggregate profit. There is, however, a limit to the capacity of households to grow their indebtedness based on negative saving. The third factor that can put a downward pressure on profit is the trade balance. This influence will depend on what drives economic growth in the country. If the country has a strategy of export-led growth, the share of the trade balance is positive, and so there is no adverse effect on profit as the economy grows other than possible market saturation or adverse developments in other countries. On the contrary, if economic growth is led by consumption and investment, the share of imports may grow at a faster rate and may represent a bigger share of GDP than exports, which has a negative impact on profit growth. Finally, one of the central forces that put a downward pressure on aggregate profit is the tendency for government deficit to go down during the expansion in order to fine-tune the economy or to meet "the imperative of balancing the budget," or because sustained expansion leads to higher tax receipts and lower government expenditures due to the built-in stabilizers.

We now turn to the factors that affect the growth of cash commitments. The level of cash commitment is composed of the unit cost of external funds and the level of outstanding liabilities:

$$CC = (a_O + i_O)L_O + (a_{NO} + i_{NO})L_{NO},$$

or, noting s_O the share of debts issued to finance and to fund production-related activities and s_{NO} the share of debts issued for purely financial activities:

$$CC = [(a_O + i_O)s_O + (a_{NO} + i_{NO})s_{NO}]L.$$

Therefore, the growth rate of cash commitments is

$$g_{CC} = g_u + g_L,$$

with $u = a + i$ the average unit cost of debts[12] and L the total amount of outstanding debts ($L = L_O + L_{NO}$). One can see that four factors affect the growth of cash commitments: two price-related factors and two volume-related factors. Starting with the latter, they are composed of liabilities created to finance and to fund the production effort of the economy (L_O), and other activities (L_{NO}). As the economy grows, refinancing loans and other purely financial maneuvering activities may grow.[13] These activities add a debt burden without generating any actual or potential increase in Π (Minsky 1975a; Lavoie 1986). Leaving aside the refinancing component of L_{NO}, Minsky argues that during a long expansionary period and a boom period, there is a "reciprocating stimulus – a positive feedback – between speculation on the exchanges and speculation by firms" (Minsky 1975a: 90). The success on the production side of the economy leads to optimism in financial markets, higher leveraging of positions by borrowing from brokers, and greater use of idle reserves and liquid assets (Minsky 1975a: 121–123, 1977c: 147). Concentrating on the refinancing side of L_{NO}, refinancing activities increase over time because of economic incentives (in terms of costs and rewards) to include refinancing operations in funding plans (Minsky 1975b: 317ff., 1986a: 213, 1993b: 80–81). A first incentive is the interest rate differential (Minsky 1986a: 201, 211). Indeed, a shortening of maturity leads, for the same amount borrowed, to a lower interest payment ($\Delta iL < 0$) and a higher principal payment ($\Delta aL > 0$). As long as the maturity is not too short to offset completely the interest-payment gain obtained from borrowing short-term, it is cheaper to ask short-term credits. However, a shorter maturity implies that it is necessary to recontract more often so that the sensitivity to adverse changes in financial conditions increases. A second force is the nature of banks. As stated earlier, banks, because of the nature of their balance sheet and competitive pressures, are speculative units and promote speculative financial structures. Finally, the innovation process may lead to a shortening of the maturity of debt contracts, this is especially the case in periods during which there is a "scarcity" of "clearing money" as reflected by its high cost (Minsky 1985a). Thus, one may conclude that the growth of purely financial operations has both volume and price effects on CC by increasing L_{NO} and a. These financial operations do not need to be driven by speculative mania. They can be the results of the normal production process. As the Circuit theory shows, in the simplest macro model, a sufficient condition for the emergence of refinancing needs for firms is households' desire to keep part of their saving in monetary form (Davidson 1978; Lavoie 1987, 1992; Parguez 1984). In this case, the short-term advances granted at the beginning of the production process to pay for wages and raw materials cannot be reimbursed completely. Banks must accept to rollover the short-term debts not reimbursed for the economic process to continue.

Turning to the price-related factors, as the economy and optimism grow, the amortization rate also grows for all types of economic activities (Minsky 1986a, 1995). Indeed, it is assumed, by optimistic bankers and entrepreneurs, that good results will come soon, and so that shorter maturity terms can be accepted. In addition, toward the end of the expansion if the liquidity preference of bankers increases, a also increases. Finally, over a prolonged expansion, interest rates may tend to rise for all maturities. This rise in interest rates is not explained by the loanable funds theory or the exogeneity of the money supply. First, we know that lending and borrowing activities are based on margins of safety, the latter being determined by conventions prevailing in the economy. If these margins are satisfied and actual margins continue to worsen, then, unless conventions change, there will be an increase in interest rates on debt contracts. This is related to the principle of increasing risk. Thus, one reason for the rise in interest rates would be that the convention of bankers has a tendency to loosen less rapidly than others. As shown earlier, bankers are the skeptics of the game, making it easier for cc_a to become inferior to cc.

Second, while the economy is still growing, earnings may fall short of what was expected. This, following Keynes (1930), puts an upward pressure on interest rate as bearishness spreads in financial markets (Ertuk 2006a, 2006b). The more prolonged an expansion, the easier it is for results to fall short of Wall Street's expectations as market-growth meets several constraints (Sterman 2000) and as expected results become less accommodative of a possible downturn, or even deceleration, in sales.

A third factor that promotes a rise in interest rates is the inelasticity of loan demand to interest rates. Indeed, the refinancing process creates a need for funds, whatever the rates of interest are. In a Ponzi position, this need grows over time, and it grows at an accelerating rate as interest rates increase and maturity decreases. In this kind of situation, unless the Ponzi process sustains an activity that ultimately will increase the cash generating power of a unit (and will grow this power to a rate superior to the growth of cash outflows), the accelerating deterioration of balance sheets will make banks more and more reluctant to lend, given the banking convention.

Fourth, monetary policy plays an important role in the rise of interest rates as the expansion proceeds:

> For interest rates not to rise during an investment boom, the supply of finance must be infinitely elastic, which implies either that a flood of financial innovation is taking place or that the central bank is supplying reserves in unlimited amounts.
>
> (Minsky 1982a: 33)

Because of the inflation barrier, the central bank may tighten its policy, which "almost always means a rise in interest rates" (Minsky 1975b: 333). Given the state of financial innovations and the liquidity preference of banks and financial-market participants, this rise in policy rates is transmitted to other interest rates, and this transmission occurs immediately if interest rates are variable. As shown in chapter 4, there is a very high correlation, and even Granger causality, between the central bank rate and other interest rates.

OTHER FACTORS THAT LEAD TO NEGATIVE NCF_O

In addition to the paradox of leverage and the forces that tend to generate an economic situation that leads $g_{CC} > g_\Pi$, there are additional factors that may lead to a situation where $\Pi < CC$, that is, that generate a dependence on position-making operations. Two extensive studies (Minsky 1964a: 252–262, 1975a: 73, 87–88, 115) suggest several reasons: (1) deliberate choice ($Q < E(CC)$), (2) errors of expectations, (3) losses of income, (4) rising labor cost, (5) higher cost of refinancing, (6) exercise of demand options, (7) exercise of contingent liabilities, and (8) decline in asset prices or malfunctioning of a market.

The first reason why an economic unit may need to refinance its position is because it chose a financial structure that incorporates the need to refinance. The reasons why economic units may want to do so have been explained before. This does not result from irrational behaviors (Minsky 1982a: 33). A second reason for the existence of refinancing needs is because the expectations of NCF_O are not realized, or are off the margin of error included in the decision process. As noted earlier, Q is equal to $E(\Pi) - \theta\sigma_\Pi$, which needs to be compared to $E(CC)$. The margin of errors $\theta\sigma_\Pi$ has a tendency to shrink during the expansionary process as θ goes down (because of increased confidence). This leads to a greater possibility of non-realization of expectations, and so a higher chance of downward correction of expectations, a reduction in investment, and lower profit (which accentuates the problem). In addition, unrealistic expectations during a euphoric state makes $E(\Pi)$ unlikely not to be realized, making even hedged financing units potentially more fragile. The third reason is due to unexpected delays or interruptions in inflows of cash because of reasons not under the control of an economic unit, like defaults of its debtors or unemployment. In an economy in which the layering of financial decisions is high, this channel reflects the possibility of a systemic risk. The fourth and fifth reasons are related to an increase in factor costs. As the economy tends toward full employment, and especially if unions are strong and their demands are not tamed by income policies and if financing is available (Minsky 1986a: 259, 1975a: 163–164), workers will have more power to raise and to meet their demands. Also, as shown earlier, the cost of refinancing in terms of interest rate and amortization speed tends to increase. If firms can pass along these higher costs on to their prices, their financial condition will not worsen but will depend on the maintenance of an inflationary process and so a bonanza. Reasons six and seven are linked to the nature of financial contracts. Demand debts may lead to a sudden large increase in the cash commitments by their issuers. The typical example is the run on banks.

A final reason that can lead to a refinancing need is related to both the cash-flow and stock impacts that asset prices entail. In terms of cash-flow, as shown earlier, liquidation is not a solution at the aggregate level and the malfunctioning of financial markets prevents a smooth liquidation process at the individual level, which affects the cash received from strategic and position-making portfolio operations. The second impact of decreasing asset prices is a decline in the net wealth of all economic units holding these assets, which affects their creditworthiness and so their access to external funds.

Factors limiting the financial weakening of the economy

There are several limits to the progress of financial weakening during the expansion, which means that Minsky's theory is not deterministic (Minsky 1986a: 211–213). Sometimes the weakening may stop or may never happen on any sides (actual or expectational). First, there are some financial limits to what can happen. These financial limits work at two different levels. Entrepreneurs will not show to bankers projects that they do not find profitable (Wolfson 1996). Therefore, as long as entrepreneurs are "conservative" they will not engage in, or will limit strongly their use of, speculative financing and funding. This is not, however, the main element that prevents financial weakening. One essential brake is the lender's risk, especially through its impact on credit rationing. Indeed, loan officers play a crucial role in determining the relevance of the positions taken, and are aware of "Bill Janeway's first law, 'Entrepreneurs lie'" (Minsky 1990d: 59, 1989c: 177, n. 10). A second factor is related to the innovative process. Indeed, there is a "financial innovations barrier" (Minsky 1986a: 212, n. 15) that puts limits on what can be financed and funded profitably. A third factor that limits the weakening is related to the paradox of leverage that frustrates expectations by limiting the need of external funds. Finally, as stated earlier, if the government is highly involved in the growth process, the weakening may never occur. Thus, on the actual side, the financial weakening depends on the source of economic growth and the degree of indebtedness, and, on the expectational side, it depends on the maintenance of conservative behaviors toward leveraging. In the end, therefore,

> The existence of profit opportunities does not necessarily mean that fragile financing patterns will emerge immediately.
>
> (Minsky 1986a: 211)

There may be situations for which the patterns of financial weakening will not emerge if the government has the right policy strategy of continuous preemptive regulations and management of the economy. As stated earlier, the right time for the government to intervene is not toward the end of expansion period or during a recession. The government should be involved all the time through policies that structurally affect the economic system and that maintain a healthy state of expectations. This is true even very early in the expansion when there is no inflation or no lack of demand, and when the private sector has its mind oriented toward pushing growth as high as possible. However, there are always tensions in the private sector that push toward the use of speculative finance. In addition, as stated earlier, government policies may also be a source of financial weakening and inflation. All this requires constant government attention and care, "there is no final solution to the problems of organizing economic life" (Minsky 1975a: 168).

Implications

The crisis and debt-deflation phases

The preceding presented in detail the forces at the origins of the financial weakening of the economy. The immediate implication for the origins of the crisis is the following:

> During a long-wave expansion each of these elements of the financial environment changes in such a manner as to increase the probability of a panic taking place; balance-sheet payments increase relative to income receipts, asset prices are bid up, and income and other financial assets grow faster than ultimate liquidity. Hence a financial panic is not something that just happens; it is an outcome of the very cyclical phase it brings to an end.
>
> (Minsky 1964b: 334)

Thus, even though a financial crisis may be the product of random shocks on the economy, the conditions that lead to a financial crisis are systematic to the way the capitalist system works (Minsky 1991c). Similarly, the crisis is not explained by "bad luck." Models sometimes conceptualize crises by using an objective probability distribution from which "Nature draws investment returns" and unfortunately happens to pick a bad distribution. This view of the crisis can be made more endogenous and more compatible with Minsky's view by combining it with subjective probability and heuristic biases in a context of uncertainty (Guttentag and Herring 1984). However, in Minsky's theory the conditions for success are endogenously determined and so is the objective probability of disaster: "the frequency distribution changes through time" in a non-random fashion (Minsky 1995: 207, n. 6).

Thus, the turning point is endogenously determined by the financial fragility of the economic system (Minsky 1982a: 30–33):

> A financial panic occurs when a not unusual decline in income or run of defaults on financial contracts occurs in a "favorable" environment.
>
> (Minsky 1964b: 334)

This "refinancing crisis" (Minsky 1983b: 112) leads to unusual ways to make positions (Minsky 1972b: 103), and, depending on the extent of the financial distress, the degree of layering, the existence of effective built-in stabilizers, the indirect effects on the wealth of hedge units, and the effect on expectations, may generate a debt-deflation. If a large proportion of economic units are in speculative financial positions, the refinancing needs are large and, therefore, large liquidations will take place in asset markets. If economic units are largely intertwined in their financial relations, defaults and liquidations will spread fast, multiplying the effects of the initial liquidation by increasing the needs for funds. If the liquidation process leads to a large decline in asset prices and a downward revision of expectations, asset prices go down and stay low as the normal price is revised downward. This leads to an enduring decrease in the net worth of all the holders of the assets being liquidated and so to a decrease in their borrowing power, which may lead to more liquidations. If no built-in stabilizers exist, the crisis creates a large instability and stops only when the financial structure has been simplified, which may take many years (Minsky 1986a: 177). Finally, depending on the effects of financial instability on expectations, economic activity will be more or less affected. The degree of revision depends on the risk aversion of economic units and on the effectiveness of built-in stabilizers, and an economy in which entrepreneurs are risk-adverse will take more time to recover. If the built-in stabilizers work, there will not be a large crisis, but, if not effective, they may also promote long-term instability by preventing a downward revision of expectations toward a more conservative view, which may create favorable conditions for the emergence of stagflation.

In conclusion, trying to predict the downturn of a business cycle is useless and impossible. It is useless because if policy makers want to implement effective policies, in the sense that they prevent both short-term and long-term instability, they have to act continuously during the whole cycle. By the time people start to worry about the downturn it is too late. Second, it is impossible because, when an economy is financially fragile, there are many different channels that can generate a crisis. Thus, neither the triggering cause of a crisis (the "why" question) nor the timing of the crisis (the "when" question) matter for policy purpose. What matters is the whole process that leads to the possibility of a crisis. Given the institutional context, specific financial developments always tend to lead to stagflation or recession, and the point of policy is to prevent, or at least to constrain, their development independently of short-term profitability and short-term welfare gains.

Empirical verification

There have been several empirical studies, in addition to those done by Minsky (for example, Minsky 1962, 1964a, 1975d, 1984b, 1986a), that have measured the financial weakening of the economy over time (Niggle 1989b; Davis 1995; Sinai and Brinner 1975; Sinai 1976). Minsky insisted that his view is empirically founded:

> At any one time, "the market" seems to operate with a consensus about the extent to which operations can be debt-financed for a particular rating, but this

consensus can be both stretched and changed: both the acceptable and the actual debt-equity ratios vary in a systematic way over the longer business-cycle swings.

(Minsky 1975a: 110–111)

However, other empirical studies do not always give clear results. For example, Isenberg (1988, 1994) studied the Great Depression period and showed that there was no aggregate financial weakening in the firm sector, but that it was concentrated in the dynamic part of the firm sector, especially in large firms. Lavoie and Seccareccia (2001) found no conclusive manifestations of the financial weakening process for the G-7 between 1971 and 1995, and no or opposite effect for real GDP, real interest rate, and debt–equity ratio. There are, however, several important points to recognize when doing an empirical analysis that aims the studying of Financial Instability Hypothesis.

First, as stated earlier, restricting Minsky's theory to a theory of investment funding is a narrow approach to Minsky's theory. The center of the problem is not in the production sector. The household sector can be a source of instability if consumption starts to be externally financed and funded, or if households are involved in Ponzi financing for their holding of stocks (Minsky 1984b, 1995):

An upturn in debt-financed consumer durable sales can lead an expansion.

(Minsky 1964a: 268)

Banks always leverage their positions and so are a great potential source of instability. In his study of the Great Depression, Minsky did not concentrate on the production sector but on the household, banking, and government sectors. He then studied four different causes for the financial weakening of the period:

(1) the uses to which credit was put in the stock market, (2) the nature of household debt and in particular the household mortgage, (3) the expansions of utility-holding companies and (4) the reduction of the government debt.

(Minsky 1984b: 247)

The willingness of the federal government to maintain "sound" fiscal principles and the structure of balance sheets of households were essential during this period. Wray showed that the tendency of the federal government to aim for a fiscal surplus has always been a main cause of instability. Each period of major fiscal surplus in the US was followed by an economic recession (Wray 1999).

Second, concerns about the financial side and financial relationships must be tested in nominal terms, not in real terms. Real interest rates, real wages, and other "real" financial variables are poor measures of financial weakening because there are cash outflows and cash inflows that are unrelated to the inflationary process, and nominal interest rates are the relevant variable for the compounding process. As shown in preceding chapters and in this chapter, the articulation between cash inflows and cash outflows is essential because it determines the liquidity of a unit.

Third, the evolution of interest rates provides only a very partial view of the change in the cost of external funds. Among other important variables is the amortization rate because of the tendency of debt maturities to decrease during the expansion (Minsky 1995). However, even if the cost of external funds does not change at all during the business cycle, this does not put into question Minsky's analysis because what matters is the growth of financial commitments relative to the growth of the sum of net cash inflows from income operations and gross cash inflows from balance-sheet operations (if required, the sum may have to include also the net cash inflows from strategic portfolio transactions). At the aggregate level, as long as cash commitments increase for reasons unrelated to national-income creation, the preceding tendencies can occur without any change in the cost of external funds.

Fourth, the fragility of the economy does not need to be observable through data because it may only concern the expectational side of the economy in the sense that margins of safety become smaller:

> Hedge, speculative, and Ponzi financing positions at current interest rates may all have the same flows of cash commitments, but they will have different margins of safety to protect them from probable changes in future interest rates and increasing future payment commitments.
>
> (Kregel 1997: 547)

In this case, an empirical analysis is not helpful, and what is needed is better in-depth supervision, which Minsky and others also advocated (Minsky 1972b, 1975c, 1986a; Campbell and Minsky 1987; Shull 1993; Phillips 1997; Guttentag and Herring 1988).

Fifth, as stated earlier, the debt–equity ratio may be misleading and has to be coupled with a more detailed analysis of balance-sheet structures. First, a speculative financial position does not increase debts necessarily, and both speculative and Ponzi positions can make positions through liquidation at the sectoral level. Second, a lower mismatch of inflows and outflows reduces financial fragility even when debt increases.[14] Thus, in both preceding cases, the debt–equity ratio cannot capture, by itself, the financial weakening process of the economy (Minsky 1963a; Davis 1995). Better ratios to calculate are those related to the cash box condition, i.e. cash-flow ratios and cash-balance ratios, because they provide a more accurate view of the articulation of flows and of the capacity to meet liquidity problems without depending on financial-market conditions. Stock-flow ratios (like debt to income ratio) may also give some better approximation of the true burden of debts if not all cash inflows and cash outflows are not measurable. Finally, all financial obligations ("debts") generated by balance-sheet and off-balance-sheet operations should be included.

Sixth, net worth may also provide some information about the situation of a unit because Ponzi financial structures lead to an automatic decrease in net worth.

However, equity capital does not provide a direct measure of the fragility of an economic unit because capital is not a source of protection against financial adversity. Only cash and liquid superficial (i.e. non-strategic) assets provide a good protection against financial difficulties and a certain level of capital does not give a clue about the composition of assets that allow this equity capital to exist. A high proportion of illiquid assets make an economic unit more fragile for a given level of capital equity.

Seventh, related to the fifth point, cash commitments have to include all kinds of outflows related to financial contracts so that one can get a financial-obligation ratio for each sector. At the practical level, however, data have large drawbacks because some cash outflows, especially for the capital account and for off-balance sheet obligations like principal payment or margin payments, are usually not available (Sahel and Vesala 2001). In addition, the data available do not provide a good evaluation of the market value of assets (Minsky 1962: 257–258). Finally, data like internal funds or profits, may not give an accurate value of the actual cash inflows in companies because of imputations and other adjustments unrelated to actual flows of cash. A national accounting framework that focuses exclusively on a cash-flow analysis is missing.

Eighth, a good analysis of the financial fragility of a system not only measures ratios but also includes a sensitivity analysis. Minsky suggested this kind of analysis (Minsky 1972b, 1975c), what he called "surprise analysis," by looking at the conditional value of assets and cash flows under different sets of assumptions:

> A conditional cash flow examination of individual and of classes of financial institutions would determine the impact upon the institution or class of institution of various policy-determined conditions.
>
> (Minsky 1972b: 129)

This procedure of analysis needs more work but is also more rewarding in terms of results because it allows to have an idea of the minimum variation in income, interest rates, asset prices, and expectations that will lead to liquidity or solvency problems (Vercelli 2001: 43). Recent developments in risk-management analysis are welcomed, but there is still a long way to go before aggregate sensitivity analysis can be applied. Currently, stress-tests only catch the first round effect of a shock on an individual bank and an aggregate framework that catches interaction among banks, and between banks and the rest of the economy, is not available for lack of data and for lack of modeling ability (Sahel and Vesala 2001; Goodhart and Tsomocos 2007; Guttmann 2006). On this last point, recent developments in terms of stock-flow consistent models provide hope even though they leave aside cash-flow interrelations.

Ninth, as stated several times earlier, if the growth of the economy is led by the government, financial weakening may not happen from the business cycle. Other forces may be involved that will lead to financial weakening like speculation in financial markets, or shock on the economy, or if financial instruments allow immediate Ponzi financing. And, if those other forces are not operative, no financial weakening occurs at the aggregate level.

Conclusion

There are behavioral (both psychological and social), economic, and policy arguments at the root of the Financial Instability Hypothesis. At the behavioral and economic levels, a hedge financial structure promotes optimism and more risky behaviors; this is all the more the case when competition is strong. At the policy level, policies that work only late in expansion or during recessions and that provide a floor for profits may promote moral hazard and economic expansion before bad debts are purged completely. At the economic level, there are forces that limit the non-inflationary growth of aggregate income. In the end, the dynamics of the Minskian analysis are complex, varied, and dialectical in nature. Two central dynamics during the expansionary phase are that cc_n increases while cc does not necessarily go up until late in the expansion. An increase in cc, however, is not necessary in order to generate a higher sensitivity of the economy to normal economic fluctuations or shocks.

If there is no increase in cc, the crisis can only be explained by an endogenously generated reversion of the state of mind, or an exogenous abrupt change in the conventions that decrease cc_n and so the borrowing power of economic units. Keynes suggested that this was the central cause of the crisis more than rising interest rates that reflect the consequences of the crisis:

> [I] suggest that a more typical, and often the predominant, explanation of the crisis is, not primarily a rise in the rate of interest, but a sudden collapse in the marginal efficiency of capital [...]. Moreover, the dismay and uncertainty as to the future which accompanies a collapse in the marginal efficiency of capital naturally precipitates a sharp increase in liquidity-preference – and hence a rise in the rate of interest.
>
> (Keynes 1936a: 315–316)

This, of course, is perfectly compatible with Minsky's theory (Minsky 1972b: 109). This is even more the case if one gets more precise by stating that a crisis generates a sharp rise in interest-rate spreads (Lavoie 1996b; Mishkin 1991), while all interest rates may rise progressively earlier *pari passu* because of tightening by the central bank during the boom period or because of an increase in liquidity preference (because of disappointing sales, banker's skepticism, the financial-innovation barrier, or any other factor presented above that affects liquidity preference).

Overall, there is what Vercelli calls a "structural instability," which is generated by profit-seeking behaviors under a competitive economic environment (Vercelli 2001: 34, 45):

> The evolution of the debt structure and of financial institutions, as well as the changes in the standards of acceptable liability structures to finance

positions in assets, are important empirical correlatives of the migration of non-linear iterative systems from producing coherent to producing incoherent results.

(Minsky 1982c: 383)

Thus, the modeling of Minsky's framework must take into account the weakening of the actual and expectational levels. One way to do this is by using non-linear equations with intrinsic cyclical properties. However, an alternative method, which seems more satisfying, is to create models with shifting behavioral parameters. In the latter case, the existence of a cycle is not imposed by non-linear equations but explained by the structure of the model and the behaviors of economic agents (Sterman 2000). Thus, there cannot be a lasting stationary or steady state in a Minskian model because tranquility leads to daring, which shifts some parameters. Two central shifting parameters are cc_n and Q that step upward in period of tranquility, and this initial upward shift is compounded by the structure of the model because "the governor mechanism by way of financing terms is often dominated by positive, disequilibrating feedbacks" (Minsky 1986a: 228).

The modeling of Minsky's framework

The following presents a macroeconomic model that captures some of the elements and dynamics of the Minskian analysis and that is used to simulate the impact of interest-rate policies. The model concentrates on several points, the financing and funding of economic activities, the formation of aggregate profit, the determination of cash commitments and the possibility of refinancing needs, the role of financial conventions in the determination of investment level, and the role of the cash box condition in the servicing of cash commitments.

To build the model, two tools are used: the stock-flow table and System Dynamics modeling. The stock-flow table, based on National Income accounting and Flow of Funds accounting, gives the basic structure of the model and is an important tool to verify that all the financial implications of economic decisions are taken into account (Godley and Lavoie 2007).[15] System Dynamics modeling focuses the analysis on the identification of the main positive and negative feedback loops that generate an observed time pattern.

A few more words about System Dynamics are necessary to make sure that the reader understands how the modeling is done. System Dynamics is a continuous-time modeling technique that emphasizes the role of time. Stocks take time to accumulate and to decline, they create time delays, and those time delays must be included in the model. A stock and a flow are related in time and so the time dimension must explicitly be modeled (dishoarding from a bank account, selling a share, etc.), and time puts a maximum upper limit on the value of inflows and outflows. Most modeling techniques assume that it is possible to add to and to remove from stocks over one unit of time.

Basic framework

The accounting framework

The model has five sectors: a household sector, a firm sector, a banking sector, the Treasury, and a central bank. Tables 5.2–5.4 present the accounting framework of the model. Table 5.2 records the flows induced by income production and income distribution, and Table 5.3 records portfolio operations (i.e. changes in the balance sheets) induced by the preceding operations. For businesses and the central bank, a distinction is made between the current account (i.e. flow impacts on the income statement) and the capital account (i.e. flow impacts on the balance-sheet statement) because of the double impact of net profit and investment.

The capital columns represent the flow implications on balance sheets; therefore, "+" and "−" in the NIPA table for these columns have to be read, respectively, as sources and uses of funds. Changes in balance sheets that are represented in the NIPA table are changes in the assets and liabilities induced by the production and distribution sides of the system. Changes recorded in the flow of funds table (Table 5.3) are changes in the financial side.[16] The consistency of stocks and flows is verified if the sum for all flows and all stocks, for each sector and across sectors, is zero. If the model does not generate this, it means that at least one important part of the model has not been taken into account.

The flow of funds table records net amounts, that is, the gross amounts of debts and demand deposits newly created, net of the reflux of bank IOUs to the banking sector via the servicing of principal and net of the amount of debts written off. Thus, the net change in the amount of debts is

$$\Delta_n L = \Delta L - aL - zL,$$

with ΔL the gross amount of loans (new debts), aL the amount of principal serviced, and zL the amount of debts written off. The gross amount of loans can be detailed more explicitly by making a difference between long-term and short-term debts:

$$\Delta L_{st} = \Delta L_W + \Delta L_{REF},$$

$$\Delta L_{lt} = \Delta L_I.$$

The gross amount of short-term loans depends on the amount of money necessary to pay the wage bill, and the amount of loans that have been granted to refinance positions. The gross amount of long-term debts depends on the amount of external funds needed by firms to fund investment. Thus, in net terms we have

$$\Delta_n L_{st} = \Delta L_W + \Delta L_{REF} - a_{st}L_{st} - z_{st}L_{st},$$

$$\Delta_n L_{lt} = \Delta L_I - a_{lt}L_{lt} - z_{lt}L_{lt}.$$

Table 5.2 National income relations

Flows

NIPA: Income Transaction Matrix
(+: Inflows, −: Outflows)

Sectors	Households	Firms Current	Firms Capital	Banks Current	Banks Capital	Treasury	Central Bank Current	Central Bank Capital	Balancing Items	Total Flows
Consumption	$-C$	$+C$								0
Investment		$+I$	$-I$							0
Gvt Expenditures		$+G$				$-G$				0
ΔInventories		$+\Delta IN$	$-\Delta IN$							0
Sales		Y								
Wage bill	$+W$	$-W_F$				$-W_G$				0
Net profit after tax		$-\Pi_{nFT}$	$+\Pi_{nFT}$	$-\Pi_{nB}$	$+\Pi_{nB}$		$-\Pi_{nCB}$	$+\Pi_{nCB}$		0
Interest on short-term loans		$-i_{st}L_{st}$		$+i_{st}L_{st}$						0
Interest on long-term loans		$-i_{lt}L_{lt}$		$+i_{lt}L_{lt}$						0
Interest on advances				$-i_A L_A$			$+i_A L_A$			0
Interest on reserves				$+i_R L_R$			$-i_R L_R$			0
Income tax receipts	$-T_W$	$-T_\Pi$				$+T_Y$				0
Wealth tax			$-T_{\text{wealth }F}$		$-T_{\text{wealth }B}$	$+T_{\text{wealth}}$				0
Financial balances	S_H	0	$+\Pi_{nFT}-I-T_{\text{wealth }F}$	0	$+\Pi_{nB}-T_{\text{wealth }B}$	$+T-G-W_G$	0	Π_{nCB}	0	0

Table 5.3 Flow of funds relations

Flows

Flow of Funds: Balance-sheet Transaction Matrix (Net Amount)
(+: Source of Funds (lower assets/higher liabilities), −: Uses of Funds (higher assets/ lower liabilities))

Sectors	Households	Firms		Banks		Treasury	Central Bank		Balancing Items	Total Flows
		Current	Capital	Current	Capital		Current	Capital		
Demand deposits	$-\Delta_n DD_H$		$-\Delta_n DD_F$		$+\Delta_n DD$				0	0
Short-term loans			$+\Delta_n L_{st}$		$-\Delta_n L_{st}$				0	0
long-term loans			$+\Delta_n L_{lt}$		$-\Delta_n L_{lt}$				0	0
Reserves					$-\Delta_n R$			$+\Delta_n R$	0	0
Treasury account						$-\Delta_n F$		$+\Delta_n F$	0	0
Advance to treasury						$+\Delta_n A_T$		$-\Delta_n A_T$	0	0
Advance to banks					$+\Delta_n A_B$			$-\Delta_n A_B$	0	0
Writing off of equity			$-zL$		$+zL$				0	0
Total sectors	0		0		0	0		0	0	0

Table 5.4 Balance-sheet relations

Stocks

Balance-Sheet Matrix
(+: Assets, −: Liabilities)

Sectors	Households	Firms Current	Firms Capital	Banks Current	Banks Capital	Treasury	Central bank Current	Central bank Capital	Balancing items	Total stocks
Fixed capital			$+P_K K_F$			$+P_K K_G$			$-P_K K$	0
Demand deposits	$+DD_H$		$+DD_F$		$-DD$					0
Reserve					$+R$			$-R$		0
Treasury account						$-F$		$+F$		0
Advances					$-A_B$	$-A_T$		$+A$		0
Debts			$-L_F$		$+L$					0
Balancing items	$-NW_H$		$-NW_F$		$-NW_B$	$-NW_T$		$-NW_{CB}$	$+P_K K$	0
Total sectors	0		0		0	0		0	0	0

The same idea can be applied to demand deposits and to the writing-off of net worth:[17]

$$\Delta_n DD = \Delta DD - aL,$$

$$\Delta_n NW_B = \Pi_{nB} - zL,$$

$$\Delta_n NW_F = \Pi_{nF} + zL.$$

One can note immediately that short-term loans do not grow exclusively to finance production-related economic activities, i.e. activities that contribute to the growth of national income. One can see also that there is no need for "unproductive"[18] indebtedness other than refinancing to generate this phenomenon.

The central bank provides advances to banks and to the Treasury. Banks need to borrow some reserves from the central bank either to meet some reserve requirements (legally defined or for clearing purposes), or to be able to pay the debt services they owe to the central bank on the advances granted by the latter. The net variation for central bank advances to banks is

$$\Delta_n A_B = \max(RR - R, 0)/t_R + \Delta L_{REFB} - a_A A_B,$$

with t_R the time necessary to adjust reserves and ΔL_{REFB} the amount of refinancing loans granted to banks. The Treasury gets its account at the central bank credited whenever the Treasury needs to spend, and this is balanced by recording an advance to the Treasury. The repayment of Treasury advances is not done on a specific schedule but when the Treasury receives tax payments. The net variation of advances to the Treasury is

$$\Delta_n A_T = G - T,$$

with G government spending and T the amount of tax receipts.

The rest of the accounting structure is straightforward. For example, the GDP and national income identity is

$$C + I + G + \Delta IN \equiv Y \equiv W_D + \Pi_{nFD} + iL + T_Y.$$

with ΔIN the change in inventories measured at prevailing market price, Π_{nFD} the net profit of firms after income tax, W_D wage earnings after income tax, iL net interest paid by firms, and T_Y the level of income tax. Net profit does not represent the amount of funds available for the funding of investment. Indeed, the net cash flow generated by net profit needs to be reduced by aL and income tax payment, and corrected for inventory valuation, which gives the net cash flow from operations ("internal funds"):

$$\Pi_{nF} = \Pi_F - iL,$$

$$\Pi_{IF} = \Pi_{nF}(1 - t_\Pi) - \Delta IN - aL.$$

Cash outflows induced by the amortization of debts are not part of the income account but part of the capital account. Net cash flow from operations is assumed to be a central variable in the decision-making process of firms, it measures the cash gain from core economic activities, rather than the increase in equity capital.

The household sector

Households consist of employed or unemployed individuals. They can be employed by firms and by the Treasury who pay a wage to households. Households' consumption pattern depends on their after-tax income and on their demand deposit:

$$C = c_W(1 - t_W)W + c_{DD}DD_H,$$

with c_W the marginal propensity to consume out of wage income, and c_{DD} the marginal propensity to consume out of demand deposits. The level of households' saving represents the net increase in their net worth, whose counterpart exclusively comes from a net increase in demand deposit:

$$S_H = \Delta_n DD_H = W - C - T_W,$$

with $T_W = t_W W$ the amount of income tax paid by households and t_W the tax rate on wage income.

The firm sector

This is the most developed sector of the model. There are two types of firms, some of them produce consumption goods, and others produce investment goods. Even though they respond to the same type of financial incentives, their production organizations are very different because investment goods are expensive and take a long time to produce and to install. As Keynes and Minsky note, this is a central source of uncertainty and financial instability.

Starting with the consumption-good sector, the production organization aims at being as flexible as possible in order to meet the demands of customers very rapidly. For this to happen, two complementary strategies are implemented by the firms of the consumption-good sector. A first strategy involves maintaining a certain level of inventory of consumption goods. Firms target an inventory coverage ratio, that is, they want to keep in inventory (in_C) a certain amount of consumption goods that is a multiple of expected demand $E(O_{Cd})$. This targeted inventory coverage is assumed to be equal to the targeted speed t_{Oin}^T at which firms wish to be able to supply consumption goods (given transportation time, time to remove from inventories, and others). All this allows to find a desired inventory level for consumption goods in_{Cd}, with $in_{Cd} = t_{Oin}^T \times E(O_{Cd})$. If inventories are not in line with desired inventories, firms will want to produce more or less

$$O_{ingap} = (in_{Cd} - in_C)/t_{ingap},$$

with t_{ingap} the time necessary to detect inventory discrepancies and O_{ingap} the production needed to meet inventory coverage (note that this value can be negative). Inventories may not be at the desired level if the time to supply consumption goods is not equal to the targeted time (and so the inventory coverage ratio is not on target) or if production is different from its targeted value. A second strategy is to anticipate expected demand, i.e. to produce in advance of what future demand is expected to be. Demand for consumption goods comes from households (C) and from the government (G_C), and expected demand is determined by smoothing past sales and by a targeted price for consumption goods P_C^T:

$$E(O_{Cd}) = E(C + G_C)/P_C^T.$$

The formation of prices will be explained later. Therefore, the total targeted production is

$$O_C^T = E(O_{Cd}) + O_{ingap}.$$

Given this targeted production, firms in the consumption-good sector determine their desired level of employment (N_{Cd}) and their desired level of capital equipment (K_{Cd}). The latter will also affect indirectly the demand for labor and so will be presented first; however, before doing so let us look at how targeted production is determined in the investment-good sector.

In the investment-good sector, production is made by order. The customers are all the firms that want to invest (I) and the government (G_I). Firms do not anticipate demand for investment goods, they wait for customers to come to knock at their door, which implies a different inventory-management strategy. Firms in the investment-good sector enter a contract to deliver goods at a specific time; therefore, they have a targeted completion time of investment goods to meet t_{OI}^T. Thus, the targeted level of production is

$$O_I^T = in_I / t_{OI}^T.$$

This formulation assumes that all goods being produced are homogeneous and can accommodate any customer. It would be possible to do a good-specific production organization but that would complicate the model too much. This formulation also simplifies the chain of production by assuming that only one stock exists, which is "inventory" of investment goods and which represents investment goods being produced and ready for delivery. More realistically, there are several stages of production and this can be modeled easily with System Dynamics. Given this targeted production, firms in the investment-good sector determine their demand for labor (N_{Id}) and their desired level of capital equipment (K_{Id}).

In both sub-sectors, the demand for labor and capital are similarly determined. The demand for capital K_d depends on the targeted capacity of production ($O^{\max T}$) and the average productivity of capital equipment (AP_K). It is also affected by a dimensionless factor that represents the effect of relative rate of return on desired capital equipment (e_{2r}).[19] The relative rate of return is the rate of return divided by the targeted rate of return (r/r^T), which will be explained more explicitly later:

$$K_d = e_{2r} \times O^{\mathrm{max}T}/AP_K.$$

e_{2r} is positively related to the relative rate of return and if the relative rate of return is equal to one (rate of return is on target) then $e_{2r} = 1$. Differences appear by sub-sector in what affects the targeted capacity of production. The simplest way to determine the latter is by dividing targeted production by the normal capacity utilization rate:

$$O^{\mathrm{max}T} = O^T/u_n.$$

However, given the production, organization additional factors influence the targeted capacity of production. In the consumption-good sector, it is affected positively by the relative utilization capacity rate (u_C/u_{nC}) and negatively by the inventory discrepancy (in_C/in_{Cd}). In the investment-good sector, it is affected positively by the relative utilization capacity rate (u_I/u_{nI}) and by the relative time to complete investment goods (t_{OI}/t_{OI}^T):

$$O_C^{\mathrm{max}T} = e_{2u}e_{\mathrm{ingap}}O_C^T/u_{nC},$$

$$O_I^{\mathrm{max}T} = e_{2u}e_{t\mathrm{gap}}O_I^T/u_{nI},$$

with e_{2u}, e_{ingap}, and $e_{t\mathrm{gap}}$, the effect on the targeted capacity of production of, respectively, relative capacity utilization rates, the inventory discrepancy in the consumption-good sector, and the relative time to complete investment goods. The capacity utilization rate (u_C, u_I) is affected by considerations regarding the relative rate of return and the need to meet production requirements (Sterman 2000). A firm is affected by more than just monetary considerations, for example, production contracts may push a firm to produce even though it is not as monetary beneficial as targeted. Inversely, current profitability may be very high but expected demand may be low, which limits the need to use production capacities. In the end, the current capacity utilization rate is determined by an average of monetary and production considerations:

$$u_C = \alpha_r e_r + (1 - \alpha_r)e_{\mathrm{ingap}},$$

$$u_I = \alpha_r e_r + (1 - \alpha_r)e_{t\mathrm{gap}},$$

with e_r the positive effect of relative rate of return on utilization capacity rate, e_{ingap} the positive effect of inventory discrepancy on utilization capacity rate in the consumption-good sector, $e_{t\mathrm{gap}}$ the positive effect of time gap on utilization capacity rate in the investment-good sector. All effects are within the zero to one range, α_r is the weight of monetary considerations and $(1 - \alpha_r)$ the weight of production/technical considerations.[20] The expected rate of return is defined as

$$r = E(\Pi_{IF})/P_K K.$$

This is an important departure from traditional modeling literature. What pushes to produce is not profitability in the sense of growing capital equity. What matters is the additional net amount of cash expected to be forthcoming. Profit, being a measure of absolute growth in capital equity, includes changes in inventories; therefore, higher inventories increase profit. However, firms may not be happy if inventories increase, especially if they increase above the targeted inventory level. What firms respond to is expected sales, and so expected additional cash inflows. Thus, the growth in equity does not tell if a firm is successful and so profit is not the relevant measure to decide if a firm should continue to produce or not.

Expectations of internal funds are formed differently in the consumption-good sector and in the investment-good sector. In the former, they are based on an extrapolation of past sales. In the latter, expected internal funds are measured on the basis of current orders. It is assumed that investment goods are paid at delivery and that producers must finance construction without any advance of funds from the economic units that ordered investment goods. Thus, current sales of investment goods do not provide a good estimation of future monetary inflows. Indeed, current sales may be nil because no investment good is finished, but if orders are high, firms in the investment-good sector will grow their capacity of production and their employment.

Once the desired capital equipment level is determined, one can determine the desired level of gross investment (O_{Id}):

$$O_{Id} = O_{Idn} + dK,$$

with O_{Idn} the desired net investment level with $O_{Idn} = (K_d - K)/t_I$ (where t_I is the time necessary to make an investment decision, most modelers assume $t_I = 1$), and dK the level of replacement investment due to physical depreciation, d is the depreciation rate of capital equipment (which is the inverse of the average life of capital equipment).

The level of employment is determined by two constraints. One is the existing level of capital equipment (firms cannot hire more employees than what their machines allow) and the other is targeted production (firms hire only if they expect to sale). As shown later, there may be a third constraint on employment, namely a finance constraint, but for the moment, the latter is left aside. Firms would like to have enough employees to meet the targeted production, given the average productivity of labor (AP_L):

$$N_d = O^T / AP_L.$$

However, this may be constrained by production capabilities, given technological and monetary considerations, uO^{max} with $O^{max} = AP_K \times K$. Thus

$$N_d = \min(O^T, uO^{max})/AP_L.$$

Firms compare the desired level of employment to the actual level of employment in order to determine if they should hire or lay off people, given the time necessary to do so: $\Delta N = (N_d - N)/t_H$, with t_H the time necessary to hire/lay off someone. Note that the time to hire and lay off is not instantaneous, which has consequences for the determination of output.

Now that targeted production, desired employment, and desired capital equipment have been determined, it is possible to explain the current level of production in each sector, which is determined as follows:

$$O = \min (N \times AP_{La}, uO^{max}).$$

There is an upper bound on production determined by production capacity and capacity utilization rate. Below that bound, output is determined by employment and the adjusted average productivity of labor (AP_{La}). The adjusted average productivity of labor is used to show that employers may sometimes ask employees to work harder or slower depending on the production needs. This allows employers to vary production and reach their target without having to hire or to lay off someone (which takes time and can be costly). Adjusted productivity of labor is determined as follows:

$$AP_{La} = \min(AP_{La}^{max}, (N/N_d) \times AP_L).$$

Again, there is an upper bound determined by production capacity $AP_{La}^{max} = uO^{max}/N_C$, but below that productivity is adjusted to compensate for discrepancies between desired and actual employment level. One should note, however, that adjusted productivity is not what employers use to determine employment. For the latter, they use what they expect employees will be able to produce on average in normal conditions (i.e. when employment is at its desired level).

Finally, in the consumption-good sector, production is put in inventories and then sold whenever there is a demand. The supply of consumption goods O_{Cs} is determined as follows:

$$O_{Cs} = \min (O_{Cd}, in_C/t_{Oin}).$$

Because supplying goods takes time and because inventories are limited by what has been produced in the past, there may be situations in which supply is too low relative to the demand for consumption goods. In this case, supply is limited by what is available in inventories and the time to destock inventories. This constraint is necessary to make sure that inventories do not go negative.

Now that production-related decisions have been presented, the pricing and financial decisions can be presented. The pricing procedure differs depending on the sector. In the consumption-good sector, prices are determined in a competitive fashion even though firms may have a target price that they would like to get. This does not mean, however, that prices are driven down to their marginal cost, we are not in a perfectly competitive market, and, as shown below, market mechanisms still lead to a mark-up pricing procedure (Kregel 1975; Weintraub 1969, 1978). In the investment sector, prices are set by following a mark-up procedure and prices do not change frequently (Eichner 1976; Lee 1998; Lavoie 1992). The contracts written down when investment goods are ordered include an agreement on prices.

Let us start with the consumption-good sector. It is assumed that each firm would like to get a target price P_C^T. This targeted price is determined by following a target-return pricing procedure. The targeted price is fixed and does not move with unit cost within a large range of time. Costs are measured at the normal output level derived from the normal capacity utilization rate and when each variable is at its targeted value. Given the definition of the targeted rate of return r^T, we have

$$r_C^T E(P_K) K_C^T = \Pi_{IFC}^T,$$

with $\Pi_{IFC}^T = P_C^T O_{nCs} - w_C N_C^T - (a_{st} + i_{st}) L_{stC}^T - (a_{lt} + i_{lt}) L_{ltC}^T - E(T_{\Pi C})$, where O_{nCs} is the normal supply of consumption goods, and $T_{\Pi C}$ is the tax on corporate profit. O_{nCs} is equal to the production made available for sale, which excludes production for inventory rebuilding $O_{nCs} = O_C - O_{ingap}$. Because all stocks are assumed to be at their target when calculating the targeted price, $O_{ingap} = 0$ and production is at the normal output level $O_C = O_{nC} = K_C^T \times APKC \times u_{nC}$. Here we assume that interest payments can be deduced from the corporate income tax base; therefore, $E(T_{\Pi C}) = t_\Pi \Pi_n^T$. Given that $\Delta IN_C = 0$, one can express internal funds as a function of net profit:

$$\Pi_n^T = \frac{\Pi_{IFC}^T + a_{st} L_{stC}^T + a_{lt} L_{ltC}^T}{(1 - t_\Pi)}.$$

By substituting this value in the targeted internal funds one gets

$$\Pi_{IFC}^T = P_C^T O_{nC} - w_C N_C^T - (a_{st} + i_{st}) L_{stC}^T - (a_{lt} + i_{lt}) L_{ltC}^T - \frac{t_\Pi}{(1 - t_\Pi)}$$
$$\times (\Pi_{IFC}^T + a_{st} L_{stC}^T + a_{lt} L_{ltC}^T).$$

Thus, assuming that, at the stationary state, the price of investment goods and the price of existing capital goods are the same, the target-return pricing procedure generates the following targeted price:

$$P_C^T = \frac{r_C^T P_I}{APKC \times u_{nC}} \left(1 + \frac{t_\Pi}{(1 - t_\Pi)}\right) + \frac{w_C N_C^T + (a_{st} + i_{st}) L_{stC}^T + (a_{lt} + i_{lt}) L_{ltC}^T}{K_C^T \times APKC \times u_{nC}}$$
$$+ \frac{t_\Pi}{(1 - t_\Pi)} \frac{a_{st} L_{stC}^T + a_{lt} L_{ltC}^T}{K_C^T \times APKC \times u_{nC}}.$$

This price allows firms in the consumption-good sector to meet a targeted rate of return over capital equipment by setting a sufficient mark-up over labor costs, financial costs and taxes.

Even though firms in the consumption-good sector would like to reach this targeted price, it is assumed that they are not necessarily able to set this price because of competitive pressures. Prices are assumed to be adjusted to be able to close the gap between demand and supply of consumption goods. At equilibrium between demand for and supply of consumption goods, we have

$$P_C O_C = C + G_C + P_C O_{\text{ingap}}.$$

Given that $O_{Cs} = O_C - O_{\text{ingap}}$ and knowing the expression of consumption, we have

$$P_C = \frac{w_C N_C}{O_{Cs}} \left(c_W + \frac{c_W(w_I N_I + w_G N_G) - c_W T_W + c_{DD} DD_H + G_C}{w_C N_C} \right).$$

The market price is determined by an aggregate mark-up over labor cost and is used to measure aggregate profit in the consumption-good sector:

$$\Pi_C = P_C O_{Cs} - W_C.$$

Given that P_C is the clearing price, $O_{Cs} = O_{Cd} = (C + G_C)/P_C$ all the time and so aggregate profit is $\Pi_C = C + G_C - W_C$. The aggregate profit is allocated among firms in the consumption-good sector according to their respective market power. Here it is assumed that all of them have the same market power, but one could assume also that some of them have more market power and so could set their price at the targeted price even though the aggregate clearing price is below the targeted price. In this case, firms with more market power would get a higher share of the aggregate profit, given market shares. If $r_C = r_C^T$, then it is easy to show that $P_C = P_C^T$.

In the model, the targeted return is fixed at the initial stationary state rate of return r_0^* in order to start the model at a stationary state. Because the latter changes over time but the targeted rate of return is left unchanged at r_0^*, actual and targeted prices may differ in the consumption-good sector. In addition, it may be difficult or impossible for some stocks to reach their targeted value (for example, inventory discrepancies may persist). However, we think it is unrealistic to assume that firms set targeted rates of return with some preoccupation regarding the stationary state. This is all the more the case that the stationary state sometimes requires that $r^* = 0$. It is best to assume that targeted rates of return are set by firms in function of their internal objectives and the pressure of shareholders.

The methodological imperative to start the model at a stationary state has some important implications for the modeling of price-setting mechanisms in the investment-good sector. Ideally, one would like to use the target-return pricing procedure presented above. However, if the targeted rate of return is set at the stationary rate of return in the investment-good sector, there is a circularity: $P^T \rightarrow r^* \rightarrow P^T$.[21] One solution would be to set numerically the targeted rate of return to the value of the stationary state, but, given that the value of the stationary state rate of return is usually inexact, it is impossible to get a stationary state through this method. To avoid all those technical problems, another mark-up pricing procedure is used in the investment-good sector. We just have a mark-up pricing over normal historic unit cost (HUC_{nI}), with an unexplained mark up. The normal historic unit cost in the I-sector is

$$\text{HUC}_{nI} = \frac{w_I N_I^T + (a_{st} + i_{st})L_{stI}^T + (a_{lt} + i_{lt})L_{ltI}^T}{O_{nI}}.$$

Given this normal historic unit cost, the targeted price of investment good is set as follows:

$$P_I^T = (1 + \lambda_I)(1 + t_\Pi)\text{HUC}_{nI}.$$

As shown below, the targeted value for long-term debts depends on the price of investment goods. Indeed, $L_{ltI}^T = \frac{cc_{ltdI}\,\Pi_I^T}{(a_{lt} + i_{lt})}$ and $\Pi_I^T = P_I^T O_{nI} - w_I N_I^T$. Given the existence of this relationship, the targeted price of investment goods is

$$P_I^T = \frac{(1 + \lambda_I)(1 + t_\Pi)}{(1 - cc_{ltd}(1 + \lambda_I)(1 + t_\Pi))} \frac{(a_{st} + i_{st})L_{stI}^T + (1 - cc_{ltd})w_I N_I^T}{K_I^T \times AP_{KI} \times u_{nI}}.$$

It is assumed that firms in the investment-good sector can set prices at their target through contractual agreements: $P_I = P_I^T$. This price is reset at a frequency based on the targeted completion time of investment goods. One may note that this price may be negative for some values of cc_{ltd}, λ_I, and t_Π. To prevent this from happening, it is assumed that the price of investment goods cannot be below their initial value P_{I0}^T. This price sustains gross profit in the investment-good sector: $\Pi_I = P_I O_{Is} - w_I N_I$, with O_{Is} the amount of investment good delivered to the government and to firms.

The last element to present concerns the financial aspects that sustain the preceding decisions. The most important financial consideration in the model concerns the determination of the funding of investment by private companies (because the government is monetarily sovereign, it does not have to deal with this issue), which is done as follows:

$$P_I O_I = f_\Pi \Pi_{IF} + \Delta_I \text{DD} + \Delta L_I.$$

Firms use some of their internal funds, some of their cash hoards and external funds. To explain how firms decide how they should fund their investment expenditures, one needs to explain how the desired funding structure is determined, that is, how $f_{\Pi d}$, $\Delta_{dI}\text{DD}$, and $\Delta_d L_I$ are determined in order to pay for a given desired level of nominal investment $I_d = P_I O_{Id}$. It is assumed that the desired proportion of internal funds used is determined last, i.e. after desired dishoarding and desired external funding are determined.

First, firms determine their desired external funding, which implies determining a desired proportion of external funding (f_{LId}), given desired investment ($P_I O_{Id}$):

$$\Delta_d L_I = f_{LId} \times P_I O_{Id}.$$

To determine f_{LId}, firms start by determining what the desired liability structure of their balance sheet should be. To do that, they first recognize that a certain level of long-term debts generates a certain level of cash commitments on long-term debts: $CC_{lt} = (a_{lt} + i_{lt})L_{lt}$. Thus, the desired level of long-term debts implies a desired level of long-term cash commitments:

$$CC_{ltd} = (a_{lt} + i_{lt})L_{ltd}.$$

Therefore, the desired debt level is

$$L_{ltd} = \frac{CC_{ltd}}{(a_{lt} + i_{lt})}.$$

One can go a little further by extracting the flow-leveraging ratio for long-term debts, i.e. the ratio of debt service on long-term debts relative to gross operational cash flow (i.e. gross profit less variation of inventories)

$$L_{ltd} = \frac{cc_{ltd}E(\Pi - \Delta IN)}{(a_{lt} + i_{lt})}.$$

Thus, given that t_I is the time to make an investment decision, the desired net increase in long-term debts is

$$\Delta_{nd}L_{lt} = \frac{L_{ltd} - L_{lt}}{t_I} = \frac{\dfrac{cc_{ltd}E(\Pi - \Delta IN)}{(a_{lt} + i_{lt})} - \dfrac{cc_{lt}(\Pi - \Delta IN)}{(a_{lt} + i_{lt})}}{t_I},$$

which gives us

$$\Delta_{nd}L_{lt} = \Delta_d L_I = f_{LId}P_I O_{Id} = \left(cc_{ltd} - cc_{lt}\frac{(\Pi - \Delta IN)}{E(\Pi - \Delta IN)}\right)\frac{E(\Pi - \Delta IN)}{t_I(a_{lt} + i_{lt})}.$$

And the desired gross increase in long-term debts is $\Delta_d L_{lt} = \Delta_d L_I + a_{lt}L_{lt-1}$. The desired flow-leveraging ratio is bounded by what is considered a normal ratio (cc_n). The latter is determined by comparing the desired flow-leveraging ratio set by firms (cc_d) and the acceptable flow-leveraging ratio set by banks (cc_a): $cc_n = \min(cc_d, cc_a)$. Therefore the financial expression of the desired gross increase in long-term debts is

$$\Delta_d L_{lt} = \left(cc_{lm} - cc_{lt}\frac{(\Pi - \Delta IN)}{E(\Pi - \Delta IN)}\right)\frac{E(\Pi - \Delta IN)}{t_I(a_{lt} + i_{lt})} + a_{lt}L_{lt-1}.$$

As explained later, cc_d and cc_a are shifting parameters that are determined by relative rates of return.

Once the proportion of external funding has been determined, firms must decide how much they will dishoard in order to fund desired investment. To do so, firms first determine their desired level of demand deposit. In the model, the latter is determined in function of transaction and precaution considerations. As Minsky notes "accidents (and recessions) can happen, and the cash flows from operations may fall short of anticipations and of the amount required by commitments on debts. To protect against such possibilities, a unit will own money and marketable financial assets beyond what is needed for transactions" (Minsky 1986a: 336). In accounting, the "defensive interval period" is defined as the ratio of outstanding cash to monetary outflows. It gives an idea of how long a firm can meet its expenses by only using its existing monetary hoards. We will call this the cash coverage ratio and we assume that firms have a given desired cash coverage ratio ccr_d. Given the latter, and given that T_F is the amount of taxes paid by firms, the desired level of demand deposit is

$$DD_d = ccr_d(wN_d + I_d + E(CC) + E(T_F)).$$

The value ccr_d is left unexplained but it probably declines when economic expansion lasts. Therefore, the amount of dishoarding to fund investment will depend on the amount of demand deposit available relative to the desired level of demand deposit. If $DD_F < DD_{Fd}$, firms do not wish to dishoard to fund desired investment. This self-imposed constraint does not hold for non-discretionary expenses like tax payments and cash commitments.

Finally, given the proportion of external funding and the available dishoarding to fund desired investment, the proportion of internal funds used to fund a desired level of investment is also known:

$$f_{\Pi d} = \frac{P_I O_{Id} - \Delta_d L_I - \Delta_{dl} DD_F}{E(\Pi_{IF})}.$$

Thus, firms may not use all their internal funds to fund investment, indeed they may want to keep part of their internal funds for precautionary motives (Niggle 1989b). The expected proportion of internal funding is $E(f_{IF}) = f_{\Pi d} E(\Pi_{IF})/P_I O_{Id}$, which is a residual variable in the model, and $E(f_{IF}) + \Delta_{dl} DD_F/I_d + f_{Lld} = 1$. It is assumed that entrepreneurs only pay attention to two proportions: f_{Lld} and $f_{\Pi d}$.

In the model, we assume that firms are constrained by financial matters when they order investment goods, not when they have to pay for them. The desired investment level depends on the expected funding available:

$$P_I O_{Id} = \min(P_I O_{Id}, f_{\Pi d} E(\Pi_{IF}) + \Delta_{dl} DD_F + \Delta_d L_I).$$

If a firm does not think that it will have enough funds to meet its desired investment level determined by production requirements, it will cut desired investment to the level of expected funds. Once the time comes to pay for investment goods, firms try to implement their desired funding structure by focusing on f_{Lld} and $f_{\Pi d}$. First, internal funds are used for an amount of $f_{\Pi d} \Pi_{IF}$. If this amount is high enough to cover all investment expenditure (e.g. if $\Pi_{IF} > E(\Pi_{IF})$), then no external funding is required and entrepreneurs' expectations in terms of funding structure are frustrated. If $f_{\Pi d}\Pi_{IF}$ is not sufficient to cover all the investment expenditure, firms will try to meet their desired level dishoarding. Finally, if there is still not enough money available to cover the investment expenditure, firms need to borrow funds. If firms reach their targeted proportion of external funding ($f_{LI} \times P_I O_I = f_{LId} \times P_I O_I$) but there is still not enough funds available, firms use a combination of additional internal funding and additional dishoarding, and ultimately, additional external funding to fill the gap. One central behavioral hypothesis is, therefore, that firms do not necessarily use all the internal funds they earned during the current period to meet their investment expenditure. Entrepreneurs constrain themselves relative to $f_{\Pi d}$ and f_{LId}. First they use the desired proportion of internal funds, then they try to meet their desired dishoarding level, and, if additional funds are necessary, they try not to borrow more than desired.

Aside of investment, the way firms meet payments is very simple. The wage bill is assumed to be completely externally funded and inventories are assumed not to require any maintenance funding. Following the cash box condition, contractual and compulsory payments (taxes and debt services) are met by a combination of internal and external sources of funds. If external funds are used to meet the latter expenses, they represent refinancing loans. In terms of cash commitments, the following condition must be true in order for all cash commitments on debts to be serviced:

$$CC_t \leq (\Pi - \Delta IN)_t + \Delta_{CC}DD_{Ft} + \Delta L_{REFt}.$$

This condition states that, in order for cash commitments to be paid, there must be enough funds available, either from new sources, i.e. gross cash flow from operations before tax or refinancing loans, or from accumulated past net cash inflows. If this is not the case, part of CC cannot be serviced and banks will record some losses (Wray 1991c).

The bank sector

The bank sector is developed to its minimum. Banks grant advances to firms in order to achieve a certain rate of return. Given that banks do not invest, do not produce any output, and do not pay any wages, the net profit is

$$\Pi_{nB} = i_{st}L_{st} + i_{lt}L_{lt} + i_R R - i_A A,$$

with $i_R R$ the interest on reserves and $i_A A$ the interest payment on central bank advances by banks. i_A is equivalent to the discount window rate. The rate of return for banks is defined as $r_B = \Pi_{nB}/L$. Note that, contrary to a single bank, $i_{st}L_{st} + i_{lt}L_{lt}$ does not represent a source of cash for the banking system (i.e. it does not represent an increase in the amount of reserves because, in the model, none of the bank customers uses central bank money). The only thing that interest payments by the private sector do is to reduce demand deposits without reducing the amount of outstanding loans; interest payments increase capital equity. Only

$i_R R - i_A A$ is a source of net cash inflow for the banking system. Thus, a successful banking system in terms of equity growth may not reflect a higher capacity to meet liquidity demands.

Banks (as well as firms when they set cc_d) use the relative rate of return to determine the acceptable flow-leveraging ratio cc_a. This ratio leads to credit rationing if it is inferior to cc_d. This is a very primitive way to determine the acceptable flow-leveraging ratio because, among others, banks do not look at the creditworthiness of borrowers or of projects. Some of the recent behaviors in the banking sector may get close to this type of behavior:

$$cc_{aT} = cc_{a0} + \sum_{t=1}^{T} e_{rt},$$

where e_r is the effect of relative rate of return on cc_a. The way the relative rate of return affects cc_a and so the supply of bank advances is not that straightforward to figure out. One may think that there is a positive relationship between e_r and cc_a, i.e. if the rate of return is below target, banks lower cc_a and so provide less advances. However, as Minsky notes, a more aggressive strategy may be to provide more advances and to expect that this will pay off. We chose to follow the first behavioral assumption but the level of capital equity and competition may be variables that influence the choice between the two strategies. The speed at which e_r pushes cc_a up or down depends on the optimism of banks. One may think that their optimism is, at least at the beginning of cycle, lower than that of firms. Thus, banks may have a downward bias in their revisions of cc_a with the latter going up less fast than it is going down. For firms, on the contrary, one may assume that there is an upward correction bias. Finally, following the Minskian tradition of destabilizing stability, if $r = r^T$ (and so $e_{rt} = 0$) for a long period of time, e_{rt} will shift upward abruptly after a certain moment has passed. In the model, we do not consider this important insight.

The government sector: Treasury and central bank

The Treasury spends on consumption goods, investment goods, and wage payments of government employees: $G = G_C + G_I + w_G N_G$. There are two types of taxes in the model, income taxes (taxes on corporate profit and wage) and a wealth tax: $T = T_Y + T_{\text{wealth}}$. The wealth tax is imposed on the demand deposit of firms and the equity of banks. Such tax does not exist in reality and is only used to make sure that there is a stationary state for demand deposits of firms and bank equity. Another solution, maybe more realistic, would have been to say that firms make donations to state funded programs in function of their wealth. Note that the wealth tax receipts do not enter in any NIPA identities. The wealth tax affects capital equity after accounting for profit and is recorded in the flow of funds relationships.

The central bank provides advances to banks (A_B) and to the Treasury (A_T), which respectively leads to the *ex nihilo* creation of reserves for an amount R (i.e. demand deposits of banks at the central bank), and to the *ex nihilo* crediting of the Treasury account at the central bank for an amount F. Banks must pay interest on central bank advances and have a certain amortization schedule to respect, and central bank advances are the only method available to borrow reserves. Banks need reserves because the central bank requires that banks keep a certain amount of reserves. The amount of required reserves to hold is a proportion of the demand deposits at the liability side of banks:

$$RR = rrr(DD_H + DD_I + DD_C),$$

with rrr the reserve requirement ratio. Banks may need additional reserves than what is required because they may not have enough funds to pay the debt service due on the reserves they borrowed. If they cannot meet those cash commitments, the central bank automatically provides refinancing loans. The central bank may pay interest on reserves but by default i_R is equal to zero.

The Treasury uses the central bank as a financial accountant; it is the financial arm of the Treasury that keeps track, through financial records, of the Treasury's daily operations induced by expenditures and tax receipts. Whenever it needs funds to spend, the Treasury orders the central bank to credit its account, which, for accounting rigorousness, requires the recording of an advance on the asset side of the central bank. However, the advances to the Treasury are in no way a burden to the latter. There is no predefined repayment schedule and no interest income to be paid on the central bank advances to the Treasury, which would be useless anyways because they would be pure internal accounting for the federal government (defined as the central bank and the Treasury). As Mr. Jordan of the FOMC noted

> One way of thinking about what we do when we conduct operations of the System Open Market Account is that we are monetizing government debt – the liability side of our balance sheet is in effect non-interest-bearing government debt. On the asset side we hold interest-bearing government debt that has effectively been canceled. When you were in Boy Scouts, Peter, Wright Patman used to say we could burn the [Treasury] bonds we hold and nobody would know the difference.
>
> (Jordan, FOMC meeting, March 2000, page 17)

Treasury advances are reduced when the Treasury receives tax payments. Once the funds from tax receipts are transferred to the Treasury account, we assume that they are destroyed immediately (deleted from the hard drive of the central bank's computer, or crossed over in the central bank books, or shredded if funds take the form of central bank notes) and advances to the Treasury are reduced accordingly.[22]

The net amount of reserves left in the system by Treasury operations is equal to

$$\Delta_n A = G - T.$$

Usually, this is called the public "deficit," but this is really a misnomer because the Treasury does not lack anything. All the spending already occurred before tax payments and was financed through an *ex nihilo* crediting of the Treasury's account at the central bank. Thus, the Treasury does not need to make up for the difference between its expenditures and taxes by borrowing more funds because the difference does not represent a shortfall of funds that the Treasury must find in order to be able to spend. A better term is the "net supply of reserves from Treasury operations." Government spending injects reserves in the banking system, while taxes remove reserves from the system. In the end, the net variation of reserves is

$$\Delta_n R = \Delta_n A_T + \Delta_n A_B - \Delta_n F - \Delta_n NW_{CB}.$$

Given the assumption we made about the structure of the model, $\Delta_n F = 0$ (the net variation of the Treasury account at the central bank is nil) and the previous equation is equal to

$$\Delta_n R = G - T + \Delta_n A_B - (i_B A_B - i_R R).$$

These financing and funding methods of the Treasury are similar to what most sovereign governments do today and the US Treasury does try to make sure that $\Delta_n F = 0$ (Lerner 1943, 1944; Meulendyke 1998: 156–157; Bell 2000; Wray 1998a, 2003a, 2003c, 2004b). The balance sheet of the central bank respects the following identity (with NW_{CB} the equity of the central bank): $A_T + A_B \equiv R + F + NW_{CB}$.

One may wonder what would happen if the Treasury continuously taxed incomes more than what it spent so that, given everything else, the stock of reserves reached zero. In this case, in the model, it would be impossible for the Treasury to credit its account at the central bank. Thus, even though the Treasury levied taxes on the private sector (which draws down demand deposits of households and firms) there would be no way to record the counterpart, which would be a decline in bank reserves and a crediting of the Treasury account. In reality, to prevent this and other problems from happening, the US Treasury records tax receipts on tax and loan accounts, which are demand deposits of the Treasury at some private banks. Through this collection method, the effect on reserves is not immediate and Bell (2000) has shown that those accounts play a strategic role in the management of reserve supply in the US (Wray 2003a, 2003c).

Shortcomings and possible developments

If the model is able to take into account some important characteristics of the Minskian analysis like conventions and the cash box condition, it leaves aside other important components. In addition, some rough simplifications have been made.

The first element that has been left aside is the financial market, which is an advantage and a disadvantage. The main advantage, besides simplifying the model greatly, is that this allows to show that financial-market speculation and other financial "wastages" are not necessary to the story of the Minskian framework. The main disadvantage is that a large part of the economic system is left unexplained, this is all the more a problem because investment is influenced by the arbitrage between old and new capital goods (P_K/P_I).

Another shortcoming concerns the lack of any distribution of dividends or interest income to households. One could think that firms and banks distribute part of their gross profit to households, and that this would affect consumption, inflation, economic growth, and employment, but this is not taken into account here. A more developed model could easily incorporate this element, which is not essential for the main argument. Of course, the imposition of a wealth tax is a very rough way to impose a stationary state on demand deposits of firms.

The model assumes that the unit cost of debts is variable for the whole outstanding debt. Thus, a change in interest rates or maturity terms affects all the existing debts and not only new debts. Following Minsky, this implies that the model can never take into account a hedge situation. In addition, the model does not integrate well the refinancing needs. Indeed, if $cc_n > 1$, the stationary state value for refinancing loans should be positive because there is an expected need to refinance. The model always starts with cc_n largely inferior to one. In addition, refinancing loans are exogenously granted but one may think that there are limits to the amount of refinancing loans that banks are willing to grant. Indeed, the more refinancing occurs, the more the net worth of borrowers goes down and the more banks carry risk on their balance sheets. Thus, the willingness of banks to grant advances to refinance positions may abruptly decline, creating a refinancing crisis in addition to credit rationing for normal economic activities.

Note that the preceding assumed that in order to determine the external funding of desired investment, firms only look at long-term debts. They, however, may make their external-funding decisions in function of the whole debt outstanding because what matters in the end is the total financial burden determined by the total flow-leveraging ratio cc. Thus, firms would start by looking at the total desired cash commitments rather than only desired long-term cash commitments. There are several ways to proceed from here. One way[23] is by determining desired level of debt for each maturity term:

$$CC_d = (a_{lt} + i_{lt})L_{ltd} + (a_{st} + i_{st})L_{std}.$$

The desired level of long-term debts is then determined by

$$L_{ltd} = \frac{cc_d E(\Pi - \Delta IN) - (a_{st} + i_{st})L_{std}}{(a_{lt} + i_{lt})}.$$

The desired level of short-term debts then has to be explained. Once this is done, a financial limit may be imposed on the employment level that can be externally financed. Indeed, one may start by recognizing that the level short-term debts desired to finance employment implies a desired level of short-term cash commitments CC_{std}. If $CC_{std} > CC_n$, with CC_n the total normal level of cash commitments including long-term debts, then firms are not allowed by banks to employ the number of individuals they want. This allows to find the maximum level of employment financially possible by using external funds. Assuming that there is no long-term debt, the maximum level of employment financially possible is such that $CC_{std} = CC_n$. If it is assumed that the desired level of short-term debt is equal to its stationary state value (defined below), then

$$N^{\max F} = \frac{a_{st}cc_nE(\Pi - \Delta IN)}{w(a_{st} + i_{st})}.$$

If one assumes that firms exclusively use external funds to pay their wage bills, this value creates a third constraint for the desired level of employment: $N_d = \min(O^T/APL, uO^{\max}, N^{\max F})$. If firms use their own funds to pay the wage bill, $N^{\max F}$ is only one element of the financial constraint on employment, the other element being the amount of money held by firms.

Finally, it was assumed that the credit constraint on firms comes only at the beginning of the investment decision, i.e. before the contracts to build machines are signed. However, while the machines are built, builders may have to cope with credit constraints, or when the time comes for customers to pay, banks may be unwilling or may be unable to meet its promise. In this case, producers record a loss because finished and unfinished investment goods are left idle, which has a strong impact on production and employment.

Some of the stationary state values

There is a stationary state when stocks do not grow, i.e. when inflows and outflows from stocks are equal so that the net variation of stocks is equal to zero. In addition, at the stationary state all the additional effects are equal to one ($e = 1$), except for flow-leveraging ratios for which $e = 0$, and all variables are at their targeted values.

Starting with capital equipment in the consumption-good sector, the stationary-state condition implies that net investment is zero:

$$\Delta_n K_C = O_{\text{In}C} = O_{IC} - d_C K_C = 0.$$

Or, given that $O_{\text{In}} = (K_d - K)/t_I$,

$$(K_{Cd} - K_C)/t_I = 0.$$

We know that, at the stationary state, $K_{Cd} = O_C^{\max T}/AP_{KC}$ and that $O_C^{\max T} = O_C^T/u_{nC}$, with $O_C^T = E(O_{Cd})$ because inventories are on target ($O_{\text{ingap}} = 0$).

Therefore, the stationary condition on capital equipment in the consumption-good sector becomes

$$\frac{\frac{E(O_{Cd})}{AP_{KC} \times u_{nC}} - K}{t_I} = 0.$$

Rearranging we get

$$K_C^* = \frac{E(O_{Cd})}{u_{nC} \times AP_{KC}}.$$

with $E(O_{Cd})$ being given at the initial time. This is consistent with Keynes's methodology of shifting equilibrium based on effective demand (Kregel 1976): the whole system rests on a given state of expectation of entrepreneurs regarding future sales. The gross demand of investment goods by the Treasury is assumed to be exogenous so that at the stationary state $d_G K_G = O_{IGd}$ and so $K_G^* = O_{IGd}/d_G$. Applying the same method to the investment-good sector one gets

$$K_I^* = \frac{d_C K_C^* + d_G K_G^*}{u_{nI} \times AP_{KI} - d_I}.$$

Once this is determined, it is possible to find the stationary state value of employment in each sector. Again, at the stationary state, in the consumption-good sector, we have

$$\Delta_n N_C = (N_{Cd} - N_C)/t_{HC} = 0.$$

And we know that, at the stationary state, $N_{Cd} = E(O_{Cd})/AP_{LC}$, therefore

$$N_C^* = \frac{E(O_{Cd})}{AP_{LC}}.$$

And for the investment-good sector, we have

$$N_I^* = \frac{d_C K_C^* + d_I K_I^* + d_G K_G^*}{AP_{LI}}.$$

Again, for the Treasury, it is assumed that the desired level of employment is exogenous; therefore, the stationary value of N_G is whatever the desired value of employment N_{Gd} is. If there was an employer of last resort program, N_{Gd} would be equal to the number of individuals seeking a job and unable to find one in the private sector.

We now need to find the stationary value for debts. Starting with short-term debts, they are composed of refinancing debts and debts obtained to finance the wage bill. At the stationary state, firms can meet all their cash commitments; therefore, $\Delta L_{REF} = 0$ and $z = 0$. In terms of the financing of wages, it is assumed that it is never credit constrained so that firms can obtain all the funds they need to employ the number of individuals desired $\Delta L_W = wN_d$. Thus, at the stationary state

$$\Delta_n L_{st} = wN_d - a_{st}L_{wC-1} = 0.$$

Given that, at the stationary state, desired values are fulfilled

$$L_{st}^* = \frac{wN^*}{a_{st}}.$$

Regarding long-term debts, we know that $L_{ltd} = \dfrac{cc_{ltd}E(\Pi - \Delta IN)}{(a_{lt} + i_{lt})}$ and that, at the stationary state, $\Delta IN = 0$ and $cc_d = cc_n$, therefore,

$$\frac{\dfrac{cc_{ltn}E(\Pi)}{(a_{lt} + i_{lt})} - L_{lt}}{t_I} = 0 \Rightarrow L_{lt}^* = \frac{cc_{ltn}E(\Pi^*)}{(a_{lt} + i_{lt})},$$

with the stationary level of gross profit in the consumption-good and investment-good sectors being, respectively,

$$\Pi_C^* = C^* + G_C - w_C N_C^*$$
$$\Pi_I^* = I^* + G_I - w_I N_I^*.$$

Finally, the stationary value for demand deposits can be found easily by equalizing inflows and outflows of cash. For the household sector

$$\Delta_n DD_H = W - T_W - C,$$
$$\Delta_n DD_H = W - T_W - c_W(1 - t_W)W - c_{DD}DD_H,$$

At the stationary state $\Delta_n DD_H = 0$, and so

$$DD_H^* = W^* \frac{(1 - t_W - c_W(1 - t_W))}{c_{DD}},$$

with $W^* = w_C N_C^* + w_I N_I^* + w_G N_G^*$. The same can be done easily for firms.

Simulations

In the first part of the simulations, we study the impact of several factors on economic activity by assuming that the central bank never changes its interest rates (and all other rates are fixed). Central bank rate on advances is zero permanently and the model starts at the stationary state. This is followed by a series of simulations that studies the impact of active uses of interest rate by the central bank. Before

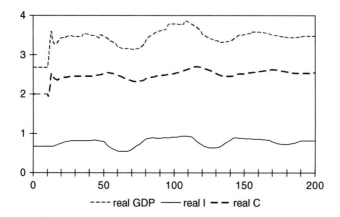

Figure 5.5 Effect of higher expected demand on economic activity.

going any further, one must remember that we concentrate exclusively on the flow-leveraging ratio of long-term debts, i.e. without including cash-commitments on short-term debts in the value of cc. Short-term debts unrelated to refinancing needs are pro-cyclical because they are related to the wage bill. On the contrary, long-term debts are the one that reflects the Minskian dynamics generated by long-term stability. Optimally one should include both short-term and long-term cash commitments in the value of cc but we were not able to do so coherently for the moment. Two possible extensions are proposed in the section related to the limits of the model.

The state of expectations and other demand-related factors

Given that the core of Keynes's framework rests on the role of expected demand for current economic activity, this is a good point of departure for the simulation. The following examines the impact of a permanent increase in expected demand for consumption goods by +0.5 good per month. It is assumed that bank rates are constant, taxes are constant, and government spending is constant (0 on investment goods, $70 on consumption goods per month, 0 on government employment). The general effect on economic activity is shown in Figure 5.5. Real GDP goes up and employment is stimulated; however, there is also a cyclical pattern.

To explain the cyclical pattern, one must look at what happens in the firm sector. Figures 5.6 and 5.7 show the implications of a permanent increase in expected demand for consumption goods in the investment-good sector and in the consumption-good sector, respectively (nominal expenditure is on the left axis, flow-leveraging ratios are on the right axis).

Starting with the investment-good sector, the dynamics of the Minskian analysis clearly are present. The reason for the procyclical fluctuations in cc_{nltI} is related to the procyclical fluctuations in the relative rate of return in the

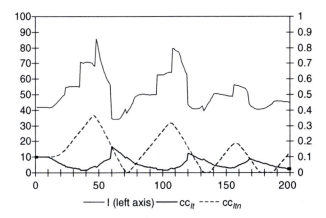

Figure 5.6 Effect of higher expected demand for consumption goods in the investment-good sector.

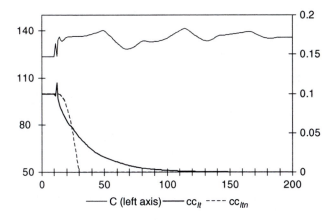

Figure 5.7 Effect of higher expected demand for consumption goods in the consumption-good sector.

investment-good sector. During the expansion, the rate of return is above target, and during the contraction, it is below target. With cc_{nltl} going up, the desired proportion of external funding of investment goes up for firms in the investment-good sector, which means that the desired use of internal funds goes down, given desired dishoarding. As shown in Figure 5.8, firms are not always borrowing what they desire to borrow because internal funds and dishoarding are sufficient to meet investment spending. At the peak of the cycle, however, external funding is usually above its desired value, as firms have to come up with additional external funding because they have used all their internal funds and all their demand deposits.

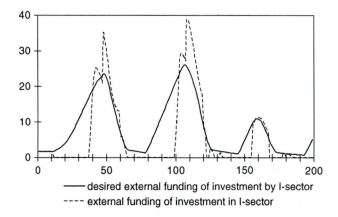

——— desired external funding of investment by I-sector

---- external funding of investment in I-sector

Figure 5.8 Desired and actual external funding of investment in the investment-good sector.

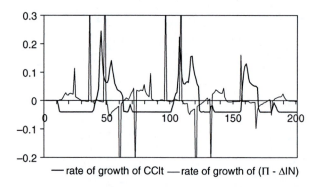

——— rate of growth of CCIt ——— rate of growth of (Π - ΔIN)

Figure 5.9 Relation between cc_{ltI} and $\Pi_I - \Delta IN_I$ in terms of growth in the investment-good sector.

Note that the flow-leveraging ratio does not go up necessarily during the expansion. Only toward the end of the expansion period does it go up and, as shown in Figure 5.9, this is due to the increase in the growth rate of cc_{ltI} (as external funding of investment grows) and the decline in the rate of growth of gross cash flow from operations ($\Pi_I - \Delta IN_I$) (which is due to a decline in the relative rate of return in both sub-sectors that causes investment demand to go down). The former eventually outweighs the latter because of a volume effect (more long-term debts) not because of a price effect (interest rates and amortization rates are constant).

In the consumption-good sector, one can see that the results are in sharp contradiction with the Minskian model and consistent with Lavoie (1997a).

Not only do firms in that sector have a financial situation that always strengthens (cc_{It} tends toward 0) but also their desired flow-leveraging ratio never goes up during the period of expansion. This is so because, following the increase in expected demand, the relative rate of return is constantly below one and so cc_{nltC} constantly declines. Given that tendency, the desired level of external funding of investment also goes down to zero. In addition, the desired amount of internal funds used, $f_{\Pi dC}\Pi_{IFC}$, is always high enough to meet all the investment expenditure in the consumption-good sector and so firms in the sector never have to borrow to fund investment. This, however, does not lead to an increase in cc_{nltC} because the latter reacts only to the relative rate of return in the consumption-good sector.

All this, however, can be made consistent with the Minskian approach if, as Isenberg (1988, 1994) and Minsky (e.g. Minsky (1984b)) note, financial fragility does not need to be generalized but may be specific to the most dynamic sector of the economy (which is the investment-good sector in the simulation). During a crisis, financial fragility may spread rapidly to the rest of the economy through the financial sector (credit rationing) and through the financial impacts on other sectors (lower cash inflows).

One may be able to reproduce the Minskian dynamics in the consumption-good sector from the same shock on expected demand by changing the weight given to monetary considerations when setting the capacity utilization rate. We know that

$$u_C = \alpha_r e_r + (1 - \alpha_r) e_{\text{ingap}}.$$

By default $\alpha_r = 0.5$, that is, firms pay equal attention to monetary and production considerations when deciding how intensively they should use their machines. As shown in Figure 5.10, if more weight is put on monetary considerations, i.e. if firms pay more attention to meet their targeted rate of return, the dynamics of the Minskian system can appear also in the consumption-good sector.

Overall, changes in expected demand have a strong impact on the dynamics of the model. This importance of expectations is not a particularity of the Minskian or Keynesian frameworks (Kregel 1977). However, the importance of conventional expectations is a particularity of the two preceding approaches. The expectations are not based on a "true" model but on a mental model that tries to explain the expected future performance of the economy. One implication of this is that the comparison between past expectations and current results (the *ex ante/ex post* distinction) is not the main way expectations affect the dynamics of the economic system. The comparison of current expectations and current state of affairs is far more important.

The same type of dynamics as presented above can be obtained simultaneously in both sectors by a general increase in nominal wage (even if the weight of monetary consideration is left at 0.5). The latter leads to an increase in demand for consumption goods and so an increase in expected demand for consumption goods over time. This leads firms in the consumption-good sector to order more investment goods and so firms in the investment-good sector do the same.

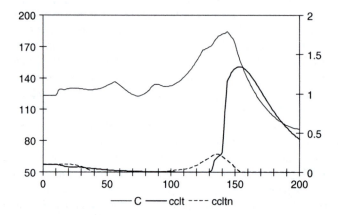

Figure 5.10 Effect of higher expected demand for consumption goods in the consumption-good sector if more weight is put on monetary considerations.

The prosperous economy results in rates of return above target, which lead to an increase in the desired proportion of external funding and so a decrease in the use of internal funds. As the investment goods are delivered and added to existing capital equipment, and as debt servicing on long-term debts starts to rise, the rate of return goes below target, which reverses the whole dynamics. The beneficial impact of higher wages depends on two conditions: first, the wage increase must be generalized (so that consumption increases enough to overweight higher cost for firms) and second, government employees must exist or some form of government spending must exist (higher government wage increases consumption without affecting the labor cost of private firms).

In the end, therefore, the dynamics of the Minskian analysis do not require any irrational exuberance in financial markets or anywhere else, or rising interest rates. A central element of the dynamics may be the relationship between actual and targeted rates of return and its effects on production and employment decisions, the rate of return being defined as the net cash flow from operations over the value of capital equipment (or any other relevant variable as denominator). Of course, the Minskian dynamics would be reinforced by the willingness of the Treasury to generate a surplus during the expansion, and the willingness of the central bank to raise interest rates to manage inflation and this is what the following section studies.

Government intervention in the economy

The Treasury spends and taxes, and it turns out to be a central component for the dynamics of the model. Indeed, it is impossible to get a non-zero stationary state for employment and production if there is not a minimum amount of government

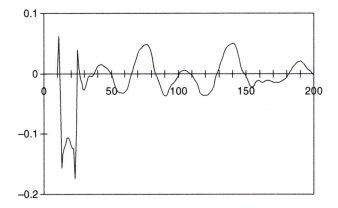

Figure 5.11 Consumer-price inflation.

spending. Indeed, net cash inflows from operations in the consumption-good sector cannot be positive unless the government spends by buying goods (in either sector) or by employing some people. By spending, the government provides cash inflows to private firms. It seems that an employer of last resort program would clearly help to sustain the economy and it would be a good point to develop in future research (Fullwiler 2007).

To study the impact of monetary policy, a good starting point is to consider the context presented in the previous section. There is an increase in expected demand for consumption goods that generates a business cycle led by the investment-good sector. As shown in Figure 5.11, this business cycle generates inflationary pressures during the expansion.

One may note that higher expected demand first leads to large deflation, not inflation. Godley and Lavoie (2007), following Gardiner Means, call this a perverse effect because one would expect that higher demand increases prices. However, here it is expected demand that rises, not current demand. The impact of higher expected demand is to raise production today, given demand, in order to be able to meet the future demand. Firms in the consumption-good sector anticipate demand, they do not follow demand. They raise production by increasing the rate of utilization of capacity of production and by investing in new capital equipment. If, instead of expected demand it is wages that go up, so that demand rises today given production, there is some inflation (even though it is moderate and there is a positive impact on production and employment for moderate increases in wages).

The central bank is assumed to respond to price instability by changing its interest rate on advances. The bank rates respond by applying a mark up to the cost of advances. The central bank has a targeted inflation rate (by default it is set at 0.5 percent) and responds more or less aggressively to deviations of inflation

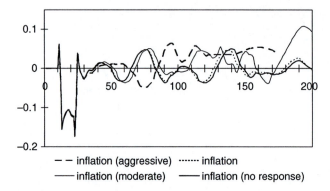

Figure 5.12 Inflation under different interest-rate policies (0.5 percent target).

Table 5.5 Performance of monetary policy in terms of inflation

	Aggressive	Moderate	Low	No response
Target 0.5%				
Average (%)	1.131	0.903	−0.714	−0.757
Std dev.	0.0436	0.0483	0.0371	0.0373
Target 0.7%				
Average	1.284	−0.403	−0.727	−0.757
Std dev.	0.0417	0.0369	0.0369	0.0373

from its targeted value. We first assume that the central bank moderately responds to expected inflation:[24]

$$i_{At} = \begin{cases} i_{At-1} - 0.01 & \text{if} \quad E(\pi) < \pi^T \\ i_{At-1} + 0.01 & \text{if} \quad E(\pi) > \pi^T \\ i_{At-1} + 0.02 & \text{if} \quad E(\pi) > 2\pi^T \end{cases}.$$

Then, it is assumed that the central bank responds aggressively to expected inflation (−0.1, 0.1, and 0.2 for the response coefficients), not very much (−0.001, 0.001, and 0.002), and finally, does not respond to inflation ($i_{At} = 0 \forall t$). Figure 5.12 shows the performance of inflation under the different rules, and the same results are presented in Table 5.5.

The more aggressive the central bank is in terms of interest-rate policy, the more it tends to promote inflation and variability of inflation. If the central bank does not respond to inflation at all, there is a tendency for deflation in the system and the variability of consumer price is the lowest. These results confirm the econometrical results of chapter 4, at least in terms of the inflationary effect of active monetary policy. The aggressiveness of a central bank can also be modeled by looking at the impact of different inflation targets, which is also done in Table 5.5. As one can note, under a higher inflation target (0.7 percent instead of 0.5 percent), i.e. a less

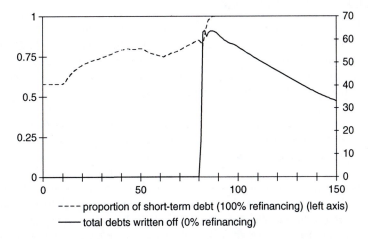

Figure 5.13 Impact of aggressive monetary policy on refinancing needs.

aggressive policy in terms of target, a moderate response by the central bank performs best. In the end, therefore, the capacity of the central bank to manage inflation depends on its aggressiveness in terms of inflation target and interest-rate manipulations. If the central bank is very aggressive in terms of target (low target), no manipulation of interest rates works best. If the central bank is very aggressive in terms of interest-rate manipulations, a higher inflation target is best. All these results suggest that the central bank should be lax in order to help to manage inflation. Aggressive monetary policy tends to generate interest-rate variability and to promote output-price inflation.

Additional analysis shows that an aggressive (and even a moderate) response is clearly not welcome. Indeed, an aggressive response leads to financial instability by raising interest rates too fast. The cash flow from operations cannot keep up with the growth of debts and, as shown in Figure 5.13, firms (and banks) have to ask for refinancing loans or to declare bankruptcy (and so some debts are written down).

Overall, one may conclude that using interest rates to try to manage inflation does not help to reduce price instability and may actually increase the latter, and in addition, may generate financial fragility and financial instability. Thus, one may conclude that an economy with a high proportion of short-term loans is far more delicate to manage via interest-rate changes. Indeed, higher interest rates can rapidly increase the cost of the whole outstanding debt as short-term debts are rolled over, and lower interest rates may be inefficient in reducing the growth of cash commitments if the growth of the latter is related to other reasons than the cost of loans.

Implications for central banking

Central banks should reorient their policy goals toward financial stability and should leave output-price stability and employment to other public policies. Using interest rates to manage the economy is very passive, can generate perverse effects, and usually is not very effective. The role of central banks is to manage, to promote, and to monitor the liquidity of the economy, which is the reason for which they have been created.

However, the financial supervision should be done in a different way than today. For the moment, it rests on a vision of banks as isolated agents whose individual problems result from their specific decisions, and it ignores the importance of behaviors based on conventions. "Bad behavior" is really not a good way to understand the dynamics involved because behaviors are socio-economically determined (Henry 2006). Under competition and uncertainty, and encouraged by existing reward mechanisms, economic units tend to follow the average behavior, which is considered to be "normal" and sensible, even though it may entail a good deal of financial fragility. In this case, what matters is not the behavior of the firms ahead of the norm, it is the norm itself that is the problem. Thus, "bad behavior" may be generalized and systematic, and may be considered normal and required in order not to lose market shares. Discovering systemic risk, not isolated bad behaviors, is the main task of regulators and supervisors. For example, a central bank knows that "new economy" conventions are fictions that will not last, and it should not have any interest in letting it go unchecked.[25] It may be true that new technologies improve economic growth, but they do not imply that the economy will grow forever, or that the growth rate of income will be always higher than the growth rate of cash commitments. There are historical and economic arguments against the new-era proponents.

A central bank can promote systemic financial prudence in several ways. One is by guiding cc_n through a supervision and regulation of banks that focuses on cash flows. One should develop a cash-flow oriented analysis of the banking system that looks at the different ways financial institutions could get into trouble, and how sensitive they are to the occurrence of shocks of a usual magnitude. This would imply supervising the expected cash inflows of financial institutions, their expected cash outflows, and the strength of the different position-making channels. In addition, the regulatory authorities should use capital requirements but be flexible by moving capital requirements with economic conditions in a counter-cyclical manner. Capital requirements should grow during economic expansion and go down during economic recession. This should be complemented by a supervision that focuses more on the assets that back a given level of net worth, and that makes sure, through a form of income policy, that demands from stakeholders are not promoting financial instability. Thus, "control over the capital-asset ratio and the pay-out ratio for banks are powerful weapons for guiding development of banking" (Minsky 1986a: 321). One should recognize, however, that significant progress toward those goals has been made over the past twenty to thirty years. CAMELS composite ratings and prompt corrective action (PAC) for undercapitalized financial institutions have been significant improvements in the supervision of financial institutions (Comptroller of the Currency 2007; Guttmann 2006). This type of supervision, however, should include all financial institutions without exception. In addition, the data obtained during the supervision could provide invaluable information about the strength of current and future cash inflows of each institution, and the refinancing channels available to financial institutions. This should be used to create a macroeconomic framework that captures the interrelationship between financial institutions, and between financial institutions and the rest of the economic system.

Currently, there is no equivalent sensitivity analysis of cash flow for the aggregate economy. Some progress has been made over the past three decades by central bankers in terms of their awareness of financial conditions but there is still much room for developments, and current analyses are made of bits and pieces that focuses on correlations that break down in periods of instability (Nelson and Passmore 2001; Sahel and Vesala 2001). Godley and Lavoie (2007) have pushed for the use of stock-flow accounting in theoretical macroeconomic models. This could be combined with computerized modeling techniques like System Dynamics, which can handle well non-linear phenomena, to study in detail the sensitivity of the economy to changes in asset prices and the interrelations among different sectors of the economy. However, a large amount of data is missing and prevents an implementation of this technique at the policy level for the moment (Sahel and Vesala 2001). The inexistence of a cash-flow oriented national accounting framework is a particularly large gap that needs to be filled.

The current emphasis on capital requirements by the Basel Accord does not really help to promote financial stability. Capital equity is not "cash" and only present and future net cash inflows represent financial strength and allow to cope with current and future liquidity problems. In this sense, a growing capital equity does not mean that a company is successful or even more solvent. Capital equity is affected by all sorts of adjustments that have nothing to do with the capacity of the company to generate cash from its core business, or to liquidate quickly assets at low costs in case of emergency. Granted, within the logic of capital requirement regulation, the purpose of Basel capital requirement is not to meet liquidity problems directly but to manage risk-taking activities. Net worth is supposed to promote financial stability by helping to prevent adverse selection, moral hazard and other agency problems. Having a certain amount of capital makes sure that loans will be limited to strong borrowers, and that the owners of the company will feel the pain financially if they let managers "behave badly" (Mishkin 1991, 1997; Davis 1995; Minsky 1977a, 1986a: 320–321). However, this position fails to recognize three central points. First, following the dialectical approach of Minsky, a too high amount of capital equity may promote a sense of safety that may encourage risk taking. Thus, more net worth does not mean more responsible behaviors and there may be a non-linear relationship between the two (Kregel 2006; Wray 2006b). Second, many authors have noted that capital requirements have procyclical properties, i.e. a financial disruption creates a need to raise capital to meet requirements which, through fire sales and credit rationing, contributes further to financial instability. Third, as Greenspan notes (2008), the main contribution of the new Basel Accord is to help financial institutions to optimize asset allocation given their amount of capital and their risk assessment. That, however, by itself does not help to promote financial stability. On the contrary, private assessments of risk tend to be procyclical. A period of good economic performance and socio-psychological factors push individuals to become very daring and so contributes to financial fragility. Thus, the willingness of the new Basel Accord to let the most developed financial institutions determine their own risk-assessment method in order to calculate capital requirements is problematic.

Aside of supervision, a central bank may be actively involved in the restructuring of balance sheets that have become illiquid or insolvent because of a large amount of non-performing debts. If central bankers do not feel that they should do this directly, they could create an institution specialized in the smoothing of the simplification process and work closely with this institution. The point is that there is an institution that is able to deal with liquidity crises (the central bank), but no institution exists to deal with solvency crises. The central bank could extend its responsibilities toward this area, especially when a lender of last resort intervention is necessary: Canceling debts in a constructive manner (by being involved in the restructuring process) is the best way to promote recovery. The Hunt crisis is the perfect example of what a central bank should not do: no participation in the discussion of the private bail out in which it does provide funds directly or indirectly (through a backing of the private rescuers), no strict imposition of conditions or restriction on the future behaviors of banks (Greider 1987).

The central bank should also orient its research toward promoting financial contracts that do not have cumulative adverse financial effects. One way of doing this is by enhancing financial contracts with highly predictable cash outflows that can be adjusted downward to account for short-term liquidity problems of creditworthy borrowers. A second way through which the central bank can promote financial stability is by promoting the matching of cash flows from assets and liabilities. It can do so by promoting a maturity matching of assets and liabilities and by providing banks with a low-cost refinancing channel. In the end, both the income and the capital components of financial instruments should be adapted to the needs of borrowers as much as possible. More generally, one needs to enlarge the spectrum of financial contracts toward those that allow flexibility in the income and capital payments as long as the source of borrower's cash inflows seems sound and is only disrupted temporarily. Clauses including automatic restructuring of loan contracts may help in this direction.

In terms of asset prices, the model provides only preliminary insights. Indeed, the model could not look into the impacts of asset prices because there was no financial market. However, the main insight we get is that speculation in financial markets does not need to exist in order for financial fragility to emerge. There is no bubble in the model. The model includes only one type of unproductive loans (refinancing) and this is sufficient to generate fragility. If they are not granted then liquidation is necessary and ultimately debts are written off. If they are granted the proportion of short-term loans increases dramatically, making the economy more sensitive to changes in financial conditions; anyways, the system is more fragile.

The preceding also shows some of the limits of the current practices of risk management in terms of their capacity to manage financial stability. As Bernstein notes "What matters in the end is not the probability that you're right, but the consequences of what happens to the client if you're wrong" (Bernstein 2001: 1). This concerns both the occurrence of a future event and its timing. The massive amount of past financial data does not provide a reliable source of information about those two crucial points. The best way to hedge against the future is to have a long position in liquid assets or to have access to liquid assets; nothing else will do, even the most sophisticated mathematical model. It is the duty of the central bank to provide an access to those liquid assets when needed.

Finally, maybe one of the central conclusions of this chapter for central banking is that financial innovations should be supervised. Innovations (drugs, mechanical innovations, etc.) in other sectors of the economy are strictly scrutinized and tested by supervisors before they are allowed to be used in daily life. The financial sector is at odds in this case because financial innovations are allowed to be implemented freely even though their consequences are not understood well, even by their creators. Innovations in any sector are central to the dynamics of a capitalist system and they should be allowed to thrive. Entrepreneurship is an essential component of economic welfare. However, innovations also alter the structure of the economic system and affect behaviors, and so may be disastrous for the economy and for the well-being of its population. Thus, financial innovations should be well understood before they can be set free in the economic system. If they tend to promote Ponzi behaviors and their cash-flow implications are extremely difficult to understand, they should not be allowed.

6 Financial matters in the decisions of the FOMC

With the Financial Modernization Act (or "Gramm-Leach-Bliley Act") of 1999, the involvement of the Federal Reserve in the financial system increased tremendously. The Fed has become "the umbrella holding company supervisor" and all federal and state regulators were brought under the oversight of the Federal Reserve System. However, members of the Federal Open Market Committee (FOMC) have still in mind a model of the world, in which financial matters are of secondary importance relative to real matters. In addition, they are more or less suspicious about the capacity of a central bank to fine-tune the economy and agree that a central bank should be mainly concerned with the long-term goal of price stability, the latter promoting sustainable growth and financial stability. However, FOMC members, as well as other central bankers, are involved heavily in the fine-tuning of the economy "to a degree that was previously unimaginable, even during the golden age of Keynesian macroeconomics in the 1950s and 1960s" (Dalziel 2002: 519).

Reading the FOMC transcripts from 1979 to 2001 gives many insights about the way financial considerations have affected the decisions of the FOMC, and helps to explain the previous contradictions. The first part of the chapter looks at the decisions of the Committee before, during, and after the occurrence of several financial problems. The aim is to see if the FOMC members anticipated these problems, and to study what they tried to do to avoid or to solve them. This will also give us an insider's view about the role played by asset prices and financial fragility in the decision process of the FOMC members. The second part of the chapter shows that FOMC members sometimes had a hard time understanding what was going on in the economy because of an inappropriate theoretical framework. This part also corroborates some of the conclusions and insights that have been reached in the previous chapters.

The Federal Reserve and financial disruptions

A series of financial problems

During the 1979–2002 period, the Federal Reserve had to deal with many financial problems. By computing trade volume and price data, Figures 6.1–6.3 show all the

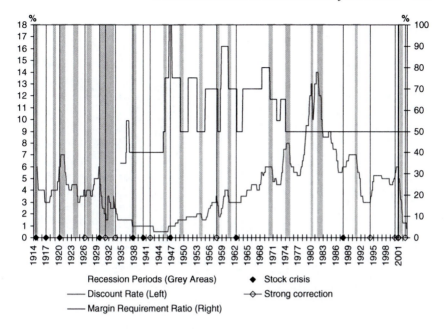

Figure 6.1 Stock market and monetary policy of the Fed.
Sources: Federal Reserve of New York (ftp website), Board of Governors, NBER, Financial Market
Center, http://www.momentumcd.com/STOCKDATA.html. Calculation by the author.

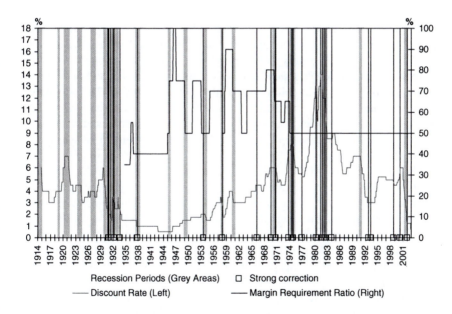

Figure 6.2 Bond market and monetary policy of the Fed.
Sources: Federal Reserve of New York (ftp website), Board of Governors, NBER, Financial Market
Center, http://www.momentumcd.com/STOCKDATA.html. Calculation by the author.

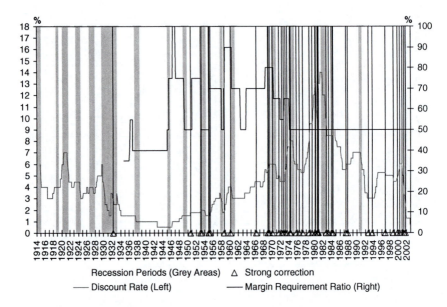

Recession Periods (Grey Areas)   Δ Strong correction
—— Discount Rate (Left)   —— Margin Requirement Ratio (Right)

Figure 6.3 Short-term-paper markets and monetary policy of the Fed.
Sources: Federal Reserve of New York (ftp website), Board of Governors, NBER, Financial Market Center, http://www.momentumcd.com/STOCKDATA.html. Calculation by the author.

strong corrections in asset prices (i.e. large and rapid decreases in prices without panic) and financial crises (strong correction plus panic) that occurred between 1914 and 2002 (see Appendix 5 for methodology). Figure 6.1 suggests that there were nine stock-market crises and ten strong corrections, and two of these events clearly can be related to the policy of the Federal Reserve: The 1947 crisis, with the margin requirement ratio going up to 100 percent, and the 1994 strong correction due to the first rise in policy rates after 5 years. Others are more related to recession periods, for example 1914, 1929, and 1937, or to other causes like speculation (1987, 2001).

Figures 6.2 and 6.3 show all the strong corrections that occurred in the bond market and in short-term-paper markets. Because of the inability to get data about trading volumes, crises could not be identified, and the number of strong corrections is certainly overstated. Several things, however, are worth noticing. First, during the 1970s, the frequency of strong corrections rose steeply in the bond market after a long period of stability following the Great Depression. The volatility in short-term-paper markets also increased a lot after 1950. Both events can be partly related to the Treasury Accord of 1951 and the change in monetary-policy strategy in the 1970s. The higher volatility in short-term-paper markets is also due to the emergence of the federal funds market in the mid-1950s and other financial innovations like negotiable certificate of deposits in 1961 in response to the change in monetary policy in the 1950s (Cargill and Garcia 1982).

Second, the data capture some well-known disturbances like the 1966 and 1969 crises in the short-term-paper markets, and the 1994 and 1998 problems in the bond market.

In addition to the previous financial disturbances, one can find the following additional problems discussed at the FOMC meetings: solvency crisis of thrift institutions during most of the 1980s and early 1990s, the financial problems of the less developed countries (LDCs crisis) in early/mid 1980s, Hunt Brothers in December 1980, Drysdale and Chase in May 1982, Penn Square Bank in July 1982, Continental Illinois in May 1984, ESM and Ohio thrift institutions in March 1985, Drexel in March 1990, Trump and RJR debt in July 1990, Olympia and York in February 1992, Tequila crisis in early 1994, Orange county financial problems in December 1994, the widespread international financial crisis of 1997–1998, and LTCM in September 1998. We will not explain the causes and consequences of those different problems; some of them are explained in details in Greider (1987), Wolfson (1994), and Mayer (2001). The point here is to study how the FOMC members anticipated the problems, if they did, and what their decisions were, given what was happening: Did the financial problems push them to modify their policy? What further regulatory or supervisory decisions did the Fed take? Did these problems take a large part of the FOMC meetings?

The reaction of the Fed

The period of analysis is divided in two sub-periods, the first one going from 1979 to 1990 and involving problems related to the savings and loan associations crisis (S&Ls crisis), the LDCs debt crisis, and the speculation in the stock market. The second period, from 1991 to 2001, contains some international financial problems and the "new era" speculation in the stock market.

The 1979–1990 period

In October 1979, the Fed decided to change its operating procedures in order to fight inflation and regain credibility in this fight. The aim was to de-emphasize interest rates as a target and to focus on reserve targets. Practically, this implied that the central bank allowed wider fluctuations in the fed funds rate. The widest target range was 13–20 percent in March 1980, and the highest range was reached in May and June 1981 with a targeted range of 16–22 percent. The policy, to the despair of Roos, was not a complete shift to Monetarism but a "hybrid," to take Volcker's words, it still took into account the importance of the federal funds rate:[1]

> We are not – at least I am not – proposing that we go to a purely mechanical reserve targeting approach. [...] We are allowing some human being to sit there and [judge] that the multiplier between reserves and deposits [used for the projections] is off and to make some adjustment for that in conducting operations in the next few weeks. There are all these elements of judgment

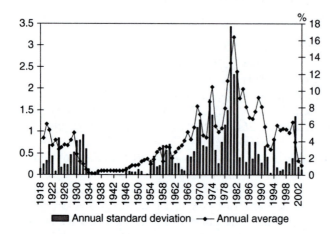

Figure 6.4 Average variability and level of the federal funds rate.
Source: Board of Governors.

that enter into the process. That, combined with the constraint on the federal funds rate, brings us to something of a hybrid.

(Volcker, October 1979, FOMC transcript, page 28)

As shown in Figure 6.4, the "brute force" (Mayer 2001) employed by the Fed involved imposing the burden of high interest rates and high variability of interest rates on an economy that was used to a relatively moderate and stable cost of external funds. The variability was essential in creating a squeeze in net cash inflows because it made it harder to anticipate the cost of external funds and to incorporate into contracts the impact of this cost.[2] This high level and variability of interest rates immediately hurt LDCs, which borrowed heavily in dollars during the 1970s, and so their creditors, the US commercial banks. This also sent an additional, and final, blow to the thrift institutions that had been suffering from the consequences of Treasury Accord since the 1960s.

In March 1980, no more than 5 months after the implementation of the new operational procedure, some FOMC members, like Morris, Partee, and Timlen, expressed concerns about the state of depository institutions in some part of the US. By May 1981, the only question left was when the crisis would occur:

VICE CHAIRMAN SOLOMON. What I hear, and what my people's analysis suggests is likely, is that between two and four of them, of which a couple is very important, are calculating that they will have a crisis early next year. They are also calculating the number of months they can take this; and, of course, if interest rates were to go significantly higher, that [crisis] might be moved up a couple of months.

[...]

MR. PARTEE. I don't think the savings banks are really quite that close. It's 1982 and 1983 for the savings banks. It's 1981 and 1982 for the savings and loans.

[…]

MR. SCHULTZ. In addition, I have the same thoughts that were expressed here a little earlier: That we are putting a lot of pressure on various parts of the economy and that it's going to be hard to get out of this without some kind of financial crisis.

[…]

MR. FORD. You said there might be a financial crisis and I thought everyone would blanch. I blanched, but nobody else did. We're obviously not going to put that in the policy record, but I really do hope that we redouble our efforts to watch very carefully for possible problems arising in the most vulnerable sectors, the housing-related sectors, and try every device we can think of to help the thrifts that is not a bail-out […].

(FOMC meeting, May 1981, pages 12, 24, 34)

Concerns about the financial position of commercial banks in LDCs and thrifts in mortgage markets actually started earlier. Taking the latter first, since the Fed started to use interest rates more actively in the mid 1950s, it had to take into account the fact that thrifts could not cope with high volatility of interest rates without being provided more flexibility in their interest-rate policies. This led to several modifications in interest-rates regulations, especially when interest rates started to rise to high and volatile levels at the end of the 1960s. One example is the progressive increase in the cap for interest rates on certificate deposits (Minsky 1969b; Cargill and Garcia 1982; Wojnilower 1980).

For commercial banks, concerns started in the mid-1970s. Greider (1987: 432ff.) shows that regulators and supervisors were increasingly alarmed by the country exposure of major US banks "but the major banks paid little attention" (Greider 1987: 437). Later Governor Wallich admitted that

It's regrettable that we didn't put any teeth in the country-exposure regulations. The banks reported to us regularly, but we didn't do anything about it. Examiners raised questions. In some cases, they got a response. Other banks said, "These stupid examiners – what do they know?"

(Wallich, quoted in Greider (1987: 438))

As Volcker recognized, this lack of capacity to have the big banks change their behaviors according to the suggestions of the examiners has political roots:

Anyone who thinks you can run bank regulation independent from the general political climate doesn't understand. Suppose the Federal Reserve would have decided to be tougher in the seventies. There would have been an outcry, from the banks and the congressmen who get their contributions, from everyone who was sold on deregulation. "What the hell are you talking about? We haven't had a banking loss for thirty years. So what the hell are you doing with new regulations?" Congressmen would come at us. "Why do you regulators think you know more than our bank CEOs?"

(Volcker, quoted in Greider (1987: 439–440))

Here, we find again the importance of the role of conventions for economic decisions. Social, economic, and political pressures limit what can be done – even the central bank, assumed to be independent of political and private wills, is subject to these pressures. Thus, the Federal Reserve is partly responsible for the LDCs problem because it failed to remind banks of the role they have in a capitalist economy. Banks should have been one of the barriers that prevent overconfidence and financial fragility. As shown later, a similar story repeated itself several times over the following 20 years. Therefore, the high level and variability of interest rates generated by the Fed were not at the source of the problem for commercial banks. They only compounded a problem that would have emerged anyways as disinflation and decrease in oil price occurred. In total, the Fed contributed to the financial problems of the period in two ways: a lack of willingness to apply and to enforce its regulatory and supervisory powers, and its brutal interest-rate policy.

The consequence was a long and painful turmoil for the saving and loans associations and commercial banks over the 1980s and early 1990s. Concerning the former, between 1986 and 1995, financial problems resulted in the closing, by the FSLIC and Resolution Trust Corporation (RTC), of 1043 institutions holding $519 billions in assets (Curry and Shibut 2000). In total, according to the FDIC, failures, mergers, and other deletions led to a reduction of the number of thrifts by 1,589, or about half of them. Commercial banks also recorded a large number of failures following the default of Mexico (that would have occurred earlier without the secret $1.5 billion total support of the Federal Reserve (Greider 1987: 485–486)), and that set off a series of defaults that included, among others, Brazil, Venezuela, Argentina, and Yugoslavia (FOMC transcripts, October 1982). Combined with consolidations and absorptions, this led to the second largest wave of commercial-bank failures in the history of the United States, as shown in Figure 6.5. Like in the 1920s–1930s, the number of head offices of commercial banks was approximately halved.

All this was predicted well in advance by FOMC members; therefore, one may wonder how this affected their monetary policy and what responses were put forward to try to prevent this type of problem from happening again. Concerning the first question, Figures 6.6 and 6.7 show that, during the early years of the crisis, FOMC members usually were worried about the financial fragility of economic sectors.

The word "liquidity," when related to the liquidity of positions, was heavily used in 1982, and "fragile" or "fragility" of financial positions was also used more

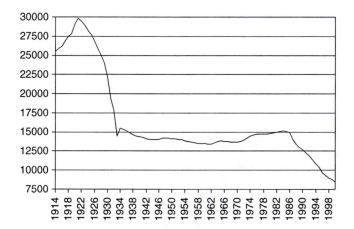

Figure 6.5 Number of head offices of commercial banks: 1914–2000.
Sources: Board of Governors of the Federal Reserve System (1943, 1976, 1981, 1991), FRASER
(http://fraser.stlouisfed.org/).

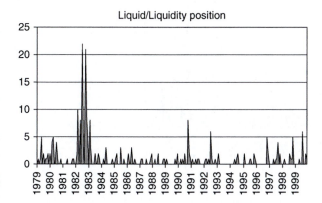

Figure 6.6 Liquidity concerns of the FOMC members.
Source: FOMC Transcripts.

frequently between 1982 and 1985.[3] These were the main motivations behind
the decrease in the fed funds rate during the period 1982–1986, even after the
1981–1982 recession. In the late 1980s, preoccupation about inflation took over
again, as shown in Figure 6.8.

However, the willingness to increase the interest rate was mitigated by
preoccupations about the fragility of the financial system, with the word-count
for "fragile" and "fragility" reaching a new maximum in late 1989/early 1990. For
example, Governors LaWare and Seger (who were among the most concerned

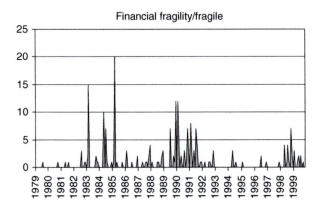

Figure 6.7 Financial fragility concerns of the FOMC members.
Source: FOMC Transcripts.

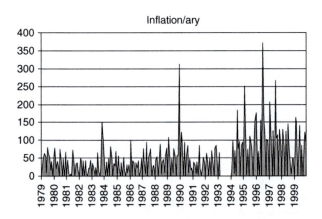

Figure 6.8 Concerns about inflation at the FOMC meetings.
Source: FOMC Transcripts.

and articulated in their reasoning about the importance of checking the liquidity of positions), stated

> I haven't heard anyone mention the thrift industry, but I think that that's a disaster area, and something we have to pay attention to, Bob Boykin, I'm sure, can speak to that, as can a number of us, and too much tightening too soon, I think, would make it a greater disaster.
>
> (Seger, FOMC meeting, May 1988, page 8)

> I'm completely in agreement with the analysis of the strength of the economy. I feel a little bit like I was in a vehicle that was accelerating down the road and I have an instinctive desire to hit the brakes a little bit and snub it down.

But the thing that worries me is that I think the road's a little slipperier than it looks in the sense that there's some fragility in the infrastructure of the economy. First of all, consumers have a heck of a lot of debt. And the most recent instruments of that debt – equity credit lines, as we call them – I think have been abused in the granting throughout a large part of the industry. [...] Probably more important, however, is the heavy debt structure in the corporate sector. If you were to look at as many of these leveraged buyouts and takeover schemes as I have, you would find that in a lot of these the cash flows that are designed to service the debt that's involved are very skinny indeed. And they depend on a relatively stable interest rate structure and the ability over a reasonably short period of time to liquidate assets in order to get debt down to manageable levels. Well, it seems to me that a significant increase in interest rates – even one as modest as the one described in the Greenbook – over the next 12 months or so could create some major problems, at least for some of the situations that I've seen. And that could have a very sobering effect, it seems to me, on the overall economy through the problems that would be incurred by some very large companies. Another one that I guess tends to slip out of our minds occasionally is the real estate situation. [...] Finally, this thrift situation – an aspect of which we intend to discuss at the luncheon today – has not gone away. It's getting worse. And a significant increase in the cost of money to these troubled thrifts is just going to accelerate the rate of loss in that industry.

(LaWare, FOMC meeting, August 1988, page 41)

In the end, their preoccupations convinced other FOMC members not to raise the fed funds rate target above 10 percent, an already harmful level.

As stated earlier, the FOMC had to consider several important failures of financial institutions in the formation of its monetary policy. It helped to solve the immediate threat of systemic risk by acting as lender of last resort but it never pushed for a restructuring of institutions in trouble in order to promote stability. In the case of the Hunt brothers, Volcker gave his support to a private bailout (Greider 1987: 191; Wolfson 1994):

The Hunts arranged a bail-out in the end. We acquiesced in permitting them to do it. Why did we acquiesce? Because we were worried about the second biggest brokerage house in the United States, and the biggest brokerage house in the country was not all that far behind. And at least one of the biggest banks in the United States was in potential jeopardy.

(Volcker, FOMC meeting, December 1980, page 62)

This preoccupation about systemic risk was also behind the lending of $12.5 billions to Continental Illinois in 1984 ($4.5 billions from the FDIC and $8 billions of advances from the Federal Reserve) (Greider 1987: 628). On the contrary, in 1982, Penn Square Bank was closed, and private banks (including Continental for $1 billion) had to write down bad loans. In October 1987, the stock market recorded almost a 25 percent decline. Greenspan acted rapidly by welcoming borrowing at the Discount Window. The next day the crisis was gone, and the market gained 15 percentage points in the next two days.

One essential response to the banking crisis was the deregulation wave that occurred with the Depository Institutions Deregulation and Monetary Control Act (DIDMCA) in 1980 and the Garn-St. Germain Act in 1982. Indeed, one essential cause of the financial problems was thought to be the segmentation of the financial system and interest-rate controls, which prevented competition and the diversification of portfolios. The Federal Reserve agreed on the 1980 Act once it was amended by some clauses that made all depository institutions, members or non-members of the Federal Reserve System, subject to reserve requirements.[4] Following the Monetarist frame of thought, the Fed was afraid of the potential loss of control over the money supply due to the decreasing proportion of member banks. Indeed, the proportion of member commercial banks dramatically decreased after Second World War from a peak of 49.1 percent in 1945–1946 to a low of 36.5 percent in 1980, and the decline accelerated after 1954 as it became costly for banks to respect Regulation Q and reserve requirements given the post-Accord monetary policy of the Fed (Board of Governors of the Federal Reserve System 1943, 1976, 1981, 1991).

The deregulation, however, only made things worse for the S&Ls that took large positions in risky and speculative markets. By allowing S&Ls to be involved in commercial lending, trust services, non-mortgage consumer lending, and to grant secured and unsecured loans in a wide range of economic activities, the deregulation gave them incentives to enter aggressively into the commercial real estate, credit cards, and junk-bonds markets (Cargill and Garcia 1982). This allowed S&L associations to get higher return but also highly increased the riskiness of their portfolio. As Kregel notes

> Investments in commercial real estate and in non-investment grade assets (junk bonds), both prompted by the 1982 Act, were the cause of most of the fraud and losses in the thrifts. Thus, although most were already insolvent as a result of the introduction of the "more level" playing field of the early 1980s, savings banks were allowed to continue to operate, raising funds through the use of brokered, government-insured, $100,000 deposits and investing in assets with the highest, and thus riskiest, returns available in order to avoid formal insolvency.
>
> (Kregel 1998b: 58)

Commercial banks already had more liberty regarding the structure of their assets before the deregulation period, and they tried to restructure their balance sheets by lending to other activities than LDCs governments. But, because of the higher cost of external funds induced by monetary policy and the end of Regulation Q, they had to look for higher and riskier returns on assets. This led them to make several mistakes:

> First, banks lent to oil and gas producers in the early 1980s, just in time for the collapse of the OPEC cartel and of the price of oil; then they moved into

commercial real estate, just in time for the tax exemptions on such projects to be withdrawn in the tax reform bill of 1986; and finally they engaged in highly leveraged transactions via bridge lending for mergers and acquisitions, just in time for the collapse of the junk bond market in 1989.

(Kregel 1998b: 58)

In the end, therefore, the deregulation of the economy led to an enormous weakening of a financial structure already highly damaged by the interest-rate policy of the Fed and its unwillingness to confront the irresponsible behaviors of banks in the 1970s. The Fed, by accepting to bargain financial deregulation for monetary control, again should bear part of the blame. In front of all these financial problems, the Fed pushed for the reregulation of banking activities. One of the main themes behind the reregulation process has been "risk management." This started with the Basel Accord of 1988 and was developed in the new 2005 Basel Accord.[5]

Concerning the 1987 financial market crash, the blame was put mainly on computers. Automated trading, via its interaction between spot and forward market, led to massive sell orders (Greenwald and Stein 1991). One could argue, however, that speculation was going on in the market. Indeed, if in December 1985 a "1,500 level on the stock market ought to be sustainable with a reasonable outlook" (Volcker, FOMC Transcripts, December 1985, page 55) and was attributed to the successful anti-inflation policy of the Fed, by July 1986 the Dow Jones Industrial Average had reached a level of 1,800 and some of the FOMC members started to be worried as the following statement of Vice Chairman Corrigan shows:

I have two overriding concerns: the first is this financial sector dichotomy that Frank Morris referred to. I too find it very hard to rationalize the patterns of behavior that we see in financial markets – not just in the United States but around the world – with what seems to be going on in the real economy. [...] I can't help but think that when we have a 62 or 63 point change in the Dow-Jones average in one day, that in itself feeds on this sense of uneasiness that a number of people have been referring to around the table.

(Corrigan, FOMC meeting, July 1986, page 33–34)

The FOMC members, however, did not do anything, even though they were deeply worried that a crash would undermine the confidence of economic agents and weaken further an already extremely fragile economy.

The 1991–2001 periods

After the recession of the early 1990s, the economy grew at the average rate of 3.7 percent from 1992 to 2000, and this long period of growth was accompanied by speculation in stock markets. The center of the speculative mania was the NASDAQ market. The rapid increase in stock prices was rationalized by arguing that new technologies had raised permanently the growth rate of productivity and had made business cycles a thing of the past. Some authors even argued that the Dow Jones would reach 36,000 points easily (Glassman and Hassett 1999).

At the beginning, FOMC members were skeptical but, over time, they progressively incorporated the productivity story into their analysis. The earliest proposition that the "the norm of long-term productivity growth, [...] has tilted upward" was stated in December 1992 by Greenspan (Greenspan, FOMC meeting, December 1992, page 28). However, the seriousness of this new-economy argument was not acknowledged by the Committee before March 1994. After that date, the argument became a central element in the discussions of the FOMC and the speeches given by some of its members. Indeed, the latter were puzzled by the fact that "sustained" economic growth had not led to any inflationary pressures:

> Everyone is concerned about a pickup in inflation, tightness and stringency picking up, and the fact that commodity prices are moving, but there is no apparent acceleration in wages or final goods prices. [...] I raise this issue because we are pretty far along in this business cycle. So why is inflation not showing its head a little more?
>
> (Greenspan, FOMC meeting, March 1994, page 42)

> To summarize my views, I would say that I consider myself a new paradigm optimist.
>
> (McTeer, FOMC, August 1997, page 26)

> I was quoted in a recent *New Yorker* article, one of the flood of articles on our Chairman and the new era, as being "mystified in a pleasant way by the recent performance of the economy." I think that describes the mood that has captured this group for quite a while now.
>
> (Rivlin, FOMC meeting, May 1999, page 50)

The members of the Committee thus, at least partly and some of them more than others, were bought into the new-economy convention and, by the end of the 1990s, advocates of a "permanent bliss", rather than a "temporary bliss," were in the majority at the FOMC (Meyer 2004: 80, 125). However, they were also increasingly preoccupied by the asset-price bubble.

In February 1994, after 4 years of easing or stable rates, the FOMC members voted for a symmetric alternative C of 25 basis points. The main concern was inflation, but during this meeting, there was an intense debate among members because many of them were not convinced that a 25 basis points raise was enough. The main reason behind the debate was what was going on in financial markets and the potential wealth-effect impact on inflation (Greenspan, FOMC meeting, March 1995, page 43). As Governor LaWare stated:

> I think the markets have already discounted a 25 basis point move and are still burning away at a great rate. I would like to see a stronger move than 25 basis

points simply to damp down without a crash the stock market particularly. [...] I believe a 50 basis point move will send an unmistakable message that will damp this enthusiasm in the stock market without causing it to crash.

(LaWare, FOMC meeting, February 1994, page 54)

However, Greenspan strongly pushed against such a move and begged other members to go only for a 25 basis point move. Indeed, he was afraid that financial markets were not anticipating any move:

I would be very concerned if this Committee went 50 basis points now because I don't think the markets expect it. [...] I am telling you – and I've seen these markets – this is not the time to do this.

(Greenspan, FOMC meeting, February 1994, page 55)

He finally convinced all the members, and on February 28, they had a telephone conference to discuss the consequences of their action:

Let me say that looking back at our action, it strikes me that we had a far greater impact than we anticipated. I think we partially broke the back of an emerging speculation in equities; it's still too soon to know whether or not that's true, but the evidence to date clearly suggests that that is at least a good possibility. In retrospect, we may well have done the same thing inadvertently in the bond market because what we were getting earlier were tremendously rapid declines in long-term rates. As we look back on this, I suspect that there was a significant overshoot in the markets. We pricked that bubble as well, I think. We also have created a degree of uncertainty; if we were looking at the emergence of speculative forces, which clearly were evident in very early stages, then I think we had a desirable effect.

(Greenspan, FOMC conference call, February 28, 1994, page 3)

Thus, the action was considered a success even though they did not anticipate such a strong reaction by the bond market and the stock market. During 1994, the stock market declined and stayed flat. Figure 6.1 also indicates that a strong correction occurred in the stock market after the February meeting.

Members of the FOMC were satisfied with this state of affairs and thought that speculation, if not over, would be greatly attenuated, which cleared the way for further and faster increases in interest rates to fight a presupposed looming inflation:[6] "I think there is a lesser danger in financial markets, although they are still precarious, this enables us to move somewhat faster than our previous planning presupposed" (Greenspan, FOMC conference call, April 18, 1994, page 7). By the end of 1995, however, concerns about overvaluation in the stock market had reemerged at the Committee, and debates about the existence or not of a bubble were going on, as exemplified by Figure 6.9 and Figure 6.10.

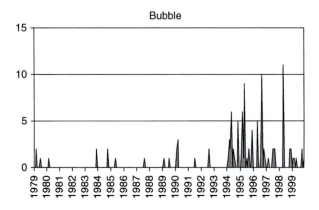

Figure 6.9 Discussion about the stock market at the FOMC.
Source: FOMC Transcripts.

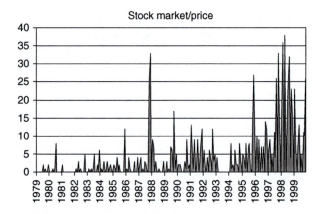

Figure 6.10 Discussion of bubble at the FOMC meetings.
Source: FOMC Transcripts.

In September 1996, Governor Lindsey pushed strongly for a bursting of the bubble:

> As in the United States in the late 1920s and Japan in the late 1980s, the case for a central bank ultimately to burst that bubble becomes overwhelming. I think it is far better that we do so while the bubble still resembles surface froth and before the bubble carries the economy to stratospheric heights.
>
> (Lindsey, FOMC meeting, September 1996, page 25)

However, Greenspan was still not convinced, not because he disagreed but because he did not know how to do it smoothly by using monetary policy, and because he thought that inflation targeting and stock-market stability were incompatible goals (see also December 5 speech for more developments around this idea):

> I recognize that there is a stock market bubble problem at this point, and I agree with Governor Lindsey that this is a problem that we should keep an eye on monetary policy when we confront stock market bubbles. That is because, to the extent that we are successful in keeping product price inflation down, history tells us that price-earnings ratios under those conditions go through the roof. What is really needed to keep stock market bubbles from occurring is a lot of product price inflation, which historically has tended to undercut stock markets almost everywhere. There is a clear tradeoff. If monetary policy succeeds in one, it fails in the other. Now, unless we have the capability of playing in between and managing to know exactly when to push a little here and to pull a little there, it is not obvious to me that there is a simple set of monetary policy solutions that deflate the bubble. We do have the possibility of raising major concerns by increasing margin requirements. I guarantee that if you want to get rid of the bubble, whatever it is, that will do it. My concern is that I am not sure what else it will do.[7]
>
> (Greenspan, FOMC meeting, September 1996, pages 30–31)

Because of this lack of a consensus on how to deal with speculation, FOMC members, under the leadership of Greenspan, resorted to moral suasion. In December 5, in a speech given at the Annual Dinner of the American Enterprise Institute, Greenspan qualified the state of the stock market as "irrational exuberance." This actually led to a freeze and even a decline in the stock-market level, but not for long. After that, Greenspan still used some form or moral suasion but "with less and less conviction" because he was criticized for expressing doubts about the "wisdom of the investors" (Meyer 2004: 142–143). After 1997, the stock market went up very rapidly and by the end of 1999 the average value of shares had doubled their 1997 level. The members of the Committee were divided, ranging from Jordan, who pushed for more emphases on asset prices (FOMC meetings, November 1997 and March 1998), to Governor Phillips, who argued in favor of ignoring them and letting "market participants do the stock market pricing" (Phillips, FOMC meeting, May 1998, page 57). In the middle was Greenspan, stating, "I do not know what to do" (FOMC meeting, August 1997, page 78). Finally, he took a position in the following way:

> The question, essentially, is whether we have any great insight into how to handle asset values as a part of monetary policy. In principle, we have to recognize that asset values have an effect, so we have to consider their impact and we certainly do so in terms of the wealth effect. But how we can alter the pattern of market valuations, as distinct from its effects on consumption and other sectors of the economy, is somewhat beyond me. I have concluded that in the broader sense we have to stay with our fundamental central

bank goal, namely, to stabilize product price levels. To the extent that the financial markets affect the factors that influence product price levels, I think monetary policy action is appropriate. But I believe the notion of merely hitting the market itself is an illusion. It may be something that we could discuss at great length as a chapter of a textbook, but I doubt very much that we know how to implement it from a policy point of view.

(Greenspan, FOMC meeting, May 1998, page 85)

Stated alternatively, as long as asset prices do not affect output prices, they should be ignored, and at this time there were no tensions on output prices, and so FOMC members could ignore asset prices. As shown in chapter 2, this represents the main view of the New Consensus.

This position left the Committee free to deal with other problems. The Committee was very concerned about inflation and paranoid about getting "behind the curve" (that is, not being the leader, relative to financial markets, in changing interest rates in response to expected inflation):

The most important policy consideration, however, is whether policy inaction at this time would put us behind the curve. What is reassuring is that we are hard pressed to find any evidence of rising inflationary pressures in the data, whether we are looking, for example, at the pipeline numbers or at the wage structure. Wherever we look, we are getting little, if any, evidence of mounting inflationary pressures, and that has to raise some questions about how we view the economy at large.

(Greenspan, FOMC meeting, July 1997, page 109)

The Committee was becoming increasingly anxious about the non-appearance of inflation after 6 years of economic growth, as shown in Figure 6.8. However, it soon had to deal with more financial troubles because of the international implications of financial turmoil in Southeast Asia and Russia. The FOMC members were afraid that this would affect the US economy by decreasing exports, by decreasing the financial strength of foreign debtors (and so that of US banks), and by spreading to the US financial markets. The latter manifested itself through a bond market crash and the LTCM insolvency. Both events occurred toward the end of 1998 as the Russian crisis was starting, the Southeast Asia crisis was unraveling, and the Japanese, Chinese, and South African asset markets were heavily affected (FOMC meeting, August 1998). The T-bond futures market recorded the largest drop of its history with a decline of $3000. At the same time, LTCM, who leverage heavily its positions in the Russian bond markets was losing a lot of its capital and it became increasingly clear that it would not be able to meet its margin calls (Mayer 2001: 7ff., 265ff.). As a consequence, the FOMC decided to ease, and they did so three times between September and November. The Federal Reserve also supervised a lending agreement between LTCM and a group of banks for $3.6 billions (Mayer 2001: 268).

Once this disastrous episode was over and the international financial crisis dissipated, concerns about inflation took over again at the FOMC meetings. As shown later, FOMC members tried to find reasons to increase interest rates, even inventing some if they could not justify their upward moves by looking at actual or expected inflation.

The speculation ended in March 2000 and stock markets dropped, especially the NASDAQ, that went from an average peak of 4,803 in February 2000 to 1,242 in September 2002, back to its level of early 1997. Following those events, Enron set off in 2001 a wave of scandals related to accounting and other irregular practices in capital markets. In 2002, WorldCom, Tyco International, AOL Time Warner, and many others were prosecuted for infractions in capital markets (Patsuris 2002). These irregularities aimed at boosting the volume of trade in shares and at maintaining the prices of shares by issuing fraudulent quarterly accounting reports. These events led the Congress to ratify the Sarbanes-Oxley Act in 2002. According to the director of the Division of Enforcement of the Security Exchange Commission (SEC) the aims of the Act are

> Holding gatekeepers responsible, aggressively pursuing obstruction of our investigations, and creating more personal accountability and deterrence in the corner offices of America's public companies.
>
> (Cutler, Speech, September 20, 2004)

The "gatekeepers" are the persons whose job it is to maintain the integrity of the capital markets by making sure that firms in those markets respect all the rules: Auditors who ensure that financial data are clean and satisfy the GAAP standards (most firms resorted to "creative" accounting, fraudulent financial statements, exotic earnings management, and other irregularities),[8] lawyers who make sure that public companies comply with the securities law requirements (disclosure standards were not respected and manipulations of quotations were practiced), research analysts who provide accurate recommendations to the public (some analysts praised publicly the soundness of some firms while privately recommending to sell their shares),[9] and the boards of directors who manage firms (some of them lied about the true state of their company and claimed knowing nothing about fraudulent accounting and security practices). The Act tried to reach its goals by imposing harsher sanctions (destroying documents vital to an investigation, as in the Enron case, and issuing unreliable financial statements can lead to long prison time), by trying to limit the possibility of conflicts of interests existing in the research analyst function, and by requiring the public company CEOs and CFOs to certify the accuracy of their financial statements (CEOs can no longer claim not knowing what is going on).

The Sarbanes-Oxley Act only put the Fed marginally in the business of carefully supervising the practices of capital-market participants. Indeed, the Act created, under section 101, the Public Company Accounting Oversight Board (PCAOB). The Board is not part of the government but is overseen by the SEC. It is composed of five members "appointed from among prominent individuals of integrity and reputation who have a demonstrated commitment to the interest of investors and the public" (Section 101(e)(1)), and no more than two of them can be public accountants. The members of the Board are determined by the SEC "after consultation with the Chairman of the Board of Governors of the Federal Reserve System, and the Secretary of the Treasury" (Section 101(e)(4)(A)).

Overall, the position of the Fed regarding its role in financial markets went in all directions, from proactive policy (1994) to moral suasion (1996), and from the incapacity to make a decision (1997) to making the decision to ignore speculation as a matter of direct concern (1998, 1999). In terms of regulation, after the accounting and financial debacle, the Fed and other regulatory authorities used the period of financial conservatism to increase their roles in the oversight of the behaviors of corporations via the Sarbanes-Oxley Act. However, this involvement of the Fed was rather minimal. The real grip on the financial system came with the Gramm-Leach-Bliley Act that allowed the Board of Governors to be at the center of the regulation of the financial system. The Federal Reserve, however, does not seem to have grasped the implications of this in terms of the role of a central bank in the financial system, and the need for an overall reformulation of regulatory rules and bodies. There should be a centralization of regulatory activities around the Federal Reserve that encompasses all the financial institutions, old and new, marginal and large, without exceptions.

A critical appraisal of the FOMC economic framework

The previous section analyzed the involvement of the Federal Reserve in the management of financial matters. This last section opens the analysis by studying how the economic framework that the FOMC members used to analyze the economy was challenged between 1979 and 2001. It will be shown that some of the insights of the Post-Keynesian view would have helped the FOMC members to understand what was going on when they were outraged or puzzled by the behaviors of economic variables. This will be done by looking at five specific topics: credibility, transparency and gradualism, money supply, interest rates, and inflation.

Credibility at the FOMC meetings

The notion of "credibility" became increasingly important for policy practice during the early 1980s and, as shown in Figure 6.11, has remained a major concern since.[10] Once a central bank has set its goal (price stability or others), it should make sure that the public is confident that the central bank will do everything in its power to achieve and maintain the goal. By reassuring the public, the central bank will achieve its goal at a minimum cost, i.e. only small changes in interest rates will be necessary to meet the goal. Independence from political pressure is assumed to be a major element necessary to secure credibility.

At the end of the 1970s, the Federal Reserve was held responsible for the double-digit inflation. The Fed, under Burns and Miller, was accused of being soft

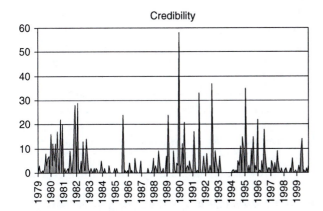

Figure 6.11 Credibility and FOMC meetings.
Source: FOMC Transcripts.

on inflation to support the Administration (Greider 1987: 67). To avoid a repetition of the experience of the 1970s and given the growing influence of Monetarist ideas, the Fed decided to strengthen its credibility as inflation fighter by shifting to the operating procedure described in the previous section. By targeting reserves more carefully, it was thought that the supply of money would be better controlled and so inflation would be lower. Some FOMC members, like Roos, even argued for an exclusive focus on reserve and monetary targets without any preoccupation for interest rates and financial stability. Speaking in July 1981, in a period of high financial fragility and at the verge of one of the worst recessions since the 1930s, Roos justified high rates in the following way:

> Paul, isn't it our purpose, though, to impose the discipline of monetary policy upon the banks? And won't the fact that they had to pay more teach them a lesson? Won't it teach them that if we want to discourage their extending credit, for example, that they have to take it seriously and not anticipate that we'll be there with the funds they need for their reserve requirements when they need them? In other words, isn't this really the strategy of our whole policy currently, and isn't the level of the fed funds rate reflecting exactly what we want to achieve, if our strategy is right?
>
> (Roos, FOMC meeting, July 1981, page 6)

This hardcore version of inflation credibility was critiqued, however, by Governor Rice and others:

> I agree with most of the varying earlier comments on the importance of credibility. However, it seems to me that credibility has several dimensions – certainly more than one. Many people I have talked to feel that it was the high

interest rate policy of the Federal Reserve that caused the current recession and they wonder what kind of institution this is that really wants to cause a recession. On unemployment there are some credibilities involved, too, except that it is negative credibility.

(Rice, FOMC meeting, December 1981, page 31)

I'm very chary of the credibility argument for all the reasons that have been stated. [We could have] a great increase of credibility with the monetarists in the short run and if the economy plunges into recession or we have a great financial crisis, we will suffer an enormous loss of credibility in a more basic sense.

(Volcker, FOMC meeting, August 1985, page 34)

I think we miss some of the environment here if we congratulate ourselves too much on the credibility that we presently enjoy and assume that that's because we are seen as fearless inflation fighters. We are seen and applauded for that only so long as nobody else gets hurt in the process of our fighting inflation. If we were to go out there and really beat inflation over the head and in the process increase the unemployment rate or dump the economy in some fashion I think that our credibility would disappear overnight. People would forget that we were inflation fighters and label us as the black knights who have ruined people's lives.

(LaWare, FOMC meeting, February 1989, page 38)

Thus, the central bank is credible if its helps to create a stable environment for the private sector, which should be the ultimate goal of any public institution. Price stability is one aspect of that goal, but full employment and financial stability are also key elements to consider.

A central bank that narrows its goal to guaranteeing price stability assumes, besides believing that it is the most appropriate institution to deal with price stability, that this is the best way it can contribute to promoting prosperity and the social interest. However, studies have shown that there is no clear correlation or causation between inflation and economic growth (Haslag 1997; Levine and Zervos 1993; Stanners 1993), and Committee members recognized this sometimes:

CHAIRMAN GREENSPAN. You are in effect raising the question that we were discussing before, namely, can we demonstrate that as the inflation rate falls, the rate of growth in productivity continues to increase?

MS. MINEHAN. Right.

CHAIRMAN GREENSPAN. Because that is the basic determinant that tells us whether in fact the system is functioning.

MS. MINEHAN. Yes.

CHAIRMAN GREENSPAN. We do not have enough data points in recent history to be able to make that judgment.

(FOMC meeting, July 1997, page 66)

If this is the case, the social interest may not be served best by a central bank that is seen as a highly credible inflation fighter and, hence, a lack of democratic legitimacy may emerge. This recognition of the lack of democratic legitimacy runs through all Greider's book but is also visible at the FOMC:

I think the people who should decide that price stability, hopefully as a means to an end, is the appropriate goal of monetary policy are not the people sitting around this table. Rather, it should be the American people through their representatives in the Congress.

(McDonough, FOMC meeting, July 1996, page 53)

I think it certainly has been the general view of the Committee, as evidenced by the nature of our discussions, that long-term price stability is our objective. It's unambiguous, unequivocal, and I would say held pretty much by everyone around this table. The only operative question is whether it is statutory or not. And were we to try to make it statutory, I suspect we'd run into some very significant resistance.

(Greenspan, FOMC meeting, December 2000, page 18)

Post-Keynesians also have critiqued the strong emphasis on the notion of inflation credibility as undemocratic, based on an inadequate theoretical framework, and empirically unfounded (Bain *et al.* 1996; Pressman 1996; Grabel 1998, 2000; Bain 1998; Cornwall and Cornwall 1998).

In addition, by pursuing too much its credibility, the central bank may have to act against inflation excessively even when there are no signs of the latter, or when it is very moderate, in order not to "lose" its credibility. This creates an upward bias toward raising interest rates:

We're rightly worried about accelerating inflation, but we're still in a deflationary world environment. [...] Turning to Peter Fisher's fourth point a while ago, I think the biggest argument for tightening at this meeting is that so many of us have threatened it that the Committee would probably lose face and lose credibility if it didn't raise the funds rate by at least ¼ point.

(McTeer, FOMC meeting, June 1999, page 46)

Thus, constantly preaching the fight against inflation puts a central bank in a situation in which it may have to tighten, not because it needs to, but because it said it would (Bell-Kelton 2006). In addition, by concentrating so much on inflation, a central bank may promote higher inflation expectations and their integration in contracts, leading to higher rates of inflation: "In terms of what's happening on the inflation front, I think in a way maybe we ourselves are contributing to it because we talk so much about it" (Seger, FOMC meeting, May 1987, page 18).

Finally, given that inflation has other sources than monetary sources and that the central bank cannot control the money supply, it is doubtful that the most direct impact, if any, of higher credibility of a central bank is an improvement of its effectiveness in managing inflation (Fisher 1994: 300):

> Nobody has been able to prove that credibility has bought the Bundesbank or any other central bank the benefit of a lower cost to reduce inflation. In fact, Stanley Fischer presented a very good paper at the 300th anniversary of the Bank of England proving rather the contrary. There is no particular benefit in the so-called credibility, and I think credibility mainly makes central bankers feel better about themselves.
>
> (McDonough, FOMC meeting, January 1995, page 54)

The most direct impact is a better control of the yield curve by reinforcing the predictability of future moves in policy rates, which is reinforced by the emphasis put on transparency as shown below. If one judges credibility this way, it has been high from the very beginning of the Federal Reserve System. Indeed, as shown in chapter 4, there always has been a very strong correlation between all interest rates. However, one still needs to prove that a better control of the yield curve implies a better control of inflation. As shown earlier and below, the relationship between interest rates and inflation is non-linear and heavily depends on the financial state of the private sector in terms of ownership of interest-earning assets, and financing and funding needs.

Rather than resulting from of a gain in credibility, the decline in inflation in the 1980s and the 1990s can be explained by the decline in energy cost and oil dependence, as well as the increasing international competition. From the anecdotal evidence reported during the "go-round" of the FOMC meetings, this seems actually quite clear. For example, Stone reports that "Manufacturers continue to report rising input prices, but many still note the inability to pass on these rising costs because of competitive pressures" (FOMC meeting, June 2000, page 50).

Transparency and gradualism

As shown below, following the abandonment of the Monetarist framework in October 1982, the FOMC entered a period of operational uncertainty until the mid-1990s. Even though it was now targeting the level of federal funds rate, the Federal Reserve was unwilling to disclose this to the public and continued to announce a targeted growth range for monetary aggregates. Very early, Ford noted that this was not an appropriate behavior and that FOMC members needed to make sure that financial market participants understand what the FOMC does:

> And I don't think it's too much of a stretch of the words to say we want to [fine] tune the economy in reality. We think we can do it. […] Mr. Chairman, it raises

the question in my mind, in line with your question: Why are we dealing with monetary aggregates at all? If you go back to how we got there, the monetary theorists who pushed this whole concept had as one of the fundamental parts of the concept that we shouldn't try to fine-tune and especially shouldn't try on a short-term basis to be flexible about a lot of things. [...] What we're doing is we are looking at the real economy, trying to manage it in real terms, and *de facto* we're using interest rates as the principal variable to attempt to do that. That's what we're doing. So, my answer to you would be: If we're going to do all these other things, then it would be in the interest of not creating more noise in the markets just to say that we are now going to attempt in our collective wisdom to manage the real economy out of a recession without managing it back into inflation and the principal thing we're going to do is move short-term rates. Because I think that's the truth. Isn't that what we're really doing? It looks that way on the charts to me.

(Ford, FOMC meeting, February 1983, page 31–32)

However, one has to wait until the early 1990s to find more discussions regarding the need to change the structure of FOMC deliberations and to increase the transparency of its decision-making process:

MS. SEGER. I'm just sitting here listening to Peter and Don talk about this fed funds fixation and the problems [that creates]. Are you sort of making the case for prompt release of our minutes? Maybe that would fix it so we could tell people what we're doing rather than make them try to read it from entrails.

MR. KOHN. I wasn't trying to make that case, no. I'm not sure that would help them in terms of trying to guess what we're going to do tomorrow, which is really what it's all about – not what we did yesterday.

MS. SEGER. It would still give them more guidance than they now get where they just really are flying by the seat of their pants.

[...]

MR. MULLINS. Would there be a benefit in going to a range from our point estimate? Or would that just–

MR. STERNLIGHT. Well, I like to think of what we have as a range anyway. But the market would immediately put the rate in the middle of the range and if they're looking for –

CHAIRMAN GREENSPAN. They'll be looking for the central point of that range.

[...]

MR. ANGELL. Mr. Chairman, in light of our abilities on the funds rate. I wonder whether it would be a little more accurate to pull that range in a bit. The 400 basis points –

CHAIRMAN GREENSPAN. We've raised this issue before.

MR. ANGELL. Okay.

CHAIRMAN GREENSPAN. I would suggest the following: May I ask Don Kohn to submit a recommendation to this Committee on that question, because we've been doing this for long time?

(FOMC meeting, October 1990, pages 7–8, 59)

This was followed by a period during which talking about the federal funds rate became a taboo and "the Committee [had] deliberately avoided explicit announced federal funds targets and explicit narrow ranges for movements in the funds rate" (Kohn, FOMC Transcripts, March 1991, page 1):

I must say I'm still quite reluctant to cave in, if you will, on this question that we can do nothing but target the federal funds rate.

(Greenspan, FOMC transcripts, March 1991, page 2)

As a practical matter we are on a fed funds targeting regime now. We have chosen not to say that to the world. I think it's bad public relations, basically, to say that that is what we are doing, and I think it's right not to; but internally we all recognize that that's what we are doing.

(Melzer, FOMC transcripts, March 1991, page 4)

To announce to the general public that the FOMC was targeting the level of the federal funds rate would be going against all the Monetarist principles. One has to wait until 1994 for a progressive increase in the transparency in the decision-making process of the FOMC. Since February 1994, the FOMC has released public statements that implicitly indicate changes in its targeted rate, and that explicitly contain a targeted value since July 1995. Progressively more information has been disclosed with higher frequency about the decision process (statements, minutes, forecasts, transcripts, etc.) and the potential future trend of the targeted federal funds rate (balance-of-risks component of the statement).

In addition to the willingness to show consistency in its deliberations, this growing concern about transparency and gradualism is explained by the dramatic impacts that unpredictable large variations of policy rates entailed in the early 1980s, and by the events in financial markets following the February 1994 meeting that reinforced the will of the FOMC members to really think hard about their communication strategy:

How that warning would or should be constructed, I do not yet know. I do remember that in the latter months of 1993 and especially in January 1994, I felt as though I was getting up on the table, jumping up and down and screaming, "Hey, we are about to raise rates." I did it three more times, and I said, "Hey, hey." [Laughter] We finally raised rates by 25 basis points on

February 4th and the markets asked, what did you do, where did that come from? I don't know whether or not we can condition markets that do not wish to be conditioned about changes in policy, but I do think we have an obligation to indicate in advance of our move why we are moving. The old notion that we will explain what we did three weeks after the fact in Humphrey-Hawkins testimony strikes me as wholly inconsistent with how long it takes the world to turn. It is far better to say in advance what we are going to do and why than the other way around.

(Greenspan, FOMC meeting, February 1997, page 99)

Indeed, even though the variability of its interest-rate target has declined a lot relative to the 1970s and 1980s, it is still significant and comparable to that of the late 1960s/early 1970s. Following Irving Fisher, this variability is assumed to be a required condition for the modern practice of monetary policy:

If we believe that monetary policy can stabilize the economy when confronted with the types of forces we are seeing, the implication is a highly volatile federal funds rate that moves against those forces on the upside and in the other direction on the downside.

(Greenspan, FOMC meeting, June 2001, page 142)

Coupled with gradualism, transparency helps to minimize surprises in the financial markets and to give a better view of future policy moves.

I see greater transparency as serving both to enhance the accountability of the Fed and to increase the effectiveness of monetary policy by improving the market's ability to anticipate future policy actions.

(Meyer, FOMC meeting, December 2001, page 89)

With transparency, monetary policy has moved from an era of unpredictable volatility to an era of planned volatility in terms of interest rates.

Following the framework developed in chapter 4, the importance of transparency and gradualism is evident if one is concerned with the stability of financial markets, and if a central bank wants to use interest rates to manage the economy. However, if a central bank is able to limit the instability generated by its monetary policy, the increase in predictability of future monetary policy may decrease the already limited capacity of central banks to manage inflation and the financial system as a whole through this means.

Indeed, in terms of inflation, higher transparency may have perverse cost and demand effects on inflation. On the cost side, transparency may reinforce the interest-rate induced inflation by inducing firms, depending on their pricing power, to include in contracts the expected impact of future policy moves on costs. This effect can be reinforced by the higher wage demands due to the expected rise in interest rates (Pigeon 2004). These two cost effects on prices are strengthened in period of financial fragility. On the demand side, a higher predictability of future monetary policy may decrease the already relatively low sensitivity of expenditures to interest rates. By allowing to plan ahead with more certainty, and given expected demand, firms may just pass the higher cost of borrowing to their prices, or hedge it by borrowing more today in expectation of future hikes, or bet that refinancing at a lower cost will be available, and just go ahead with whatever they planned to do. In addition, higher interest rates increase the income of interest earners and so may lead to higher demand.

In terms of the management of the financial system, the unpredictable volatility of policy rates, combined with the uniform capital requirements by the 1988 Basel Accord, has led to a boom in securitization and derivative markets. Financial institutions have learned to profit from interest-rate instability and to thrive upon it. Now that the central bank has moved to planned volatility, the capacity of financial institutions to make profit out of interest-rate volatility has increased tremendously and has facilitated additional layering to make even more profit (ABS, CDO, CDO^2, CDS, and other similar financial innovations) (Watterson 2005).[11] All this has created a higher dependence of financial institutions on the continuation of planned volatility, and has increased the opacity of the financial interrelations because of the development of off-balance sheet accounting and of the incapacity of the issuers of those complicated securities to understand fully their cash-flow implications (Morgenson 2008a).

Money and reserve supply endogeneity and monetary targets

The Post-Keynesian tradition rejects the idea that the money supply is a variable that can be controlled by the central bank. The only things that a central bank can target with certainty through open-market operations, by coordinating its action with the issuer of the main securities it buys and sells,[12] are the market rates of interest (and usually central bankers concentrate on the short range of the market). In March 1979, there is a recognition of this by the FOMC:

> MR. EASTBURN. The other part of my question is: How much validity is there to the idea that what is happening to money is supply induced and not demand induced?
>
> MR. AXILROD. Well, it's very difficult to give an answer to that, President Eastburn, because we don't control the supply of money and we make no effort to control it.
>
> [...]
>
> MR. AXILROD. President Eastburn, the only way I think I can answer is to say that, as you know, the System does no more than accommodate to whatever amount of money the public wants to hold at today's interest rates. So in that sense we could always have more money [growth] if the System were to provide reserves more aggressively and let interest rates go down in

the short run. That's the way I would answer. [As for] whether it's a demand or a supply phenomenon, it's very difficult to disassociate the two.

(FOMC meeting, March 1979, page 7–8)

These insights were lost when the new procedure was adopted in October 1979 and Roos, from the St. Louis Fed, was among the most impatient with the incapacity of the Federal Reserve to control total reserves and money supply:

MR. ROOS. Well, if the level of borrowing comes in higher than we would anticipate, [can't] you reduce the level of the nonborrowed reserves path accordingly? Can't you adjust your open market operations for the unexpected bulge in borrowing or the unexpectedly low borrowing if you ignore the effect on the fed funds market? Can't you just supply or withdraw reserves to compensate for what has happened?

MR. STERNLIGHT. Yes we could. There's always that question of how much we want to compensate for that high borrowing. We faced that kind of decision in [this statement] week.

CHAIRMAN VOLCKER. The Desk can't [adjust] in the short run. It's fixed. In a sense they could do it over time if people are borrowing more, as they may be now. They seem to be borrowing more than we would expect, given the differential from the discount rate. But in any particular week it is fixed.

MR. ROOS. Do we have to supply the reserves?

CHAIRMAN VOLCKER. We have to supply the reserves.

MR. ROOS. [Why] do we have to supply the reserves? If we did not supply those reserves, we'd force the commercial banks to borrow or to buy fed funds, which would move the fed funds rate up.

(FOMC meeting, September 1980, page 6)

Thus, Roos ignored the tremendous potential impact on the economy and insisted on letting interest rates go up as high, and vary as much, as necessary.[13] He was deeply dissatisfied with the "hybrid" approach and argued for a total elimination of any interest-rate target:

I think there's a very basic contradiction in trying to control interest rates explicitly or implicitly and achieving our monetary target objectives. And I would express myself as favoring the total elimination of any specification regarding interest rates.

(Roos, FOMC meeting, February 1981, page 54)

All the other Committee members strongly disagreed with his position (even if some of them, like Black, shared Roos's view but in a softer way), which argued that the Fed would just abandon any pretension to maintaining financial stability (the reason for which it was created). They acknowledged that high interest-rate variability is harmful and that, ultimately, what people care about is the cost of money, not the level of growth of money supply:[14]

> MR. WALLICH. The central banks that have the most credibility, such as the Swiss National Bank and the Bundesbank are pretty relaxed with respect to their targets. Sometimes one of them even abandons its targets. And yet they do not lose credibility because there is that basic belief that they will achieve better stability.

> MS. TEETERS. More people perceive that we have $15\frac{1}{2}$ percent interest rates and 17 percent mortgage rates than whether we are [fostering growth of] the money supply at 1 percent or 2 percent or 3 percent.

> VICE CHAIRMAN SOLOMON. The trouble is that everything we say here is true.

> MS. TEETERS. Yes.

> VICE CHAIRMAN SOLOMON. Even when we say different things.
> (FOMC meeting, February 1982, page 91)

If this did not push toward reconsidering the policy, their incapacity to target "money" did lead them to reconsider their view about money:

> MR. MORRIS. Well, Mr. Chairman, I think it is ironic that the Federal Reserve has switched to monetarism at the very time when our ability to measure the money supply has eroded dramatically and our ability to differentiate money from liquid assets is rapidly disappearing.

> [...]

> MR. BALLES. I share Frank's frustration on knowing what money is these days.

> (FOMC meeting, December 1981, pages 32, 43)

Eventually, they could not answer the question and finally abandoned the policy:

> [In response] to talk that says we can significantly influence this – or as the phraseology goes that if we lower rates, we will move M2 up into the range – I say "garbage." Having said all of that, I then ask myself: 'What should we be doing?' Well, we have a statute out there. If we didn't have the statute, I would argue that we ought to forget the whole thing. If it doesn't have any policy purpose, why are we doing it? By law [we have] to make such forecasts. And if we are to do so, I suggest that we do them in a context which does us the least harm, if I may put it that way.
> (Greenspan, FOMC meeting, February 1993, page 39)

We do not, in fact, discuss monetary policy in terms of the Ms between Humphrey-Hawkins meetings. Don Kohn dutifully mentions them because he thinks he ought to, but that is not the way we think about monetary policy.

(Rivlin, FOMC meeting, February 1998, page 91)

One may wonder, however, why they persisted so long to apply a policy that most of them knew would fail from the beginning. Indeed, even though the Federal Reserve abandoned in October 1982 the operating procedure it adopted in October 1979, the institutional structure of the FOMC deliberation established at that time was not really reconsidered until the end of 1990:

Our present structure was set up to target M1, which then ceased to be a good indicator. We have all this institutional set-up in effect and it's not useful.

(Black, FOMC meeting, October 1990, page 6)

Thus, the policy directive contained in the transcripts[15] has a range of 6 to 10 percent for the federal funds rate until October 1990, and numerical target for M2 and M3 growth until December 1992, but large fluctuations in federal funds rate were not allowed anymore. Besides the unwillingness to abandon a monetary framework that only a few of them deeply believed in, one has to look for political reasons to understand why FOMC members were so slow to change their way of deliberating and of presenting their action to the public.

In terms of politics, in 1979, the FOMC did not want to take responsibility for the recession because of financial instability that it knew would have to occur to break inflation expectations. The FOMC members protected themselves behind monetary targets, thinking they would not be made responsible for the high interest rates:

I do think that the monetary aggregates provided a very good political shelter for us to do the things we probably couldn't have done otherwise.

(Teeters, FOMC meeting, February 1983, page 26)

I think the important argument, and really the reason why we went to this procedure, was basically a political one. We were afraid that we could not move the federal funds rate as much as we really felt we ought to, unless we obfuscated in some way: We're not really moving the federal funds rate, we're targeting reserves and the markets have driven the funds rate up. That may have had some validity at the time, and I had some sympathy for it. But as time goes on, I've become more and more concerned about a procedure that really involves trying to fool the public and the Congress and the markets, and at times fooling ourselves in the process.

(Black, FOMC meeting, March 1988, page 12)

In December 1989, following a period of tightening and expected further tightening, Stern suggested to go back to a monetary target for precisely the same reason:

> Well, I have only a little to add to all of this. I think Tom Melzer is probably right: We're going to need to shift the focus to some measure or measures of the money supply as we proceed here if we can, both for substantive reasons and also because that has some political advantages as well, as we go forward.
>
> (Stern, FOMC meeting, December 1989, page 50)

In terms of economics, targeting the federal funds rate was not seen as a good method to implement monetary policy and the apparent lack of direct control of money supply seemed to let the devil of inflation enter by the front door. In addition, they had no theoretical framework that could justify the use of an interest-rate target as a good means to manage the economy:

> CHAIRMAN GREENSPAN. No, I would say that we have a specific operational problem that we have to find a way of resolving. Just to be locked in on the federal funds rate is to me simplistic monetary policy: it doesn't work.
>
> MR. BLACK. As I've said before, it's a modern day version of the real bills doctrine. We set a particular rate and the market gets all the money it wants at that rate. The only way we have to encourage it to take more is to lower that rate, or the only way to discourage it is to raise the rate, which is what we had under the real bills doctrine. And I don't like the initiative for the generation of the money supply to come from the market. It ought to be supply determined rather than demand determined since the long-term velocity of M2 looks like a pretty stable function to me now. So, I've always endorsed that, I don't have the answer, as I indicated earlier. We just don't have any reserve measure that can be expected to control M2, so I don't know what the alternative is. And I am very frustrated over that.
>
> (FOMC meeting, October 1990, pages 55–56)

With the abandonment of the monetary-target framework, they were left with no core framework to justify their decisions from 1982 to until the end of the 1990s:

> We've advanced from pragmatic monetarism to full-blown eclecticism.
>
> (Corrigan, FOMC meeting, October 1985, page 33)

> In a world where we do not have monetary aggregates to guide us as to the thrust of monetary policy actions, we are kind of groping around just trying to characterize where the stance is.
>
> (Jordan, FOMC meeting, March 1994, page 49)

With the expiration of the Humphrey-Hawkins legislation in the early 2000s, formal discussion and reporting of long-term growth ranges of monetary aggregates to the Congress completely disappeared from the FOMC framework of operation. However, even after recognizing their irrelevance, FOMC members still felt the need to look at monetary aggregates in an informal way:

> But obviously, as you suggest, I don't believe we would be credible central bankers if we didn't all in our own individual ways look at the aggregates at every meeting. And, in fact, I certainly did look at them coming into this meeting. So, I think continuing to keep track of them is part of what we are expected to do.
>
> (Ferguson, FOMC meeting, June 2000, page 92)

In June 2000, Broaddus proposed to replace Humphrey-Hawkins annual discussion of long-term policy by discussions surrounding inflation targeting but met the resistance of most members of the Committee. From the end of the 1990s, the Wicksellian/Fisherian framework progressively gained more and more favor among FOMC members and finally provided a theoretically grounded justification for interest-rate targeting that could include the 1990s productivity story of the "new era":

> Knowledge of trend productivity growth is very important, to me at least and I think to many people, in terms of giving us an estimated range for the equilibrium real funds rate at any point in time, given whatever situation we face. We've talked about this many times before: The higher the productivity growth rate, and hence the faster the expected growth of future income, the more businesses and households are going to borrow money to try to bring some of that expected higher future income forward; and hence the higher the equilibrium real rate needs to be to make people and business firms be patient and wait until the actual higher income arises.
>
> (Greenspan, FOMC meeting, June 2001, page 29)

This framework of analysis, however, is used by most FOMC members as a qualitative framework, not as a means of knowing by how much real interest rates have to be raised: "What they tell you is direction and rough orders of magnitude" (Greenspan, FOMC meeting, February 2000, page 112).

Looking at what Post-Keynesians have to say, we can understand that monetary targets are not only irrelevant but also dangerous. As the preamble of the 1914 Federal Reserve Act states, the Federal Reserve System was set up mainly to maintain financial stability through "an elastic currency" and an "effective supervision" of the banking system. Other economic preoccupations were secondary and characterized as "other purposes." In fact, one has to wait a 1977 amendment of the Federal Reserve Act with section 2A to find a clear statement that justifies the involvement of the Federal Reserve in the management of inflation, employment, and economic growth. Given the true purpose of the

Federal Reserve and given the nature of money, controlling the money supply is impossible. The only thing a central bank can do is to set interest rates, and to supply and withdraw reserves on demand in such a way as to maintain its policy rate on target.

Today, FOMC members have gone from a Monetarist to a Fisherian framework. In both cases, the nominal interest rate is unimportant for the management of the economy. What matters in the second framework are the real long-term interest rate and its relationship to a natural rate of interest. Chapters 2 and 4 have argued that these two concepts are irrelevant for understanding the way a monetary economy works. Nominal interest rates are a good characterization of monetary policy if the cash flows they generate are compared to the nominal cash inflows of deficit-spending private economic units.

Interest rates

Even though FOMC members understand that there are other transmission mechanisms for monetary policy, the belief in the capacity of the central bank to influence expenditure, and so inflation, through the impact of policy rates on the cost of borrowing is the core component of current monetary policy:

> The essence of monetary policy is through the interest rate-cost of capital channel. In the Goldman Sachs financial conditions index this interest rate channel gets 90 percent of the weighting. In the FRB/US model its weighting ranges from 76 percent to 90 percent, depending on whether one takes one-quarter impacts or long-run impacts. [...] I will agree with the critics that there are both theoretical and empirical questions about some of the other ways that monetary policy allegedly stimulates the economy.
>
> (Gramlich, FOMC meeting, November 2001, page 63)

We have seen that in the Post-Keynesian analysis, there is no straightforward relationship between interest rates and demand for loans. We have shown also that the central bank has a leading role in determining the yield curve, much more than inflation, and that inflation and interest rates are loosely related and even can be positively related. FOMC members sometimes dwelled upon the previous "heresies."

If one starts with the yield curve, this may be the area in which FOMC members' beliefs have been the most challenged. At the end of 1970s and early 1980s, all of them believed that a central bank could not affect long-term rates directly. The latter were assumed to depend only on expected inflation and so if a central bank decreased its targeted short-term rates, long-term rates would increase because financial market participants would expect higher inflation in the future (the central bank is "flooding money" in the economy). The same effect would be reached if the federal fiscal deficit grew:

> Also, with respect to the comments a little earlier on where long-term rates are headed, with special attention to the mortgage rate, I am distressed to see

how high those rates are forecast to be. But I am also convinced that we won't get those rates lower than that 12 to 13 plus percent for both the corporate bond issues as well as mortgage rates until we get the inflation rate down. Obviously, long-term interest rates are very heavily influenced by both actual and expected inflation.

(Balles, FOMC meeting, August 1980, page 18)

Well, I think one of the main reasons rates are high is because we have put out what the public perceives as too much money. If we show that we are going to deal with that, I would expect interest rates to come down largely in response to the elimination of part of the expectations effect problem.

(Black, FOMC meeting, December 1980, page 35)

It seems to me that there are two main reasons why rates are staying up. The first would be the uncertainties concerning what might be done by Congress on the present budget impasse: I guess all we can do in that area is to jawbone, as I think you've done very effectively from time-to-time, with the rest of us chiming in whenever we could. But the second reason is a fear that the System at some point may be forced toward some materially easy monetary policy.

(Black, FOMC meeting, May 1982, page 28)

In this context, they could not understand why their harsh monetary policy did not bring down long-term rates, and by 1983, inflation had decreased considerably but long-term rates were still very high, as Figure 6.12 shows, because of the lower limit imposed on long-term rates by the federal funds rate.

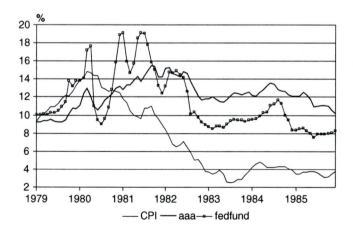

Figure 6.12 AAA bond, federal funds rate, and CPI inflation.
Sources: BLS, Federal Reserve System.

Eventually, the FOMC had to recognize that it was responsible for the situation and that the central bank rate is one of the leading factors in the determination of the whole range of interest rates:

> I think it's wrong to read every wriggle in the bond market as a sign of inflation or inflation psychology. Having worked with investments for 10 years, I can tell you a lot of people who trade bonds don't have anything in mind; they are just throwing pieces of paper around.
>
> (Seger, FOMC meeting, May 1987, page 18)

> I don't think there's anything sacred about the yield curve in terms of inflation expectations. I think basically all that says is that the markets are betting that short-term rates in the future are going to be lower than they are today. I think you really have to isolate more on the long bond itself to get some sort of notion of what they're thinking. It doesn't necessarily mean lower inflation expectations: it does mean that they think the short rates are going to be lower in the future for various reasons.
>
> (Johnson, FOMC meeting, February 1989, page 53)

> The long bond doesn't just represent inflation expectations: it also represents expectations as to Fed policy. And when we shift from easing to tightening we have a real tough deal to play.
>
> (Angell, FOMC meeting, December 1989, page 93)

Some members had some difficulty accepting this, but the staff of the Committee reminded them of this:

> MR. JORDAN. I'm left a little uncomfortable with part of your explanation about expectations of short rates as they relate to long rates. Earlier this year, and beginning last year, some academics testifying in Congress argued that the reason intermediate and long rates are as high as they are was the fear that the fed was going to raise the funds rate. They said all we had to do was take the pledge that we wouldn't raise short rates and bond yields would fall.
>
> MR. PRELL. Well, there may be some element of truth to that. In fact, one story that we've heard is that the change in the perception about the likelihood of the Fed tightening over the next year has provided the bond markets with some encouragement.
>
> MR. JORDAN. That's starkly in contrast to the view that longer-term expectations about debt monetization and inflation –
>
> (FOMC meeting, March 1993, page 11)

Overall, therefore, the explanation given in chapter 4 about the relationship between interest rates and inflation had to be recognized by FOMC members, as "incoherent" as it seemed. It was shown that there is no incoherence if one can recognize that real rates are not a primary matter of concern for financial market participants. More precisely, real considerations are included in a broader strategy regarding solvency and liquidity.

The next idea that has been challenged is related to the cost aspect of interest rates. The Federal Reserve assumes that higher interest rates increase the cost of borrowing and so decrease the amount of loan demand. We have already argued that this negative relationship has no reason to hold because what matters is not the interest rate itself but its relationship to the main cash-flow generating factor of the activity financed and funded with external funds, the cash inflows being or not being related to what will happen to output price growth. FOMC members do not seem to understand that as the following shows:

> In addition to the input that we bring to these meetings and the usual sources of our own research staff and directors, last Friday when Vice Chairman Schultz visited us in San Francisco we called in a special small group of bankers, businessmen, and academicians for a very frank exchange of views. We sounded them out about their feelings on the economy and on Fed policy, and I must say, Fred, that I thought the reactions were quite candid and somewhat humiliating in a way. The bankers generally expressed the view that as yet there's very little evidence that the high level of interest rates is having any significant total effect on cutting off credit demand. Now, one has to add to that the expressions we got from them in our usual go-around with bankers and bank directors that these high rates are having a cutting effect on the so-called middle market for business borrowers – the smaller firms – and for mortgage loans and some small farmers. That's where the incidence of the high interest rate effect has been felt thus far in our part of the country. But as a general matter, even if the businessmen present were mostly from big concerns, they simply indicated that the higher rates per se are not having any effect at all on their capital projects. If a project is worthwhile, it's not going to get cut off by a one or two percentage point increase in the cost of funds. A minority expressed the view that this is leading to some greater caution on inventory policy, which is already being viewed as quite cautious. One major real estate developer present indicated that the higher rates are just built into their projects and aren't having any dampening effect at all.
>
> (Balles, FOMC meeting, September 1979, page 27)

In 1989, Vice Chairman Corrigan made a similar comment, apparently not aware of what Balles reported 10 years earlier:

> The anecdotal material on the inflation side is, frankly, a bit sour right now. Virtually all companies – small and large – that we've talked to in the recent past do point to both labor and non-labor cost pressures. And consistent with Gary's comment [they report] less difficulty in passing costs through.

I don't think I would characterize these impressions as symptomatic of a 1979-80 type outburst of inflation.

(Corrigan, FOMC meeting, March 1989, page 26)

Thus, as long as borrowers can pass the cost of their loans to their cash-flow generating activity, or the latter is highly effective in generating cash so that the former does not matter, borrowers have no reason to be preoccupied by the cost of borrowing. However, more importantly, even if they know they cannot afford high borrowing cost for a long period, economic agents may still have an incentive to borrow in order to avoid declaring insolvency. Refinancing needs are a source of loan demand that is not negatively related to interest rates. In the end, therefore, high interest rates can lead to higher inflation. Again, hard pressed by real events, some FOMC members recognized that but most of them saw this as an anomaly:

Interest rates may be [low] after tax, or in real terms, but they are still contributing to cost and are creating, I think, some of the upward pressure on prices.

(Teeters, FOMC meeting, May 1981, page 10)

In other words, tighter credit leads to higher prices!

(Greenspan, FOMC meeting, May 1990, page 16)

There is deterioration in the inflation rate stemming from interest costs and energy costs, and those are not trivial sources of deterioration. At the end of the day it doesn't have to be labor costs that are causing the overall inflation deterioration.

(Greenspan, FOMC meeting, November 2000, page 85)

Overall, many of the conclusions of the Post-Keynesian approach regarding interest rates have been verified in practice, but most of the FOMC members cannot accept them because they go against their theoretical framework.

Monetary policy and inflation

Given that the Schwartz hypothesis seems to be widely shared among academics and central bankers, inflation is the central preoccupation of modern central banks. Focusing on inflation is supposed to bring higher long-term sustainable economic growth and financial stability. As stated earlier, and as FOMC members recognized, the former causation is not supported by data, and Greenspan presented the 1990s bubbles as an example for which price stability and stock-market stability are incompatible. This was noted several times by FOMC members:

I will now commit a little heresy in the minds of some folks. In current circumstances, the absence of consumer price inflation is not a sufficient condition for financial stability in my view. It is ultimately financial stability, as we have seen in our own history and in other economies around the world that is the key to maximum sustainable growth.

(Jordan, FOMC meeting, August 1998, page 48)

The problem as we learned is that the longer we maintain a degree of stability, the lower the risk premiums become. So there is a question of whether we have an internal problem in policymaking, namely that if we indeed stabilize the system for too long, risk premiums fall, speculation tends to emerge, and we face the type of problem that we ran into. That may be, and I suspect it is an inevitable consequence of any form of discretionary monetary policy. Unless we go back to the gold standard or adopt some automatic mechanism, or conduct a black box type of monetary policy, I don't see how we can get around this problem.

(Greenspan, FOMC Meeting, June 2001, page 142)

Following Minsky's theory, one can understand clearly the dynamics that are involved in the sentence above. Contrary to what Greenspan argues, those dynamics are not mainly the product of discretionary policy and the unwillingness of politician to make tough decisions at the right time. There are internal dynamics to the capitalist economic system that make stability destabilizing. However, once again, these points usually are treated as anomalies, or "heresies," and output-price inflation is assumed to be the first objective that will promote growth and financial stability:

First, let me raise a heretical issue. Is price stability really what we are after or are we after financial stability? Even more generally, going back over time we have tended to argue, I think correctly, that the objective of monetary policy is to create maximum sustainable economic growth, and we have argued, again I think quite correctly, that price stability is a necessary condition to reach that goal. But price stability may indeed be a proxy for something else, which I suspect is financial stability. [...] So, I think the problems that we will have to deal with in defining what we are stabilizing are going to increase in the years ahead. What I want to suggest is that we confront the question of whether we are trying to stabilize prices or trying to stabilize the financial system. That is where the issue of asset prices comes in; it is in a certain sense positioned on a continuum that begins with spot prices for units of goods and services.

(Greenspan, FOMC meeting, July 1997, pages 49–50)

We have had cases in our history and cases in other countries' history where the present price of claims to future consumption moved very substantially – sometimes too far up and then sometimes very rapidly down. This creates financial instabilities that are unhealthy for the performance of an economy. Otherwise, 1907 would not have happened; 1893 would not have happened.

(Jordan, FOMC meeting, February 1999, page 123)

This book has argued that actually the causation runs both ways because price stability promotes financial stability by making the future more certain, and financial stability generates price stability (avoid debt-deflation process and inflationary refinancing spiral). But the book has argued also that the central bank should concentrate its efforts on financial stability, not price stability, because it is more suited for that task.

The supposition of the contrary assumes a quantity theory approach of money in which the central bank can control money directly or indirectly (which it cannot) and a causal link between money and price (which does not necessarily exist).[16] We have already seen that FOMC members have been disabused about the capacity to do the former. However, some of them have also been skeptical about the incapacity of the Fed to control inflation. The Fed, which is so often acclaimed for its victory against the mid-1970s inflationary economy, has in fact very little contribution in this decline according to Teeters:

> May I remind you that we shouldn't take too much credit for the price easing? I never thought we were totally at fault for the price increases that we suffered from OPEC and food; and I don't think the fact that OPEC and food have calmed down has a great deal to do with monetary policy per se, except in the very long run.
>
> (Teeters, FOMC meeting, July 1981, page 46)

This claim, of course, was made before the large recession of 1982 that broke inflation and for which the Fed is partly responsible, but it shows that inflation is not directly under the control of monetary factors. The decrease in inflation was due to "special factors," as they are called by the FOMC members, like lower oil price or appreciation of the dollar. As stated earlier, credibility and other central-bank related elements may account for little of the decline in inflation over the 1980s and 1990s.

Another problem concerns the appropriate definition of inflation, which has become an even more important concern with the progressive move toward inflation targeting after 2000. We are back to the dilemma of the monetary targets:

> To clarify our goal, we need to get our inflation measurement straight. How can we answer the question about whether current inflation is consistent with price stability without being clear about what we are talking about: CPI, core CPI, median CPI, experimental CPI, GDP or PCE price indexes, or something else? We certainly need to be specific among ourselves if not before the public. How should we interpret the current 1997 and 1998 forecasts in the Greenbook of an acceleration in the GDP chain-weighted price index and the core CPI and a deceleration in the overall consumer price index? Is inflation accelerating or decelerating?
>
> (Melzer, FOMC meeting, May 1997, page 39)

Different indicators give different signals about what the central bank should do and Greenspan recognizes that the CPI is not a good indicator for monetary policy: "I hope that within two years the CPI rarely will be discussed at these meetings." (Greenspan, FOMC meeting, February 1997; Papadimitriou and Wray 1996). Rather than measuring inflation directly some FOMC members, especially recently, have relied on the differential between market rates and the natural rate of interest rate to have an indication of the stand of monetary policy:

> The level, of course, is important because we need to know where the funds rate stands relative to some perception of the natural rate. That's crucial in assessing whether we are injecting a sufficient amount of liquidity for the macroeconomic circumstances to achieve the outcome we want.
>
> (Jordan, FOMC meeting, November 2001, page 58)

> The temporary disinflationary effect of the supply shock may at first limit the increase in interest rates, but given that the productivity upturn carries with it an increase in the equilibrium real rate, the cyclical rise in rates required to contain inflation may ultimately be larger than otherwise. Wicksell's framework of natural versus market rates provides a useful perspective on this development. The recent productivity upturn implies an increase in the economy's natural rate. At unchanged market rates the gap between natural and market rates has widened, and monetary policy has in effect become more stimulative. Only when monetary policy moves market rates enough to close this gap will the expansion begin to slow.
>
> (Meyer, FOMC meeting, February 2000, page 76)

However, here again there are measurement problems and widely different values of the natural rate can be identified, making this intermediate target impractical for monetary policy, either qualitatively or quantitatively (Cuaresma and Gnan 2007; Weber 2006; Ferguson 2004; Orphanides and Williams 2002). Of course, besides the measurement problems of the natural rate of interest, its intrinsic qualitative merits for the analysis of monetary economies are questionable.

The biggest challenge to the idea that inflation is mainly a monetary phenomenon occurred at the end of the 1990s. After 6 years of growth, FOMC members were wondering why inflation had not occurred yet and why expected inflation was not significant. They tried, especially Greenspan, to find many different indicators that could support their view and could justify a preemptive increase in interest rates, but nothing was available:

> The second is that lots of times in our meetings people have come up with new indicators that we ought to look at that don't quite suggest what some of the other indicators have suggested. The Chairman does this more than anybody else, but everybody does it to some degree.
>
> (Gramlich, FOMC meeting, June 1999, pages 97–98)

The big difficulty I see is in acting preemptively, which I think is necessary if we really are to stabilize inflation at present low levels. In order to act preemptively we must be able to forecast inflation, and that can present a problem. We could rely on modeling approaches to forecast inflation, but these have not been very successful precisely because of the supply shocks that have made the inflation-targeting approach attractive. We could rely on leading indicators, but there aren't many reliable leading indicators that are not already considered in models. We could rely on the forecasts of inflation of others, but those other forecasters may have the same trouble with their models or their leading indicators that we have.

(Gramlich, FOMC meeting, December 1999, page 36)

Eventually, FOMC members were forced to conclude that something was wrong in their economic framework. One of them was that it failed to take into account the interaction between supply and demand of goods:

Let me just say very simply – this is really a repetition of what I've been saying in the past – that we have all been brought up to a greater or lesser extent on the presumption that the supply side is a very stable force. [...] In my judgment our models fail to account appropriately for the interaction between the supply side and the demand side largely because historically it has not been necessary for them to do so.

(Greenspan, FOMC meeting, October 1999, pages 46–47)

Post-Keynesians reject this independence of supply and demand of goods, and the concept of "effective demand" is the best way to understand that. The actual and potential supply capacities depend on expected demand, which is affected progressively by, and largely independent of, current actual demand.[17] One implication of this is that the notions of NAIRU and potential output become irrelevant for policy practice:

I must say I am a little puzzled by the fascination with NAIRU. I thought work done by Stock and Watson and others suggested that if there is a NAIRU, it lies somewhere between 4 to 7 percent or some range like that, which is quite wide. If that is right, it is not a terribly useful concept for policy. So, I have been reluctant for some time to go down that path very aggressively.

(Stern, FOMC meeting, February 1999, page 112)

In the end, therefore, the FOMC members have had to question their economic understanding regarding the origins of inflation, but unfortunately, this did not lead to any change in the framework used.

Conclusion

The theoretical framework of FOMC members has been challenged in many ways over the past 30 years. Looking at what Post-Keynesians have to provide in terms of analytical framework would have helped them to figure out what is going on and how to improve their policy. One can doubt, however, that pure economic arguments guide the decisions of a supposedly independent Federal Reserve. For example, it is often assumed that the change of procedure in October 1979 was a change of economic paradigm at the Federal Reserve. The preceding showed that this was not the case. The Federal Reserve never became a ("pragmatic") Monetarist only for economic reasons; political reasons were at the root, and a good portion of the FOMC members knew that the adoption of the Monetarist framework opened a road toward disasters. They were pushed, however, in this direction by the shared idea among most economists that a central bank can "pump money" in the economy and is the main source of inflation. Neither of those two ideas is right: Central banks cannot force banks to grant advances, and cannot provide an additional net supply of reserves if banks do not want them unless it is prepared to lower its policy rates; the maintenance of a high policy rate may require the net injection of more reserves than a low policy rate, and inflation has many non-monetary causes.

All this also provides additional support to the idea that the management of inflation, employment, and economic growth is not the domain of central banks. If policy rates are manipulated constantly, a central bank has to go through a tremendous amount of effort of communication in order not to create large volatilities in financial markets. All this for not much in return because the final effects of interest rates on economic activity are highly uncertain and non-linear; worse still, the manipulation of policy rates can result in interest-induced inflation as well as higher financial fragility. One more time, one is forced to conclude that monetary policy should be left aside and a central bank should concentrate its effort on developing a strong encompassing supervision of the financial system that puts major emphasis on the determination of systemic risk and socially beneficial activities. Through this means it would have a more direct and straightforward impact on the economic system.

General conclusion

Over the 1980s and the 1990s, the FOMC sometimes had to alter or to moderate its interest-rate policy in order to take into account financial problems in the economy. The FOMC, however, discussed financial matters only marginally, spending most of its time on inflation-related matters via a theoretical framework that does not accommodate financial issues well and that provides a distorted explanation of inflation, interest rates, and the monetary-creation process, among others. In the 1970s, this led to great instability in financial markets as the Federal Reserve decreased its concern about providing a smooth refinancing source of reserves. At the end of the 1970s, FOMC members decided mostly to ignore financial matters and to go for highly variable interest rates, knowing that the precarious state of the banking system that the Federal Reserve and other examiners failed to supervise correctly probably would lead to large financial problems. This policy directly led to the crisis of the thrift institutions and contributed to the economic recessions of the early 1980s.

Some members like Teeters, LaWare, Jordan, or McTeer did have a way of analyzing the economic situation that puts more weight on the importance of checking the financial positions of economic sectors and the liquidity of the economy, but they usually were not the dominant voice in the Committee. Large financial problems were dealt with more closely by the FOMC, usually by one or several conference call(s), and by private meeting with the parties. However, those meetings did not lead to a restructuring of the management of banks toward safer financial practices. Some Governors, like Blinder and Meyer, complained to Greenspan about being left in the dark when major financial disturbances were unfolding, but other members were largely indifferent (Meyer 2004: 118). Regarding the LTCM crisis, Meyer states "I can't even tell you if the Chairman was kept adequately informed, though my suspicion is that he was not as involved as he ought to have been" (Meyer 2004: 118). In addition, a proactive policy was rarely tried because of political and social pressures to let the money machine go until it breaks. This again was illustrated recently with the developments in the mortgage market and the ensuing general debacle over the whole US and international financial system (Wray 2008; Kregel 2008; Whalen 2008). Accordingly, all Committee members assumed, by default or not, that the interest rate is the best tool to use to influence economic decisions.

Overall, the 1979–2001 period witnesses several main problems with current central banking. First, whatever the regulatory measures are and however accurate they are, and whatever the relevance of the economic framework used, if the regulatory authority does not take any corrective actions to stop some financial excesses because of political and social pressures, no improvement can be made. The central bank is a crucial component for the stability and soundness of the financial system. This is especially the case in the US institutional framework that has been created by the Financial Modernization Act, where the Federal Reserve is now at the center of the financial system. It should influence proactively the evolution of the financial system by analyzing financial innovations as they appear and rapidly including them into, or dismissing them from, the regulatory framework. Financial innovations that promote financial instability should be banned immediately, independently of the potential profitability that they may generate for their issuer. Maybe a "Financial Innovation Committee" should be created within the Federal Reserve where all financial innovations created have to be tested and fully understood before they can be used in daily life. If the cash-flow implications cannot be understood well or if they are Ponzi in nature, those financial innovations should not be authorized.

Second, fine-tuning the economy is not an adequate role for a central bank. The latter has a role of contrarian; however, the main way it should do this is not by using interest rates but by intervening dynamically in the credit and financial policies of the financial institutions. The interest rate is a rather ineffective tool because of its passivity, cumulative effects, and *ex post* response to the problem. The interest rate is passive because the main factors affecting decisions are expectations, as Greenspan himself recognized:

> Prolonged periods of expansion promote a greater *rational* willingness to take risks, a pattern very difficult to avert by a modest tightening of monetary policy.
>
> (Greenspan, Speech, August 30, 2002)

The interest rate is an *ex post* tool because once decisions have been implemented and affect the economic system (via inflation, employment, speculation, or any other ways) those decisions are irreversible and have to be financed and funded. It is cumulative because higher interest rates may promote borrowing when agents are indebted. In addition, constant fluctuations in policy rates create financial disruptions through their effect on debt burden and on asset prices, and also through the disincentive for financial institutions to hold fixed-income claims.

Third, asset prices are important, but the Committee was never able to find a comfortable way to integrate them in its reasoning and always used extreme measures. It acted either bluntly without any, or only few, considerations for the impacts on asset prices, or timidly via small changes in interest rates and a few comments about the speculative situation. A better understanding of the sensitivity of positions to changes in asset prices would have given the Committee a more reliable way to act and to argue about the economic situation.

Fourth, in the dynamic approach, a central bank is not the "dumb" or "ignorant" person in the valuation of what lies ahead. On the contrary, a central bank should be viewed as holding a key position because of its capacity to look far into the past, because of its experience in dealing with macroeconomic problems, and because of its role as a lender of last resort. The central bank knows something because it is more aware than the CEOs or any other financial analysts of what happened in the past, and that human nature and competition give an incentive to ignore lessons from the past. What is needed is a productive cooperation between financial institutions and central banks, each sharing their own experience for a better financial policy. This cooperation, however, may be difficult, especially in the current monetary-policy setting, because of the profit motive that drives private financial institutions. Today, interest volatility has been internalized by financial institutions through the development of securitization and re-securitization, and they have learned to profit from the constant changes in interest rates. This is even more the case now that the Federal Reserve tries to suggest well in advance what it plans to do. Thus, Wojnilower notes that

> The Fed wants a smoothly growing economy, but the securities industry thrives on volatility that generates trading volume and profits. The Fed and financial markets are adversaries, not allies.
>
> (Wojnilower 2005: 1)

In this case, central bankers should have the nerve to use the vast regulatory and supervisory power given to them to make sure that their policy bites and promotes financial stability. They will only have the strength to do so if they have the right tool to state clearly and convincingly their point of view, and if they have the will to go against the strong social and political pressures that promote short-term wealth accumulation against long-term financial stability. The new Basel Accord, by letting big banks assess their own risk, does not go in this direction because, among other problems, it presupposes that big banks know more about their business than supervisors and regulators. The experience of the 1970s–1990s, however, should have provided a clear counter example of this idea. Big banks cannot, or more probably do not, want to take into account the systemic risk that grows out of their individualistic behavior because this goes against their profit-oriented activities. The convention prevailing in the banking system and competitive pressures pushes them to follow the average behavior and to fall together, knowing that the central bank will rescue the majority of them. Bankers know the game of privatization of gains and socialization of losses very well, and the central bank should redefine the rules of this game.

Finally, one has to recognize that supervision and regulation concentrate only on the "expectational" part of the problem. We have seen, however, that fragility can occur without any expectational problems. The working of compounding and the shortening of maturity terms are central to the dynamics of financial weakening. The search for financial instruments and institutions that promote financial stability should be a major goal of central banks. In addition, a central bank should be highly involved in any emergency lending agreement and restructuring process in which public funds are involved, in order to guarantee that the solution reached is in the best interests, not of the particular institutions involved nor of its own (like in the early 1980s with DIDMCA), but of the financial stability of the economic system.

7 Conclusion

A new role for the central bank

Contrary to most of the macroeconomic literature on central banking, this book focuses on financial considerations in order to discuss the appropriate role of a central bank in the management of the economy. The main conclusion that has been reached is that central banks should reform their current way of operating by changing their goal and their instruments of intervention. Their main objective should not be price stability but financial stability, and their main tool should not be interest rates but a proactive financial policy oriented toward understanding systemic risk. Interest rates on overnight central bank advances should be set at zero forever. Interest rates, as an operating tool, are grossly ineffective to manage the economic system and may promote economic fragility, inflation, speculation, misdistribution of income, and economic recession. This is especially the case in an economic system in which refinancing loans and short-term loans are in high proportion, policy rates are changed frequently and widely, and financial markets are dominated by fund managers. Financial policy should replace monetary policy and should be included in a broader policy of permanent and stable full-employment.

This vision of the role of a central bank is the complete opposite of the main view of New Neoclassical Synthesis for several reasons. First, it does not assume that inflation has only, or even mainly, monetary origins; second, interest rates are guided by monetary forces, and there is no real anchor toward which they tend; third, we live in a monetary production economy in which agents care about nominal values and compare nominal values for the sake of nominal values; fourth, the world is uncertain, and the future is not written in stone but created by current economic decisions; and fifth, there are other structural public institutions that are better suited for the goal of price stability and to affect the production side of the economic system. Central banks have been created to deal with the financial side of the economic system and should focus their attention exclusively on this side. While concentrating their attention on the financial side of the economy system, central bankers should understand that the rationality of economic agents is different from the traditional economic rationality. Individual rationality is social, not individualistic. This implies that the role of social conventions becomes central for economic decisions, which has several implications for the conduct of central banking.

First, a central bank should be an anchor for financial decisions by trying to influence the existing financial conventions about the appropriate way to leverage expectations. The central bank should be at the center of a financial policy that guides the financial practices of financial institutions: portfolio strategies, methods of granting loans, and refinancing channels. More generally, a central bank should influence the social rationality in a way that promotes financial stability by discouraging the use of speculative finance.

Second, this role of guidance is essential because private economic agents are driven by a profit motive that prevents them from recognizing, or acknowledging, the potential social disruptions and inefficiencies induced by the combination of individual search for accumulation and social base of justification. Without this guiding role, a central bank is condemned to be a follower in the game of privatizing gains and socializing losses via inflation, unemployment, and a prolonged recession. As a lender of last resort, the central bank should be the one that writes and redefines the rule of this game.

Third, because a convention is arbitrary in nature, even though the justification process that sustains it may be well grounded and may lead to economic decisions that realize the future envisioned by the convention, the level of asset prices is not what matters. There is no a priori fundamental value for asset prices, and the notion of bubble is not a relevant concept for central banking. It is a dangerous concept to focus on for political reasons when there is speculation; and it is an inadequate concept to focus on for economic reasons when assets are assumed to be well priced. In the latter case, problems may be accumulating in financial markets if balance sheets become highly dependent on changes in asset prices. What matters is the sensitivity of balance sheets to changes in asset prices.

The problem becomes to figure out a way by which central banks can guide the financial system toward behaviors that are more socially responsible. We have argued that central banks can do this in several ways. First, one has to recognize that part of this guiding principle already exists through the myriad of regulators and supervisors. For example, pension funds cannot place their funds in some assets in more than a certain proportion, and more reliable information has been made available to individual agents about the risk of placing money in the stock market. However, cases like Enron and the new economy bubble show that this is not enough, and individuals are ready to bet, and have been encouraged by financial institutions to bet, their future savings on arbitrary conventions without checking for the implications of their choices. The recent emergence of financial holding companies also has not been matched by a broader financial regulation. Taking for example the United States, the Fed has been declared the umbrella supervisor, but the regulatory framework is still largely scattered and compartmentalized, a product of continuous *ex post* responses to financial innovations. Thus, more *ex post* regulation never really helps to stabilize the system and what is needed is a regulatory body that continuously and proactively responds to changes in the financial sector.

Thus, the first thing that should be done is to create a regulatory body that can deal with highly diversified and broad financial institutions, and that is proactive in dealing with systemic risks. In terms of the United States, it would be good to merge all the relevant federal regulatory bodies into one central regulatory institution like a Financial Oversight and Resolution Commission (FORC) that would be part of the central bank. This Commission would be headed by a Committee composed of financial analysts, financial engineers, accountants, economists, labor-union representatives, and lawyers. They would be selected for their achievements, not in terms of their capacity make lots of money or to manage businesses, but in terms of their capacity to deal with or to analyze financial matters in a broad and systemic way. Committee members would have a long mandate and the Commission would regulate and supervise all financial institutions, without exceptions.

The Commission would have several central duties. The first one will be to put a stamp of approval on any financial innovation (i.e. new financial instrument, or new financial institution, or new ways of using existing financial instruments/institutions) that the Commission considers safe. Anytime any financial institution comes up with an idea, it would have to submit the idea to the FORC. The latter would inspect and test extensively proposed innovations and would approve those that promote financial stability (i.e. hedge financing) while rejecting immediately Ponzi-like financial innovations, especially those based on collateral-oriented loans. It would operate in the same way the Food and Drug Administration operates when a new drug is created. By doing this the FORC, and so the central bank, will be constantly informed about changes in the financial system, and will be able to pass promptly the appropriate legislations to avoid regulatory arbitrages and to promote safe financial practices. Thus, unlike today, the implicit validation of financial innovations would not be done *ex post* by reluctantly granting access to the lender of last resort facility because of the fear of a systemic failure but, instead, would be proactive to avoid systemic risk in the first place.

The second duty of the Commission would be to be actively engage in the search for new financial instruments or institutions that promote hedge financing and that allow a smooth refinancing of positions when needed. Instruments with income and capital components that are made compatible with the main cash inflows of borrowers would help to achieve that goal. Thus, financial instruments with a maturity adapted to that of main cash-flow generating activities of borrowers, and an income component proportional to the cash inflows of borrowers, would improve greatly the stability of the system. This would work both in the interests of borrowers (who could continue their activities while solving short-term liquidity problems) and of lenders (who depend, directly or indirectly, on the continuation of economic activity for their income). To promote those financial innovations, the Commission could provide monetary incentives for the private sector to use them. Community banking is one area where the development of socially beneficial financial innovations could be highly successful and should be encouraged further.

A third duty of the Commission would be to be involved heavily in the resolution of insolvency problems if the intervention of the central bank is required. If necessary, because some financial institutions are too big to fail and a major restructuration is needed, the Commission should nationalize them, and possibly, resell them at a fair price to the private sector when they have been restructured properly. When financial restructuring is necessary, the FORC should have in mind the public interest, not the interest of troubled financial institutions nor its own interest (like when the Fed bargained deregulation for mandatory reserve requirements in the 1980s).

Fourth, the Commission also should put much more emphasis on cash-flow monitoring rather than capital requirements or reserves. Capital equity in itself does not provide any direct protection against financial fragility, may promote financial instability through the procyclical effect of capital requirements, and has non-linear effect on risk-taking behaviors by reducing moral hazard but also by giving a sense of safety. In addition, supervision should aim at promoting an awareness of the social consequences of individual choices. This type of supervision should replace the "bad bank" approach to supervision that assumes that there is necessarily something wrong with the managers of financial institutions. In an uncertain world, in which competition is a driving force, general conformism, even toward dangerous financial practices, is inherent. Thus, the Commission should make sure that reward mechanisms and managerial practices do not promote short-termism. The Uniform Financial Institutions Rating System, which checks the performance of financial institution in terms of capital adequacy, asset quality, management, earnings, liquidity, and sensitivity to market risk (CAMELS), is an essential component of the supervisory system to develop and to apply to all existing financial companies and should include all off-balance sheet items (maybe off-balance sheet accounting should be forbidden). Data collected through CAMELS should be used to develop a supervisory framework that focuses on aggregate systemic risk and CAMELS should be used and developed to analyze immediately financial innovations. One of the central elements to develop would be a cash-flow oriented macroeconomic accounting that would complement flow of funds and national income accounting.

Finally, the Commission would have to monitor broad financial fragility constantly. A good way to do that would be for the Committee of the FORC to meet on a regular basis, maybe as frequently as the FOMC does today, to discuss the financial conditions of the system. These meetings would be a good way to understand the general direction toward which the financial system is heading, would help the FORC to stay up to date with the latest financial developments, and would be a means to decide what part of the financial sector needs more attention.

All this could be done by relying on the expertise of each member of the Commission. However, its power of argumentation and conviction would be greatly increased if a new tool could be provided to the Commission. This tool would measure systemic risk in any part of the system. This would need a lot more research and we are far from achieving this goal in terms of either data availability or modeling techniques. Central banks should devote most of their research to the understanding of the aggregate financial frame and of the financial interactions between different sectors of the economy. We have argued that this requires a change of economic paradigm and so a change in the methodological tools used to analyze economic activity. A monetary economy is fundamentally different from a barter economy with money. The first step would be to understand some basic principles like the difference between financing and funding, the origins of aggregate monetary profit, and the implication of fiscal policy for financial matters: Saving cannot finance investment, federal fiscal deficit usually is a necessity and is good for aggregate private saving, and capital assets have value because they are scarce. The second step is to retreat from the search for formal models that are mathematically tractable in terms of equilibrium. What we want are models with more realistic assumptions and detailed institutional framework, and models that grasp the complexity of economic mechanisms. We have suggested that the stock and flow consistency approach, combined with computerized modeling technique, provides methodological tools that seem useful in the search for a comprehensive understanding of the interactions and dynamics of an economic system.

Once this research has been developed, a better understanding of how and where systemic risk could emerge would be available. This could allow the Commission to develop aggregate stress tests to study the sensitivity of balance sheets, cash flows, and position-making sources, to changes in asset prices, output prices, income, interest rates, foreign exchange rates, criteria of creditworthiness, and other types of crucial factors for the cash inflows and cash outflows. This would also give the central bank a better understanding of the refinancing sources that are used and potentially useable by the private sectors. In the end, thus, a central bank would have a comprehensive understanding of the risk of illiquidity and insolvency for the economy or a particular sector of the economy.

By doing all the preceding, the role and authority of the central bank in the financial management of the economic system would be greatly strengthened. First, moral suasion, if thought appropriate, would be based on a stronger argument than "there is bubble" or "irrational exuberance." Second, the lender of last resort policy of the central bank would be greatly improved because it would be easier to understand the state of financial fragility of an economic system, and so to improve the timing of a lender of last resort intervention. The central bank could let asset prices go down more easily if the fragility is not too high. Private agents would understand that an intervention would not be immediate, and that they could record substantial losses before the central bank intervenes. This should promote more prudent financial behaviors by all economic agents. At the same time, once a central bank has decided to provide advances, it would do so by having a broad lender of last resort policy toward financial institutions. This is all the more the case that financial innovations would have been approved previously.

In total, a central bank has to work at both the expectational level and the actual level of the financial side of the economy. At the expectation level, it should take part in the formation and guidance of financial conventions, by guiding financial decisions and practices, by reminding actors of the past, by showing how sensitive positions are to changes or to non-realizations of expectations, and by not having a premature lender of last resort policy if it knows that the system can sustain some financial losses. This would imply a comprehensive and systematic supervision and regulation of all financial institutions, and new types of institutions would be analyzed as fast, and as thoroughly, as possible and would be integrated immediately in the supervisory framework. At the actual level, a central bank should check and manage the fragility of the financial frame of the economy, both at the aggregate and individual levels. The central bank would have an impact at the actual level by promoting smooth financial instruments for borrowers, by guiding the refinancing practices through the daily acceptance of certain types of assets at the Discount Window, and by making the simplification process smoother once it has decided to intervene as lender of last resort. Finally, to promote stability, the central bank should take part in any restructuring process that requires the intervention of the central bank.

There are, however, limits to what a central bank can do. Indeed, unless a central bank is prepared to do so, it will not encumber itself with illiquid assets and non-performing assets, and so is not an adequate institution to deal with wide solvency crises. In this case, a complementary institution like a government investment bank would be necessary (like the Reconstruction Finance Corporation of the 1930s and the Resolution Trust Corporation of the 1990s).

In the end, therefore, we have reached the conclusion that a central bank has a central role in the management of the economic system, but it is not the role that is attributed to it today. The central bank should be more involved in financial matters, both as a guide and as a reformer. The central bank then would go from a passive to a dynamic approach to central banking that would be included in the broader policy agenda for stable full employment.

Appendices

Appendix 1: Own rates of interest, real rates of interest, and money rates of interest

The real rate of interest of Fisher and the own rate of interest of Keynes are different concepts. In both theories, the money-interest rate is a relationship between a forward price (current price for future delivery) and a spot price (current price for immediate delivery). However, the real rates are calculated from the production process, whereas the own rates are derived from the relation between two money rates of interest.

In Fisher's theory, the real rates of return are obtained from the productive use of assets. These real returns are compared to the time preference of individuals in terms of output in order to determine a required, or natural, rate of return. Thus, the real rate of interest is the relation between the present quantity (Q_p) and the future quantity (Q_f) of an asset j (Fisher 1930: 36):

$$r_j = (Q_{jf} - Q_{jp})/Q_{jp}.$$

For example, when someone buys wheat in order to obtain a real rate of 4 percent, this means that, by planting 100 bushels of wheat, he will harvest 104 bushels of wheat in the future. Thus, the real rate of interest on wheat is

$$r_w = (104B - 100B)/100B = 4\%.$$

Over time, the law of diminishing returns applies, but, in the "first approximation," one can assume that r_w is fixed.

However, arbitragers are not usually the direct producers, and so everything goes through the spot and forward markets. The money rate of an asset j is determined by its spot-forward price relationship, which combines the expected rate of increase in the price of asset j and the real rate of interest of this asset (Fisher 1930: 69):

$$E(\pi_j) = (F_j - S_j)/S_j,$$

$$R_j = r_j + E(\pi_j) + r_j \cdot E(\pi_j) = \frac{F_j Q_{jf} - S_j Q_{jp}}{S_j Q_{jp}},$$

Table A1.1 Money and real rates of wheat

	Present (lend/borrow)	Future (liquidate)	Rates (obtained/paid)
Money contract	$100	$104	4%
Wheat contract	B100	B104	4%
Price per bushel			
No increase expected	$1	$1	0%
Increase expected	$1	$1.01	1%
Total monetary gain/cost from the wheat contracts			
No inflation expected	$100	$104	4%
Inflation expected	$100	$105.04	5.04%

with F_j the forward price of asset j, and S_j the spot price of asset j. This is illustrated in Table A1.1, which reproduces Fisher's example (Fisher 1907: 80).

When no inflation is expected, the real rate on wheat and the money rate on wheat are equal, and the latter is equal to the money rate on money. In this case, individuals are indifferent between having a position in wheat or in money, and no borrowing and lending occur to smooth real income over time. When individuals expect an increase in the price of wheat, this expectation not being integrated by individuals, money rates are different: 5.04 percent on wheat > 4 percent on money. Given those current expectations, a money return (cost) on wheat of 5.04 percent obtained (paid) from lending (borrowing) wheat spot and liquidating (redeeming) it forward is considered to be equivalent to the wheat return (cost) of 4 percent obtained (paid) by buying, growing, and harvesting wheat over the same period of time. Thus, given that the money yield on wheat contracts is higher than the money yield on money contracts, borrowers have an incentive to borrow money while lenders prefer to lend in wheat terms. In the end, the process stops when both money rates are equal, which goes through an adjustment of expected inflation as defined by the relation between forward and spot prices.

In Keynes's theory, the money rates of interest are also relations between spot and forward prices but the own rates are not relations between a future quantity and a present quantity obtained from the production process. The own rate (Γ) is a relation between the forward quantity of a commodity and the spot quantity of commodity:

$$\Gamma_j = (Q_{jF} - Q_{jS})/Q_{jS}.$$

This is derived from the relationship between two money rates: the money rate on money and the money rate on asset j. It is impossible to calculate an own rate without having those two money rates first. In Keynes, Rs are the starting point and Γs are just an image, in terms of physical forward quantity, of the money rates, and there is no use of r. To see this, an example in Table A1.2 is provided. Say

Table A1.2 Money rates and own rates

	Spot	Forward	Rates
Bushels obtained	100	100	0%
Money obtained (per $100)	$100	$105	5%
Price (per B100)	$100	$107	7%
Bushels equivalent	100	Q_{wF}	Γ_w

that there is both a forward and a spot market for wheat and money. The contracts are written per 100 bushels of wheat and per $100 of money. If one places $100 today, he will receive $105 in the future, and if one buys 100 bushels spot and sells them forward today, he will receive $107. One can see that the physical quantity of bushels obtained does not change over time. This is so because this quantity is determined by contract, not by physical production.

Thus, because $Q_{jf} = Q_{jp}$, the money rate has a simpler definition than Fisher's:

$$R_j = (F_j - S_j)/S_j.$$

The calculation of the own rate of wheat involves asking the following question: How many bushels will an individual be able to get in the future, given the forward prices of money and wheat? (Kregel 1982). In the future, one is expected to have to pay $107 for 100 bushels and to receive $105 for placing $100. Thus, in the future one is expected to be able to buy $Q_{wF} = \$105/\$107 \approx 98.13$ bushels. The own rate of wheat is

$$\Gamma_w = (98.13 - 100)/100 = -1.87\%.$$

This rate depends on the expected net quantity of wheat available in the future (which influences F_w) and the net quantity available today (which affect S_w). For producible assets, these quantities depend on the production (expected production for forward market) net of the carrying cost (destruction during the stocking period).

Therefore, the method used is the reverse of Fisher's. In the latter, the given rs are the starting point and one wants to know the Rs in order to make arbitrages properly. In Keynes, everything starts with money rates determined in spot and forward markets that have defined contract size. The "real rates" on those markets are zero, or more precisely, the additional quantity obtained is nil because it is defined by contract, not by the production process. However, the production process affects the money rates via its influence on the spot and forward markets. The own rates are just an image of those money rates in quantitative terms. They do not represent a physical yield. In addition, given that in a period of expansion the lowest money rate is the money rate on money, this means that all money rates on other assets have a negative own rate of interest. Indeed for $R_j > R_m$,

$$\Gamma_j = \frac{Q_{jF} - Q_{jS}}{Q_{jS}} = \frac{F_m/F_j - S_m/S_j}{S_m/S_j} = \frac{R_m - R_j}{R_j + 1} \Rightarrow \left| \begin{array}{l} \Gamma_j < 0 \ \forall j \neq m \\ \Gamma_m = 0 \end{array} \right. .$$

Thus, own rates of interest cannot be positive as long as money has the lowest rate of interest, which led Keynes to contend that "it is the *greatest* of the own rates of interest [...] which rules the roost" (Keynes 1936a: 233). Stated alternatively, it is the *lowest* of the money rates of interest that rules the roost. Positive own rates reflect a period of recession.

Appendix 2: The aggregate liquidity preference ratio with K assets

To calculate $\bar{\alpha}_M$, it is necessary to define the appropriate notation:

$$\bar{\alpha}_M = \bar{\alpha}_M$$
$$(1 \times 1)$$

$$M = \begin{bmatrix} M_1 \\ \vdots \\ M_J \end{bmatrix} \quad \tilde{S} = \begin{bmatrix} \tilde{S}_1 \\ \vdots \\ \tilde{S}_J \end{bmatrix} \quad \alpha_M = \begin{bmatrix} \alpha_{M1} \\ \vdots \\ \alpha_{MJ} \end{bmatrix} \quad P_A^* = \begin{bmatrix} P_{A1}^* \\ \vdots \\ P_{AK}^* \end{bmatrix} \quad \Lambda_J = \begin{bmatrix} 1 \\ \vdots \\ 1 \end{bmatrix}.$$
$$(J\times1) \qquad (J\times1) \qquad (J\times1) \qquad (K\times1) \qquad (J\times1)$$

$$\alpha = \begin{bmatrix} \alpha_{11} & \cdots & \alpha_{1J} \\ \vdots & \ddots & \vdots \\ \alpha_{K1} & \cdots & \alpha_{KJ} \end{bmatrix} \quad A = \begin{bmatrix} A_{11} & \cdots & A_{1J} \\ \vdots & \ddots & \vdots \\ A_{K1} & \cdots & A_{KJ} \end{bmatrix}$$
$$(K\times J) \qquad\qquad\qquad (K\times J)$$

For each asset i, the null price is

$$P_{A_i}^* = \frac{\sum_{j=1}^{J} \alpha_{ij}(M_j - \tilde{S}_j)}{\sum_{j=1}^{J} \alpha_{Mj} A_{ij}} = (M - \tilde{S})'\alpha'(A\alpha_M)^{-1}.$$

The average liquidity preference ratio of the economy is, at equilibrium, equal to the ratio of the existing money supply to the total wealth of the economy, that is to say

$$\bar{\alpha}_M \equiv \frac{\sum_{j=1}^{J} M_j}{\sum_{j=1}^{J}\sum_{k=1}^{K} P_{A_k}^* A_{kj} + \sum_{j=1}^{J} M_j} = (\Lambda_J' M)((P_A^*)' A \Lambda_J + \Lambda_J' M)^{-1}.$$

We know that

$$P_A^* = \begin{bmatrix} P_{A1}^* \\ \vdots \\ P_{AK}^* \end{bmatrix} = \begin{bmatrix} [(M - \tilde{S})'\alpha'(A\alpha_M)^{-1}]_1 \\ \vdots \\ [(M - \tilde{S})'\alpha'(A\alpha_M)^{-1}]_K \end{bmatrix}.$$
$$(K\times1)$$

Let us rename the preceding matrix:

$$(M - \tilde{S})'\alpha'(A\alpha_M)^{-1} = \begin{bmatrix} [(M - \tilde{S})'\alpha'(A\alpha_M)^{-1}]_1 \\ \vdots \\ [(M - \tilde{S})'\alpha'(A\alpha_M)^{-1}]_K \end{bmatrix}.$$

Then, by replacing the value of the average liquidity ratio of the economy, we have

$$\overline{\alpha}_M = \Lambda_J'M[((M - \tilde{S})'\alpha'(A\alpha_M)^{-1})'A\Lambda_J + \Lambda_J'M]^{-1}.$$

One can see that the aggregate desired liquidity ratio is, at equilibrium, a function of the quantity of money in the economy, the quantity of assets, and the level of transactions in different capital markets.

Appendix 3: Immunization procedure with consols

Let us assume that someone buys a consol in order to get a targeted total rate of return $\bar{\imath}$ over a holding period of h years. The total rate of return $\check{\imath}$ from coupons, reinvested coupons, and the sale of the bond is such that

$$V_0(1 + \check{\imath})^h = C\left[\frac{(1 + i)^h - 1}{i}\right] + V_h,$$

with C the periodic coupon on the bond, i the prevailing interest rate in the financial market, and V_t the fair price of the consol at time t. The fair price of a consol is $V_{Pt} = C/i_t$ and so a change in interest rate leads to the following change in the bond price:

$$dV_P/di = -C/i^2.$$

After having held a consol for h years and placed all the coupons at the same rate i, the reinvestment income is

$$RI = C\left[\frac{(1 + i)^h - 1}{i}\right] - hC.$$

Thus, the impact of a change in interest rate on reinvestment income is

$$\frac{dRI}{di} = \frac{C}{i^2}(1 + ih(1 + i)^{h-1} - (1 + i)^h).$$

Let us now assume that the interest rate is at the targeted rate of return when the individual buys the bond ($i = \bar{\imath}$). If the market rate never changes during the holding period, all the coupons are reinvested at $\bar{\imath}$ and the price of the consol never changes ($V_0 = V_h$); therefore, the individual will be able to get a rate of return $\check{\imath}$ from coupons and reinvestment income that is equal to the targeted rate (which is equal to the market rate). However, if the interest rate changes, the rate of return on the consol will be affected by the opposite impact on reinvestment income and the price of the bond. In this case, in order for the total rate of return on the consol to be unaffected by a change in interest rate, the following must hold:

$$|dRI/di| = |dV_P/di|.$$

That is

$$\frac{C}{i^2}\left(1+ih(1+i)^{h-1}-(1+i)^h\right) = \frac{C}{i^2},$$

which leads to the following condition:

$$i = 1/(h-1).$$

It is also easy to show that $|dRI/di| < |dV_P/di|$ if

$$i < 1/(h-1).$$

All this can be used to implement an immunization strategy that prevents the total rate of return $\check{\imath}$ from going below $\bar{\imath}$, whatever the change in i. The strategy consists in holding the bond for a time at least equal to the duration calculated at the targeted rate of return. For a consol, the duration is $D_P = (1 + i)/i$; therefore, if someone targets a rate of return $\bar{\imath}$, then, in order to immunize this targeted rate of return from changes in i, the targeted holding period should be

$$h^T = D_P(\bar{\imath}) = (1+\bar{\imath})/\bar{\imath}.$$

Therefore, by replacing h by h^T in the previous condition, one gets

$$1+ih(1+i)^{h-1}-(1+i)^h \begin{vmatrix} > 1 \text{ if } i > \bar{\imath} \\ < 1 \text{ if } i < \bar{\imath} \end{vmatrix}.$$

That is

$$|dRI/di| \begin{vmatrix} > |dV_P/di| \text{ if } i > \bar{\imath} \\ < |dV_P/di| \text{ if } i < \bar{\imath} \end{vmatrix}.$$

Thus, if one holds a consol for at least the duration term calculated at a targeted return, one is sure to secure at least a rate of return of $\bar{\imath}$ because, assuming that i is first on target, if i decreases relative to $\bar{\imath}$, the decline in reinvestment income is more than compensated by capital gains after h^T years: $-dRI < dV_P$. Inversely, if i increases relative to $\bar{\imath}$, the gain in reinvestment income more than compensates the capital loss after h^T years: $dRI > -dV$. Therefore, if $h \geq D_P(\bar{\imath})$, there is, as shown in Figure A3.1, the following relationship between the market rate and the difference between the actual rate $\check{\imath}$ and targeted rate for a coupon bond.

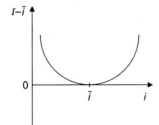

Figure A3.1 Immunization strategy.

The convexity of the relation depends on the sensitivity of the price and reinvestment income to changes in interest rates. The lower the coupon rate, the flatter the relationship, and for zero-coupon bonds, the relationship is a flat relationship: $\check{\imath} = \bar{\imath}$, whatever the market rate is. The higher the maturity, the higher the sensitivity of the bond price to market changes and so the higher the convexity and duration are (i.e. the longer it takes to break even for a given targeted rate of return).

Appendix 4: Econometric analysis of inflation and interest rates

Table A4.1 Lag test
VAR lag order selection criteria
Endogenous variables: EXPFEDFUNDS CP3M TBI3M TB10Y AAA
Exogenous variables: C
Sample: 1914:01 2004:02
Included observations: 1001

Lag	LogL	LR	FPE	AIC	SC	HQ
0	−6011.595	NA	0.114381	12.02117	12.04569	12.03049
1	977.3816	13894.17	1.04E−07	−1.892870	−1.745755	−1.836959
2	1453.538	941.8477	4.21E−08	−2.794282	−2.524570	−2.691777
3	1543.565	177.1758	3.70E−08	−2.924206	−2.531897*	−2.775108
4	1595.979	102.6296	3.50E−08	−2.978980	−2.464075	−2.783289
5	1637.360	80.61244	3.39E−08	−3.011709	−2.374208	−2.769426
6	1698.118	117.7513	3.15E−08	−3.083152	−2.323055	−2.794276
7	1761.501	122.2074	2.92E−08	−3.159842	−2.277149	−2.824373*
8	1804.962	83.36215*	2.81E−08*	−3.196727*	−2.191438	−2.814666

* Indicates lag order selected by the criterion.
LR, sequential modified LR test statistic (each test at 5% level); FPE, Final prediction error; AIC, Akaike information criterion; SC, Schwarz information criterion; HQ, Hannan-Quinn information criterion.

Table A4.2 Granger test among market rates

Pairwise Granger causality tests
Sample:1914:012004:02

Null hypothesis	Obs. (2 lags)	Probability (1 lag)	Probability (2 lags)	Probability (4 lags)	Probability (5 lags)
DAAA does not Granger cause DEXPFEDFUNDS	1036	0.09901	0.24978	0.31060	8.9E-08
DEXPFEDFUNDS does not Granger cause DAAA		0.00000	1.40E-15	6.7E-15	1.3E-16
DTB10Y does not Granger cause DEXPFEDFUNDS	1018	0.66726	0.27286	0.04613	0.00084
DEXPFEDFUNDS does not Granger cause DTB10Y		0.00000	0	0	0.00000
DTBI3M does not Granger cause DEXPFEDFUNDS	1006	4.3E-06	0.13437	0.01469	1.2E-05
DEXPFEDFUNDS does not Granger cause DTBI3M		0.00000	0	0.14340	0.00000
DCP3M does not Granger cause DEXPFEDFUNDS	1036	2.5E-07	0.05341	0.14340	5.6E-05
DEXPFEDFUNDS does not Granger cause DCP3M		0.00000	0	0	0.00000
DTB10Y does not Granger cause DAAA	1019	8.8E-14	1.20E-11	3.7E-14	3.0E-15
DAAA does not Granger cause DTB10Y		0.02700	0.5385	0.32571	0.58947
DTBI3M does not Granger cause DAAA	1007	0.97287	0.11173	0.00206	0.01275
DAAA does not Granger cause DTBI3M		8.6E-05	1.00E-08	1.3E-07	2.8E-07
DCP3M does not Granger cause DAAA	1072	0.04965	0.18627	0.02506	0.09948
DAAA does not Granger cause DCP3M		6.6E-09	1.70E-10	3.5E-09	1.9E-08
DTBI3M does not Granger cause DTB10Y	1007	0.09064	0.0151	2.3E-05	0.00023
DTB10Y does not Granger cause DTBI3M		2.1E-10	1.00E-11	1.4E-10	1.3E-11
DCP3M does not Granger cause DTB10Y	1019	0.00062	0.00114	4.3E-07	7.4E-06
DTB10Y does not Granger cause DCP3M		0.00000	0	7.6E-16	8.9E-16
DCP3M does not Granger cause DTBI3M	1007	0.51373	0.05658	0.09846	0.13469
DTBI3M does not Granger cause DCP3M		3.2E-12	1.80E-11	9.8E-14	4.3E-13

Table A4.3 Inflation and changes in federal funds rate: 1914–1952

Pairwise Granger causality tests
Sample: 1914:01 1952:12

Null hypothesis	Obs. (3 lags)	Probability (3 lags)	Probability (6 lags)	Probability (12 lags)	Probability (18 lags)
INFLATION does not Granger cause DFEDFUNDS	421	0.15472	0.28680	0.69304	0.38635
DFEDFUNDS does not Granger cause INFLATION		0.49973	0.50037	0.69898	0.35111

Table A4.4 Inflation and changes in federal funds rate: 1953–2004

Pairwise Granger causality tests
Sample: 1953:01 2004:02

Null hypothesis	Obs. (3 lags)	Probability (3 lags)	Probability (6 lags)	Probability (12 lags)	Probability (18 lags)
INFLATION does not Granger cause DFEDFUNDS	614	0.10977	0.13273	0.13679	0.40792
DFEDFUNDS does not Granger cause INFLATION		6.2E-06	2.7E-05	9.8E-08	3.0E-06

Table A4.5 Changes in expected inflation and changes in federal funds rate

Pairwise Granger causality tests
Sample: 1978:02 2004:02

Null hypothesis	Obs. (3 lags)	Probability (2 lags)	Probability (3 lags)	Probability (12 lags)	Probability (18 lags)
DFEDFUNDS does not Granger cause DEXPINFL	308	0.00018	8.7E-06	2.3E-07	4.9E-06
DEXPINFL does not Granger cause DFEDFUNDS		0.88040	0.00690	2.1E-05	6.5E-08

Table A4.6 Lag length

VAR lag order selection criteria
Endogenous variables: FEDFUNDS EXPINFL
Exogenous variables: C
Sample: 1914:01 2004:02
Included observations: 304

Lag	LogL	LR	FPE	AIC	SC	HQ
0	−1347.912	NA	24.66162	8.881002	8.905456	8.890784
1	−586.9013	1507.002	0.169469	3.900667	3.974029	3.930013
2	−544.4584	83.48979	0.131599	3.647752	3.770023	3.696664
3	−530.6025	27.07369	0.123338	3.582911	3.754090*	3.651387
4	−520.3354	19.92629	0.118358	3.541680	3.761767	3.629720
5	−512.0665	15.93941	0.115084	3.513595	3.782591	3.621200
6	−506.5590	10.54396	0.113953	3.503677	3.821581	3.630846
7	−493.3203	25.17095*	0.107239*	3.442896*	3.809708	3.589630*
8	−489.6536	6.923229	0.107482	3.445089	3.860810	3.611387

* Indicates lag order selected by the criterion.

Table A4.7 Cointegration

Sample (adjusted): 1920:05 2004:01
Included observations: 1005 after adjusting endpoints
Trend assumption: No deterministic trend (restricted constant)
Series: EXPFEDFUNDS CP3M TBI3M TB10Y AAA
Lags interval (in first differences): 1 to 3

Unrestricted cointegration rank test

Hypothesized no. of CE(s)	Eigenvalue	Tracestatistic	5% critical value	1% critical value
None**	0.096167	216.6055	76.07	84.45
At most1 **	0.054172	114.9888	53.12	60.16
At most 2**	0.036798	59.01581	34.91	41.07
At most 3*	0.018413	21.33605	19.96	24.60
At most 4	0.002642	2.658506	9.24	12.97

(**) Denotes rejection of the hypothesis at the 5% (1%) level.
Trace test indicates 4 cointegrating equation(s) at the 5% level.
Trace test indicates 3 cointegrating equation(s) at the 1% level.

Continued

Table A4.7 Cont'd

Hypothesized no. of CE(s)	Eigenvalue	Max-Eigen statistic	5% critical value	1% critical value
None**	0.096167	101.6167	34.40	39.79
At most 1**	0.054172	55.97300	28.14	33.24
At most 2**	0.036798	37.67976	22.00	26.81
At most 3*	0.018413	18.67754	15.67	20.20
At most 4	0.002642	2.658506	9.24	12.97

*(**) Denotes rejection of the hypothesis at the 5% (1%) level.
Max-eigenvalue test indicates 4 cointegrating equation(s) at the 5% level.
Max-eigenvalue test indicates 3 cointegrating equation(s) at the 1% level.

Table A4.8 Interest rates, expected inflation, and inflation: Jan 1978–Dec 2003

Sample (adjusted): 1978:06 2003:12
Included observations: 307 after adjusting endpoints
Trend assumption: No deterministic trend (restricted constant)
Series: FEDFUNDS EXPINFL
Lags interval (in first differences): 1 to 4

Unrestricted cointegration rank test

Hypothesized no. of CE(s)	Eigenvalue	Trace statistic	5% critical value	1% critical value
None*	0.049280	20.75923	19.96	24.60
At most 1	0.016938	5.244636	9.24	12.97

*(**) Denotes rejection of the hypothesis at the 5% (1%) level.
Trace test indicates 1 cointegrating equation(s) at the 5% level.
Trace test indicates no cointegration at the 1% level.

Table A4.9 Cointegration equations, speed of adjustment parameters

Vector error correction estimates
Sample (adjusted) (2 lags): 1920:04 2004:01
Included observations (2 lags): 1006 after adjusting endpoints

	2 lags	*3 lags*	*7 lags*
CointEq1 in eq. for			
D(EXPFEDFUNDS)	−0.058194	0.031991	−0.034882
D(AAA)	0.075894***	−0.018824***	−0.002725***
D(TB10Y)	0.096833***	−0.004493***	−0.01242***
D(TBI3M)	0.132329***	0.000593***	0.007203***
D(CP3M)	0.129301***	0.01076***	−0.026556***
CointEq2 in eq. for			
D(EXPFEDFUNDS)	−0.056979***	0.031104**	−0.038822*
D(AAA)	0.075245***	−0.014489***	−0.013985***
D(TB10Y)	0.097863	0.00266	−0.028655*
D(TBI3M)	0.112937	0.000168	0.006208
D(CP3M)	0.103048	0.016604**	−0.033771
CointEq3 in eq. for			
D(EXPFEDFUNDS)	−0.010699***	0.018687**	−0.031703***
D(AAA)	0.075281	−0.016015***	−0.011698***
D(TB10Y)	0.091115**	−0.007934***	−0.013345***
D(TBI3M)	0.107636	−0.006127	0.00727
D(CP3M)	0.109493***	0.000423***	−0.017263***

* Significant at 10%, **significant at 5%, *** significant at 1%.

Table A4.10 F-test on lagged variables

VEC pairwise Granger causality/block exogeneity Wald tests
Sample: 1914:01 2004:02
Included observations (2 lags): 1006

Dependent variable: D(EXPFEDFUNDS)

Exclude	*Prob. (2 lags)*	*Prob. (3 lags)*	*Prob. (7 lags)*
D(AAA)	0.5021	0.4076	0
D(TB10Y)	0.0728	0.0129	0.0001
D(TBI3M)	0.0089	0.0143	0
D(CP3M)	0.2461	0.2274	0.324
All	0.0059	0.0003	0

Continued

Table A4.10 Cont'd

Dependent variable: D(AAA)

Exclude	Prob. (2 lags)	Prob. (3 lags)	Prob. (7 lags)
D(EXPFEDFUNDS)	0.0118	0.0231	0.0003
D(TB10Y)	0	0	0
D(TBI3M)	0.0041	0.0001	0
D(CP3M)	0.0002	0.0005	0
All	0	0	0

Dependent variable: D(TB10Y)

Exclude	Prob. (2 lags)	Prob. (3 lags)	Prob. (7 lags)
D(EXPFEDFUNDS)	0.0007	0.0021	0
D(AAA)	0.7904	0.1153	0.1969
D(TBI3M)	0.1055	0.0074	0.0003
D(CP3M)	0.0003	0.0004	0
All	0	0	0

Dependent variable: D(TBI3M)

Exclude	Prob. (2 lags)	Prob. (3 lags)	Prob. (7 lags)
D(EXPFEDFUNDS)	0	0	0
D(AAA)	0.0056	0.0262	0.3351
D(TB10Y)	0.0002	0.0001	0
D(CP3M)	0.0001	0	0
All	0	0	0

Dependent variable: D(CP3M)

Exclude	Prob. (2 lags)	Prob. (3 lags)	Prob. (7 lags)
D(EXPFEDFUNDS)	0	0	0
D(AAA)	0.078	0.0788	0.2987
D(TB10Y)	0	0	0
D(TBI3M)	0.4003	0.5726	0.0098
All	0	0	0

Table A4.11 Cointegration equation and speed of adjustment parameters

Vector Error Correction Estimates (excluding TBI3M), 2 lags
Sample (adjusted): 1919:04 2004:01
Included observations: 1018 after adjusting endpoints
t-statistics in [ ]

Error correction	D(EXPFEDFUNDS)	D(CP3M)	D(TB10Y)	D(AAA)
CointEq1	−0.005860	0.117444	0.083801	0.064741
	[−0.18191]	[7.23582]	[5.61722]	[5.74497]
CointEq2	−0.025914	−0.116029	−0.067937	−0.045013
	[−0.79510]	[−7.06610]	[−4.50127]	[−3.94825]
CointEq3	0.080506	−0.003828	−0.040774	−0.009482
	[2.32123]	[−0.21906]	[−2.53869]	[−0.78159]

Table A4.12 F-test on lagged variables

VEC pairwise Granger causality/block exogeneity Wald
Tests (excluding TBI3M)
Sample: 1914:01 2004:02
Included observations: 1018

Dependent variable: D(EXPFEDFUNDS)

Exclude	Chi-sq	df	Prob.
D(CP3M)	6.483580	2	0.0391
D(TB10Y)	2.733254	2	0.2550
D(AAA)	0.979088	2	0.6129
All	10.31002	6	0.1122

Dependent variable: D(CP3M)

Exclude	Chi-sq	df	Prob.
D(EXPFEDFUNDS)	894.7633	2	0.0000
D(TB10Y)	28.25997	2	0.0000
D(AAA)	4.021679	2	0.1339
All	1040.065	6	0.0000

Continued

Table A4.12 Cont'd

Dependent variable: D(TB10Y)

Exclude	Chi-sq	df	Prob.
D(EXPFEDFUNDS)	19.91972	2	0.0000
D(CP3M)	28.84574	2	0.0000
D(AAA)	0.089033	2	0.9565
All	49.37727	6	0.0000

Dependent variable: D(AAA)

Exclude	Chi-sq	df	Prob.
D(EXPFEDFUNDS)	11.94838	2	0.0025
D(CP3M)	24.39055	2	0.0000
D(TB10Y)	49.93347	2	0.0000
All	81.55211	6	0.0000

Table A4.13 Cointegration equation

Vector error correction estimates
Sample (adjusted) (2 lags): 1978:04 2003:12
Included observations (2 lags): 309 after adjusting

	2 lags	6 lags	12 lags
CointEq1 in eq. for			
D(FEDFUNDS)	−0.051536***	−0.059826***	−0.032787***
D(EXPINFLATION)	0.010032	−0.005175	0.01804*

*Significant at 10%, **significant at 5%, ***significant at 1%.

Table A4.14 F-test

VEC pairwise Granger causality/block exogeneity Wald tests
Sample: 1914:01 2004:02
Included observations (2 lags): 309

Dependent variable: D(FEDFUNDS)

Exclude	Prob. (2 lags)	Prob. (6 lags)	Prob. (12 lags)
D(EXPINFL)	0.3269	0	0
All	0.3269	0	0

Dependent variable: D(EXPINFL)

Exclude	Prob. (2 lags)	Prob. (6 lags)	Prob. (12 lags)
D(FEDFUNDS)	0.0001	0.0001	0
All	0.0001	0.0001	0

Appendix 5: Financial disturbances and financial crises in the US

To determine when financial crises or large financial corrections occurred in the stock market, the bond market, and the short-term-paper markets, the following procedure has been followed.

First, we collected data that were available at different websites for the period 1900–2003. For shares, the monthly average close value of the Standard and Poor 500, the NASDAQ composite index, and the Dow Jones Industrial Average were selected. The monthly volume of transactions, in terms of share volume (i.e. the number of shares transacted) on the NYSE and NASDAQ were also collected. For interest bearing securities or similar instruments, the average monthly yield rate of AAA bonds (AAA), BAA bonds (BAA), 3-month maturity Treasury bills (tb3m), eurodollar deposits (ed3m), commercial papers (cp3m), and certificates of deposits (cd3m) were collected. When data about 3-month maturity security were not available, an average of short-term maturities was calculated. Data about the volume of transactions of bonds and of short-term papers would have been of great interest, but we could not find them.

Second, data were treated in the following way. For shares, the monthly average growth rate of each index was calculated, as well as the average volume of transactions over each year for each market. The latter was used as denominator to calculate the following ratio for the NASDAQ and NYSE:

Monthly share volume/Annual average share volume

The average monthly growth rates and the preceding ratios were combined to determine when a financial crisis or a strong correction occurred in the share market. The combination was the following. First, the average and standard deviation of each growth rate and ratio were calculated for the whole period. Then, these averages and standard deviations were used to determine a financial-crisis bound and a financial-correction bound. For the rate of growth, the bounds were calculated as follows:

$$\text{Financial-crisis bound} = 2^*(\text{Average} - \text{Standard deviation})$$

$$\text{Financial-correction bound} = (\text{Average} - \text{Standard deviation}) - 1$$

For the volume ratios, the financial-crisis bound was calculated as follows (no financial-correction bound was calculated):

$$\text{Financial-crisis bound} = (\text{Average} + \text{Standard deviation}) + 10$$

This implies that a financial crisis will be recorded in the share market if, at a given date, one of the index decreases by more than twice its "normal" lower bound, that is the bound determined by the difference between the average rate of growth and its standard deviation, and if the volume of transactions for the market of this index is 10 points higher than the "normal" higher bound of transaction ratio. If one takes, for example, the SP500 and the volume on the NYSE, one has Figures A5.1 and A5.2. One can see that the critical value of the financial-crisis bound is passed quite often on each graph; however, both volume and growth rate criteria must be satisfied at the same time to record a financial crisis. Thus, if, at a given data, the share market, as summarized by the SP500, decreases by more than 7.7 percent (the critical bound for rate of growth of the SP500) but the volume ratio is less than 139 (the critical value for the share volume on the NYSE), then one cannot consider that a financial crisis occurred.

Of course, critical to this treatment of the information is the choice of the multiplicative factor for the rate of growth (why 2 rather than 1.5 or 3?) and

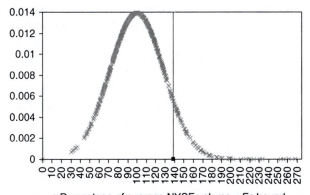

Figure A5.1 Distribution of the monthly volume expressed as a percentage of yearly average volume on the NYSE: 1900–2003.

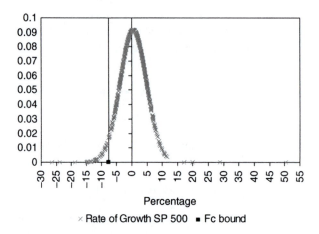

Figure A5.2 Distribution of the rate of growth of the SP500: 1900–2003.

for the volume (why 10 points rather than 5 or 20?). One has to recognize that some arbitrariness exists in the selection of the financial-crisis bound. We have tried to decrease this by checking the relevance of the results with what happened actually in the past. A factor of 2 and a mark up of 10 points seem to extract the correct dates for known share-market crises.

The same procedure was followed for the fixed income assets. First, the following yield differentials were calculated: BAA – AAA, ed3m – tb3m, cp3m – tb3m, cd3m – tb3m. Second, the rates of growth of those spreads were calculated, as well as their respective average and standard deviation for the whole period. Because no data were available for the volumes of transactions of these securities, we could not calculate a financial-crisis bound. More precisely, the financial-crisis bound based on the rate of growth only is not sufficient to make any decisions. Indeed, volumes are important because they add some information about the state of mind of market participants. Financial crises reflect a sense of panic and so high volume of transactions must exist as many people try to sell to market makers:[1] A large increase in a spread with a low volume of transactions does not reflect a sense of panic and so should be disqualified as financial crisis. This cannot be extracted from the data available. Thus, the only bound calculated is the large-correction bound:

Financial-correction bound = (Average + Standard deviation) + 1

This bound states that if the spread increases by more than 1 percentage point over its "normal" higher bound, this reflects a large correction in the bond market or short-term-paper market. Figure A5.3 shows the result for the BAA–AAA spread.

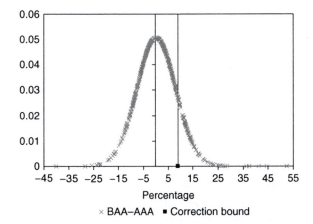

Figure A5.3 Rate of growth of the BAA–AAA spread: 1919–2003.

Thus, if BAA–AAA grows by more than 9.1 percent over a month, then one can assume that there has been a large correction in the bond market. Again, the choice of the bound is arbitrary and tries to point at some of the known financial problems in those markets.

Notes

2 Central banking, asset prices, and financial fragility

1 See Gordon (1990) for a summary of the rigidities existing in the labor and goods markets, and Gertler (1988) for a review of the role of imperfections in the credit markets.

2 Fisher was careful to state his theory in terms of three "approximations." The first one assumes perfect foresight and constant income, the second one assumes risk and variable income, and the third one assumes uncertain income streams (Fisher 1907: 221). As Fisher recognized, "the great shortcoming of the first and second approximations, from the standpoint of real life, is the complete ruling out of uncertainty" (Fisher 1930: 206) but "we must [...] give up as a bad job any attempt to formulate completely the influences which really determine the rate of interest" (Fisher 1930: 321).

3 The rate on wheat can then be obtained either by growing wheat or by lending the wheat to a farmer. More generally, one can write contracts specified in terms of quantities of wheat.

4 This assumes that an arbitrage between present and future enjoyable income is possible at the macroeconomic level. See chapter 4.

5 Svensson (2003) shows two different ways this framework of analysis can be used for policy implementation: instrumental rule and targeting rule. Le Héron (2003) and Le Héron and Carré (2005, 2006) provide a detailed analysis of two possible monetary-policy strategies to influence price expectations.

6 As shown in chapter 6, the 1979–1982 period does not represent a pure experiment with monetary target.

7 Fair (2005) empirically shows that a weight superior to one is not necessary to get stability. In addition, he finds that there is a strong trade-off between interest-rate variability and inflation variability. The model, which is purely a real model, cannot deal with the consequence of interest-rate variability on the financial side of the economy.

8 All this generates questions about the stability of the equilibrium and the capacity of the inflation target to be a strong attractor for inflation expectation (Lavoie 2004; Setterfield 2004a).

9 The measurement of the natural rate of interest is difficult and results differ widely, which leads some authors to doubt the relevance of this notion for policy practice (Weber *et al.* 2008; Cuaresma and Gnan 2007; Weber 2006; Ferguson 2004; Orphanides and Williams 2002).

10 This provides a direct critique of the functional theory of distribution. Remuneration is based "on account of pecuniary serviceability to the employer, not on grounds of material serviceability to mankind at large. The product is value, sought and paid for on account of and in some proportion to its vendibility, not for more recondite reasons of ulterior human welfare at large" (Veblen 1901: 214–215).

11 "I cannot agree with Adam Smith, or with Mr. Malthus, that it is the nominal value of goods, or their prices only, which enter into the consideration of the merchant" (Ricardo 1820 (1951): 26).

12 Say that in the first period $C = PQ_c = \$1 \times 3 = \$3$, workers consume all their net income. In the second period, if Q_c is the same $C = \$6$ and so workers can save \$2. This increase in their financial wealth improves the collateral they can offer to bankers when they ask for loans.

13 Dow (1997) shows that the money supply is endogenous in the *General Theory*. The finance motive is not a way to introduce the endogeneity of money, and overdrafts already are taken into account in the *General Theory*. The role of this motive is to explain how aggregate income is generated and to add the influence of expected transactions on interest rates (Tymoigne 2003). See King (2002) for more historical details about endogenous money in the Post-Keynesian framework.

14 Lavoie and Seccareccia (2004) and Fontana and Palacio-Vera (2002) compare the similarities and differences of the New Consensus and Post-Keynesian frameworks. Wray (1990) and Palley (2002) study the different views of the endogeneity of money.

15 In a country that is monetarily sovereign, the creation of central bank money is not limited by gold, the supply of a foreign currency, or anything else. Central bank money, and all other monetary instruments tied to it, maintain their value because of federal government taxes that withdraw central bank money from the system (Wray 1998a; Tymoigne 2007b). The whole book is based on the assumption that the government of country does not have a significant amount of foreign-currency denominated debts and follows a flexible exchange rate regime (or, at least, has a very wide band for its exchange-rate management policy).

16 More broadly, this conclusion tells us that *ex nihilo* credit creation is not the "abnormal" or "unnatural" method of starting economic activities; it is the implicit counterpart of the fact that any economic activity is implemented on the basis of a bet: taking risks today to improve one's position in the future.

17 Here one has to be very careful about what is meant by Keynes. "Productivity" does not refer to capacity to produce physical output, it means "purposeful." "No one would pay this premium [on money loans] unless the possession of cash served some purpose, i.e. had some efficiency" (Keynes 1937a (1973): 101). "To deny the productivity of money is the opposite of my view" (Keynes 1936b (1973): 92).

18 The risk premium could be introduced in q but for theoretical purpose they are separated. $q_j + r_j$ represents the "gross yield" of an asset j (Keynes 1936a: 68, 221).

19 If there is no forward market for an asset j, the expected price replaces the forward price.

20 The decline in q_1 is not due necessarily to an increase in costs of production. It is the saturation of the market that reduces the price at which output can be sold and leads to a decline in the quantity demanded. Increasing cost of production is a factor that significantly affects q only toward full employment.

21 Those are low elasticity of production, low elasticity of substitution, and low carry cost relative to the liquidity premium. Sometimes, the first condition is said to contradict the idea that the money supply is endogenous. However, Wray notes "This should not be interpreted as a fixed quantity of money in the face of rising demand for money, but rather means that an increase of liquidity preference cannot keep labor employed by shifting it to production of money" (Wray 2006a: 186).

22 Judd and Scadding (1982) show that even Friedman's enlarged demand function is not stable because of the influence of financial innovations.

23 Mathematically one needs to solve $\dfrac{a}{b}(1 + g_{a/b}) = \dfrac{a + g_a a}{b + g_b b} \Rightarrow g_{a/b} = \dfrac{g_a - g_b}{1 + g_b}$

24 Here a circularity exists because current demand affects $g_{\Pi nD}$, which progressively influences expected profit and so g_Q. The latter affects employment and so current income, which influences current demand and so $g_{\Pi nD}$. This circularity is broken easily

by following the principle of effective demand: current economic activity depends on long-term profit expectations by entrepreneurs. These long-term expectations are largely independent of current profit, which implies that the whole economic system hangs by a given initial set of expectations by entrepreneurs (Keynes 1936a; Kregel 1976, 1986b).

25 See, for example, Lavoie (1995) for a rapid summary and comparison of different contemporary theories of distribution in the Post-Keynesian/Post Classical school. Kregel (1971a) and Baranzini (1991) provide a broader account of the Post-Keynesian contribution to distribution theory.

26 Kalecki (1971a), Sawyer (1985a), and Minsky (1986a) provide a more detailed explanation. See also Levy and Levy (1983) for a different way to explain the same thing.

27 They, however, can be added to complement the explanation given to financial crises and credit crunches (Wolfson 1996). Keynes already included them by taking into account the role of moral hazard (Keynes 1936a: 144).

3 Asset-price theories and central banking

1 The following is not a review of the literature; the purpose is not so much to review the literature but to show the consequences of each position in terms of central bank policy.

2 Campbell (2000) reviews the studies of the past twenty years.

3 This supposes that the speculators cannot influence V. See below and see Kregel (1992b) for the hypotheses used by Marshall to justify this position.

4 The support theory, developed by Tversky and others (Rottenstreich and Tversky 1997; Tversky and Koehler 1994), has been less successful because it implies a departure from economic rationality as defined above. It seems, however, to be much closer to Keynes's vision of decisions under uncertainty as developed in *Treatise on Probability*.

5 This is so for two reasons: first, an increase in interest rates raises the cost of the funds they borrow to speculate, and second, it puts a downward pressure on the price of the assets they hold.

6 Bernstein (1997a, 1997c) and Arnott and Bernstein (2002a, 2002b) show that the current assumption that shares are more profitable to carry over the long run than bonds is based on a narrow analysis of past data. Most financial analysts until the 1950s would have argued the opposite.

7 Trade can still occur because of differences in expectations regarding future prices, or because of different allocations of assets.

8 This point, present in Keynes (1936a), was systematized by Kahn (1954) and will be developed further in chapter 4. Boulding (1944) also showed that the Marshallian supply/demand approach is not appropriate because the supply and demand curves are interdependent.

4 Against the instrumental use of interest rates

1 For large variations in i, a better approximation is obtained by adding convexity, i.e. the second-order derivative of V relative to i.

2 One may need to be reminded that in economics, "investment" has nothing to do with the common use of the term as "financial investment." In this book, the latter is called "placement" and it is made possible by saving money. "Investment" means increasing or maintaining capacities of production (i.e. "buying machines," not "buying financial assets"). As stated in chapters 3 and 2, placement and investment activities are unrelated and the former does not promote automatically the latter.

3 A strict test of Fisher's theory would imply taking time ranges for inflation expectations that are equal to the maturity term of each asset.

4 If, before any change in interest rates, everybody is already bull or bear, then the interest rate is undetermined and the elasticity of money demand relative to interest rate is zero. Indeed, all the financial wealth is already devoted to trying to buy bonds (so that $L = 0$ at the aggregate level) or to sell bonds (L is at its maximum at the aggregate level); therefore, additional changes in the rate of interest will not have a large effect on the desired demand for money for speculation. As Kahn stated it, unanimous opinion is only "a *sufficient* condition [...]. The *necessary* condition is a high concentration, measured in terms of wealth, in the neighbourhood of the margin, of persons with identical views: idiosyncratics can be ignored if their idiosyncracies are based on complete conviction" (Kahn 1954 (1972): 87, n .1).

5 This led Robertson (1940) and Hicks (1946: 164) to argue that Keynes's theory of the rate of interest contains a circular argument and led Hicks, Kaldor (1939), and Kalecki to propose an alternative explanation of the yield curve based on expectations of monetary policy. However, Kahn (1954), Robinson (1951), and Kregel (1998a) have critiqued this approach, and have confirmed the importance of expectations of long-term rates for the determination of the current level of long-term rates. Moreover, Keynes already took into account expectations of short-term rates for the determination of long-term rates.

6 "[T]he individual, who believes that future rates of interest will be above the rates assumed by the market, has a reason for keeping actual liquid cash, whilst the individual who differs from the market in the other direction will have a motive for borrowing money for short periods in order to purchase debts of longer term" (Keynes 1936a: 170). If everybody agrees with the convention in the market then $E(\Delta i) = i_n - i$, but otherwise the expected change will be influenced by the difference. This is so because i_n is an anchor for individuals' expectations but it does not imply that everybody agrees with i_n: individuals adjust their expectation relative to the market convention.

7 The reasoning could be done also from the point of view of a bondholder who checks the benefit of selling today. In this case, he compares the cost of losing some income and missing potential capital gains to the benefit of avoiding capital losses. Thus, if he expects that $E(-\Delta i) > i^2$, he should not sell today because the net cost is positive (misses capital gains and loses income).

8 This situation is hardly probable as people are always concerned about their solvency and liquidity, even pure rentiers.

9 Arestis and Howells (1992) have shown that the emergence of substitutes to bank loans has decreased this elasticity.

10 In 1994, the average amount of excess reserves was 2.7 billions of yen, and this amount grew dramatically in 1998 to reach 699.2 billions of yen. In 2004, the average amount of excess reserves reached 22.8 trillions of yen, according to the Bank of Japan.

11 As Robinson (1951) shows, if gentlemen-rentiers were dominant, the normal yield curve would be negatively slopped; something that does not represent the current state of affairs in financial markets.

12 Rochon and Setterfield recently compared the performance of each of the previous interest-rate rules. They show that a permanent zero central bank rate "always yields the highest rate of growth and the lowest rate of inflation" (Rochon and Setterfield 2007a: 25). This result is reached in the context of a real economy, without reference to the financial implications of interest rates. One may argue that taking into account the financial side of the economy would reinforce this result.

5 An analysis of financial fragility in the Minskian tradition

1 Conventions can be modified to accommodate occurring events. There is an *ex post* rationalization, and only when there is a prolonged period of disappointments, or an extreme unexpected shock, do conventions break. The state of expectations is largely independent of current economic results.

2 If the federal government promises to convert its IOUs on demand into a foreign currency, the latter is at the top of IOUs. In this case, the federal government does not have a monetary sovereignty.

3 Therefore, another way to define "euphoria" is when loan officers start to believe that recessions are things of the past, that is, when they fail to correct overwhelmingly optimistic expectations.

4 Actually, an increase in the unit cost of external funds is not a necessary condition for cash commitments to increase relative to cash inflows.

5 A primitive version of this downward instability can be found in Minsky's early articles (Minsky 1957b, 1959, 1965a). In this case, investment is affected by a financial accelerator that depends on the financial fragility of firms (represented by the equity and liquidity ratios). Later, this was replaced by the P_{Id}/P_{Is} framework, which, contrary to the previous articles and Tobin's q (which also ignores the role of the funding structure), does not ignore the role of uncertainty for economic decisions (Minsky 1972b: 98).

6 In today's world, this occurs far before full employment because of the obsession with low inflation, even when there is no sign of inflation at all. As shown in chapters 2 and 6, the role of monetary policy is now to act in advance of any inflationary pressure, potential or not.

7 Past and current experiences of big governments in developed capitalist economies have not been implemented in a way consistent with Minsky's recommendation and Keynes's ideas (Minsky 1975a: 166; Wray 1994; Kregel 1994).

8 Dymski and Pollin (1992, 50–53) argue that distributive questions are of secondary importance in Minsky's approach. This is not the case; from very early in his career (mid-1960s), Minsky pushed for a more equitable capitalism and, for him, the best way to do so was to promote stable full employment (Minsky 1965b, 1966, 1973).

9 The employer of last resort, by fixing the lowest wage rate, will already contribute to the stabilization of wages (Minsky 1983a: 276). An income policy may improve this control and may also complement it on the mark-up side (Davidson 1968c; Kaldor 1950).

10 Note that the mechanism at work is not a comparison between past expectations and current results. It is a comparison between what is going on in the economy and what is expected in the future. The comparison between past expectations and actual results, the *ex ante/ex post* distinction, is not directly relevant for the analysis of current economic activity. Indeed, current economic activity is determined by current expectations, "*realised* results are only relevant in so far as they influence ensuing expectations in the next production period" (Keynes 1937f. (1973): 179).

11 As shown below, this expectation may be misled because of the paradox of leverage but all that matters for decisions is what bankers and others think will happen, nothing else matters. As stated earlier, the principle of increasing risk works on the same basis: the increasing risk perceived from increasing external borrowing may not be well founded but it is the expected result, given a convention about appropriate leveraging, that matters.

12 The growth rate of the average unit cost is more formally $g_u = g_{u_{OSO}} \cdot \dfrac{u_{OSO}}{u_{OSO} + u_{NOSNO}} + g_{u_{NOSNO}} \cdot \dfrac{u_{NOSNO}}{u_{OSO} + u_{NOSNO}}$, with u the unit cost of debt.

13 The Circuit approach has usually a narrow view of what needs to be financed and funded. Graziani (2003b) recognizes the problem by showing the necessity to include financial asset acquisitions in the analysis but still leaves aside the problem of refinancing.

14 Isenberg (1988: 1066) concurs in her study of the Great Depression: "These [debt] ratios, while exhibiting the proper quantitative relationship for the Minskian hypothesis over the cycle, did not reflect a move into speculative or Ponzi finance. As has been stated, the maturities of debts and assets were matched."

15 One important element left aside by this table, however, is the cash-flow analysis, but the latter can be introduced easily, notably in relation to the cash box condition.

16 Remember that the asset side of a balance sheet can be separated into current assets and fixed assets. Current assets contain inventories and financial assets.

17 This direct impact on equity assumes that all loans are unsecured loans and that banks do not provision for expected losses on loans. Adding secured loans would imply taking into account changes in the value of collaterals, which would affect the willingness to lend.

18 The dichotomy productive/unproductive can be misleading because it may assume that unproductive activities are necessarily wasteful and "bad." In this book, "unproductive" only means that an activity does not contribute to grow national income. However, an unproductive activity (like refinancing operations) can be essential to sustain production-related activities.

19 System Dynamics uses those effects to account for additional impacts on a variable besides the direct impact given by the technical definition of a variable. The effects are most of the time not a constant and they are equal to one when the relative variable by which they are affected is equal to one (Sterman 2000).

20 These technical/production considerations are of different nature than the Neoclassical analysis. What drives the decisions to use machines is not the physical gain (AP_K) from capital equipment, it is the need to meet the demand of customers and to make sure that they are satisfied. Firms of the investment-good sector try to deliver goods on time and firms in the consumption-good sector try to meet all the demand. All this prevents customers' frustration and so helps to create a long-term relationship with customers. In the end, caring about meeting current demand and contractual requirements, and not purely about the rate of return, is all about money too.

21 This circularity does not exist in the consumption-good sector because aggregate profit does not depend on P_C^T. Aggregate profit is determined by the structure of aggregate demand rather than from the point of view of firms.

22 One may note that this implies that taxes are not a source of funds for the Treasury (Wray 1998a; Bell 2000).

23 Another way, which may be more fruitful, is to find the desired proportion of long-term debts by starting with $CC_d = (a_{lt} + i_{lt})f_{ltd}L + (a_{st} + i_{st})(1 - f_{ltd})L$ and expressing f_{ltd} as a function of cc_d.

24 This could have been modeled as $i_A = i_{A0} + \Sigma e_\pi$, with e_π the effect of relative expected inflation (expected inflation relative to its targeted value) on the central bank rate, but we want to show more clearly to the reader the exact increments involved because we are interested in the impact of the aggressiveness of the central bank.

25 There are, of course, political and financial pressures that will affect the behaviors of central bankers. See chapter 6.

6 Financial matters in the decisions of the FOMC

1 All quotes are copied and pasted from the FOMC transcripts without any editing. Transcripts are raw and unedited recordings of FOMC discussions.

2 The main consequence of this high variability of interest rates has been the development of variable-interest-rate loan contracts, interest-rate swaps, and other derivative financial instruments (Wojnilower 1980; Markham 2002: 191ff.). Also, the development of mortgage-backed securities and other securitization processes has been a way for financial institutions to avoid the interest-rate uncertainty generated by the change in the Fed policy.

3 The word-counting procedure is based on the discussion between members that appeared in the FOMC transcripts between 1979 and 1999. The procedure excludes all appendices and documents read during the meeting by the staff and by FOMC members. In addition, the transcripts of the September 1980 meeting and March 1993 to February 1994 meetings do not allow the word-counting function of *Adobe Reader* and so were

excluded from the counting. Finally, when a word was used in an irrelevant way it was not counted. For example, in a sentence like, "the most liquid monetary aggregate" "liquid" does not reflect a discussion of the liquidity of the economy, or of the financial position of economic sectors; therefore, it was ignored.

4 This amendment to the Federal Reserve Act is in section 103 of the DIDMCA. In addition, all depository institutions with transaction deposits are given access to the Discount Window (Section 103(b)(7)).

5 Gallati (2003) gives an in-depth review of the Basel Accord, and Earl (1990), Goodhart *et al.* (1998), Mayer (2001), Brealey (2001), Wray (2006b), Kregel (2006), Guttmann (2006), and Palley (2000, 2004, 2006) critically review this Accord and discuss its limits in detail.

6 As shown later, inflation never showed up, either in expectations or in reality, and this put the Committee in an awkward position.

7 In a speech given on August 30, 2002, Greenspan actually changed his mind and argued that margin requirements have no significant effects on asset prices. Vice-Chairman Ferguson made the same case in a February 2000 speech. Fortune (2000) also shows that changes in initial margins requirements may calm down the most aggressive speculators but, overall, will not prevent a speculative mania. This is all the more the case if speculation is not based on borrowed funds (Kindleberger 1997; Toporowski 1999).

8 Mulford and Comiskey (2002) provide a good account of those different accounting practices and the incentives to practice them: "Often the desired reward is an upward move in a firm's share price. For others, the incentive may be a desire to improve debt ratings and reduce interest costs on borrowed amounts or create additional slack and reduce restrictions from debt covenants. An interest in boosting a profit-based bonus may drive some. Finally, for high-profile firms, the motivation may be lower political costs, including avoiding more regulation or higher taxes" (Mulford and Comiskey 2002: 2).

9 Shiller (2000) clearly explains what the incentives behind this practice are.

10 Le Héron (2006) and Le Héron and Carré (2005, 2006) argue that the Federal Reserve follows a "confidence strategy" rather than a "credibility strategy." There is a complex interaction with the financial market participants in order to influence expectations of future monetary-policy moves.

11 ABS stands for asset-backed security, CDO stands for collateralized debt obligation, CDO^2 stands for collateralized debt obligation squared, and CDS stands for credit default swap.

12 This coordination is central for open-market operations. There must be an overall positive net supply of new securities used in those operations in order for central banks and financial institutions to have a substantial stock of those securities, and so to be able to practice these operations (Wray 1998a: 118–119, 167, 2003a; Marshall 2002). The January 2001 FOMC transcript contains a long discussion of those problems.

13 The March 1980 meeting contains a similar debate and concentrates on the idea that the impossibility to control total reserves is due to lagged reserve requirements. The question of lag led to the imposition of "contemporaneous" reserve requirements on M1 in the hope that it would help to improve the control of M1. Moore (1991) shows the irrelevance of this view, and actually, most FOMC members were not fooled by this, Volcker included:

> Well, the contemporaneous reserve accounting issue is going to be on our desks very quickly. I will tell you my view of contemporaneous reserve accounting very simply. I do not think it is going to make a lot of difference in and of itself.
>
> (Volcker, FOMC meeting, February 1982, page 92)

In the March 1983 meeting, members like Guffey, Corrigan, Teeters, and Gramley also expressed strong reservations.

14 From Greider's description (1987: 204–205) of the relationship of Roos with other members, one can note that they never took him seriously. The FOMC members never became pure Monetarists under Volcker because they knew that this economic framework was not coherent with economic reality. Mayer (2001) also reaches the same conclusion: most Federal Reserve staff did not believe in the Monetarist prescriptions but there was a strong pressure to go for it.

15 The directive in the transcripts may differ from the one released in the minutes of the meeting by being far less detailed. The former directive, however, really shows what matters for FOMC members. For example, FOMC members had continued to release M-growth targets in the minutes until February 2000 because they were required to do so by the Humphrey-Hawkins legislation; however, their policy decisions were no longer discussed in relation to those targets and were not present in the directive of the transcripts after 1992.

16 There are, of course, multiple studies by Friedman about the "long-term" relation between price and money but there are two qualifications to make here: first, "short-term" real effects last actually around 3 to 10 years (Friedman 1987 (1989): 32) and second, the relation is just a correlation that needs to be interpreted in relation to the state of the economy and to the endogeneity of the money supply (Kaldor 1982).

17 The independence of long-term sales expectations relative to current sales implies, contrary to bastard Keynesianism, that temporary higher aggregate spending today may not promote economic activity today because entrepreneurs may be pessimistic about the future.

Appendix 5: Financial disturbances and financial crises in the US

1 One should note that if market makers did not exist, then a financial crisis would be reflected by a nil or near zero volume of transactions, as everybody or most people try to sell, whatever the price of securities is: supply faces no demand and so no transaction can occur.

References

Adelson, M. (2006) "MBS basics," Nomura Securities International Inc., Research Paper, March 31.

Aglietta, M. (2001) *Macroéconomie Financière*, 2nd edn, Paris: Editions La Découverte.

Alchian, A. A. and Klein, B. (1973) "On a correct measure of inflation," *Journal of Money, Credit and Banking*, 5 (1), Part 1: 173–191.

Alsonso-González, L. A. and Palacio-Vera, A. (2002) "Monetary policy, Taylor's rule and instability," *Metroeconomica*, 53 (1): 1–24.

Anthony, M. (1986) "On the non-existence of a natural rate of unemployment and Kaleckian micro underpinnings to the Phillips curve," *Journal of Post Keynesian Economics*, 8 (3): 447–462.

Arestis, P. and Howells, P. (1992) "Institutional developments and the effectiveness of monetary policy," *Journal of Economic Issues*, 26 (1): 135–157.

—— (1994) "Monetary policy and income distribution in the UK," *Review of Radical Political Economics*, 26 (3): 56–65.

Arestis, P. and Sawyer, M. C. (2004a) "Can monetary policy affect the real economy?," *European Review of Economics and Finance*, 3 (3): 9–32.

—— (2004b) "On the effectiveness of monetary policy and of fiscal policy," *Review of Social Economy*, 62 (4): 441–463.

—— (2006) "The nature and role of monetary policy when money is endogenous," *Cambridge Journal of Economics*, 30 (6): 847–860.

Argitis, G. and Pitelis, C. (2001) "Monetary policy and distribution of income: Evidence for the United States and the United Kingdom," *Journal of Post Keynesian Economics*, 23 (4): 617–638.

Arnott, R. D. and Bernstein, P. L. (2002a) "Past and present flaws in the mantra of stocks-for-the-long-run," *Pensions & Investments*, 30 (4): 12.

—— (2002b) "What risk premium is 'normal'?," *Financial Analysts Journal*, 58 (2): 64–85.

Arrow, K. J. and Hahn, F. H. (1971) *General Competitive Analysis*, San Francisco: Holden-Day Inc.

Artus, P. (2000) "Faut-il introduire les prix d'actifs dans la fonction de réaction des banques centrales ?," *Revue d'Economie Politique*, 110 (6): 787–807.

—— (2003) "Pourquoi la politique monétaire ne réagit-elle pas aux prix d'actifs?," *Economie et Prévision*, 2 (158): 61–71.

Atesoglu, H. S. (2003) "Monetary transmission—federal funds rate and prime rate," *Journal of Post Keynesian Economics*, 26 (2): 357–362.

—— (2005) "Monetary policy and long-term interest rates," *Journal of Post Keynesian Economics*, 27 (3): 533–539.

—— (2007) "The neutral rate of interest and a new monetary policy rule," *Journal of Post Keynesian Economics*, 29 (4): 689–697.

Avery, C. and Zemsky, P. (1998) "Multidimensional uncertainty and herd behavior in financial markets," *American Economic Review*, 88 (4): 724–748.

Bain, K. (1998) "Some problems with the use of 'credibility' and 'reputation' to support the independence of central banks," in P. Arestis and M. C. Sawyer (eds) *The Political Economy of Central Banking*, 38–48, Northampton: Edward Elgar.

Bain, K., Arestis, P. and Howells, P. (1996) "Central banks, governments and markets: An examination of central bank independence and power," *Economies et Sociétés*, 30 (2–3), MP 10: 229–246.

Banerjee, A. V. (1992) "A simple model of herd behavior," *Quarterly Journal of Economics*, 107 (3): 797–817.

Bank of International Settlements (1997) *67th Annual Report*, Geneva: Bank of International Settlements.

—— (2007) *77th Annual Report*, Geneva: Bank of International Settlements.

Baranzini, M. (1991) *A Theory of Wealth Distribution and Accumulation*, Oxford: Oxford University Press.

Barberis, N., Sheilfer, A. and Vishny, R. (1998) "A model of investor sentiment," *Journal of Financial Economics*, 49 (3): 307–343.

Barro, R. J. and Gordon, D. B. (1983) "A positive theory of monetary policy in a natural rate model," *Journal of Political Economy*, 91 (4): 589–610.

Bean, C. (2003) "Asset prices, financial imbalances and monetary policy: Are inflation targets enough?," in A. Richards and T. Robinson (eds) *Asset Prices and Monetary Policy*, 48–76, Sydney: Reserve Bank of Australia.

Beard, T. R. (1964) "Debt management: Its relationship to monetary policy, 1951–1962," *National Banking Review*, 2 (September): 61–76; reprinted in H. A. Wolf and R. C. Doenges (eds) (1968) *Readings in Money and Banking*, 367–384, New York: Appleton-Century-Croft.

Bell, S. A. (2000) "Do taxes and bonds finance government spending?," *Journal of Economic Issues*, 34 (3): 603–620.

—— (2001) "The role of the state and the hierarchy of money," *Cambridge Journal of Economics*, 25 (2): 149–163.

Bell, S. and Quiggin, J. (2006) "Asset price instability and policy responses: The legacy of liberalization," *Journal of Economic Issues*, 40 (3): 629–649.

Bell, S. A. and Wray, L. R. (2004) "The war on poverty forty years on," *Challenge*, 47 (5): 6–29.

Bell-Kelton, S. A. (2006) "Behind closed doors: The political economy of central banking in the United States," *International Journal of Political Economy*, 35 (1): 5–23.

Benston, G. J. and Kaufman, G. G. (1995) "Is the banking and payments system fragile?," *Journal of Financial Services Research*, 9 (3–4): 209–240; reprinted in H. A. Benink (ed.) (1995) *Coping with Financial Fragility and Systemic Risk*, 15–46, Boston: Ernst & Young.

Berger, W., Kißmer, F. and Wagner, H. (2007) "Monetary policy and asset prices: More bad news for 'Benign Neglect'," *International Finance*, 10 (1): 1–20.

Bernanke, B. S. (1983) "Nonmonetary effects of the financial crisis in the propagation of the Great Depression," *American Economic Review*, 73 (3): 257–276.

—— (2002) "Asset-price 'bubbles' and monetary policy," remarks before the New York Chapter of the National Association for Business Economics, New York, October 15, 2002.

Bernanke, B. S. and Gertler, M. (1989) "Agency costs, net worth, and business fluctuations," *American Economic Review*, 79 (1): 14–31.

—— (1990) "Financial fragility and economic performance," *Quarterly Journal of Economics*, 105 (1): 87–114.

—— (1995) "Inside the black box: The credit channel of monetary policy transmission," *Journal of Economic Perspectives*, 9 (4): 27–48.

—— (1999) "Monetary policy and asset price volatility," Federal Reserve Bank of Kansas City *Economic Review*, 4th quarter: 17–51.

—— (2001) "Should central banks respond to movements in asset prices?," *American Economic Review*, 91 (2): 253–257.

Bernanke, B. S. and Mishkin, F. S. (1997) "Inflation targeting: A new framework for monetary policy?," *Journal of Economic Perspectives*, 11 (2): 97–116.

Bernanke, B. S., Gertler, M. and Gilchrist, S. (1999) "The financial accelerator in a quantitative business cycle framework," in J. B. Taylor and M. Woodford (eds) *Handbook of Macroeconomics*, vol. 1, 1341–1393, New York: Elsevier.

Bernstein, P. L. (1993) "Is investing for the long term theory or just mumbo-jumbo?," *Journal of Post Keynesian Economics*, 15 (3): 387–393; reprinted in P. Davidson (ed.) (1993) *Can the Free Market Pick Winners?*, 75–81, Armonk: M. E. Sharpe.

—— (1997a) "What rate of return can you reasonably expect ... or what can the long run tell us about the short run?," *Financial Analysts Journal*, 53 (2): 20–28.

—— (1997b) " 'Off' the average," *Journal of Portfolio Management*, 24 (1): 3.

—— (1997c) "How long can you run—and where are you running?," *Journal of Post Keynesian Economics*, 20 (2): 183–189.

—— (1998a) *Against the Gods*, New York: Wiley.

—— (2000) "Risk management: Facing the consequences," *Trusts & Estates*, 139 (11): 42–50.

—— (2001) "Risky business," *On Wall Street*, October: 1.

Bibow, J. (2006) "Liquidity preference theory," in P. Arestis and M. C. Sawyer (eds) *A Handbook of Alternative Monetary Economics*, 328–345, Northampton: Edward Elgar.

Biefang-Frisancho Mariscal, I. and Howells, P. (2002) "Central banks and market interest rates," *Journal of Post Keynesian Economics*, 24 (4): 569–585.

Bikhchandani, S., Hirsheilfer, D. and Welch, I. (1992) "A theory of fads, fashion, custom, and cultural change as informational cascades," *Journal of Political Economy*, 100 (5): 992–1026.

Black, F. (1986) "Noise," *Journal of Finance*, 41 (3): 529–543.

Blanchard, O. (1979) "Speculative bubbles, crashes and rational expectations," *Economic Letters*, 3 (4): 387–389.

Blanchard, O. and Watson, M. (1982) "Bubbles, rational expectations and financial markets," in P. Wachtel (ed.) *Crises in the Economic and Financial Structure*, 295–316, Lexington: D. C. Heath and Company.

Board of Governors of the Federal Reserve System (1943) *Banking and Monetary Statistics: 1914–1941*, Washington, DC: Federal Reserve System.

—— (1976) *Banking and Monetary Statistics: 1941–1970*, Washington, DC: Federal Reserve System.

—— (1981) *Annual Statistical Digest: 1970–1979*, Washington, DC: Federal Reserve System.

—— (1991) *Annual Statistical Digest: 1980–1989*, Washington, DC: Federal Reserve System.

Bordo, M. D., Dueker, M. J. and Wheelock, D. C. (2002) "Aggregate price shocks and financial instability: A historical analysis," *Economic Inquiry*, 40 (4): 521–538.

Bordo, M. D. and Jeanne, O. (2002) "Monetary policy and asset prices: Does 'Benign Neglect' make sense?," *International Finance*, 5 (2): 139–164.

Bordo, M. D. and Wheelock, D. C. (1998) "Price stability and financial stability: The historical record," Federal Reserve Bank of St. Louis *Review*, September/October: 41–62.

Borio, C. E. V. and Lowe, P. (2002) "Asset prices, financial and monetary stability: Exploring the nexus," Bank of International Settlements, Working Paper No. 114.

—— (2003) "Imbalances or 'bubbles'? Implications for monetary and financial stability," in W. C. Hunter, G. G. Kaufman and M. Pomerleano (eds) *Asset Price Bubbles: The Implications for Monetary Regulatory and International Policies*, 247–270, Cambridge, MA: MIT Press.

Borio, C. E. V., English, W. and Filardo, A. (2003) "A tale of two perspectives: Old or new challenges for monetary policy?," Bank of International Settlements, Working Paper No. 127.

Borio, C. E. V., Kennedy, N. and Prowse, S. D. (1994) "Exploring aggregate asset price fluctuations across countries: Measurement, determinants and monetary policy implications," Bank of International Settlements, Economic Paper No. 40.

Boulding, K. E. (1944) "A liquidity preference theory of market prices," *Economica*, 11 (42): 55–63.

—— (1950) *A Reconstruction of Economics*, New York: Wiley.

—— (1966) *Economic Analysis: Macroeconomics*, New York: Harper and Row.

Brealey, R. A. (2001) "Bank capital requirements and the control of bank failure," in Bank of England (ed.) *Financial Stability and Central Banks: A Global Perspective*, 144–165, New York: Routledge.

Brennan, M. J. (1998) "Stripping the S&P 500 index," *Financial Analysts Journal*, 54 (1): 12–22.

Brossard, O. (1998) "L'instabilité financière selon Minsky: L'incertitude et la liquidité au fondement du cycle?," *Revue Economique*, 49 (2): 407–435.

—— (2001) *D'un Krach à l'Autre: Instabilité et Régulation des Economies Monétaires*, Paris: Editions Grasset & Fasquelle/Le Monde de l'Education.

Brousseau, V. and Detken, C. (2001) "Monetary policy and fears of financial instability," European Central Bank, Working Paper No. 89.

Brown, C. (2007) "Financial engineering, consumer credit, and the stability of effective demand," *Journal of Post Keynesian Economics*, 29 (3): 427–453.

Bryan, M. F., Cecchetti, S. G. and O'Sullivan, R. (2001) "Asset prices in the measurement of inflation," *De Economist*, 149 (4): 405–431.

Bullard, J. B. and Schaling, E. (2002) "Why the Fed should ignore the stock market," Federal Reserve Bank of St. Louis *Review*, March/April: 35–41.

Campbell, C. and Minsky, H. P. (1987) "How to get off the back of a tiger or, do initial conditions constrain deposit insurance reform?," in Federal Reserve Bank of Chicago (ed.) *Proceedings of a Conference on Bank Structure and Competition*, 252–266, Chicago: Federal Reserve Bank of Chicago.

Campbell, J. Y. (2000) "Asset pricing at the millennium," *Journal of Finance*, 55 (4): 1515–1567.

Cargill, T. F. and Garcia, G. G. (1982) *Financial Deregulation and Monetary Control: Historical Perspective and Impact of the 1980 Act*, Stanford: Hoover Institution Press.

Carter, M. (1989) "Financial innovation and financial fragility," *Journal of Economic Issues*, 23 (3): 779–793.

Caskey, J. and Fazzari, S. (1986) "Macroeconomics and credit markets," *Journal of Economic Issues*, 20 (2): 421–429.

Cecchetti, S. G. (2003) "What the FOMC says and does when the stock market booms," in A. Richards and T. Robinson (eds) *Asset Prices and Monetary Policy*, 77–96, Australia: Reserve Bank of Australia.

Cecchetti, S. G., Genberg, H., Lipsky, J. and Wadhwani, S. (eds) (2000) *Asset Prices and Central Bank Policy*, London: Centre for Economic Policy Research.

Cecchetti, S. G., Genberg, H. and Wadhwani, S. (2003) "Asset prices in a flexible inflation targeting framework," in W. C. Hunter, G. G. Kaufman and M. Pomerleano (eds) *Asset Price Bubbles: The Implications for Monetary Regulatory and International Policies*, 427–444, Cambridge, MA: MIT Press.

Chick, V. (1983) *Macroeconomics After Keynes*, Cambridge, MA: MIT Press.

—— (1986) "The evolution of the banking system and the theory of saving, investment and interest," *Economies et Sociétés*, 20 (8–9), MP 3: 111–126; reprinted in P. Arestis and S. C. Dow (eds) (1992) *On Money, Method and Keynes: Selected Essays*, 193–205, London: Macmillan.

—— (1992) "Some methodological issues in the theory of speculation," in P. Arestis and S. C. Dow (eds) *On Money, Method and Keynes: Selected Essays*, 181–192, London: Macmillan.

Christoffersen, P. F. and Schinasi, G. J. (2003) "Using asset prices to assess inflationary pressures: Constructing a broad-based price measure for Japan, 1970–2003," mimeograph.

Clarida, R., Galí, J. and Gertler, M. (1999) "The science of monetary policy: A New Keynesian perspective," *Journal of Economic Literature*, 37 (4): 1661–1707.

—— (2000) "Monetary policy rules and macroeconomic stability: Evidence and some theory," *Quarterly Journal of Economics*, 115 (1): 147–180.

Clarke, J. A. and Mirza, S. (2006) "A comparison of some common methods for detecting Granger noncausality," *Journal of Statistical Computation and Simulation*, 76 (3): 207–231.

Cogley, T. (1999) "Should the Fed take deliberate steps to deflate asset price bubbles?," Federal Reserve Bank of San Francisco *Economic Review*, No. 1: 42–52.

Commons, J. R. (1934) *Institutional Economics*, New York: Macmillan. Reprinted in two volumes, in 1959 (Vol. 1) and 1961 (Vol. 2), Madison: The University of Wisconsin Press.

Comptroller of the Currency (2007) *Bank Supervision Process: Comptroller's Handbook*, Washington, DC: Office of the Comptroller of the Currency.

Cook, T. and Hahn, T. (1989) "The effect of changes in the federal funds rate target on market interest rates in the 1970s," *Journal of Monetary Economics*, 24 (3): 331–351.

Cooray, A. (2002) "The Fisher effect: A review of the literature," Macquarie University-Sidney, Department of Economics, Research Paper No. 6/2002.

Cornwall J. and Cornwall, W. (1998) "Unemployment costs of inflation targeting," in P. Arestis and M. C. Sawyer (eds) *The Political Economy of Central Banking*, 49–66, Northampton: Edward Elgar.

Cottrell, A. (1994) "Keynes and the Keynesians on the Fisher effect," *Scottish Journal of Political Economy*, 41 (3): 416–433.

—— (1997) "The Fisher effect: Phenomenology, theory and policy," in A. J. Cohen, H. Hagemann and J. Smithin (eds) *Money, Financial Institutions and Macroeconomics*, 55–65, Boston: Kluwer.

Crockett, A. (2008) "Market liquidity and financial stability," Banque de France *Financial Stability Review*, Special Issue, No. 11: 13–17.

Crotty, J. R. (1992) "Neoclassical and Keynesian approaches to the theory of investment," *Journal of Post Keynesian Economics*, 14 (4): 483–496; reprinted in P. Davidson (ed.) (1993) *Can the Free Market Pick Winners?*, 61–74, Armonk: M. E. Sharpe.

—— (1994) "Are Keynesian uncertainty and macrotheory compatible? Conventional decision making, institutional structures, and conditional stability in Keynesian macromodels," in G. A. Dymski and R. Pollin (eds) *New Perspectives in Monetary Macroeconomics: Explorations in the Tradition of Hyman P. Minsky*, 105–139, Ann Arbor: University of Michigan Press.

Crow, J. (2002) *Making Money: An Insider's Perspective on Finance, Politics and Canada's Central Bank*, Etobicoke: John Wiley & Sons Canada.

Cuaresma, J. C. and Gnan, E. (2007) "The natural rate of interest: Which concept? Which estimation method? Which policy conclusions?," *Journal of Post Keynesian Economics*, 29 (4): 667–688.

Curry, T. and Shibut, L. (2000) "The cost of the savings and loan crisis: Truth and consequences," *FDIC Banking Review*, 13 (2): 26–35.

Cutler, S. M. (2004) "The themes of Sarbanes-Oxley as reflected in the Commission's enforcement program," Speech at UCLA School of Law, Los Angeles, September 20, 2004.

Dalziel, P. (1996) "Central banks and monetary control when credit-money finances investment," *Economies et Sociétés*, 30 (2–3), MP 10: 117–135.

—— (1999) "A Post Keynesian theory of asset price inflation with endogenous money," *Journal of Post Keynesian Economics*, 22 (2): 227–245.

—— (2001) *Money, Credit, and Price Stability*, London: Routledge.

—— (2002) "The triumph of Keynes: What now for monetary policy research?," *Journal of Post Keynesian Economics*, 24 (4): 511–527.

Daniel, K., Hirsheifler, D. and Subrahmanyam, A. (1998) "Investor psychology and security market under- and overreactions," *Journal of Finance*, 53 (6): 1839–1885.

Davidson, P. (1968a) "Money, portfolio balance, capital accumulation, and economic growth," *Econometrica*, 36 (2): 291–321.

—— (1968b) "The demand and supply of securities and economic growth and its implications for the Kaldor-Pasinetti versus Samuelson-Modigliani controversy," *American Economic Review*, 58 (2): 252–269.

—— (1968c) "The role of monetary policy in the overall economic policy," reprinted in L. Davidson (ed.) (1991) *The Collected Writings of Paul Davidson*, vol. 1, 95–109, New York: New York University Press.

—— (1974) "A Keynesian view of Friedman's theoretical framework of economic analysis," in R. J. Gordon (ed.) *Milton Friedman's Monetary Framework: A Debate with His Critics*, 90–110, Chicago: University of Chicago Press.

—— (1978) *Money and the Real World*, 2nd edn, London: Macmillan.

—— (1982) "Rational expectations: A fallacious foundation for studying crucial decision-making processes," *Journal of Post Keynesian Economics*, 5 (2): 182–198; reprinted in L. Davidson (ed.) (1991) *The Collected Writings of Paul Davidson*, vol. 2, 123–138, New York: New York University Press.

—— (1985) "Policies for prices and incomes," in A. Barrère (ed.) *Money, Credit and Prices in Keynesian Perspective*, 182–188; reprinted in L. Davidson (ed.) (1991) *The Collected Writings of Paul Davidson*, vol. 2, 87–93, New York: New York University Press.

—— (1986a) "A Post Keynesian view of theories and causes for high real interest rates," *Thames Papers in Political Economy*, Spring; reprinted in L. Davidson (ed.) (1991) *The Collected Writings of Paul Davidson*, vol. 1, 342–364, New York: New York University Press.

—— (1986b) "Finance, funding, saving, and investment," *Journal of Post Keynesian Economics*, 9 (1): 101–110.

—— (1988a) "A technical definition of uncertainty and the long run non-neutrality of money," *Cambridge Journal of Economics*, 12 (3): 329–337.

—— (1988b) "Financial markets, investment and employment," in E. Matzner, J. A. Kregel and S. Roncaglia (eds) *Barriers to Full Employment*, 73–92, New York: St. Martin's Press; reprinted in L. Davidson (ed.) (1991) *The Collected Writings of Paul Davidson*, vol. 1, 611–628, New York: New York University Press.

—— (1991) "Is probability theory relevant for choice under uncertainty?: A Post Keynesian perspective," *Journal of Economic Perspectives*, 5 (1): 129–143.

—— (1993) "Asset deflation and financial fragility," in P. Arestis (ed.) *Money and Banking: Issues for the Twenty-First Century*, 21–33, London: Macmillan; reprinted in L. Davidson (ed.) (1999) *The Collected Writings of Paul Davidson*, vol. 3, 232–245, London: Macmillan.

—— (1994) *Post Keynesian Macroeconomics Theory*, Northampton: Edward Elgar.

—— (1995) "Uncertainty in economics," in S. C. Dow and J. Hillard (eds) *Keynes, Knowledge, and Uncertainty*, 107–116, Aldershot: Edward Elgar.

—— (1998) "Volatile financial markets and the speculator," *Economic Issues*, 3 (2): 1–18; reprinted in L. Davidson (ed.) (1999) *The Collected Writings of Paul Davidson*, vol. 3, 276–295, London: Macmillan.

—— (2002) *Financial Markets, Money, and the Real World*, Northampton: Edward Elgar.

—— (2006) "Can, or should, a central bank inflation target?," *Journal of Post Keynesian Economics*, 28 (4): 689–703.

Davis, E. P. (1995) *Debt, Financial Fragility, and Systemic Risk*, 2nd edn, Oxford: Oxford University Press.

De Bondt, W. F. M. (2003) "Bubble psychology," in W. C. Hunter, G. G. Kaufman and M. Pomerleano (eds) *Asset Price Bubbles: The Implications for Monetary Regulatory and International Policies*, 205–216, Cambridge, MA: MIT Press.

De Bondt, W. F. M. and Thaler, R. H. (1985) "Does the stock market overreact?," *Journal of Finance*, 40 (3): 794–805.

—— (1995) "Financial decision-making in markets and firms: A behavioral perspective," in R. Jarrow, V. Maksimovil and W. T. Ziemba (eds) *Handbook in Operations Research and Management Science*, vol. 9, 385–410, San Diego: Elsevier.

De-Juan, O. (2007) "The conventional versus the natural rate of interest: Implications for central bank autonomy," *Journal of Post Keynesian Economics*, 29 (4): 645–666.

De Long, J. B., Sheilfer, A., Summer, L. H. and Waldmann, R. J. (1990) "Noise trader risk in financial markets," *Journal of Political Economy*, 98 (4): 703–738.

—— (1991) "The survival of noise traders in financial markets," *Journal of Business*, 64 (1): 1–19.

Detken, C. and Smets, F. (2004) "Asset price booms and monetary policy," European Central Bank, Working Paper No. 364.

Dickens, E. (1999) "A political-economic critique of Minsky's financial instability hypothesis: The case of the 1966 financial crisis," *Review of Political Economy*, 11 (4): 379–398.

Disyatat, P. (2005) "Inflation targeting, asset prices and financial imbalances: Conceptualizing the debate," Bank of International Settlements, Working Paper No. 168.

Dos Santos, C. H. (2005) "A stock-flow consistent general framework for formal Minskyan analyses of closed economies," *Journal of Post Keynesian Economics*, 27 (4): 711–735.

Dow, S. C. (1986) "Speculation and the monetary circuit: With particular attention to the euro-currency market," *Economies et Sociétés*, 20 (8–9), MP 3: 95–109; reprinted in S. C. Dow (ed.) (1993) *Money and the Economic Process*, 43–54, Northampton: Edward Elgar.

—— (1995) "Uncertainty about uncertainty," in S. C. Dow and J. Hillard (eds) *Keynes, Knowledge, and Uncertainty*, 117–127, Aldershot: Edward Elgar.

—— (1996) "Horizontalism: A critique," *Cambridge Journal of Economics*, 20 (4): 497–508.

—— (1997) "Endogenous money," in G. C. Harcourt and P. A. Riach (eds) *A 'Second Edition' of the General Theory*, vol. 2, 61–78, New York: Routledge.

—— (2006) "Endogenous money: Structuralist," in P. Arestis and M. C. Sawyer (eds) *A Handbook of Alternative Monetary Economics*, 35–51, Northampton: Edward Elgar.

Dunn, S. P. (2001) "Bounded rationality is not fundamental uncertainty: A Post Keynesian perspective," *Journal of Post Keynesian Economics*, 23 (4): 567–587.

Dupor, B. (2002) "Nominal price versus asset price stabilization," mimeograph.

—— (2005) "Stabilizing non-fundamental asset price movements under discretion and limited information," *Journal of Monetary Economics*, 52 (4): 727–747.

Dupuy, J.-P. (1989) "Convention et Common Knowledge," *Revue Economique*, 40 (2): 361–400.

Dymski, G. A. (1994) "Asymmetric information, uncertainty, and financial structure: 'New' versus 'Post-' Keynesian microfoundations," in G. A. Dymski and R. Pollin (eds) *New Perspectives in Monetary Macroeconomics: Explorations in the Tradition of Hyman P. Minsky*, 77–103, Ann Arbor: University of Michigan Press.

Dymski, G. A. and Pollin, R. (1992) "Hyman Minsky as hedgehog: The power of the Wall Street paradigm," in S. Fazzari and D. B. Papadimitriou (eds) *Financial Conditions and Macroeconomic Performance*, 27–61, Armonk: M. E. Sharpe.

Earl, P. E. (1990) *Monetary Scenarios: A Modern Approach to Financial Systems*, Aldershot: Edward Elgar.

Eichner, A. S. (1976) *The Megacorp and Oligopoly: Microfoundations of Macro Dynamics*, Cambridge: Cambridge University Press.

Ellsberg, D. (1961) "Risk, ambiguity, and the Savage axioms," *Quarterly Journal of Economics*, 75 (4): 643–669.

Enders, W. (2004) *Applied Econometric Times Series*, Hoboken: Wiley.

Ertuk, K. A. (2006a) "Asset price bubble, liquidity preference and the business cycle," *Metroeconomica*, 57 (2): 239–256.

—— (2006b) "On the Minskyan business cycle," Levy Economics Institute, Working Paper No. 474.

European Central Bank (2005) *Monthly Bulletin*, April.

Fabozzi, F. (1993) *Fixed Income Mathematics*, 3rd edn, Chicago: Probus.

Fair, R. C. (2005) "Estimates of the effectiveness of monetary policy," *Journal of Money, Credit, and Banking*, 37 (4): 645–660.

Fama, E. F. (1965) "The behavior of stock-market prices," *Journal of Business*, 38 (1): 34–105.

—— (1970) "Efficient capital markets: A review of theory and empirical work," *Journal of Finance*, 25 (2): 383–417.

—— (1975) "Short-term interest rates as predictors of inflation," *American Economic Review*, 65 (3): 269–282.

Fazzari, S. (1992) "Keynesian theories of investment and finance: Neo, Post, and New," in S. Fazzari and D. B. Papadimitriou (eds) *Financial Conditions and Macroeconomic Performance*, 121–132, Armonk: M. E. Sharpe.

—— (1993) "The investment-finance link: Investment and U.S. fiscal policy in the 1990s," Levy Economics Institute, Public Policy Brief No. 9/1993.

Fazzari, S. and Caskey, J. (1989) "Debt commitments and aggregate demand: A critique of the Neoclassical synthesis and policy," in W. Semmler (ed.) *Financial Dynamics and Business Cycles*, 188–199, New York: M. E. Sharpe.

Fazzari, S. and Minsky, H. P. (1984) "Domestic monetary policy: If not Monetarism, what?," *Journal of Economic Issues*, 18 (1): 101–116.

Fazzari, S., Hubbard, R. G. and Petersen, B. (1988) "Financing constraints and corporate investment," *Brookings Papers on Economic Activity*, 1988 (1): 141–195.

Federal Open Market Committee (1979–2001) *Transcripts of the FOMC Meetings*, Washington, DC: Federal Reserve System.

Ferguson, R. W., Jr. (2000) "The new economy: Unanswered questions for 2000," remarks before the Downtown Economists Club, New York, February 17, 2000.

—— (2004) "Equilibrium real interest rate: Theory and application," remarks to the University of Connecticut School of Business Graduate Learning Center and the SS&C Technologies Financial Accelerator, Hartford, October 29, 2004.

—— (2005) "Recessions and recoveries associated with asset-price movements: What do we know?," remarks at the Stanford Institute for Economic Policy Research, Stanford, January 27, 2005.

Ferri, P. and Minsky, H. P. (1989) "The breakdown of the IS-LM synthesis: Implications for Post-Keynesian economic theory," *Review of Political Economy*, 1 (2): 123–143.

—— (1992) "Market processes and thwarting systems," *Structural Change and Economic Dynamics*, 3 (1): 79–91.

Fields, M. J. (1933) "Speculation and the stability of stock prices," *Quarterly Journal of Economics*, 47 (2): 357–367.

Filardo, A. J. (2000) "Monetary policy and asset prices," Federal Reserve Bank of Kansas City *Economic Review*, 3rd quarter: 11–37.

—— (2001) "Should monetary policy respond to asset price bubbles? Some experimental results," Federal Reserve Bank of Kansas City, Research Working Paper No. 01–04.

—— (2004) "Monetary policy and asset price bubbles: Calibrating the monetary policy trade-offs," Bank of International Settlements, Working Paper No. 155.

Fisher, I. (1907) *The Rate of Interest: Its Nature, Determination and Relation to Economic Phenomena*, New York: Macmillan.

—— (1930) *The Theory of Interest: As Determined by Impatience to Spend Income and Opportunity to Invest It*, New York: Macmillan.

—— (1932) *Booms and Depressions: Some First Principles*, New York: Adelphy.

—— (1933) "The debt-deflation theory of great depressions," *Econometrica*, 1 (4): 337–357.

Fisher, S. (1994) "Modern central banking," in F. Capie, C. A. E. Goodhart, S. Fisher and N. Schnadt (eds) *The Future of Central Banking*, 262–308, Cambridge: Cambridge University Press.

Fontana, G. (2006) "The 'New Consensus' view of monetary policy: A New Wicksellian connection?," Levy Economics Institute, Working Paper No. 476.

Fontana, G. and Palacio-Vera, A. (2002) "Monetary policy rules: What are we learning?," *Journal of Post Keynesian Economics*, 24 (4): 547–568.

—— (2003) "Is there an active role for monetary policy in the endogenous money approach?," *Journal of Economics Issues*, 37 (2): 511–517.

—— (2007) "Are long-run price stability and short-run output stabilization all that monetary policy can aim for?," *Metroeconomica*, 58 (2): 269–298.

Fortune, P. (2000) "Margin requirements, margin loans, and margin rates: Practice and principles," *New England Economic Review*, September/October: 19–44.

Franke, R. and Semmler, W. (1989) "Debt-financing of firms, stability, and cycles in a dynamical macroeconomic growth model," in W. Semmler (ed.) *Financial Dynamics and Business Cycles*, 38–64, Armonk: M. E. Sharpe.

Friedman, M. (1953) "The case for flexible exchange rate," in M. Friedman (ed.) *Essays in Positivism*, 157–203, Chicago: University of Chicago Press.

—— (1968) "The role of monetary policy," *American Economic Review*, 58 (1): 1–17.

—— (1974) "A theoretical framework for monetary analysis," in R. J. Gordon (ed.) *Milton Friedman's Monetary Framework: A Debate with His Critics*, 1–62, Chicago: University of Chicago Press.

—— (1987) "Quantity theory of money," in P. Newman, M. Milgate and J. Eatwell (eds) *The New Palgrave*, vol. 4, 3–20, New York: Norton; reprinted in P. Newman, M. Milgate and J. Eatwell (eds) (1989) *The New Palgrave: Money*, 1–40, New York: Norton.

Friedman, M. and Schwartz, A. J. (1963) *A Monetary History of the United States, 1867–1960,* Princeton: Princeton University Press.

—— (1976) "From Gibson to Fisher," *Exploration in Economics*, 3 (2): 288–291.

Fuhrer, J. and Moore, G. (1992) "Monetary policy rules and the indicator properties of asset prices," *Journal of Monetary Economics*, 29 (2): 303–336.

Fullwiler, S. T. (2006) "Setting interest rates in the modern money era," *Journal of Post Keynesian Economics*, 28 (3): 495–525.

—— (2007) "Macroeconomic stabilization through an employer of last resort," *Journal of Economic Issues*, 41 (1): 93–134.

Galbraith, J. K. (1961) *The Great Crash*, 3rd edn, Cambridge, MA: The Riverside Press.

—— (1993) *A Short Story of Financial Euphoria*, 2nd edn, New York: Viking Penguin.

Gale, D. (1982) *Money: In Equilibrium*, Cambridge: Cambridge University Press.

Gallati, R. R. (2003) *Risk Management and Capital Adequacy*, New York: McGraw Hill.

Gertler, M. (1988) "Financial structure and aggregate economic activity: An overview," *Journal of Money, Credit and Banking*, 20 (3), Part 2: 559–588.

—— (1998) Discussion in Centre for Economic Policy Research (ed.) *Asset Prices and Monetary Policy: Four Views*, 1–9, London: Centre for Economic Policy Research.

Gervais, S. and Odean, T. (2001) "Learning to be overconfident," *Review of Financial Studies*, 14 (1): 1–27.

Ghazali, N. A. and Ramlee, S. (2003) "A long memory test of the long-run fisher effect in the G7 countries," *Applied Financial Economics*, 13 (10): 763–769.

Gilchrist, S. and Leahy, J. V. (2002) "Monetary policy and asset prices," *Journal of Monetary Economics*, 49 (1): 75–97.

Glassman, J. K. and Hassett, K. A. (1999) *Dow 36,000: The New Strategy for Profiting from the Coming Rise in the Stock Market*, New York: Times Business.

Glickman, M. (1994) "The concept of information, intractable uncertainty, and the current state of the 'efficient markets' theory: A Post Keynesian view," *Journal of Post Keynesian Economics*, 16 (3): 325–349.

—— (2000) "Seeking explanations not preserving theorems: Corporate finance, confidence, asymmetric information, and the UK macroeconomy," *Journal of Post Keynesian Economics*, 23 (2): 201–233.

Glyn, A. (1997) "Does aggregate profitability *really* matter?," *Cambridge Journal of Economics*, 21 (5): 593–619.

Gnos, C. and Rochon, L.-P. (2007) "The New Consensus and Post-Keynesian interest rate policy," *Review of Political Economy*, 17 (3): 369–386.

Godley, W. and Lavoie, M. (2007) *Monetary Economics: An Integrated Approach to Credit, Money, Income, Production and Wealth*, New York: Palgrave Macmillan.

Godley, W. and Shaikh, A. (1998) "An important inconsistency in the heart of the standard macroeconomic model," Levy Economics Institute, Working Paper No. 236.

Goldsmith, R. W. (1982) Comment on "The financial-instability hypothesis: Capitalist processes and the behavior of the economy," in C. P. Kindleberger and J.-P. Laffargue (eds) *Financial Crises: Theory, History, Policy*, 41–43, Cambridge: Cambridge University Press.

Goldstein, D. (1995) "Uncertainty, competition, and speculative finance in the eighties," *Journal of Economic Issues*, 29 (3): 719–746.

Goodfriend, M. (1998a) Discussion in Centre for Economic Policy Research (ed.) *Asset Prices and Monetary Policy: Four Views*, 10–19, London: Centre for Economic Policy Research.

—— (1998b) "Using the term structure of interest rates for monetary policy," Federal Reserve Bank of Richmond *Economic Quarterly*, 84 (3): 13–30.

—— (2001) "Financial stability, deflation, and monetary policy," Bank of Japan *Monetary and Economic Studies*, 19 (S-1): 143–167.

—— (2003) "Interest rate policy should not react directly to asset prices," in W. C. Hunter, G. G. Kaufman and M. Pomerleano (eds) *Asset Price Bubbles: The Implications for Monetary Regulatory and International Policies*, 445–457, Cambridge, MA: MIT Press.

Goodhart, C. A. E. (1988) *The Evolution of Central Banks*, Cambridge, MA: MIT Press.

—— (1989) *Money, Information and Uncertainty*, 2nd edn, Cambridge, MA: MIT Press.

—— (1992) "The objectives for, and conduct of, monetary policy in the 1990s," in A. Blundell-Wignall (ed.) *Inflation, Disinflation and Monetary Policy*, 314–333, Sydney: Reserve Bank of Australia; reprinted in C. A. E. Goodhart (ed.) (1995) *The Central Bank and the Financial System*, 216–235, Cambridge, MA: MIT Press.

—— (1993) "Price stability and financial fragility," in K. Sawamoto, Z. Nakajima and H. Taguchi (eds) *Financial Stability in a Changing Environment*, 439–497, New York: St. Martin's Press; reprinted in C. A. E. Goodhart (ed.) (1995) *The Central Bank and the Financial System*, 263–302, Cambridge, MA: MIT Press.

—— (1999) "Time, inflation and asset prices," London School of Economics, Financial Market Group, Special Paper No. 117.

—— (2001) "What weight should be given to asset prices in the measurement of inflation?," *Economic Journal*, 111 (472): F335–F356.

Goodhart, C. A. E. and Hofmann, B. (2000) "Do asset prices help to predict consumer price inflation?," *Manchester School*, 68 (s1): 122–140.

—— (2001) "Asset prices, financial conditions, and the transmission of monetary policy," paper prepared for the conference on *Asset Prices, Exchange Rates, and Monetary Policy*, Stanford University, March 2–3, 2001.

Goodhart, C. A. E. and Tsomocos, D. P. (2007) "Analysis of financial stability," seminar paper presented at the Fondation Banque de France, February 20, 2008.

Goodhart, C. A. E., Hartmann, P., Llewellyn, D., Rojas-Suárez, L. and Weisbrod, S. (eds) (1998) *Financial Regulation: Why, How and Where Now?*, London: Routledge.

Gordon, R. J. (1973) Comment on "Interest rates and prices in the long-run," *Journal of Money, Credit and Banking*, 5 (1), Part 2: 460–463.

—— (1990) "What is New-Keynesian economics?," *Journal of Economic Literature*, 28 (3): 1115–1171.

Grabel, I. (1998) "Coercing credibility: Neoliberal policies and monetary institutions in developing and transitional economies," in P. Arestis and M. C. Sawyer (eds) *The Political Economy of Central Banking*, 83–100, Northampton: Edward Elgar.

—— (2000) "The political economy of 'policy credibility': The New-Classical macroeconomics and the remaking of emerging economies," *Cambridge Journal of Economics*, 24 (1): 1–19.

Granger, C. W. J. (1988) "Some recent developments in a concept of causality," *Journal of Econometrics*, 39 (1–2): 199–211.

Graziani, A. (1990) "The theory of the monetary circuit," *Economies et Sociétés*, 24 (6), MP 7: 7–36.

—— (2003a) *The Monetary Theory of Production*, Cambridge: Cambridge University Press.

—— (2003b) "Finance motive," in J. E. King (ed.) *The Elgar Companion to Post Keynesian Economics*, 142–145, Northampton: Edward Elgar.

Greenspan, A. (1996) "The challenge of central banking in a democratic society," remarks at the Annual Dinner and Francis Boyer Lecture of The American Enterprise Institute for Public Policy Research, Washington, DC, December 5, 1996.

—— (1999) "Measuring financial risk in the twenty-first century," remarks before a conference sponsored by the Office of the Comptroller of the Currency, Washington, DC, October 14, 1999.

—— (2002) "Economic volatility," remarks at a symposium sponsored by the Federal Reserve Bank of Kansas City, Jackson Hole, August 30, 2002.

—— (2008) "We will never have a perfect model of risk," *Financial Times*, March 17, 2008, page 9.

Greenwald, B. C. and Stein, J. C. (1991) "Transactional risk, market crashes, and the role of circuit breakers," *Journal of Business*, 64 (4): 443–462.

Greider, W. (1987) *Secrets of the Temple*, New York: Simon and Schuster.

Gruen, D., Plumb, M. and Stone, A. (2003) "How should monetary policy respond to asset-price bubbles?," in A. Richards and T. Robinson (eds) *Asset Prices and Monetary Policy*, 260–280, Sydney: Reserve Bank of Australia; reprinted and amended in *International Journal of Central Banking*, December 2005, 1 (3): 1–31.

Guttentag, J. and Herring, R. (1984) "Credit rationing and financial disorder," *Journal of Finance*, 39 (5): 1359–1382.

—— (1988) "Prudential supervision to manage systemic vulnerability," in Federal Reserve Bank of Chicago (ed.) *Proceedings of a Conference on Bank Structure and Competition*, 602–633, Chicago: Federal Reserve Bank of Chicago.

Guttmann, R. (2006) "Basel II: A new regulatory framework for global banking," mimeograph.

Hahn, F. H. (1982) *Money and Inflation*, Oxford: Basil Blackwell.

Haliassos, M. and Tobin, J. (1990) "The macroeconomics of government finance," in B. M. Friedman and F. H. Hahn (eds) *Handbook of Monetary Economics*, vol. 2, 889–959, Amsterdam: North-Holland.

Hannsgen, G. (2004) "Gibson's paradox, monetary policy, and the emergence of cycles," Levy Economics Institute, Working Paper No. 410.

—— (2005) "Minsky's acceleration channel and the role of money," *Journal of Post Keynesian Economics*, 27 (3): 471–489.

—— (2006a) "The transmission mechanism of monetary policy: A critical review," in P. Arestis and M. C. Sawyer (eds) *A Handbook of Alternative Monetary Economics*, 205–223, Northampton: Edward Elgar.

—— (2006b) "Gibson's paradox II," Levy Economics Institute, Working Paper No. 448.

Harcourt, G. C. (1972) *Some Cambridge Controversies in the Theory of Capital*, Cambridge: Cambridge University Press.

Harrod, R. (1971) Discussion in G. Clayton, J. C. Gilbert and R. Sedgwick (eds) *Monetary Theory and Monetary Policy in the 1970s*, 58–63, Oxford: Oxford University Press.

Hart, O. D. and Kreps, D. M. (1986) "Price destabilizing speculation," *Journal of Political Economy*, 94 (5): 927–952.

Harvey, J. (1998) "Heuristic judgment theory," *Journal of Economic Issues*, 32 (1): 47–64.

—— (2001) "Exchange rate theory and 'the fundamentals'," *Journal of Post Keynesian Economics*, 24 (1): 3–15.

Haslag, J. H. (1997) "Output, growth, welfare, and inflation: A survey," Federal Reserve Bank of Dallas *Economic Review*, 2nd quarter: 11–21.

Heffernan, S. A. (1997) "Modelling British interest rate adjustment: An error correction approach," *Economica*, 64 (254): 211–231.

Henry, J. F. (2003) "Say's economy," in S. Kates (ed.) *Two Hundred Years of Say's Law: Essays on Economic Theory's Most Controversial Principle*, 187–198, Northampton: Edward Elgar.

—— (2006) "'Bad' Decisions, poverty, and economic theory: The individualist and social perspectives in light of 'the American Myth'," paper presented at the Association for Institutional Thought conference, Phoenix, April 2006.

Herring, R. J. (1999) "Credit risk and financial instability," *Oxford Review of Economic Policy*, 15 (3): 63–79.

Hicks, J. R. (1946) *Value and Capital*, 2nd edn, Oxford: Oxford University Press.

Hunter, W. C., Kaufman, G. G. and Pomerleano, M. (2003) Overview in W. C. Hunter, G. G. Kaufman and M. Pomerleano (eds) *Asset Price Bubbles: The Implications for Monetary Regulatory and International Policies*, xiii–xxvi, Cambridge, MA: MIT Press.

Illing, G. (2001) "Financial fragility, bubbles and monetary policy," Center for Economic Studies and Ifo Institute for Economic Research, Working Paper No. 449.

Innes, A. M. (1913) "What is money?," *Banking Law Journal*, 30 (5): 377–408; reprinted in L. R. Wray (ed.) (2004) *Credit and State Theories of Money: The Contributions of A. Mitchell Innes*, 14–49, Northampton: Edward Elgar.

—— (1914) "Credit theory of money?," *Banking Law Journal*, 31 (2): 151–168; reprinted in L. R. Wray (ed.) (2004) *Credit and State Theories of Money: The Contributions of A. Mitchell Innes*, 50–78, Northampton: Edward Elgar.

International Monetary Fund (2000) *World Economic Outlook: Asset Prices and the Business Cycle*, May 2000, Washington, DC: International Monetary Fund.

—— (2007) *Global Financial Stability Report*, October 2007, Washington DC: International Monetary Fund.

Isaac, A. G. (1993) "Is there a natural rate?," *Journal of Post Keynesian Economics*, 15 (4): 453–470.

Isenberg, D. L. (1988) "Is there a case for Minsky's financial fragility hypothesis in the 1920s?," *Journal of Economic Issues*, 22 (4): 1045–1069.

—— (1994) "Financial fragility and the Great Depression: New evidence on credit growth in the 1920s," in G. A. Dymski and R. Pollin (eds) *New Perspectives in*

Monetary Macroeconomics: Explorations in the Tradition of Hyman P. Minsky, 201–229, Ann Arbor: University of Michigan Press.

Issing, O. (1998) Discussion in Centre for Economic Policy Research (ed.) *Asset Prices and Monetary Policy: Four Views*, 20–22, London: Centre for Economic Policy Research.

Judd, J. P. and Scadding, J. L. (1982) "The search for a stable money demand function: A survey of the post-1973 literature," *Journal of Economic Literature*, 20 (3): 993–1023.

Kahn, R. F. (1954) "Some notes on liquidity preference," *Manchester School of Economic and Social Studies*, 22 (3): 229–257; reprinted in R. F. Kahn (ed.) (1972) *Essays on Employment and Growth*, 72–96, Cambridge: Cambridge University Press.

—— (1956a) "Full employment and British economic policy," reprinted in R. F. Kahn (ed.) (1972) *Essays on Employment and Growth*, 97–102, Cambridge: Cambridge University Press.

—— (1956b) "Lord Keynes and contemporary economic problems," reprinted in R. F. Kahn (ed.) (1972) *Essays on Employment and Growth*, 103–123, Cambridge: Cambridge University Press.

—— (1959) "Memorandum of evidence submitted to the Radcliffe Committee," reprinted in R. F. Kahn (ed.) (1972) *Essays on Employment and Growth*, 124–152, Cambridge: Cambridge University Press.

—— (1984) *The Making of Keynes's General Theory*, Cambridge: Cambridge University Press.

Kahneman, D. and Tversky, A. (1973) "On the psychology of prediction," *Psychological Review*, 80 (4): 237–251.

—— (1979) "Prospect theory: An analysis of decision under risk," *Econometrica*, 47 (2): 263–292.

—— (1992) "Advances in prospect theory: Cumulative representation of uncertainty," *Journal of Risk and Uncertainty*, 5 (4): 297–323.

Kaldor, N. (1939) "Speculation and economic stability," *Review of Economic Studies*, 7 (1): 1–27; reprinted and revised in N. Kaldor (ed.) (1960) *Essays on Economic Stability and Growth*, 17–58, London: Duckworth.

—— (1950) "A positive policy for wages and dividends," memorandum; reprinted in N. Kaldor (ed.) (1964) *Essays on Economic Policy*, vol. 1, 111–127, New York: W. W. Norton & Co., Inc.

—— (1958) "Monetary policy, economic stability and growth," memorandum; reprinted in N. Kaldor (ed.) (1964) *Essays on Economic Policy*, vol. 1, 128–153, New York: W. W. Norton & Co., Inc.

—— (1982) *The Scourge of Monetarism*, Oxford: Oxford University Press.

Kalecki, M. (1971a) "The determinants of profits," in M. Kalecki (ed.) *Selected Essays on the Dynamics of the Capitalist Economy*, 78–92, Cambridge: Cambridge University Press.

—— (1971b) "Enterpreneurial capital and investment," in M. Kalecki (ed.) *Selected Essays on the Dynamics of the Capitalist Economy*, 105–109, Cambridge: Cambridge University Press.

Kanter, J. (2007) "Europeans plan to investigate ratings agencies and their warnings," *New York Times*, August 17, 2007.

Kaufman, G. G. (1998) "Central banks, asset bubbles, and financial stability," Federal Reserve Bank of Chicago, Working Paper No. 98–12.

Kelton, S. A. and Wray, L. R. (2006) "What a long, strange trip it's been: Can we muddle through without fiscal policy?," in C. Gnos and L.-P. Rochon (eds) *Post-Keynesian Principles of Economic Policy*, 101–119, Northampton: Edward Elgar.

Kent, C. and Lowe, P. (1997) "Asset-price bubbles and monetary policy," Reserve Bank of Australia, Research Discussion Paper No. 9709.

Kenway, P. (1980) "Marx, Keynes and the possibility of crisis," *Cambridge Economics Journal*, 4 (1): 23–36.

Keynes, J. M. (1921) *A Treatise on Probability*, London: Macmillan; reprinted in D. E. Moggridge (ed.) (1971) *The Collected Writings of John Maynard Keynes*, vol. 8, London: Macmillan.

—— (1930) *A Treatise on Money*, London: Macmillan; reprinted in D. E. Moggridge (ed.) (1971) *The Collected Writings of John Maynard Keynes*, vol. 5 and vol. 6, Macmillan: London.

—— (1933a) "A monetary theory of production," reprinted in D. E. Moggridge (ed.) (1973) *The Collected Writings of John Maynard Keynes*, vol. 13, 408–411, London: Macmillan.

—— (1933b) "The characteristics of an entrepreneur economy," reprinted in D. E. Moggridge (ed.) (1979) *The Collected Writings of John Maynard Keynes*, vol. 29, 87–101, London: Macmillan.

—— (1933c) "The distinction between a co-operative economy and an entrepreneur economy," reprinted in D. E. Moggridge (ed.) (1979) *The Collected Writings of John Maynard Keynes*, vol. 29, 76–87, London: Macmillan.

—— (1936a) *The General Theory of Employment, Interest, and Money*, New York: Harcourt Brace; reprinted in D. E. Moggridge (ed.) (1971) *The Collected Writings of John Maynard Keynes*, vol. 7, London: Macmillan.

—— (1936b) Letter to D. H. Robertson, 13 December 1936; reprinted in D. E. Moggridge (ed.) (1973) *The Collected Writings of John Maynard Keynes*, vol. 14, 89–95, London: Macmillan.

—— (1937a) "The theory of the rate of interest," in A. D. Gayer (ed.) *The Lessons of Monetary Experience: Essays in Honor of Irving Fisher*, 145–152, New York: Farrar & Rinehart, Inc; reprinted in D. E. Moggridge (ed.) (1973) *The Collected Writings of John Maynard Keynes*, vol. 14, 101–108, London: Macmillan.

—— (1937b) "The general theory of employment," *Quarterly Journal of Economics*, 51 (2): 209–223; reprinted in D. E. Moggridge (ed.) (1973) *The Collected Writings of John Maynard Keynes*, vol. 14, 109–123, London: Macmillan.

—— (1937c) "Alternative theories of the rate of interest," *Economic Journal*, 47 (186): 241–252; reprinted in D. E. Moggridge (ed.) (1973) *The Collected Writings of John Maynard Keynes*, vol. 14, 201–215, London: Macmillan.

—— (1937d) "The 'ex ante' theory of the rate of interest," *Economic Journal*, 47 (188): 663–669; reprinted in D. E. Moggridge (ed.) (1973) *The Collected Writings of John Maynard Keynes*, vol. 14, 215–223, London: Macmillan.

—— (1937e) Letter to J. R. Hicks, 31 March 1937; reprinted in D. E. Moggridge (ed.) (1973) *The Collected Writings of John Maynard Keynes*, vol. 14, 79–81, London: Macmillan.

—— (1937f) "Ex post and ex ante," reprinted in D. E. Moggridge (ed.) (1973) *The Collected Writings of John Maynard Keynes*, vol. 14, 179–183, London: Macmillan.

—— (1938a) Letter to E. S. Shaw, 4 April 1938; reprinted in D. E. Moggridge (ed.) (1979) *The Collected Writings of John Maynard Keynes*, vol. 29, 280–281, London: Macmillan.

—— (1938b) Letter to E. S. Shaw, 13 April 1938; reprinted in D. E. Moggridge (ed.) (1979) *The Collected Writings of John Maynard Keynes*, vol. 29, 281–282, London: Macmillan.

—— (1938c) Comments on "Mr. Keynes and 'finance,'" *Economic Journal*, 48 (190): 318–322; reprinted in D. E. Moggridge (ed.) (1973) *The Collected Writings of John Maynard Keynes*, vol. 14, 229–233, London: Macmillan.

—— (1938d) Letter to H. Townshend, 7 December 1938; reprinted in D. E. Moggridge (ed.) (1979) *The Collected Writings of John Maynard Keynes*, vol. 29, 293–294, London: Macmillan.

—— (1939) "The process of capital formation," *Economic Journal*, 49 (195): 569–574; reprinted in D. E. Moggridge (ed.) (1973) *The Collected Writings of John Maynard Keynes*, vol. 14, 278–285, London: Macmillan.

—— (1943) Letter to J. Wedgwood, 7 July 1943; reprinted in D. E. Moggridge (ed.) (1980) *The Collected Writings of John Maynard Keynes*, vol. 27, 350–351, London: Macmillan.

Kindleberger, C. P. (1992) "The quality of debt," in D. B. Papadimitriou (ed.) *Profits, Deficits and Instability*, 189–201, New York: St. Martin's Press.

—— (1995) "Asset inflation and monetary policy," *Banca Nazionale del Lavoro Quarterly Review*, 48 (192): 17–37.

—— (1996) *Mania, Panics, and Crashes*, 3rd edn, New York: Wiley.

—— (1997) "Manias and how to prevent them: Interview with Charles P. Kindleberger," *Challenge*, 40 (6): 21–31.

King, J. E. (2002) *A History of Post Keynesian Economics Since 1936*, Cheltenham: Edward Elgar.

Kiyotaki, N. and Moore, J. (1997) "Credit Cycles," *Journal of Political Economy*, 105 (2): 211–248.

Knight, F. H. (1921) *Risk, Uncertainty and Profit*, Boston: Houghton Mifflin Company.

Kónya, L. and Singh, J. P. (2006) "Exports, imports and economic growth in India," La Trobe University, School of Business, Discussion Paper No. A06.06.

Koustas, Z. and Serletis, A. (1999) "On the Fisher effect," *Journal of Monetary Economics*, 44 (1): 105–130.

Kregel, J. A. (1971) *Rate of Profit, Distribution and Growth: Two Views*, New York: Aldine.

—— (1975) *The Reconstruction of Political Economy: An Introduction to Post-Keynesian Economics*, 2nd edn, London: Macmillan.

—— (1976) "Economic methodology in the face of uncertainty: The modeling methods of Keynes and the Post-Keynesians," *Economic Journal*, 86 (342): 209–225.

—— (1977) "On the existence of expectations in English Neoclassical economics," *Journal of Economic Literature*, 15 (2): 495–500.

—— (1982) "Money, expectations and relative prices in Keynes' monetary equilibrium," *Economie Appliquée*, 35 (3): 449–465.

—— (1984) "Monetary production economics and monetary policy," *Economies et Sociétés*, 18 (4), MP 1: 221–232.

—— (1985) "Hamlet without the prince: Cambridge macroeconomics without money," *American Economic Review*, 75 (2): 133–139.

—— (1986a) "Shylock and Hamlet or are there bulls and bears in the circuit?," *Economies et Sociétés*, 20 (8–9), MP 3: 11–22.

—— (1986b) "Conceptions of equilibrium: The logic of choice and the logic of production," in I. Kirzner (ed.) *Subjectivism, Intelligibility, and Economic Understanding*, 157–170, New York: New York University Press; reprinted in P. Boettke and D. Prychitko (eds) (1998) *Market Process Theories*, vol. 2, 89–102, Northampton: Edward Elgar.

—— (1987) "Rational spirits and the Post Keynesian macrotheory of microeconomics," *De Economist*, 135 (4): 520–532.

—— (1988a) "The multiplier and liquidity preference: Two sides of the theory of effective demand," in A. Barrère (ed.) *The Foundations of Keynesian Analysis*, 231–250, New York: St. Martin Press.

—— (1988b) "Irving Fisher, great-grandparent of the *General Theory*: Money, rate of return over cost and efficiency of capital," *Cahiers d'Economie Politique*, No. 14–15: 59–68.

—— (1992a) "Minsky's 'two price' theory of financial instability and monetary policy: Discounting vs. open market intervention," in S. Fazzari and D. B. Papadimitriou (eds) *Financial Conditions and Macroeconomic Performance*, 85–103, Armonk: M. E. Sharpe.

—— (1992b) "Walras' auctioneer and Marshall's well-informed dealer: Time, market prices, and normal supply prices," *Quaderni di Storia dell'Economia Politica*, 10 (1): 531–551.

—— (1994) "The viability of economic policy and the priorities of economic policy," *Journal of Post Keynesian Economics*, 17 (2): 261–272.

—— (1996) "The theory of value, expectations and chapter 17 of *The General Theory*," in G. C. Harcourt and P. A. Riach (eds) *A 'Second Edition' of the General Theory*, vol. 1, 261–282, London: Routledge.

—— (1997) "Margins of safety and weight of the argument in generating financial crisis," *Journal of Economic Issues*, 31 (2): 543–548.

—— (1998a) "Aspects of a Post Keynesian theory of finance," *Journal of Post Keynesian Economics*, 21 (1): 111–133.

—— (1998b) *The Past and Future of Banks*, Quaderni di Ricerche, No. 21, Rome: Ente Luigi Einaudi.

—— (1999) "Capital and income in the theory of investment and output: Irving Fisher and John Maynard Keynes," in H. E. Loef and H. G. Monissen (eds) *The Economics of Irving Fisher*, 268–278, Northampton: Edward Elgar.

—— (2003) "Krugman on the liquidity trap: Why inflation will not bring recovery in Japan," in R. Arena and N. Salvadori (eds) *Money, Credit, and the Role of the State*, 225–238, Aldershot: Ashgate.

—— (2006) "Can the Basel revised framework succeed where Basel I failed?," remarks prepared for the International Seminar *Global Finance and Strategies of Developing Countries* organized by the Institute of Economics University of Campinas, March 13–14, 2006.

—— (2008) "Minsky's cushions of safety: Systemic risk and the crisis in the U.S. subprime mortgage market," Levy Economics Institute, Public Policy Brief No. 93/2008.

Kregel, J. A. and Nasica, E. (1999) "Alternative analyses of uncertainty and rationality: Keynes and modern economics," in S. Marzetti Dall-Aste Brandolini and R. Scazzieri (eds) *La Probabilità in Keynes: Premesse e Influenze*, 115–137, Bologna: Clueb.

Kriesler, P. and Lavoie, M. (2007) "The New Consensus on monetary policy and its Post-Keynesian critique," *Review of Political Economy*, 19 (3): 387–404.

Kydland, F. E. and Prescott, E. C. (1977) "Rules rather than discretion: The inconsistency of optimal plans," *Journal of Political Economy*, 85 (3): 473–492.

Kyle, A. S. and Wang, F. A. (1997) "Speculation duopoly with agreement to disagree: Can overconfidence survive the market test?," *Journal of Finance*, 52 (6): 2073–2090.

Laubach, T. and Williams, J. C. (2003) "Measuring the natural rate of interest," *Review of Economics and Statistics*, 85 (4): 1063–1070.

Lavoie, M. (1983) "Loi de Minsky et loi d'entropie," *Economie Appliquée*, 36 (2–3): 287–331.

—— (1984) "The endogenous flow of credit and the Post Keynesian theory of money," *Journal of Economic Issues*, 18 (3): 771–797.

—— (1985) "La distinction entre l'incertitude keynésienne et le risque néoclassique," *Economie Appliquée*, 38 (2): 493–518.

—— (1986) "Minsky's law or the theorem of systemic financial fragility," *Studi Economici*, 41 (29): 3–28.

—— (1987) "Monnaie et production: Une synthèse de la théorie du circuit," *Economies et Sociétés*, 21 (9), MP 4: 65–101.

—— (1992) *Foundations of Post Keynesian Economic Analysis*, Aldershot: Edward Elgar.

—— (1995) "Interest rates in Post-Keynesian models of growth and distribution," *Metroeconomica*, 46 (2): 146–177.

—— (1996a) "Monetary policy in an economy with endogenous credit money," in G. Deleplace and E. J. Nell (eds) *Money in Motion: The Post Keynesian and Circulation Approaches*, 532–545, London: Macmillan.

—— (1996b) "Horizontalism, Structuralism, liquidity preference and the principle of increasing risk," *Scottish Journal of Political Economy*, 43 (3): 275–300.

—— (1997a) "Loanable funds, endogenous money, and Minsky's financial fragility hypothesis," in A. J. Cohen, H. Hagemann and J. Smithin (eds) *Money, Financial Institutions, and Macroeconomics*, 67–82, Boston: Kluwer Nijhoff.

—— (1997b) "Fair rates of interest in Post-Keynesian political economy," in J. Teixeira (ed.) *Issues in Modern Political Economy*, 123–137, Brasilia: University of Brasilia Press.

—— (1999) "Fair rates of interest and Post-Keynesian economics: The Canadian case," paper presented at Clarkson University, May 1999.

—— (2004) "The New Consensus on monetary policy seen from a Post-Keynesian perspective," in M. Lavoie and M. Seccareccia (eds) *Central Banking in the Modern World: Alternative Perspectives*, 15–34, Northampton: Edward Elgar.

—— (2005) "Monetary base endogeneity and the new procedures of the asset-based Canadian and American monetary systems," *Journal of Post Keynesian Economics*, 27 (4): 689–709.

—— (2006) "Endogenous money: Accomodationist," in P. Arestis and M. C. Sawyer (eds) *A Handbook of Alternative Monetary Economics*, 17–34, Northampton: Edward Elgar.

Lavoie, M. and Seccareccia, M. (1988) "Money, interest and rentiers: The twilight of rentier capitalism in Keynes's *General Theory*?," in *Keynes and Public Policy After Fifty Years*, vol. 2, 145–158, New York: New York University Press.

—— (1999) "Interest rate: Fair," in P. O'Hara (ed.) *Encyclopedia of Political Economy*, vol. 1, 543–545, London: Routledge.

—— (2001) "Minsky's financial fragility hypothesis: A missing macroeconomic link?," in R. Bellofiore and P. Ferri (eds) *Financial Fragility and Investment in the Capitalist Economy: The Economic Legacy of Hyman Minsky*, vol. 2, 76–96, Cheltenham: Edward Elgar.

—— (eds) (2004) *Central Banking in the Modern World: Alternative Perspectives*, Northampton: Edward Elgar.

Lawson, T. (1985) "Uncertainty and economic analysis," *Economic Journal*, 95 (380): 909–927.

—— (1988) "Probability and uncertainty in economic analysis," *Journal of Post Keynesian Economic*, 11 (1): 38–65.

Leach, J. (1991) "Rational speculation," *Journal of Political Economy*, 99 (1): 131–144.

Lee, F. S. (1998) *Post Keynesian Price Theory*, Cambridge: Cambridge University Press.

—— (2000) "The organizational history of Post Keynesian economics in America, 1971–1995," *Journal of Post Keynesian Economics*, 23 (1): 141–162.

—— (2002) "Mutual aid and the making of heterodox economics in Postwar America: A Post Keynesian view," *History of Economics Review*, 35: 45–62.

Le Héron, E. (1986) "Généralisation de la préférence pour la liquidité et financement de l'investissement," *Economies et Sociétés*, 20 (8–9), MP 3: 65–93.

—— (1991) "Les approches traditionnelles de l'inflation et leur dépassement par les post-keynésiens," *Economies et Sociétés*, 25 (11–12), MP 8: 11–31.

—— (2003) "A New Consensus on monetary policy?," *Brazilian Journal of Political Economy*, 23 (4): 3–27.

—— (2006) "Alan Greenspan, the confidence strategy," *Brazilian Journal of Political Economy*, 26 (4): 502–517.

Le Héron, E. and Carré, E. (2005) "The monetary policy of the ECB and the Fed: Credibility versus confidence, a comparative approach," in P. Arestis, J. Ferriero and F. Serrano (eds) *Financial Developments in National and International Markets*, 77–102, London: Palgrave-Macmillan.

—— (2006) "Credibility versus confidence in monetary policy," in L. R. Wray and M. Forstater (eds) *Money, Financial Instability and Stabilization Policy*, 58–84, Northampton: Edward Elgar.

Lerner, A. P. (1943) "Functional finance and the federal debt," *Social Research*, 10 (1): 38–51; reprinted in D. Colander (ed.) (1983) *Selected Economic Writings of Abba L. Lerner*, 297–310, New York: New York University Press.

—— (1944) *The Economics of Control*, New York: Macmillan.

—— (1961) "Sellers' inflation and inflationary depression," in A. P. Lerner *Everybody's Business*, 81–92, Michigan: Michigan State University Press; reprinted in D. Colander (ed.) (1983) *Selected Economic Writings of Abba L. Lerner*, 469–480, New York: New York University Press.

—— (1979) "The market antiinflation plan: A cure for stagflation," in J. H. Gapinski and C. E. Rockwood (eds) *Essays in Post-Keynesian Inflation*, 217–229, Cambridge, MA: Ballinger.

Levine, R. and Zervos, S. J. (1993) "What we have learned about policy and growth from cross-country regressions?," *American Economic Review*, 83 (2): 426–430.

Levy, S. J. and Levy, D. A. (1983) *Profits and the Future of American Society*, New York: Mentor.

Livet, P. and Thévenot, L. (1994) "Les catégories de l'action collective," in A. Orléan (ed.) *Analyse Economique des Conventions*, 139–167, Paris: Presses Universitaires de France.

Markham, J. W. (2002) *A Financial History of the United States*, vol. 3, Armonk: M. E. Sharpe.

Marshall, D. (2002) "Origins of the use of Treasury debt in open market operations: Lessons for the present," Federal Reserve Bank of Chicago *Economic Perspectives*, 26 (1st quarter): 45–54.

Mayer, M. (1984) *The Money Bazaars: Understanding the Banking Revolution Around Us*, New York: E.P. Dutton, Inc.

—— (2001) *The Fed: The Inside Story of How the World's Most Powerful Financial Institution Drives the Market*, New York: Free Press.

Mayer, C. P. (1988) "New issues in corporate finance," *European Economic Review*, 32 (5): 1167–1183.

McGee, R. T. (2000) "What should a central bank do?: The case of Japan," manuscript presented at the Eastern Economic Association meetings in New York City, February 24, 2001.

Meiselman, D. (1967) "Strotz and Minsky on monetary variables and aggregate demand," in G. Horwich (ed.) *Monetary Process and Policy*, 322–329, Homewood: Richard D. Irwin, Inc.

Meulendyke, A.-M. (1998) *U.S. Monetary Policy and Financial Markets*, New York: Federal Reserve Bank of New York.

Meyer, L. H. (2001) "Does money matter?," *Federal Reserve Bank of St. Louis Review*, September/October: 1–15.

—— (2004) *A Term at the Fed: An Insider's View*, New York: Harper-Collins.

Minsky, H. P. (1957a) "Central banking and money market changes," *Quarterly Journal of Economics*, 71 (2): 171–187.

—— (1957b) "Monetary systems and accelerator models," *American Economic Review*, 47 (6): 859–883.

—— (1959) "A linear model of cyclical growth," *Review of Economics and Statistics*, 41 (2), Part 1: 133–145.

—— (1962) "Financial constraints upon decisions, an aggregate view," *Proceedings of the Business and Economic Statistics Section*, 256–267, Washington, DC: American Statistical Association.

—— (1963a) "Can 'It' happen again?," in D. Carson (ed.) *Banking and Monetary Studies*, 101–111, Homewood: Richard D. Irwin; reprinted in H. P. Minsky (ed.) (1982) *Can "It" Happen Again?*, 3–13, Armonk: M. E. Sharpe.

—— (1963b) Discussion of "Financial institutions and monetary policy," *American Economic Review*, 53 (2): 411–412.

—— (1964a) "Financial crisis, financial systems and the performance of the economy," in Commission on Money and Credit (ed.) *Private Capital Markets*, 173–380, Englewood Cliffs: Prentice-Hall.

—— (1964b) "Longer waves in financial relations: Financial factors in the more severe depressions," *American Economic Review*, 54 (3): 324–335.

—— (1965a) "The integration of simple growth and cycle models," in M. J. Brennan (ed.) *Patterns of Market Behavior*, 175–192, New England: University Press of New England; reprinted in H. P. Minsky (ed.) (1982) *Can "It" Happen Again?*, 258–277, Armonk: M. E. Sharpe.

—— (1965b) "The role of employment policy," in M. S. Gordon (ed.) *Poverty in America*, 175–200, San Francisco: Chandler Publishing Company.

—— (1965c) "Poverty: The 'Aggregate Demand' solution and other non-welfare approaches," report MR-41, Institute of Government and Public Affairs, Los Angeles: University of California.

—— (1966) "Tight full employment: Let's heat up the economy," in H. P. Miller (ed.) *Poverty: American Style*, 294–300, Belmont: Wadsworth Publishing Company.

—— (1967a) "Money, other financial variables, and aggregate demand in the short run," in G. Horwich (ed.) *Monetary Process and Policy*, 265–294, Homewood: Richard D. Irwin.

—— (1967b) "Financial intermediation in the money and capital markets," in G. Pontecorvo, R. P. Shay and A. G. Hart (eds) *Issues in Banking and Monetary Analysis*, 31–56, New York: Holt, Rinehart and Winston, Inc.

—— (1969a) "Private sector asset management and the effectiveness of monetary policy: Theory and practice," *Journal of Finance*, 24 (2): 223–238.

—— (1969b) "The new uses of monetary powers," *Nebraska Journal of Economics and Business*, 8 (2): 3–15; reprinted in H. P. Minsky (ed.) (1982) *Can "It" Happen Again?*, 179–191, Armonk: M. E. Sharpe.

—— (1969c) Discussion of "Financial model building and Federal Reserve policy," *Journal of Finance*, 24 (2): 295–297.

—— (1971) "Notes on user cost," mimeograph.

—— (1972a) "An exposition of a Keynesian theory of investment," in G. P. Szegö and K. Shell (eds) *Mathematical Methods in Investment and Finance*, 207–233, Amsterdam: North-Holland; reprinted in H. P. Minsky (ed.) (1982) *Can "It" Happen Again?*, 203–230, Armonk: M. E. Sharpe.

—— (1972b) "Financial instability revisited: The economics of disaster," in Board of Governors of the Federal Reserve System (ed.) *Reappraisal of the Federal Reserve Discount Mechanism*, vol. 3, 95–136, Washington, DC: Board of Governors of the Federal Reserve System.

—— (1972c) "An evaluation of recent monetary policy," *Nebraska Journal of Economics and Business*, 11 (4): 37–56.

—— (1973) "The strategy of economic policy and income distribution," in S. Weintraub (special ed.) *The Annals: Income Inequality*, 92–101, Philadelphia: American Academy of Political and Social Science.

—— (1974) "The modeling of financial instability: An introduction," *Modeling and Simulation*, 5, Part 1: 267–272; reprinted in Committee on Banking, Housing, and Urban Affairs (ed.) (1975) *Compendium of Major Issues in Bank Regulation*, 354–364, Washington, DC: U.S. Government Printing Office.

—— (1975a) *John Maynard Keynes*, Cambridge: Cambridge University Press.

—— (1975b) "Financial instability, the current dilemma, and the structure of banking and finance," in Committee on Banking, Housing, and Urban Affairs (ed.) *Compendium of Major Issues in Bank Regulation*, 310–353, Washington, DC: U.S. Government Printing Office.

—— (1975c) "Suggestions for a cash flow-oriented bank examination," in Federal Reserve Bank of Chicago (ed.) *Proceedings of a Conference on Bank Structure and Competition*, 150–184, Chicago: Federal Reserve Bank of Chicago.

—— (1975d) "Financial resources in a fragile financial environment," *Challenge*, 18 (3): 6–13.

—— (1977a) "Banking and a fragile financial environment," *Journal of Portfolio Management*, Summer: 16–22.

—— (1977b) "The financial instability hypothesis: An interpretation of Keynes and an alternative to 'standard' theory," *Nebraska Journal of Economics and Business*, 16 (1): 5–16; reprinted in *Challenge* 20 (1), March–April 1977: 20–27, and in H. P. Minsky (ed.) (1982) *Can "It" Happen Again?*, 59–70, Armonk: M. E. Sharpe.

—— (1977c) "A theory of systemic fragility," in E. I. Altman and A. W. Sametz (eds) *Financial Crises*, 138–152, New York: Wiley.

—— (1978) "The financial instability hypothesis: A restatement," *Thames Papers in Political Economy*, Autumn; reprinted in P. Arestis and T. Skouras (eds) (1985) *Post Keynesian Economic Theory*, 24–55, Armonk: M. E. Sharpe.

—— (1979) "Financial interrelations and the balance of payments, and the dollar crisis," in J. D. Aronson (ed.) *Debt and the Less Developed Countries*, 103–122, Boulder: Westview Press.

—— (1980a) "Finance and profit: The changing nature of American business cycles," in Joint Economic Committee (ed.) *The Business Cycle and Public Policy, 1929–1980*, Washington, DC: U.S. Government Printing Office; reprinted in H. P. Minsky (ed.) (1982) *Can "It" Happen Again?*, 14–58, Armonk: M. E. Sharpe.

—— (1980b) "Capitalist financial processes and the instability of capitalism," *Journal of Economic Issues*, 14 (2): 505–523.

—— (1981) "Financial markets and economic instability, 1965–1980," *Nebraska Journal of Economics and Business*, 20 (4): 5–16.

—— (1982a) "The financial-instability hypothesis: Capitalist processes and the behavior of the economy," in C. P. Kindleberger and J.-P. Lafargue (eds) *Financial Crises: Theory, History, and Policy*, 13–39, New York: Cambridge University Press.

—— (1982b) "Can 'It' happen again? A reprise," *Challenge*, 25 (3): 5–13.

—— (1982c) "Debt deflation processes in today's institutional environment," *Banca Nazionale Del Lavoro Quarterly Review*, 35 (143): 375–393.

—— (1983a) "Institutional roots of American inflation," in N. Schmukler and E. Marcus (eds) *Inflation Through the Ages: Economic, Social, Psychological and Historical Aspects*, 265–277, New York: Brooklyn College Press.

—— (1983b) "Pitfalls due to financial fragility," in S. Weintraub and M. Goodstein (eds) *Reaganomics in the Stagflation Economy*, 104–119, Philadelphia: University of Pennsylvania Press.

—— (1984a) "Financial innovations and financial instability: Observations and theory," in Federal Reserve Bank of St. Louis (ed.) *Financial Innovations*, 21–45, Boston: Kluwer-Nijhoff.

—— (1984b) "Banking and industry between the two wars: The United States," *Journal of European Economic History*, 13 (Special Issue): 235–272.

—— (1985a) "Money and the lender of last resort," *Challenge*, 28 (1): 12–18.

—— (1985b) "An introduction to Post-Keynesian economics," *Economic Forum*, 15 (2): 1–13.

—— (1986a) *Stabilizing an Unstable Economy*, New Haven: Yale University Press.

—— (1986b) "Global consequences of financial deregulation," *Marcus Wallenberg Papers on International Finance*, 2 (1): 1–19.

—— (1986c) "The evolution of the financial institutions and the performance of the economy," *Journal of Economic Issues*, 20 (2): 345–353.

—— (1989a) "Financial crises and the evolution of capitalism: The crash of '87—what does it mean?," in M. Gottdiener and N. Komninos (eds) *Capitalist Development and Crisis Theory: Accumulation, Regulation and Spatial Restructuring*, 391–403, New York: St Martin's Press.

—— (1989b) "The macroeconomic safety net: Does it need to be improved?," in H. P. Gray (ed.) *Research in International Business and Finance*, vol. 7, 17–27, Greenwich: JAI Press.

—— (1989c) Comments on "Economic implications of the extraordinary movements in stock prices," *Brookings Papers on Economic Activity*, 1989 (2): 173–182.

—— (1989d) "Financial structures: Indebtedness and credit," in A. Barrère (ed.) *Money, Credit and Prices in Keynesian Perspective*, 49–70, New York: St. Martin's Press.

—— (1990a) "Sraffa and Keynes: Effective demand in the long run," in K. Bharadwaj and B. Schefold (eds) *Essays on Piero Sraffa: Critical Perspectives on the Revival of Classical Theory*, 362–369, London: Unwin Hyman.

—— (1990b) "Money manager capitalism, fiscal independence and international monetary reconstruction," in M. Szabó-Pelsőczi (ed.) *The Future of The Global Economic and Monetary System*, 209–218, Budapest: Institute for World Economics of the Hungarian Academy of Sciences.

—— (1990c) "Debt and business cycles," *Business Economics*, 25 (3): 23–28.

—— (1990d) "Schumpeter: Finance and evolution," in A. Heertje and M. Perlman (eds) *Evolving Technology and Market Structure: Studies in Schumpeterian Economics*, 51–74, Ann Arbor: University of Michigan Press.

—— (1991a) "The endogeneity of money," in E. J. Nell and W. Semmler (eds) *Nicholas Kaldor and Mainstream Economics*, 207–220, New York: St. Martin's Press.

—— (1991b) "The instability hypothesis: A clarification," in M. Feldstein (ed.) *The Risk of Economic Crisis*, 158–166, Chicago: University of Chicago Press.

—— (1991c) "Financial crises: Systemic or idiosyncratic," Levy Economics Institute, Working Paper No. 51.

—— (1992) "The capital development of the economy and the structure of financial institutions," Levy Economics Institute, Working Paper No. 72.

—— (1993a) "Schumpeter and finance," in S. Biasco, A. Roncaglia and M. Salvati (eds) *Market and Institutions in Economic Development*, 103–115, New York: St. Martin's Press.

—— (1993b) "On the non-neutrality of money," Federal Reserve Bank of New York *Quarterly Review*, 18 (1): 77–82.

—— (1994) "Financial instability and the decline (?) of banking: Public policy implications," Levy Economics Institute, Working Paper No. 127.

—— (1995) "Financial factors in the economics of capitalism," *Journal of Financial Services Research*, 9 (3–4): 197–208; reprinted in H. A. Benink (ed.) (1995) *Coping with Financial Fragility and Systemic Risk*, 3–14, Boston: Ernst and Young.

—— (1996) "The essential characteristics of Post Keynesian economics," in G. Deleplace and E. J. Nell (ed.) *Money in Motion: The Post Keynesian and Circulation Approaches*, 70–88, New York: St. Martin's Press.

Mishkin, F. S. (1988) Commentary on "Causes of changing financial market volatility," in Federal Reserve Bank of Kansas City (ed.) *Financial Market Volatility*, 23–32, Kansas City: Federal Reserve Bank of Kansas City.

—— (1991) "Asymmetric information and financial crises: A historical perspective," in R. G. Hubbard (ed.) *Financial Markets and Financial Crises*, 69–108, Chicago: University of Chicago Press.

—— (1997) "The causes and propagation of financial instability: Lessons for policymakers," in Federal Reserve Bank of Kansas City (ed.) *Maintaining Financial Stability in a Global Economy*, 55–96, Kansas City: Federal Reserve Bank of Kansas City.

Mishkin, F. S. and White, E. N. (2003a) "Stock market bubbles: When does intervention work?," *Milken Institute Review*, 2nd quarter: 44–52.

—— (2003b) "U.S. stock market crashes and their aftermath: Implications for monetary policy," in W. C. Hunter, G. G. Kaufman and M. Pomerleano (eds) *Asset Price Bubbles: The Implications for Monetary Regulatory and International Policies*, 53–79, Cambridge, MA: MIT Press.

Mitchell, W. F. (1998) "The buffer stock employment model and the NAIRU: The path to full employment," *Journal of Economic Issues*, 32 (2): 547–555.

Mitchell, W. F. and Watts, M. J. (2004) "Restoring full employment: The job guarantee," in E. Carlson and W. F. Mitchell (eds) *The Urgency of Full Employment*, 94–114, Sydney: University of New South Wales Press.

Moore, B. J. (1988) *Horizontalists and Verticalists: The Macroeconomics of Credit Money*, Cambridge: Cambridge University Press.

—— (1989) "The effects of monetary policy on income distribution," in P. Davidson and J. A. Kregel (eds) *Macroeconomic Problems and Policies of Income Distribution: Functional, Personal, International*, 18–41, Aldershot: Edward Elgar.

—— (1991) "Contemporaneous reserve accounting: Can reserves be quantity-constrained?," *Journal of Post Keynesian Economics*, 7 (1): 103–113.

—— (1996) "The money supply process: A historical reinterpretation," in G. Deleplace and E. J. Nell (eds) *Money in Motion: The Post Keynesian and Circulation Approaches*, 89–101, London: Macmillan.

Morgenson, G. (2008a) "Arcane market is next to face big credit test," *New York Times*, February 17, 2008.

—— (2008b) "A road not taken by lenders," *New York Times*, April 6, 2008.

Mosler, W. B. and Forstater, M. (2004) "The natural rate of interest is zero," Center for Full Employment and Price Stability, Working Paper No. 37.

Mulford, E. E. and Comiskey, C. W. (2002) *The Financial Numbers Game: Detecting Creative Accounting Practices*, New York: Wiley.

Mullineux, A. W. (1990) *Business Cycles and Financial Crises*, Ann Arbor: University of Michigan Press.

Mundell, R. (1963) "Inflation and real interest," *Journal of Political Economy*, 71 (3): 280–283.

Mussa, M. (2003) "Asset prices and monetary policy," in W. C. Hunter, G. G. Kaufman and M. Pomerleano (eds) *Asset Price Bubbles: The Implications for Monetary Regulatory and International Policies*, 41–50, Cambridge, MA: MIT Press.

Nelson, W. and Passmore, W. (2001) "Pragmatic monitoring of financial stability," paper presented at BIS conference *Marrying the macro- and micro-prudential dimensions of financial stability*, March 2001.

Niggle, C. J. (1989a) "Monetary policy and changes in income distribution," *Journal of Economic Issues*, 23 (3): 809–822.

—— (1989b) "The cyclical behavior of corporate financial ratios and Minsky's financial instability hypothesis," in W. Semmler (ed.) *Financial Dynamics and Business Cycles*, 203–220, New York: M. E. Sharpe.

Norris, F. (2007) "Market shock: AAA rating may be junk," *New York Times*, July 20, 2007.

Orléan, A. (1999) *Le Pouvoir de la Finance*, Paris: Odile Jacob.

Orphanides, A. (2004) "Monetary policy rules, macroeconomic stability, and inflation: A view from the trenches," *Journal of Money, Credit, and Banking*, 36 (2): 151–175.

Orphanides, A. and Williams, J. C. (2002) "Robust monetary policy rules with unknown natural rates," *Brookings Papers on Economic Activity*, 2002 (2): 63–118.

Palacio-Vera, A. (2005) "The 'modern' view of macroeconomics: Some critical reflections," *Cambridge Journal of Economics*, 29 (5): 747–767.

Palley, T. I. (1994) "Debt, aggregate demand, and the business cycle: An analysis in the spirit of Kaldor and Minsky," *Journal of Post Keynesian Economics*, 16 (3): 371–390.

—— (1995) "Safety in numbers: A model of managerial herd behavior," *Journal Economics Behavior and Organization*, 28 (3): 443–450.

—— (2000) "Stabilizing finance: The case for asset-based reserve requirements," report in the Financial Markets and Society series issued by the Financial Markets Center, August 2000, Philomont, VA.

—— (2002) "Endogenous money: What it is and why it matters," *Metroeconomica*, 53 (2): 152–180.

—— (2004) "Asset–based reserve requirements: Reasserting domestic monetary control in an era of financial innovation and instability," *Review of Political Economy*, 16 (1): 43–58.

—— (2006) "A Post-Keynesian framework for monetary policy: Why interest rate operating procedures are not enough," in C. Gnos and L.-P. Rochon (eds) *Post-Keynesian Principles of Economic Policy*, 78–98, Northampton: Edward Elgar.

—— (2007) "Macroeconomics and monetary policy: Competing theoretical frameworks," *Journal of Post Keynesian Economics*, 30 (1): 61–78.

Palma, G. (1994) "Kahn on buffer stocks," *Cambridge Journal of Economics*, 18 (1): 117–127.

Papadimitriou, D. B. and Wray, L. R. (1994) "Monetary policy uncovered: Flying blind, the Federal Reserve experiment with unobservables," Levy Economics Institute, Public Policy Brief No. 15/1994.

—— (1996) "Targeting inflation: The effects of monetary policy on the CPI and its housing component," Levy Economics Institute, Public Policy Brief No. 27/1996.

—— (1997) "The institutional prerequisites for successful capitalism," *Journal of Economic Issues*, 31 (2): 493–500.

Parguez, A. (1984) "La dynamique de la monnaie," *Economies et Sociétés*, 18 (4), MP 1: 83–118.

—— (2003) "The pervasive saving constraint in Minsky's theory of crisis and the dual profits hypothesis: Minsky as a Post Keynesian Hayekian," in L.-P. Rochon and S. Rossi (eds) *Modern Theories of Money*, 475–505, Cheltenham: Edward Elgar.

Pasinetti, L. (1981) *Structural Change and Economic Growth: A Theoretical Essay on the Dynamics of the Wealth of the Nations*, Cambridge: Cambridge University Press.

Patsuris, P. (2002) "The corporate scandal sheet," *Forbes*, August 26, 2002.

Pearlstein, S. (2007) "'No Money Down' falls flat," *Washington Post*, March 14, 2007, page D01.

Phillips, R. J. (1997) "Rethinking bank examinations: A Minsky approach," *Journal of Economic Issues*, 31 (2): 509–516.

Pigeon, M.-A. (2004) "Interest rate policy at the Bank of Canada: Setting the agenda," in M. Lavoie and M. Seccareccia (eds) *Central Banking in the Modern World: Alternative Perspectives*, 112–126, Northampton: Edward Elgar.

Pollin, R. and Dymski, G. A. (1994) "The costs and benefits of financial instability: Big government capitalism and the Minsky paradox," in G. A. Dymski and R. Pollin (eds) *New Perspectives in Monetary Macroeconomics: Explorations in the Tradition of Hyman P. Minsky*, 369–401, Ann Arbor: University of Michigan Press.

Posen, A. (2006) "Why central banks should not burst bubbles," *International Finance*, 9 (1): 109–124.

Pressman, S. (1996) "What do capital markets really do?: and what should we do about capital markets?," *Economies et Sociétés*, 30 (2–3), MP 10: 193–209.

Raines, J. P. and Leathers, C. G. (2000) *Economists and the Stock Market: Speculative Theories of Stock Market Fluctuations*, Northampton: Edward Elgar.

Rambaldi, A. N. (1997) "Multiple time series models and testing for causality and exogeneity: A review," University of New England, Department of Econometrics, Working Paper No. 96.

Ricardo, D. (1820) *Notes on Malthus's "Principles of Political Economy"*, in P. Sraffa (ed.) (1951) *The Works and Correspondence of David Ricardo*, vol. 2, Cambridge: Cambridge University Press.

Roberston, D. H. (1940) "Mr. Keynes and the rate of interest," in D. H. Roberston (ed.) *Essays in Monetary Theory*, 1–38, London: Staples Press.

Robinson, J. V. (1943) "Planning full employment," reprinted in J. V. Robinson (ed.) (1966) *Collected Economic Papers*, vol. 1, 81–88, Oxford: Basil Blackwell.

—— (1945) "Obstacles to full employment," reprinted in J. V. Robinson (ed.) (1966) *Collected Economic Papers*, vol. 1, 105–114, Oxford: Basil Blackwell.

—— (1951) "The rate of interest," *Econometrica*, 19 (2): 92–111.

Rochon, L.-P. (1999) *Credit, Money and Production: An Alternative Post-Keynesian Approach*, Northampton: Edward Elgar.

—— (2003a) "On money and endogenous money: Post Keynesian and Circulation approaches," in L.-P. Rochon and S. Rossi (eds) *Modern Theories of Money*, 115–141, Cheltenham: Edward Elgar.

—— (2003b) "Financial instability hypothesis," in J. E. King (ed.) *The Elgar Companion to Post Keynesian Economics*, 145–149, Northampton: Edward Elgar.

Rochon, L.-P. and Setterfield, M. (2007a) "Post Keynesian interest rate rules and macroeconomic performance: A comparative evaluation," paper presented at the Eastern Economic Association meetings, February 23–25, 2007.

—— (2007b) "Interest rates, income distribution, and monetary policy dominance: Post Keynesians and the 'fair rate' of interest," *Journal of Post Keynesian Economics*, 30 (1): 13–42.

Rogers, C. (1989) *Money, Interest and Capital: A Study in the Foundations of Monetary Theory*, Cambridge: Cambridge University Press.

Roley, V. V. and Sellon, G. H., Jr. (1995) "Monetary policy actions and long-term interest rates," Federal Reserve Bank of Kansas City *Economic Review*, 4th quarter: 73–89.

Rottenstreich, Y. and Tversky, A. (1997) "Unpacking, repacking, and anchoring: Advances in support theory," *Psychological Review*, 104 (2): 406–415.

Roubini, N. (2006) "Why central banks should burst bubbles," *International Finance*, 9 (1): 87–107.

Rousseas, S. (1994) "The spheres of industrial and financial circulation revisited," *Economies et Sociétés*, 28 (1–2), MP 9: 315–328; reprinted in G. Deleplace and E. J. Nell (eds) (1996) *Money in Motion: The Post Keynesian and Circulation Approaches*, 672–683, London: Macmillan.

Rowthorn, R. E. (1977) "Conflict, inflation and money," *Cambridge Journal of Economics*, 1 (3): 215–239.

Runde, J. (1995) "Risk, uncertainty and Bayesian decision theory: A Keynesian view," in S. C. Dow and J. Hillard (eds) *Keynes, Knowledge, and Uncertainty*, 197–210, Aldershot: Edward Elgar.

Sahel, B. and Vesala, J. (2001) "Financial stability analysis using aggregated data," paper presented at BIS conference *Marrying the macro- and micro-prudential dimensions of financial stability*, March 2001.

Sargent, T. J. (1972) "Anticipated inflation and the nominal rate of interest," *Quarterly Journal of Economics*, 86 (2): 212–225.

—— (1976) "Interest rates and expected inflation: A selective summary of recent research," *Explorations in Economic Research*, 3 (3): 303–325.

Sawyer, M. C. (1985a) *The Economics of Michal Kalecki*, Armonk: M. E. Sharpe.

—— (1985b) "On the nature of the Phillips curve," *British Review of Economic Issues*, 7 (16): 63–86.

—— (1999) "The NAIRU: A critical appraisal," in P. Arestis and M. Sawyer (eds) *Money, Finance and Capitalist Development*, 220–254, Northampton: Edward Elgar.

—— (2002) "Economic policy with endogenous money," in P. Arestis, M. Desai and S. C. Dow (eds) *Money, Macroeconomics, and Keynes*, 35–44, London: Routledge.

Schinasi, G. J. (1994) "Asset prices, monetary policy and the business cycle," International Monetary Fund, Papers on Policy Analysis and Assessment No. 94/6.

—— (2006) *Safeguarding Financial Stability: Theory and Practice*, Washington, DC: International Monetary Fund.

Schwartz, A. J. (1988) "Financial stability and the federal safety net," in W. S. Haraf and R. M. Kushmeider (eds) *Restructuring Banking and Financial Services in America*, 34–62, Washington, DC: American Enterprise Institute for Public Policy and Research.

—— (1998) "Why financial stability depends on price stability," in G. Wood (ed.) *Money, Prices and the Real Economy*, 34–41, Northampton: Edward Elgar.

—— (2003) "Asset price inflation and monetary policy," *Atlantic Economic Journal*, 31 (1): 1–14.

Seccareccia, M. (1998) "Wicksellian norm, central bank real interest rate targeting and macroeconomic performance," in P. Arestis and M. C. Sawyer (eds) *The Political Economy of Central Banking*, 180–198, Northampton: Edward Elgar.

Seccareccia, M. and Lavoie, M. (1989) "Les idées révolutionnaires de Keynes en politique économique et le déclin du capitalisme rentier," *Economie Appliquée*, 42 (1): 47–70.

Setterfield, M. (2004a) "Central banking, stability and macroeconomic outcomes: A comparison of New Consensus and Post-Keynesian monetary macroeconomics," in M. Lavoie and M. Seccareccia (eds) *Central Banking in the Modern World: Alternative Perspectives*, 35–56, Northampton: Edward Elgar.

—— (2004b) "Financial fragility, effective demand and the business cycle," *Review of Political Economy*, 16 (2): 207–223.

—— (2006) "Is inflation targeting compatible with Post Keynesian economics?," *Journal of Post Keynesian Economics*, 28 (4): 653–671.

Setterfield, M., Gordon, D. V. and Osberg, L. (1992) "Searching for a will o' the wisp: An empirical study of the NAIRU in Canada," *European Economic Review*, 36 (1): 119–136.

Shackle, G. L. S. (1955) *Uncertainty in Economics and Other Reflections*, Cambridge: Cambridge University Press.

—— (1974) *Keynesian Kaleidics: The Evolution of a General Political Economy*, Edinburgh: Edinburgh University Press.

Shell, K. and Stiglitz, J. E. (1967) "The allocation of investment in a dynamic economy," *Quarterly Journal of Economics*, 81 (4): 592–609.

Shiller, R. J. (1981) "Do stock prices move too much to be justified by subsequent changes in dividends?," *American Economic Review*, 71 (3): 421–436.

—— (1995) "Conversation, information, and herd behavior," *American Economic Review*, 85 (2): 181–185.

—— (1999) "Human behavior and the efficiency of the financial system," in J. B. Taylor and M. Woodford (eds) *Handbook of Macroeconomics*, vol. 1c, 1305–1340, Amsterdam: North-Holland.

—— (2000) *Irrational Exuberance*, Princeton: Princeton University Press.

Shiratsuka, S. (1999) "Asset price fluctuation and price indices," Bank of Japan *Monetary and Economic Studies*, 17 (3): 103–128.

Shull, B. (1993) "The limits of prudential supervision: Reorganizing the federal bank regulatory agencies," Levy Economics Institute, Public Policy Brief No. 5/1993.

Simon, H. A. (1955) "A behavioral model of rational choice," *Quarterly Journal of Economics*, 69 (1): 99–118.

Sims, C. A., Stock, J. H. and Watson, M. W. (1990) "Inference in linear time series models with some unit roots," *Econometrica*, 58 (1): 113–144.

Sinai, A. (1976) "Credit crunches—an analysis of the postwar experience," in O. Eckstein (ed.) *Parameters and Policies in the U.S. Economy*, 244–274, Amsterdam: North-Holland Publishing Co.

Sinai, A. and Brinner, R. E. (1975) *The Capital Shortage: New Term Outlook on Long-Term Prospects*, Lexington: Data Resources, Inc.

Siscú, J. (2001) "Credible monetary policy: A Post Keynesian approach," *Journal of Post Keynesian Economics*, 23 (4): 669–687.

Small, D. H. and Clouse, J. A. (2005) "The scope of monetary policy actions authorized under the Federal Reserve Act," *B.E. Journal of Macroeconomics*, 5 (1): 1–41.

Smets, F. (1997) "Financial-asset prices and monetary policy: Theory and evidence," in P. Lowe (ed.) *Monetary Policy and Inflation Targeting*, 212–237, Sydney: Reserve Bank of Australia.

Smithin, J. (2003) *Controversies in Monetary Economics*, Northampton: Edward Elgar.

—— (2004) "Interest rate operating procedures and income distribution," in M. Lavoie and M. Seccareccia (eds) *Central Banking in the Modern World: Alternative Perspectives*, 57–69, Northampton: Edward Elgar.

—— (2006) "The theory of interest rates," in P. Arestis and M. C. Sawyer (eds) *A Handbook of Alternative Monetary Economics*, 273–290, Northampton: Edward Elgar.

—— (2007) "A real interest rate rule for monetary policy," *Journal of Post Keynesian Economics*, 30 (1): 101–118.

Spaventa, L. (1998) Discussion in Centre for Economic Policy Research (ed.) *Asset Prices and Monetary Policy: Four Views*, 23–27, London: Centre for Economic Policy Research.

Spotton, B. (1997) "Financial instability reconsidered: Orthodox theories versus historical facts," *Journal of Economic Issues*, 31 (1): 175–195.

Stanfield, J. R. and Phillips, R. J. (1991) "Economic power, financial instability, and the Cuomo report," *Journal of Economic Issues*, 25 (2): 347–354.

Stanners, W. (1993) "Is low inflation an important condition for high growth?," *Cambridge Journal of Economics*, 17 (1): 79–107.

Steindl, J. (1952) *Maturity and Stagnation in American Capitalism*, New York: Monthly Review Press.

Sterman, J. D. (2000) *Business Dynamics: Systems Thinking and Modeling for a Complex World*, Boston: McGraw-Hill.

Stock, J. H. and Watson, M. W. (2003) "Forecasting output and inflation: The role of asset prices," *Journal of Economic Literature*, 41 (3): 788–829.

Suarez, J. and Sussman, O. (1997) "Endogenous cycles in a Stiglitz-Weiss economy," *Journal of Economic Theory*, 76 (1): 47–71.

—— (1999) "Financial distress and the business cycle," *Oxford Review of Economic Policy*, 15 (3): 39–51.

—— (2007) "Financial distress, bankruptcy law and the business cycle," *Annals of Finance*, 3 (1): 5–35.

Summers, L. H. (1983) "The nonadjustment of nominal interest rates: A study of the Fisher effect," in J. Tobin (ed.) *Macroeconomics, Prices, and Quantities: Essays in Memory of Arthur M. Okun*, 201–241, Washington, DC: The Brooking Institution.

Svensson, L. E. O. (2003) "What is wrong with Taylor rules? Using judgment in monetary policy through targeting rules," *Journal of Economic Literature*, 41 (2): 426–477.

Tauheed, L. and Wray, L. R. (2006) "System dynamics of interest rate effects on aggregate demand," in L. R. Wray and M. Forstater (eds) *Money, Financial Instability, and Stabilization Policy*, 37–57, Cheltenham: Edward Elgar.

Taylor, L. and O'Connell, S. (1985) "A Minsky crisis," *Quarterly Journal of Economics*, 100 (Supplement): 871–885; reprinted in W. Semmler (ed.) (1989) *Financial Dynamics and Business Cycles*, 3–17, Armonk: M. E. Sharpe.

Thompson, J. R., Williams, E. E. and Findlay, M. C. (2003) *Models for Investors in Real World Markets*, Hoboken: Wiley.

Tillmann, P. (2007) "Do interest rates drive inflation dynamics? An analysis of the cost channel of monetary transmission," forthcoming in the *Journal of Economic Dynamics and Control*.

Tirole, J. (1982) "On the possibility of speculation under rational expectations," *Econometrica*, 50 (5): 1163–1182.

—— (1985) "Asset bubbles and overlapping generations," *Econometrica*, 53 (6): 1499–1528.

Tobin, J. (1958) "Liquidity preference as behavior towards risk," *Review of Economic Studies*, 25 (2): 65–86.

—— (1965) "Money and economic growth," *Econometrica*, 33 (4): 671–684.

Toporowski, J. (1999) "Monetary policy in an era of capital market inflation," Levy Economics Institute, Working Paper No. 279.

—— (2000) *The End of Finance: The Theory of Capital Market Inflation, Financial Derivatives and Pension Fund Capitalism*, London: Routledge.

—— (2002) "Keynes and monetary policy in speculative markets," *Investigación Económica*, 42 (242): 13–32.

Townshend, H. (1937) "Liquidity-premium and the theory of value," *Economic Journal*, 47 (185): 157–169.

Trichet, J.-C. (2003) "Asset price bubbles and their implications for monetary policy and financial stability," in W. C. Hunter, G. G. Kaufman and M. Pomerleano (eds) *Asset Price Bubbles: The Implications for Monetary Regulatory and International Policies*, 15–22, Cambridge, MA: MIT Press.

—— (2005) "Asset price bubbles and monetary policy," speech at the Mas lecture, Monetary Authority of Singapore, Singapore, June 8, 2005.

Tversky, A. and Kahneman, D. (1974) "Judgment under uncertainty: Heuristics and biases," *Science*, 185 (27 September): 1124–1131.

—— (1983) "Extensional versus intuitive reasoning: The conjunction fallacy in probability judgment," *Psychological Review*, 90 (4): 293–315.

Tversky, A. and Koehler, D. (1994) "Support theory: A nonextensional representation of subjective probability," *Psychological Review,* 101 (4): 547–567.

Tymoigne, E. (2003) "A note on finance: Linking Post Keynesian and Circuitist approaches," mimeograph.

—— (2007a) "A hard-nosed look at worsening U.S. household finance," *Challenge*, 50 (4): 88–111.

—— (2007b) "An inquiry into the nature of money: An alternative to the functional approach," mimeograph.

Valcourt, J. (2007) "Chrysler faces financial pinch, sees asset sales," *Wall Street Journal*, December 21, 2007, page A10.

Veblen, T. B. (1898) "Why is economics not an evolutionary science?," *Quarterly Journal of Economics*, 12 (4): 373–397.

—— (1899) *The Theory of the Leisure Class: An Economic Study of Institutions*, New York: Macmillan.

—— (1901) "Industrial and pecuniary employments," *Publications of the American Economic Association*, 3rd Series, 2 (1): 190–235.

—— (1904) *The Theory of Business Enterprise*, New York: Charles Scribner's Sons.

—— (1908) "Fisher's capital and income," *Political Science Quarterly*, 23 (1): 112–128.

—— (1909) "Fisher's rate of interest," *Political Science Quarterly*, 24 (2): 296–303.

Vercelli, A. (2001) "Minsky, Keynes and the structural instability of a sophisticated monetary economy," in R. Bellofiore and P. Ferri (eds) *Financial Fragility and Investment in the Capitalist Economy*, vol. 2, 33–52, Cheltenham: Edward Elgar.

Walsh, C. E. (2002) "Teaching inflation targeting: An analysis for Intermediate Macro," *Journal of Economic Education*, 33 (4): 333–346.

Wärneryd, K.-E. (2001) *Stock-Market Psychology: How People Value and Trade Stocks*, Northampton: Edward Elgar.

Watterson, P. N. Jr. (2005) "The evolution of the CDO squared," *Journal of Structured Finance*, 11 (1): 6–12.

Weber, A. A. (2006) "The role of interest rates in theory and practice—how useful is the concept of the natural real rate of interest for monetary policy?," paper presented at the G.L.S. Shackle Biennial Memorial Lecture 2006, St. Edmund's College, Cambridge, 9 March 2006.

Weber, A. A., Lemke, W. and Worms, A. (2008) "How useful is the concept of the natural real rate of interest for monetary policy?," *Cambridge Journal of Economics*, 32 (1): 49–63.

Weintraub, S. (1969) "A macro theory of pricing, income distribution and employment," reprinted in S. Weintraub (ed.) (1978) *Keynes, Keynesians and Monetarists*, 196–214, Philadelphia: University of Pennsylvania Press.

—— (1978) *Capitalism's Inflation and Unemployment Crisis*, Reading: Addison-Wesley.

—— (1979) "A TIP for MAP," in J. H. Gapinski and C. E. Rockwood (eds) *Essays in Post-Keynesian Inflation*, 231–247, Cambridge, MA: Ballinger.

Welch, I. (1992) "Sequential sales, learning, and cascades," *Journal of Finance*, 57 (2): 695–732.

Whalen, C. J. (1997) "Money-manager capitalism and the end of shared prosperity," *Journal of Economic Issues*, 31 (2): 517–525.

—— (2008) "Understanding the credit crunch as a Minsky moment," *Challenge*, 51 (1): 91–109.

Wojnilower, A. M. (1977) "L'envoi," in E. I. Altman and A. W. Sametz (eds) *Financial Crises: Institutions and Markets in a Fragile Environment*, 234–237, New York: Wiley.

—— (1980) "The central role of credit crunches in recent financial history," *Brookings Papers on Economic Activity*, 1980 (2): 277–339.

—— (1991) "Some principles of financial regulation: Lessons from the United States," in I. Macfarlane (ed.) *The Deregulation of Financial Intermediaries*, 203–216, Sydney: Reserve Bank of Australia.

—— (2005) "Why monetary policy?," manuscript prepared for the 15th Hyman Minsky Conference at the Levy Economics Institute, April 21, 2008.

Wolfson, M. H. (1994) *Financial Crises*, 2nd edn, Armonk: M. E. Sharpe.

—— (1996) "A Post Keynesian theory of credit rationing," *Journal of Post Keynesian Economics*, 18 (3): 443–470.

Wray, L. R. (1990) *Money and Credit in Capitalist Economies: The Endogenous Money Approach*, Aldershot: Edward Elgar.

—— (1991a) "Savings, profits, and speculation in capitalist economies," *Journal of Economic Issues*, 25 (4): 951–975.

—— (1991b) "Endogenous money and a liquidity preference theory of asset prices," *Review of Radical Political Economics*, 23 (1–2): 118–125.

—— (1991c) "The inconsistency of Monetarist theory and policy," *Economies et Sociétés*, 25 (11–12), MP 8: 259–276.

—— (1992a) "Commercial banks, the central bank, and endogenous money," *Journal of Post Keynesian Economics*, 14 (3): 297–310.

—— (1992b) "Alternative theories of the rate of interest," *Cambridge Journal of Economics*, 16 (1): 69–89.

—— (1992c) "Alternative approaches to money and interest rates," *Journal of Economic Issues*, 26 (4): 1145–1178.

—— (1992d) "Minsky's financial instability hypothesis and the endogeneity of money," in S. Fazzari and D. B. Papadimitriou (eds) *Financial Conditions and Macroeconomic Performance*, 161–180, Armonk: M. E. Sharpe.

—— (1993) "Money, interest rates, and Monetarist policy: Some more unpleasant Monetarist arithmetic?," *Journal of Post Keynesian Economics*, 15 (4): 541–569.

—— (1994) "Is Keynesian policy dead after all these years?," *Journal of Post Keynesian Economics*, 17 (2): 285–306.

—— (1995) "If free markets cannot 'efficiently allocate credit', what monetary policy could move us closer to full employment?," *Review of Political Economy*, 7 (2): 186–211.

—— (1996a) "Flying swine: Appropriate targets and goals of monetary policy," *Journal of Economic Issues*, 30 (2): 545–552.

—— (1996b) "Monetary theory and policy for the twenty-first century," in C. Whalen (ed.) *Political Economy for the 21st Century*, 125–148, Armonk: M. E. Sharpe.

—— (1996c) "Government deficits and appropriate monetary policy," *Economies et Sociétés*, 30 (2–3), MP 10: 269–300.

—— (1996d) "The 1966 financial crisis: Financial instability or political economy?," *Review of Political Economy*, 11 (4): 415–425.

—— (1997a) "Deficits, inflation, and monetary policy," *Journal of Post Keynesian Economics*, 19 (4): 543–571.

—— (1997b) "Flying blind: Recent Federal Reserve policy," in A. J. Cohen, H. Hagemann and J. Smithin (eds) *Money, Financial Institutions and Macroeconomics*, 203–217, Boston: Kluwer Academic Publishers.

—— (1998a) *Understanding Modern Money: The Key to Full Employment and Price Stability*, Northampton: Edward Elgar.

—— (1998b) "Zero unemployment and stable prices," *Journal of Economic Issues*, 32 (2): 539–545.

—— (1999) "Surplus mania: A reality check," Levy Economics Institute, Policy Note No. 1999/3.

—— (2001) "Money and inflation," in S. Pressman and R. P. F. Holt (eds) *A New Guide to Post Keynesian Economics*, 79–91, London: Routledge.

—— (2003a) "Functional finance and US government budget surpluses in the new millennium," in E. J. Nell and M. Forstater (eds) *Reinventing Functional Finance: Transformational Growth and Full Employment*, 141–159, Northampton: Edward Elgar.

—— (2003b) "Monetary policy: An Institutionalist approach," in M. R. Tool and P. D. Bush (eds) *Institutional Analysis and Economic Policy*, 85–113, Boston: Kluwer Academic Publishers.

—— (2003c) "Seigniorage or sovereignty?," in L.-P. Rochon and S. Rossi (eds) *Modern Theories of Money*, 84–102, Northampton: Edward Elgar.

—— (2004a) "International aspects of current monetary policy," Center for Full Employment and Price Stability, Working Paper No. 31.

—— (2004b) "Conclusion: The credit money and state money approaches," in L. R. Wray (ed.) *Credit and State Theories of Money: The Contributions of A. Mitchell Innes*, 223–262, Northampton: Edward Elgar.

—— (2004c) "The Fed and the New Monetary Consensus: The case for rate hikes, part two," Levy Economics Institute, Public Policy Brief 80/2004.

—— (2006a) "Keynes's approach to money: An assessment after seventy years," *Atlantic Economic Journal*, 34 (2): 183–193.

—— (2006b) "Can Basel II enhance financial stability? A pessimistic view," Levy Economics Institute, Public Policy Brief No. 84/2006.

—— (2007a) "Endogenous money: Structuralist and Horizontalist," Levy Economics Institute, Working Paper No. 512.

—— (2007b) "A Post Keynesian view of central bank independence, policy targets, and the rules versus discretion debate," *Journal of Post Keynesian Economics*, 30 (1): 119–141.

—— (2008) "Lessons from the subprime meltdown," *Challenge*, 51 (2): 40–68.

Index

Page references followed by f indicate an illustrative figure; t indicates a table